LAW

IN THE

MIDDLE EAST

EDITED BY

MAJID KHADDURI

AND

HERBERT J. LIEBESNY

With a Foreword by

JUSTICE ROBERT H. JACKSON

VOL. I [All published]

Origin and Development of
Islamic Law

THE LAWBOOK EXCHANGE, LTD.
Clark, New Jersey

ISBN 9781584778646 (hardcover)
ISBN 9781616191177 (paperback)

Lawbook Exchange edition 2010

The quality of this reprint is equivalent to the quality of the original work.

THE LAWBOOK EXCHANGE, LTD.
33 Terminal Avenue
Clark, New Jersey 07066-1321

Please see our website for a selection of our other publications and fine facsimile reprints of classic works of legal history:
www.lawbookexchange.com

Library of Congress Cataloging-in-Publication Data

Law in the Middle East. Vol. 1, Origin and development of Islamic law / edited by Majid Khadduri and Herbert J. Liebesny ; with a foreword by Justice Robert H. Jackson.
p. cm.
Originally published: Washington : Middle East Institute, 1955-
Includes bibliographical references and index.
ISBN-13: 978-1-58477-864-6 (cloth : alk. paper)
ISBN-10: 1-58477-864-4 (cloth : alk. paper)
1. Islamic law. 2. Law--Middle East. I. Khadduri, Majid, 1908- II. Liebesny, Herbert J., 1911- III. Title: Origin and development of Islamic law.
KBP144.L39 2007
340.5'9--dc22

2007041101

Printed in the United States of America on acid-free paper

LAW
IN THE
MIDDLE EAST

EDITED BY

MAJID KHADDURI
AND
HERBERT J. LIEBESNY

With a Foreword by
JUSTICE ROBERT H. JACKSON

VOL. I [All published]

Origin and Development of Islamic Law

THE MIDDLE EAST INSTITUTE
Washington, D. C.
1955

PRINTED BY THE WILLIAM BYRD PRESS, INC.
RICHMOND, VIRGINIA

Foreword

ROBERT HOUGHWOUT JACKSON
Associate Justice, Supreme Court of the United States*

Every matured legal system records a store of experience with the problems of maintaining an ordered society among men. The opinion that the similarities and contrasts found in the teachings of different legal systems are among the best sources for illuminating one's understanding of his own law and suggesting means of its improvement has won increasing acceptance in the United States.

Comparison of our particular laws with those of other common-law countries has been easy and frequent, facilitated as it is by common language and tradition. Having the same foundation, their disparities are chiefly matters of detail. Wider and more fundamental differences, both substantive and procedural, separate the Anglo-American system and that of the modern civil law derived from Roman law as received and adapted to their conditions by the countries of Continental Europe. Early American writers on jurisprudence such as Kent and Story frequently cited with respect and drew lessons from analogies which were found in French or Dutch texts but which were part of the great stream of legal learning which has flowed from the Romans down through the ages. Such comparisons offer little difficulty once that of language is surmounted, because this Western law, however modified by national considerations, is conceived and developed within the framework of Western civilization and compatible with its familiar cultural and religious ideas.

Greater barriers have discouraged any general interest in Islamic law. Though our debt to Arabic culture is exhibited in the customary enumeration of our astonishing output of law reports, we long held the impression that the Muslim world had nothing

* At the time of his death on October 9, 1954, Mr. Justice Jackson had substantially completed the preparation of a Foreword which he had been invited to contribute to this volume. This text is the manuscript of that Foreword in its form at that time.

to contribute to what was inside the covers. Islamic law was regarded as of speculative rather than of practical interest and received attention from a relatively few specialists and scholars. But a review of the reasons we have deemed such knowledge too alien to be useful to us may show that they really are reasons why we should abandon the smug belief that the Muslim experience has nothing to teach us. This comprehensive and authoritative exposition of "Law in the Middle East" ought to dispel that impression wherever it still exists.

In any broad sense, Islamic law offers the American lawyer a study in dramatic contrasts. Even casual acquaintance and superficial knowledge—all that most of us at bench or bar will be able to acquire—reveal that its striking features relative to our law are not likenesses but inconsistencies, not similarities but contrarieties. In its source, its scope and its sanctions, the law of the Middle East is the antithesis of Western law. We may find divergence in legal experience as instructive as parallelism if instead of allowing it to repel our inquiry we accept it as a challenge to understanding.

To the American, the most fundamental of differences lies in the relation between law and religion. In the West, even those countries which do not accept the idea of rigid separation of church and state still regard the legal system as mainly a secular concern in which expediency plays a large part. Of course, religious influences have been powerful in shaping the law. The Hebrew law of the Pentateuch, the teachings of Christ, the canon law—each has contributed to our legal thought. In earlier times it was not uncommon to draw influential statesmen, chancellors and legislators from the ranks of the churchmen. But, in spite of all this, the law has remained a temporal affair, the legislatures for its making and the courts for its enforcement—worldly institutions, identified with and responsible to the state and not the church. Hence, our American law does not prescribe religious duties; indeed, it consciously omits them. It does not make more than a limited approach to enforcing ethical duties. Indeed, one may at the same time be a law-abiding citizen and a thoroughly shabby character.

Islamic law, on the contrary, finds its chief source in the will of Allah as revealed to the Prophet Muḥammad. It contemplates one community of the faithful, though they may be of various tribes and in widely separated locations. Religion, not nationalism or geography, is the proper cohesive force. The state itself is subordinate to the Qur'ān, which leaves little room for additional legislation, none for criticism or dissent. This world is viewed as but the vestibule to another and a better one for the faithful, and the Qur'ān lays down rules of behavior toward others and toward society to assure a safe transition. It is not possible to separate political or juristic theories from the teachings of the Prophet, which establish rules of conduct concerning religious, domestic, social and political life. This results in a law of duties rather than of rights, of moral obligation binding on the individual, from which no earthly authority can relieve him, and which he disobeys at peril of his future life. Since Americans do not accept the religious or philosophical foundations of Islamic law, they are apt to think nothing of the superstructure can interest us.

But the fact is that this system which seems so unworkable to us has an amazing record of accomplishment. Such was the cohesive and animating power of Muḥammadanism that within a century of the Prophet's death his tribal people, who had no real organized state or standing army or common political ambitions, had overrun the African shores of the Mediterranean, had conquered Spain, and had threatened France until the victory of Charles Martel at Poitiers in 732. Christendom and Islam faced each other, each believing in the One God but each accepting different revelations of His will, each considering its own the true and universal faith, each bound thereby to proselyte and convert the world. The Christian led his Crusades against the "infidel," the Muslim his Holy Wars against the Christian. Had either not been weakened by a mixture of political, religious and personal rivalries, intrigues and rifts, their history might have been differently written. The East at intervals had gifted leadership, especially after the phenomenal rise of the Ottoman Empire, which penetrated Europe to the walls of Vienna, took Constantinople, seat of the ancient Byzantian Empire, and made it the capital of Turkey. These long and fanatical hostilities, often shamefully conducted on both sides, engraved on the racial memory of the West a fierce and hateful rejection of Islam and all its works as alien to our civilization, our religion and our law. I do not doubt these wars similarly embittered the Muslim memory.

These unfriendly attitudes were the more persistent in our own time, since our commercial interchange with the Muslim countries was relatively slight, and practical necessities of trade did not supply the strong motives for study of their cultures or their laws that stimulated interest in the systems of others.

Many of these barriers have ceased to obstruct our intercourse and understanding. Both Christendom and Islam are stirred with new yearnings and unrest. Today the anxious countries of the West find in the Islamic world some of their most bold and uncompromising allies in resisting the drive for world supremacy by those whose Prophet is Marx. We have become more objective about history and more tolerant of religious differences. Trade with the Middle East adds the element of expediency to other motives for study of its laws and institutions.

It is indicative of an increasing interest in the jurisprudence of Islam that the Washington Foreign Law Society devoted its first year to a series of lectures on that subject, to which the editors of the present volume made important contributions. It is creditable, if belated, that we begin to recognize that this youngest of the great world religions has produced a jurisprudence that seems to satisfy the sense of justice of many millions of people who live under the burning skies of Asia and Africa and of many thousands who dwell in the United States. Skeptical as we may be about the religious inspiration of their law, it still may hold important lessons in law enforcement for us who rely on the word of man to become law. It is time that we stopped thinking of ourselves as the only peoples in the world who love justice or who understand what justice is, who in their legal systems strive to attain it, or whose experiences hold lessons of value.

However, the barrier of language presents more than the usual difficulty of comparative law studies in the case of Islamic law. A competent scholar engaged in translating for English readers what Muslims hold to be the meaning of the words of the Qur'ān despaired of the effort to convey its spirit and declared that the Qur'ān cannot be translated so as to be made plain to one who disbelieves its inspiration and its message. I suspect that the same difficulty of communication carries over into the effort to expound Islamic law to American readers. The writers of this work, as those of all others I have seen, find it necessary to use many words which probably convey to the Muslim a whole complex of meaning, a cluster of ideas, but which do not have an English equivalent. In course of time it is the custom that legal expressions come to carry a whole bundle of ideas to the initiate as do our phrases "due process of law," "equity jurisprudence," "trial by jury," or "judicial review." It appears to be true of many Islamic legal terms that they wrap volumes of meaning into a single word, which may be expounded to us, but we, not having the same concept in our law, have no legal term to fit it. The present work finds an extensive glossary necessary to explain the terms that seem indispensable but are without English counterparts.

The American profession should welcome this exhaustive and authentic work edited by two scholars who are authorities on the law of Islam and also students of the law of the United States. These editors have enlisted leading authorities on special subjects and have presented the whole in a manner that should appeal to American interest and understanding. Dr. Khadduri and Dr. Liebesny are entitled to our thanks and to our congratulations. It is to be hoped that *Law in the Middle East* will be widely read and pondered by the American legal profession and all who believe understanding begets good will.

Background and Development of the Project

GEORGE CAMP KEISER

Chairman of the Board of Governors, The Middle East Institute

When I was asked by the Editors of this work on law in the Middle East to write an account of its incubation, I felt at first that such a foreword, if read at all, would contribute little to the subject matter that follows, which has been so admirably treated by eminent legal specialists. On second thought, however, I believe it might be interesting to those readers who are curious about origins of projects of this kind, to know that such a highly specialized work did not receive its first impetus within the legal profession. Its initial stimulus came from a small group of American laymen who were sincerely interested in making the Middle East better understood in the West, and particularly in the United States.

One pleasant summer evening in 1949, a few of us, under the hospitable roof of the Joseph Lindon Smiths at Loon Point in Dublin, New Hampshire, were discussing ways and means of bridging the wide gap between the attitudes of the people in the Muslim world and those in the Christian. Various suggestions were made as to how this might be best accomplished when Mrs. Smith, for some time a student of the Qur'ān during her long sojourns in Egypt, brought forward the idea of translating the basic works on the sharī'a into English. Because of her familiarity with Islam she knew, naturally enough, what an important bearing this law has on the Muslim people. Feeling that if the sharī'a were made known to Westerners, they would be so much better able to interpret the actions of Muslims, her thought was to have the Arabic texts made available in English to Western readers. With this ambitious suggestion, the idea of bringing an understanding of Muslim law to the English-speaking world took root.

When I returned to Washington not long after this stimulating conversation, I brought the suggestion to the attention of a number of scholars in this field and asked their opinion as to the feasibility of approaching the matter in this fashion. Bearing in mind how little was known about Muslim law, and indeed of law in the Middle East in general, among Western peoples, it was felt that a broad introductory work was needed first to pave the way for a possible future translation of the basic law books of the four Schools, even if they were to have extensive annotations. Among those who became particularly interested in this work, and who later formed themselves into a committee, were Majid Khadduri and Herbert J. Liebesny, both with excellent legal background for such a task, who subsequently became the Editors of the volume; also Mortimer Graves of the American Council of Learned Societies; Philip W. Thayer, Dean of the School of Advanced International Studies of The Johns Hopkins University; Robert F. Ogden, Chief of the Near East Section of the Library of Congress; and myself, serving as Chairman.

At first, this Committee acted as an independent unit, sponsored by The George C. Keiser Foundation, as it had not been decided whether it would be feasible to have it included as an activity of a more widely known American institution with special Middle East interests. It was finally planned, however, that it should become a Middle East Institute project and publication and the work has since been carried through under the Institute's auspices.

Rather than for the book to have a single author, the Committee believed that it would have broader scope if each chapter or section were written by a specialist chosen for his knowledge of the subject treated. The result is that it presents viewpoints of a number of the most outstanding authorities on Middle East law in America and Europe, as well as in the Middle East.

The Committee has had many difficult decisions to make and problems to solve, and while not all of the members were in the legal profession, each one has contributed to the numerous decisions with which it has been confronted. However, the Committee would have been curtailed indeed in its activities, if it had not had cooperation from many sources. Particularly outstanding in this category has been the assistance of President Floyd Black of Robert College, who located one of the contributors to the section on Turkish law, and that of The Rockefeller Foundation, which made it possible to complete the research required under the supervision of the work's two Editors.

It is not surprising, when we consider that the numerous contributors to this volume are physically so widely separated, that it has taken almost four years to complete the work, and we feel that the authors of the chapters which were among the first to be received have shown great patience and understanding in waiting so long to see their work published. It is the Committee's hope that the appearance of this volume will stimulate an interest in this broad subject, and that at some future date the time may be ripe for the undertaking Mrs. Joseph Lindon Smith visualized having produced, namely an annotated English translation of the basic classics of the sharīʿa.

Especial appreciation is due to the Editors of this work, Majid Khadduri and Herbert J. Liebesny. They have spared no effort in doing all within their power to coordinate the various chapters of this book into a well balanced study of the background of law in the Middle East. Unfortunately, during the last stages of preparation before the book went to press, Dr. Liebesny was out of the country on a tour of the Arab countries of the Middle East. This meant that, since there was a time limit in completing the volume, the main responsibility of getting the manuscript ready for press was placed in Dr. Khadduri's hands. It is therefore with the fullest gratitude that the Committee wishes to express its thanks to him for preparing the work in its finished form for presentation to many interested readers as a published volume.

It is hoped and planned that, circumstances permitting, a second volume on the modern legal systems of the Middle East countries will be published.

Editors' Preface

It should be unnecessary to justify the preparation of a volume on Islamic law or overemphasize its significance, both on the theoretical and practical planes, as the two preceding forewords have dealt respectively with the importance of this branch of knowledge and the spontaneous need felt by a few conscientious Americans, not of the legal profession, who were convinced that a balanced understanding of the Middle East would not be achieved if it did not include a knowledge of classical Islamic law and its development, based on its original source materials.

As soon as it was formed, the Committee on Law in the Middle East began to prepare the broad outline of this volume and consider the contributors to it. It was felt that a work of this kind should be the product of a group of collaborators, enlisted from the world of scholarship in the Islamic countries as well as from among Western scholars interested in matters Islamic. The Committee therefore began at once to solicit contributors with this view in mind, inviting them to give it their suggestions if collaboration proved to be impossible. At the same time it entrusted us with the development of a detailed plan and the preparation of this volume.

Correspondence with possible contributors proved to be much more time consuming then we had at first anticipated and our work was on more than one occasion interrupted, as several of our contributors, for circumstances beyond their control no less than for personal preoccupations, could not meet our deadlines. It was necessary to consider other possible contributors; this made it imperative that our contemplated time limits be extended more than once.

Nor could the task of piecing together the contributions of fourteen writers be discharged within a short period of time. The papers, as originally received, varied greatly in length as well as in the languages and styles in which they were written. We had, therefore, to undertake the work of translating them—helped by several translators—and to try to reduce the variations to a minimum. We have, however, abstained from changing the ideas and views of the writers and made no significant change in the contributions of each writer, especially those originally written in the English language, save that of unifying the spelling and transliteration to conform to the American style.

A particular difficulty in presenting discussions of Islamic law to the English and American reader lies in the rendering of Arabic legal terms into English. Not infrequently the Islamic institution does not have an exact equivalent in English or American law, and to render an Arabic term by an English technical term not entirely fitting the institution described would increase confusion rather than understanding. The Editors have therefore felt that it was wiser to use more general English terms or, at times, even utilize French or Latin terms which described the Islamic institution more fully.

We have been greatly helped in the process of preparing this volume by several friends and assistants, whether by advice or by lending a hand in the editorial work; to them we are indeed very grateful. Mention must be made in particular of Mr. C. Thomas Thorne and of several colleagues in the Middle East Institute, as well as others, whose constant counsel and assistance rendered our task less difficult.

Washington, D. C. MAJID KHADDURI
January, 1955 HERBERT J. LIEBESNY

Contributors

CHOUCRI CARDAHI, Docteur en Droit, formerly Minister of Justice, Lebanese Government, and now Professeur à la Faculté de Droit de Beyrouth, Lebanon. Author of *Droit et Morale* (Beyrouth, 1954).

HENRY CATTAN, LL.M., Member of the Bars of Jerusalem and Damascus.

S. G. VESEY-FITZGERALD, LL.D., Professor Emeritus at the School of Oriental and African Studies, the University of London. Author of *Muhammadan Law* (London, 1931).

ASAF A. A. FYZEE, LL.B., M.A., formerly Principal and Perry Professor of Jurisprudence at the Government Law College, Bombay; Chairman of the Union Public Service Commission, New Delhi; and author of *Outlines of Muhammadan Law* (Oxford, 1949).

SIR HAMILTON GIBB, M.A., LL.D., Laudian Professor of Arabic at the University of Oxford. Author of *Modern Trends in Islam* (Chicago, 1947), and other works.

MAJID KHADDURI, Ph.D., Director of Research and Education at The Middle East Institute, Washington, D.C.; and Professor at the School of Advanced International Studies, the Johns Hopkins University. Author of *The Law of War and Peace in Islam* (London, 1941) and other works.

HERBERT J. LIEBESNY, Jur.D., member of the Advisory Board of the *Middle East Journal* and author of *The Government of French North Africa* (Philadelphia, 1944).

SUBHI MAHMASANI, LL.B., Docteur en Droit, formerly Attorney-General of the Muslim Court of Appeal, and Lecturer at the American University of Beirut, Lebanon. Author of *The Philosophy of Jurisprudence in Islam* (Beirut, 1946), and other works.

RIYAD MAYDANI, LL.B., of the Department of Justice of the Syrian Government.

EBÜL'ULÂ MARDIN, Ord. Professor Emeritus of Civil and Land Law at the University of Istanbul, Turkey. Author of several legal works in Turkish.

S. S. Onar, Ph.D., Ord. Professor and Director of the Institute of Administrative Law and Sciences at the University of Istanbul, Turkey.

Joseph Schacht, Ph.D., LL.D., formerly at the University of Oxford, now Professor at the University of Leiden, Holland. Author of *Origins of Muhammadan Jurisprudence* (Oxford, 1950), and other works.

Emile Tyan, Docteur en Droit, Professeur à la Faculté de Droit de Beyrouth, Lebanon. Author of *Histoire de l'Organisation judiciaire en pays d'Islam* (Paris, 1938), and other works.

Muhammad Abu Zahra, Professor of Islamic Law at the University of Cairo, Egypt, and author of several works in Arabic on Islamic jurisprudence.

Contents

CHAPTER PAGE

I. Constitutional Organization. H. A. R. Gibb 3

II. Pre-Islamic Background and Early Development of Jurisprudence. Joseph Schacht 28

III. The Schools of Law and Later Developments of Jurisprudence. Joseph Schacht 57

IV. Nature and Sources of the Sharī'a. S. G. Vesey-Fitzgerald 85

V. Shī'ī Legal Theories. A. A. A. Fyzee 113

VI. Family Law. Muhammad Abu Zahra 132

VII. Transactions in the Sharī'a. Subhi Mahmasani 179

VIII. The Law of Waqf. Henry Cattan 203

IX. 'Uqūbāt: Penal Law. Riyad Maydani 223

X. Judicial Organization. Emile Tyan 236

XI. Development of the Sharī'a under the Ottoman Empire. Ebül'ulâ Mardin 279

XII. The Majalla. S. S. Onar 292

XIII. The Development of Western Judicial Privileges. Herbert J. Liebesny 309

XIV. Conflict of Law. Choucri Cardahi 334

XV. International Law. Majid Khadduri 349

Glossary of Legal Terms 373

Select Bibliography 378

Index 383

LAW IN THE MIDDLE EAST

Volume I

Origin and Development of Islamic Law

CHAPTER I

Constitutional Organization

THE MUSLIM COMMUNITY AND THE STATE

AT THE root of all Islamic political concepts lies the doctrine of the umma, the Community of Muslims. In its internal aspect, the umma consists of the totality (jamā'a) of individuals bound to one another by ties, not of kinship or race, but of religion, in that all its members profess their belief in the One God, Allah, and in the mission of His Prophet Muḥammad. Before God, and in their relation to Him, all are equal, without distinctions of rank, class, or race. Differences of function are recognized, but "the noblest among you is the most godfearing" (Qur'ān XLIX,13). In its external aspect, the umma is sharply differentiated from all other social organizations. Its duty is to bear witness to Allah in the relations of its members with one another and with all mankind. They form a single indivisible organization, charged to uphold the True Faith, to instruct men in the ways of God, to persuade them to the good and to dissuade them from evil by word and deed.

The Head of the umma is Allah, and Allah alone. His rule is immediate, and His commands, as revealed to Muḥammad, embody the Law and Constitution of the umma. Since God is Himself the sole Legislator, there can be no room in Islamic political theory for legislation or legislative powers, whether enjoyed by a temporal ruler or by any kind of assembly. There can be no "sovereign state," in the sense that the state has the right of enacting its own law, though it may have some freedom in determining its constitutional structure. The Law precedes the State, both logically and in terms of time; and the State exists for the sole purpose of maintaining and enforcing the Law.

Consistently with this position it follows that in the strict legal view there are definite limits to speculation on constitutional organization. The function and general form of the State have been laid down once and for all, irrespective of historical circumstances, local traditions, political aptitudes, or other social factors. The minor details of application remain open to discussion, but the main principles of Islamic government are conceived as divinely ordained institutions, valid in all circumstances and for all time, and they cannot be questioned on penalty of heresy or sin. Should the Community deviate from these principles, it falls into error and exposes itself to the chastisement of God.

THE LAW AND THE CALIPHATE

The sharī'a, then, by virtue of its character as the expression of God's Will, and by the common acceptance of its prescriptions and their implications on the part of all Muslims, supplies the authority, sanctions, and moral basis for the unity and constitution of the umma as a political entity. But neither in the Qur'ān nor in the sunna of the Prophet are there to be found precise instructions as to the forms and institutions by which the unity of the umma as a political organization should be expressed and maintained. On the Prophet's death (A.D. 632), therefore, the Community itself, by the first and most decisive exercise of ijmā' (consensus of the community), took the step of electing Abū Bakr as its temporal head or imām, with the designation of "Successor (caliph, or khalīfa) of the Prophet of God."

This step had two important consequences. In the first place, it brought the historical process into constitutional theory. The action taken by the Community had to be reconciled with and justified by the principles of the sharī'a. In the second place, together with the subsequent historical development, it focused the constitutional theory of the jurists upon the person of the khalīfa-imām (Caliph).

The rationalization of the imāmate offered little difficulty. The perpetual necessity of an imām was admitted by all schools of Islamic thought, except for a few isolated individuals, on the same fundamental reasoning as the necessity of the Law. Just as Law, i.e., the setting of limits to man's liberty of action, is necessary because man is essentially weak and inclined to evil, so no social order is possible unless these limits are observed. To ensure this and to protect the Faith itself, there is need for a governor to watch over and to restrain men, and to compel them, if necessary, to obey the Law. Consequently, God has supplemented the Law by setting an imām over the Community, and prescribing the duty of obedience to him. The imām is thus the means whereby the Law is translated from the sphere of potentiality into actuality and provided with temporal sanctions; he typifies or stands as the representative of the Law in the sphere of human relations, but does not embody it, since it exists independently of him and of his will and he is himself subject to it.

The fortuitous choice of the term khalīfa, and afterwards, of that of Amīr al-Mu'minīn, "Commander of the Faithful," to designate the successors of Muḥammad in the temporal government of the Community also provided the jurists with scriptural authority for their doctrine. In the Qur'ān, Adam is described as "a khalīfa" (Q. II, 28-30); more significantly, David is addressed with the words: "We have made thee a khalīfa on the earth, therefore judge righteously between men" (Q. XXXVIII, 25-26). Since in these and similar passages the meaning of the term is "vicegerent," the jurists drew the deduction that the khalīfa of the Prophet was the vicegerent of Allah upon earth, charged with the duty of judging righteously, i.e., of applying the sharī'a, between men. For the further duty of the Community to render him obedience a proof-text was found in the verse: "O ye Faithful, obey God and the Apostle and those set in command amongst you" (Q. IV, 62).

The authority of the imām is thus derived not from the Community, but directly from God, who as sole Head of the Community has alone the power to confer authority of any kind; and this authority rests primarily not on military strength or political skill but on religious obligation. Nor is that obligation dependent upon the capacity of the imām to carry out his main duty of guaranteeing the observance of the Law; it is by the Will of God that he possesses the right of command, and he continues to possess it (and with it the right to obedience) until God deprives him of it, in accordance with the verse: "O God, the possessor of the kingly rule, Thou givest the rule to whom Thou wilt and withdrawest the rule from whom Thou wilt" (Q. III, 25-27).

So, in the second century of the hijra, we find the Qāḍī Abū Yūsuf addressing the Caliph Harūn al-Rashīd in these words:

> Verily God, in His grace and mercy and indulgence, has made those who exercise command vicegerents upon His earth, and has furnished for them a light that illuminates for the subjects those matters in their mutual relations which are obscure to them, and that makes manifest what is confused in the duties laid upon them. The illumination of the light of those who exercise command consists in maintaining the Divine ordinances and giving to all men their rights with resolution and clear command. And the quickening of the sunnas which the pious men of old have established as precedents is of chiefest importance, for the quickening of the sunnas is of the good which lives and dies not.[1]

[1] Abū Yūsuf, *Kitāb al-Kharāj* (Cairo, A. H. 1346), p. 6.

Yet from these principles it is possible to deduce many different political systems, both monarchical and republican, and a wide variety of mechanisms of government, provided only that the supreme law of the State, the sharī'a, is respected. In historical fact the Community of Believers was, even within the first generation, rent by dissensions and split into factions, each of which placed its own interpretation upon the common doctrine of the imāmate. At one extreme the Shī'a or Party of 'Alī maintained the sole legitimacy of the imāmate of the Prophet's descendants through the marriage of his daughter Fāṭima with 'Alī, and ascribed to these hereditary imāms not only divine right to the succession but also powers of interpretation of the Qur'ān. At the other extreme, the puritan "Seceders" (Khawārij, Khārijīs) maintained the right of the Community to pronounce on the fitness of the imām for his office and to refuse obedience to him or to depose him. Both doctrines, in varying formulations, found many supporters; but these extreme factions, by their frequent resort to violence, forced the general body of the Community to take up positions not only against their armies but also against the doctrines which they proclaimed, and thereby contributed to consecrate the very systems against which they revolted.

Thus the historical process forced its way into constitutional theory on a much more massive scale. For the representatives of the "orthodox" middle way it was no longer sufficient to prove the necessity of the imāmate. The precise methods by which the historical caliphs had been elected or appointed must be justified, against the Shī'ī claim that those who recognized the historical imāmate had deviated into error and sin. Likewise, in relation to the egalitarianism of the Khārijī sectaries and the anarchical consequences which it produced through fanatical revolts, the "orthodox" defenders of the Community were forced increasingly to deprecate the right of rebellion against an unjust imām. To the far-reaching consequences of this attitude we shall revert later.

THE SUNNĪ DOCTRINE OF THE CALIPHATE

The practical outcome of this development was that the orthodox Sunnī constitutional theory formed a blend of abstract general doctrines deduced from first principles, and of concrete provisions derived from the historical experience of the Islamic State. For the legal arguments in favor of their views, the Sunnī jurists adopted generally the method of drawing deductions and analogies from the rules applied to what seemed relevant cases, especially in regard to delegation of authority (wilāya) and contracts ('uqūd). The earliest precise formulations of the theory were apparently drawn up by the followers of the jurist al-Ash'arī towards the end of the fourth century A. H. Since they furnished what is generally regarded as the "classical" Islamic doctrine of the caliphate, it is important to present them in adequate detail. For this purpose, the most satisfactory statement of their general argument, and of the rival theories, is to be found in the authoritative exposition by the Ash'arī, 'Abd al-Qāhir al-Baghdādī (d. 428/1037), part of whose chapter devoted to this subject follows in a simplified translation:[2]

On the Doctrines of the Imāmate and Conditions of Leadership

1 *On the necessity of the imāmate.* There is disagreement as to the necessity of the imāmate and the necessity of seeking out and setting up an imām. The general body of the Sunnīs, both theologians and canonists, together with the Shī'a, the Khāwarij, and most of the Mu'tazila, hold the imāmate to be compulsory, that to set up an imām and to submit to him are necessary, and that it is essential for the Muslims to have an imām to execute their ordinances, enforce legal penalties, direct their armies, marry off their widows, and divide the revenues of conquest amongst them. They are opposed only by a handful of the Qadariyya, such as Abū Bakr al-Aṣamm, who asserted that if people were to refrain from mutual injury they would have no need of an imām, and Hishām al-Fuwaṭī, who held that an imām was necessary only when the Community was united in the way of right, but not at a time of civil war.

Those who hold the imāmate to be a compulsory obligation disagree as to the reason for its necessity. Those of the Mu'tazila who maintain the doctrine of divine bounty (luṭf) assert it to be compulsory only because it is a divine bounty for the maintenance of the revealed laws. Al-Ash'arī argued that the imāmate is itself an ordinance of the revealed Law, and that though it can be demonstrated by reason that subordination to it is admissible, the necessity of it is known only by the authority of the Revelation. Furthermore, the Companions of the Prophet were unanimous on its necessity, and in view of their unanimity no regard is to be paid to the opposition of isolated individuals. Again, the sharī'a contains ordinances which none can carry out except an imām or a governor appointed by him, such as enforcing the legal penalties against freemen, giving in marriage women who have no guardians, etc. Even if the Community were to act with perfect mutual equity, as al-Aṣamm postulates, yet it would still require someone to guard the property of orphans and lunatics, to despatch troops against enemies, and to carry out many other functions which only the imām or a person appointed by the imām can perform.

2. *On the circumstances of the appointment of the Imām.* The Sunnīs assert the necessity of appointing an imām in every circum-

[2] 'Abd al-Qāhir al-Baghdādī, *Uṣūl al-Dīn* (Istanbul 1928), Vol. I, pp. 270-85.

stance in which there is no visible imām, and of rendering obedience to him if he is visible. In opposition to the belief of various Shī'ī sects in the continued existence of concealed imāms, they do not admit that there should ever come upon men a time in which there is an imām who must be obeyed but who is concealed and not manifest.

3. *On the number of the Imāms at one time.* There is disagreement amongst those who hold for the necessity of the imāmate as to the number of imāms at any one time. Our associates maintain that it is not permissible that there should be two imāms to whom obedience is obligatory at one and the same time, but that the imāmate of one only is duly contracted at that time and the remainder are under his standard. Further, should they come forth against him for no cause that calls for his deposition, they are rebels, unless there be between them a sea which prevents the supporters of each one from gaining the victory over the others, in which case it is lawful for the people of each of the two lands to make a contract of imāmate with one of the inhabitants of that region. The Shī'a maintain that there cannot be two "speaking" imāms at the same time, but that there may be one "speaking" imām and one "silent" imām; and certain of the Karrāmiyya maintain the lawfulness of two or more imāms at one time. . . . But if it were lawful to have two or more imāms, it would be lawful for every person qualified for the imāmate to exercise, each one, independent rule in his own province or tribe—a state of affairs which would lead to the complete voiding of the obligation of the imāmate.

4. *On the race and tribe of the Imām.* There is disagreement on this question. Our associates maintain that the sharī'a has prescribed the attribution of the imāmate to Quraysh and has indicated that Quraysh will never fail to produce some member of the tribe who is qualified for the imāmate, therefore it is not lawful to set up an imām for the whole Community from any other group. Al-Shāfi'ī has stated this categorically in one of his writings, and Zuraqān has transmitted the same from Abū Ḥanīfa. The followers of Ḍirār[3] argued for the legality of the imāmate from outside Quraysh, though there might be found amongst Quraysh one who was fitted for it. Al-Ka'bī[4] asserted that a Qurayshī had more claim to it than any one not of Quraysh who was qualified for it, but if there were danger of civil strife it was lawful to give the contract for it to another; but Ḍirār said, "If there is equality of condition between the man of Quraysh and the non-Arab, then the non-Arab has the better claim to it, the client being more worthy of it than the true-born Arab." The Khawārij asserted that the imāmate might be lawfully contracted to men of any race, but only to an upright man who could carry out its duties fittingly. Amongst the Shī'ī sects, the Zaidiyya asserted that it could be attributed to none of Quraysh except the descendants of 'Alī, and that any descendants of al-Ḥasan or al-Ḥusayn who should openly revolt and draw the sword, being equipped with the knowledge required for

[3] An independent theologian of the second century, connected with the beginnings of the Mu'tazilī movement.

[4] A Mu'tazilī contemporary of al-Ash'arī, d. 319/931.

the imāmate, is the imām. The Imāmiyya assert that it is held at this day by a particular person among the descendants of ʿAlī, but they disagree on the precise individual whose manifestation they look for. The Shīʿī extremists held that the imāmate originally belonged to ʿAlī and his descendants but they later transferred it to a number of non-Qurayshites on the ground either of the claim that he was nominated to the succession by testament of one or other of the imāms, or of the claim to the transmigration of the soul from the imām to that person to whom they asserted that the imāmate had been transferred. . . .

The argument of the Sunnīs for the limitation of the Imāmate to Quraysh is the word of the Prophet, "The imāms are of Quraysh." It was in deference to this tradition that the Muslims of Medina surrendered the Succession to Quraysh on the occasion of the election of Abū Bakr; wherefore this Tradition and the Consensus of the Companions of the Prophet furnish two proofs that the khilāfa is not within the competence of any persons other than Quraysh, and no heed is to be paid to the disagreement of those who oppose the consensus after it has been established. . . .

5. *On the conditions required for the imāmate.* Our associates hold that one who is competent to occupy the imāmate must possess the four following qualities: (i) knowledge, the minimum requirement being that he should reach the degree of the mujtahids in regard to things lawful and unlawful and all other ordinances; (ii) probity of character and piety, the minimum incumbent on him in this respect being that he should be one whose witness is acceptable before a qāḍī, at the time both of witnessing the act and of giving evidence thereon; (iii) good judgment in the various functions of government and administrative capacity, in that he knows the ranks and classes (marātib) of his subjects and holds them to their proper offices, not seeking aid in great matters of state from junior officers; and also an acquaintance with the organization of warfare; (iv) descent from Quraysh.

To these conditions the Shīʿa add impeccability.

6. *On impeccability in the imāmate.* Our associates hold, in common with the majority of the Community, that sinlessness is of the conditions of prophethood and the transmission of Revelation, but not one of the conditions of the imāmate. All that is stipulated in regard to the latter is outward probity of character; consequently, when the outward behavior of the imām remains in congruence with the sharīʿa his tenure of the imāmate is in regular order. When he deviates from this standard, the Community has to choose between two courses of action in regard to him: either to turn him from his error towards the right, or to turn away from him and give allegiance to another. Their action in relation to him is on the same footing as his action in relation to his substitutes, judges, officers and couriers; if they deviate from his directions he sets them right or dispenses with them. The Shīʿa on the other hand hold unanimously to the necessity of the sinlessness of the imām as a general principle, though they disagree on this claim in detail. . . . Finally, if the sinlessness of the imām is postulated, there must be postulated also the sinlessness of his substitutes

and assistants; and if every one of these were sinless they would have no need of a sinless imām to keep them on the highway of the right.

7. *On the means whereby the imām is established in office.* There is disagreement also on the method whereby the imāmate is established, whether it is by designation or by election. The vast generality of our associates and of the Mu'tazila, the Khawārij, and the Najjāriyya[5] hold that the method of its establishment is by election on the part of the Community, through the exercise of responsible judgment (ijtihād) by those of them who are qualified to do so and their selection of one who is fitted for the office. Its establishment by designation would have been permissible, but in fact no designation of any individual is known to have been made in regard to it, and therefore the Community had recourse to selection for it.

The Imāmiyya and other Shī'ī sects assert that the method of establishment of the imāmate was by designation of the imām from God through the mouth of His Prophet, and thereafter by each imām's designation of his successor as imām, although these sects disagree as to the reason why designation of the imām is indispensable. . . .

The argument for the doctrine of the majority is that, if announcement of the designation of the imām had been incumbent on the Prophet, he would have announced it in such a manner that the Community had public knowledge of it and no grounds for disagreement. For the obligation of the imāmate is one of which the knowledge is obligatory on every member of the Community, in exactly the same manner as knowledge of the qibla and of the number of prostrations to be made at each hour of prayer. . . . But since there is nothing in the Traditions sponsored by the Shī'a on the designation of 'Alī which constitutes authoritative information, the question becomes one of ijtihād, and the exercise of selection and of ijtihād in regard to it is justified.

Since, then, the establishment of the imāmate by the method of election is accepted by us as valid, there is a further disagreement among the partisans of election as to the number of actual electors of the imām. Al-Ash'arī held that the imāmate is validly contracted on behalf of one who is fitted for it by the contract of a single pious man who is qualified to exercise ijtihād, when he does so in favor of one fitted for it, and when he does so, then it is incumbent on the remainder to render him obedience. If, however, the contract is made by one who exercises ijtihād but is an evildoer, or by a learned and pious person in favor of one who is unfitted for it, such an imāmate is not validly contracted, just as a marriage can be validly contracted by a single guardian of legal probity but is not valid contracted by an evildoer, in the view of this school. Sulaymān b. Jarīr, the Zaydī,[6] and certain of the Mu'tazilīs held that the least number of those who may make the contract of the imāmate is two persons of piety and ijtihād, just as the contract of marriage is not established by less than two

[5] The followers of al-Najjār, a scholastic opponent of the Mu'tazila at the beginning of the third century.

[6] An early Zaydī leader, who held a position intermediate between the Shī'ī and Sunnī doctrines on this question.

witnesses. Al-Qalānisī[7] and those of our associates who follow him hold that the contract of the imāmate is validly made by the 'ulamā' of the Community who are present at the residence of the imām, irrespective of their number.

If one or more make a contract of imāmate in favor of one person while others make a contract in favor of another, and each of the two persons is fitted for it, then the prior contract is valid. If the two contracts are made simultaneously or it is not known which is the prior, the contract must be renewed in favor of one of them or of some other person, and God knows best.

8. *On the appointment of the imām after the death of the Prophet.* [Summary of the arguments for the legality of the imāmate of Abū Bakr against the doctrine of the Shī'a.]

9. *On inheritance and testament in regard to the imāmate.* There is disagreement as to whether the imāmate passes by inheritance, but every one who maintains the imāmate of Abū Bakr holds that it does not pass by inheritance. . . . There is disagreement also as to the legality of bequeathing the imāmate by testament to a specified person who is fitted for it. Our associates, together with some of the Mu'tazila, the Murji'a and the Khawārij, hold that the bequest of the imāmate is valid and lawful but not obligatory. If the imām bequeaths it to one who is fitted for it, it is obligatory on the Community to execute his testament, as Abū Bakr bequeathed it to 'Umar, and the Companions of the Prophet unanimously agreed to 'Umar's succession to the office. But if the imām leaves it to consultation (shūra) among certain persons after his death, this too is lawful, as was done by 'Umar. Sulaymān b. Jarīr, the Zaydī, asserted that the imām has the right of bequeathing the imāmate by testament to a specified person, but the Community must not execute his testament in that person's favor except after consultation about him; but the instance of Abū Bakr's nomination of 'Umar proves the unsoundness of his contention in view of his acceptance of the validity of their imāmates.

Before going on to discuss the later developments of this juristic theory, there are several points in connection with it which deserve some examination. The extent to which the doctrine that it expounds is an apologia, explicitly or by implication, for the historical caliphate against the charges of the Shī'ī and Khārijī oppositions, calls for no demonstration. Of its adaptation to contemporary circumstances, the clearest instance is seen in the admission that two imāms may exist simultaneously if their territories are separated by sea, a condition which manifestly applied to the Umayyad caliphate in Spain.

Equally striking are the omissions from the argument. Al-Baghdādī, for example, discusses only the particular bay'a or oath of allegiance taken to the caliph-imām by the electors, whoever

[7] An Ash'arī contemporary of the writer.

they may be, which constitutes the "contract," and never alludes to the general bay'a taken subsequently by the representatives of the Community as a whole, except for its probative value in the cases of Abū Bakr and 'Umar. It is true that practically all the Muslim jurists assume the contract to be valid and complete when it has been made by the "electors," and the subsequent general bay'a to be merely supplementary, expressing the ratification of the election by the general body of the subjects and their acceptance of the obligation of obedience. There may be some inconsistency between this position and the argument for the validity of the elections of Abū Bakr and 'Umar, as well as in the implications of the fourth sentence in 6 above. But more important is the failure to elucidate the constitutional significance of the general bay'a, and the effect upon a "contract" for the imāmate if this ratification is refused. Similarly, there is no discussion of the deposition of an evil-doing imām. Though the Community may lawfully "turn away from him and give allegiance to another," the question of how this is to be done without provoking civil war is left unanswered. The fact is that the historical precedents that could have been cited on these points were too confused, and sometimes too embarrassing, to be used as precedents, and the general rule of Sunnī constitutional theory is that when no clear precedents exist no rules can be laid down, but only general principles.

Behind these omissions, however, lies another factor. In their almost exclusive concentration upon the personality and duties of the caliph-imām as leader of the Community, the Muslim jurists present, at first sight, a striking contrast to the Greek political thinkers. These started, as a rule, from the individual and built up their systems with the aim of defining the kind of state in which he could find the widest scope for his moral development as an active citizen or, as they put it, "live the good life." This contrast has led many investigators to the conclusion that Islamic theory gives the citizen as such no place or function in the state except as taxpayer and submissive subject, and no scope for his moral development.

The explanation lies largely in the distinction between the Greek and the Muslim concepts of the state. For the Greeks the state was a secular organism; for the Muslims it was fundamental that life on earth was only a preliminary stage or preparation for the fuller life hereafter. Their ideal state was also, therefore, one that gave the fullest means to all its citizens to "live the good life," such a life, that is, as would fit them for participation in the future life, by due performance of their religious and ethical duties, by mutual cooperation in their respective functions according to the ordinances of the sharī'a, and by the development of their moral personalities on the lines ordained by God.

This distinction is most clearly and emphatically expressed by the greatest of Islamic political thinkers, Ibn Khaldūn (d. 808/1406)[8]:

In political associations it is imperative to have recourse to imposed laws, accepted and followed by the masses, as was the case amongst the Persians and other peoples, and no state can establish itself and consolidate its control without such laws. If these laws are laid down by men of intelligence and insight, the polity is founded on reason [and subserves the temporal well-being of the subjects]. But if they are laid down by God and promulgated by an inspired Lawgiver, the polity is founded on religion and is beneficial both for this world and the next. For men have not been created solely for this world since it is wholly vanity and futility, and its end is death and annihilation. Revealed laws have been sent to lead men to observe that conduct which will bring them to felicity in the future life, in all their affairs, whether of worship or of mutual dealings, and even in matters of kingship—which is a phenomenon natural to human society—so that it should be conducted on the pattern of religion, in order that the whole body may be protected by the supervision of the Revealed Law.

That state, therefore, whose law is based on violence and coercion and gives full play to the irascible nature is tyranny and injustice and in the eyes of the Law blameworthy, a judgment in which political wisdom also concurs. Furthermore, that state whose law is based upon rational statecraft and its principles, *but lacks the supervision of the Revealed Law,* is likewise blameworthy, since it is the product of speculation without the light of God. For the Lawgiver knows best the interests of men in all that relates to the other world, which is concealed from them. The principles of rational government aim solely at apparent and worldly interests, whereas the object of the Lawgiver is men's salvation in the hereafter. It is imperative, therefore, by the very nature of Revealed Laws, to bring the whole people to conform themselves to their ordinances in all matters of this world and the next. And this rule is the rule of the Lawgivers, that is to say, the Prophets, and of their successors, that is to say, the caliphs, and this is the true meaning of the caliphate.

Natural kingship, then, forces the people to conform to the private ambitions and uncontrolled desires of the ruler. Political government induces the people to conform to the dictates of reason for the promotion of worldly interests and the warding off of evils. The caliphate leads the people to conform to the insight of the Revealed Law in regard to their interests both in the world to come and those in this world which relate to it, since all the affairs of this world are assessed

[8] Ibn Khaldūn, *al-Muqaddima,* Book 3, Chap. 25, omitting the Qur'ānic citations and allusions by which the argument is supported.

by the Lawgiver in the light of their relation to the interests of the future life. Thus it is truly an office of replacement (khilāfa) of the promulgator of the Revealed Law in the guardianship of the Faith and the government of the world by its provisions.

THE CALIPH AND HIS SUBJECTS

Since, then, this ideal caliphate is the highest type of political organization on earth, and its laws are those of the Divine Wisdom, it follows that the highest welfare of its subjects is to be found in absolute obedience to its ordinances. The subject can have no rights or claims against it; his positive functions are practically confined to his private and social duties, and have no necessary relation to the political constitution of the State. Except insofar as a subject may be appointed to perform the duties of a particular office by delegation from the caliph, the development of his moral personality by the exercise of political functions is practically excluded. Consequently, Islamic political theory tends to neglect the citizen in its pursuit of the ideal of government which will conduce to his ultimate good.

Islamic political thought does not, of course, entirely lose sight of the individual. Apart from his religious duties and obligations of obedience to the imām, it recognizes his rights of personal security, freedom, and property (even if he is not a Muslim); in return for his services in fighting on behalf of the Community and the Faith, he has certain claims on the revenues for his maintenance and upon any booty that may accrue. Patriotism in the political or geographical sense is irrelevant; apostasy is the equivalent of treason and is punished with death.

But at the very heart of their theory there lay a contradiction of which the Muslim jurists were well aware, though it seldom found expression in their expositions. For the fundamental loyalty of the Muslim is given not to the imām but to the sharī'a. The Qur'ān lays upon the Believers not only religious, social, and military duties, but also the obligation to summon or persuade men to the good and restrain them from the evil and forbidden, and the moral responsibility thus imposed upon them is not limited in any way. To require of the citizen complete submission to the ideal imāmate postulated by the jurists was logical enough, since it was practically identical with the rule of the sharī'a. The historical caliphate, on the other hand, not only fell notoriously short of the ideal, but had progressively diverged from it. In principle, the jurists admitted the maxim of "No obedience in sin," and the civil wars and rebellions of the first two centuries of the caliphate grimly illustrated the extent to which it found adherents in practice.

It would seem that even in conformist circles there was great reluctance to exclude the operation of this principle from the political life of the community. As late as the end of the second century A. H., Abū Yūsuf still included in his selection of political admonitions two that asserted the moral responsibility of subjects to reprove and correct evil conduct on the part of their leaders. A century later, on the other hand, al-Ash'arī explicitly denounced "the error of those who hold it right to rise against the imāms whensoever there may be apparent in them a falling away from right."[9]

Two reasons may be discerned why the jurists failed to build upon this foundation of moral duty a doctrine of civic duty. The first, and most important, was the excesses committed by the Khārijīs, who asserted the moral obligation to resist an evildoing imām as the pretext for their repeated rebellions, and who fanatically classed all Muslims who failed to support their cause as unbelievers and wreaked a bloody vengeance upon them. In reaction, the orthodox could not but lean towards the other extreme, and this attitude was further strengthened by the revival of the old political traditions of Persia under the 'Abbāsid caliphs.

For a considerable period, it is true, the Persian influences were confined to the new secretarial class at the capital, who remained aloof from and even hostile to the Arabic culture of Islamic juristic circles. This is reflected in the exclusively religious and Arabic content of Abū Yūsuf's admonitions to Harūn al-Rashīd, in contrast to the contemporary manuals of political advice written by the secretarial officials, and is openly expressed in his injunction to the caliph to "quicken the sunnas" (see above, p. 5). But the two currents of political thought gradually converged, and assimilated elements from one another. Since the Persian tradition fixed an impassable gulf between sovereign and subjects and taught the divine right of kings in its most absolute form, subject only to open religious apostasy on his part, it fostered the belief that rebellion was the most heinous of crimes, and its doctrine came to be consecrated in the juristic maxim, "Sixty years of tyranny are better than an hour of civil strife."

Another equally effective, and perhaps more insidious, Persian contribution to Islamic thought was the rigid division of the subject population into classes: military, official, religious, mercantile,

[9] Ash'arī, *Kitāb al-Ibāna* (Hyderabad, A. H. 1321), p. 12.

and masses, each confined to its proper functions and status. Such a hierarchical organization of society was never completely accepted by the early Islamic jurists but, as will be seen presently, it dominated later political thought and has left its traces even in al-Baghdādī's exposition of the "classical" juristic theory.[10]

In consequence of their neglect of the rights of the individual against arbitrary government, the classical jurists have been reproached, both by some later mediaeval writers and especially by modern critics, with consecrating a theory of absolutism. By disregarding the stipulation that the imām's authority is bound up with his maintenance of the sharī'a on the one hand, and insisting upon the unchanged obligation of submission to him on the other, they emptied the "contract" of all moral content and left only the factor of power operative in the political organization of the Community.

The criticism is, in itself, more than justified, especially in view of the later developments of the juristic theory. But modern criticism has not, as a rule, fastened upon the failure of the jurists to assert democratic rights in the widest sense; rather, it regrets that they did not develop the germ of republican institutions, which appeared at one moment in the history of the caliphate, into an effective organ of constitutional government. The occasion was the election of the third caliph, in succession to 'Umar in 644, when (whether on the instructions of 'Umar or not) all the probable candidates for the succession assembled to debate the matter in a shūra or committee. Together with this instance, some modern writers have deduced from the references in the historical sources to 'Umar's consulting with other Companions (read in the light of the injunctions to consultation between the Believers found in the Qur'ān,[11] the existence of something like a regular shūra during his caliphate.

But there is, in fact, nothing in the texts to justify the suggestion that 'Umar's consultation was more than informal, or that there was at Medina any recognized consultative committee, still less a cabinet. The striking successes of the Muslim armies and the expansion of the Arab empire had thrust upon the successors of Muḥammad vast new responsibilities which, in their capacity as imāms, they were compelled to shoulder in person and which (since all authority was concentrated in them) could be shouldered by no other person except by delegation (wilāya) from them. In

10 See above, pp. 7-11.

11 Especially III, 153-9, and XLII, 36-8.

the early decades they had perforce devolved on their governors in the provinces extensive powers of subdelegation; but as the government became increasingly centralized with the building-up of a bureaucratic structure, it became possible for the 'Abbāsid caliphs to delegate directly all the principal administrative and judicial offices throughout the empire.

THE CALIPH AS AN ABSOLUTE RULER

The actual historical system, therefore, with which the jurists were confronted was a system in which all political authority was centered in the caliph-imām, and no authority was valid unless exercised by delegation from him, directly or indirectly. This system is explicitly assumed in the first juristic exposition of government, that of Abū Yūsuf, and there is little indication that any Sunnī jurist ever imagined the possibility of any other system of government. Even had they done so, the same motives which determined their defense of the historical caliphate would have forced them to defend its fundamental principle of administration through wilāya; but as their sectarian opponents seldom, if ever, questioned this principle, and "free" speculation on political theory was, if not impossible, at least discouraged by the very nature of Sunnī apologetics, the historical argument reinforced the religious argument in concentrating all authority on the caliph and confining discussion to his person and functions.

It has often been regarded as ironic that so much of this discussion was historically contemporary with the period of the greatest weakness of the caliphate, when it was, from about 950 to 1050, under the control of Shī'ī princes from the Caspian highlands and deprived of all power and administrative influence. More especially, this comment has been made in regard to the famous work on the "Institutions of Government" (al-aḥkām al-sulṭāniṭyya) by a younger contemporary of al-Baghdādī, the qāḍī Abu'l-Ḥasan al-Māwardī (d. 450/1058). In this work, al-Māwardī combined the Ash'arī juristic arguments relating to the imāmate with an elaborate and extremely detailed exposition of the rules to be observed in the various delegated functions of government and administration (vizierate, military command in the provinces, command of the Holy War, judiciary, prayer leadership, command of the Pilgrimage, collection and distribution of taxes, and public censorship). Of these offices a few—notably the caliph's vizierate—no longer existed at the time, and most of the others were controlled not by the caliph but by the temporal princes.

At the beginning of this chapter, however, it was pointed out that the constitutional organization of the state according to the principles of the sharī'a was regarded by the Islamic jurists as immutable in principle, and unaffected by historical circumstances except in the minor details of application at a given time. Right is right, though might may gain a temporary triumph; and it is possible, as has been suggested, that al-Māwardī's work was in reality in the nature of a program, which looked forward to an early restoration of the full powers of the caliphate and set out to define what those powers were and how they should be exercised.

There is no need to discuss in detail the points on which al-Māwardī differs from his predecessors in his exposition of the imāmate, except to note that (probably with an eye to discrediting the rival Fāṭimid caliphate at Cairo) he decisively rejects the admissibility of two imāms at the same time.[12] Much more pertinent are the admissions which he makes in discussing the "delegation" of government of the provinces. Here again the problem was one of validating an actual state of affairs. In the "classical" theory, a governor of a province, duly invested with the caliph's wilāya, is entitled to the same unqualified obedience from his subjects as is due to the imām, and all his acts and decisions are legally valid, unless revoked by the imām. For some two centuries, however, many provinces had been governed by independent princes, whose rule was based on their own military power. This was technically usurpation, but its illegality was concealed by a device somewhat resembling a concordat. In return for a formal recognition of his own dignity, chiefly by the inclusion of his name on the coinage and in the khuṭba, or Friday allocution in the congregational mosques, and of his right to administer all religious affairs, the caliph issued to the prince a diploma conferring the wilāya of the province upon him, sometimes making the delegation hereditary.

Before al-Māwardī, it seems, no jurist had formally recognized this practice, but if, as has been suggested, his work had a programmatic purpose, it was necessary for him to regularize the situation to the best of his ability. He admits, accordingly, such an "Amirate by Usurpation" (as he frankly terms it), but only in the outer provinces, and only subject to stringent stipulations, intended to guarantee that the concordat is a genuine agreement and not a mere outward formality, such as the conclusion of an alliance for mutual

[12] See H. A. R. Gibb, "Al-Māwardī's Theory of the Khilāfah," *Islamic Culture*, Vol. XI (July, 1937), pp. 291-302.

assistance and the display of a pious obedience towards the caliph by the provincial ruler.

These concessions, al-Māwardī admits, are contrary to the principles of the Law, and can be justified only on two grounds: that necessity dispenses with stipulations which cannot be fulfilled, and that fear of injury to public interests justifies a relaxation of conditions. But by justifying disregard of the law on the grounds of political necessity and expediency, al-Māwardī in effect admits that in certain cases might is to be given the semblance of right. Once this is allowed, the whole superstructure of the juristic system breaks down, and by the end of the same century its collapse is bluntly confessed by the great theologian al-Ghazzālī (d. 505/1111):[13]

> An evil-doing and barbarous sultan, so long as he is supported by military force, so that he can only with difficulty be deposed and that the attempt to depose him would create unendurable civil strife, must of necessity be left in possession and obedience must be rendered to him, exactly as obedience is required to be rendered to those who are placed in command. For in the ḥadīths regarding the duty of obedience to those invested with command and the prohibition of withdrawing one's hand from assisting them there are expressed definite commands and restraints. We consider, then, that the caliphate is contractually assumed by that member of the 'Abbāsid house who is charged with its functions, and that the office of government (wilāya) in the various lands is validly executed by sultans who profess allegiance to the caliph. . . . In short, we have regard to the qualifications and stipulations regarding sultans for the sake of the interest of public welfare. For if we were to decide that all wilāyāt are now null and void, all institutions of public welfare would also be absolutely null and void. How should the capital be dissipated in straining after the profit? Nay, but the wilāya in these days is a consequence solely of military power, and whosoever he may be to whom the holder of military power professes his allegiance, that person is the caliph. And whosoever exercises independent authority, while he shows allegiance to the caliph by mentioning his name in the khuṭba and on the coinage, he is a sultan, whose orders and judgments are executed in the several parts of the earth by a valid wilāya.

For the justification of this statement he refers his readers to his argument in an earlier work:[14]

> These concessions which we make are involuntary, but necessities make allowable even what is prohibited. . . . Who is there, I ask, who would not support this, but would argue for the voidance of the

13 Ghazzālī, *Iḥyā 'ulūm al-dīn* (Cairo 1933), Vol. II, p. 124.

14 Ghazzālī *Kitāb al-Iqtiṣād* (Cairo A. H. 1320), p. 107.

imāmate in our day because of the lack of the requisite qualifications? . . . Which is the better part, that we should declare that the qāḍīs are divested of their functions, that all wilāyāt are invalid, that no marriages can be legally contracted, that all executive actions in all parts of the earth are null and void, and to allow that the whole creation is living in sin—or to recognize that the imāmate is held by a valid contract, and that all executive acts and jurisdictions are valid, given the circumstances as they are and the necessity of these times?

It is possible, however, to read too much into these passages. Al-Ghazzālī was not arguing that the caliphate had become merely a formal symbol for the legitimation of rights acquired by force, although his language shows that in some circles, at least, it was already so regarded. On the contrary, the whole point of his argument is that, although the caliphate was shorn of all its political functions, yet, by whomsoever it was held, it continued to represent the supremacy of the sharī'a as the law of the Islamic Community. This was the "capital," the rest was but the "profit." The guarantee of maintenance of the sharī'a was formally assumed in the bay'a given by the sultans to the caliph; so long as that was done, then in all its public acts and relationships the Community was still living under the Law.

THE CALIPHATE AND THE SULTANATE

There is no reason to regard this as yet one more legal fiction. Rather, it followed in the path of Sunnī tradition by adjusting the juristic theory to the circumstances of its time. The rise of the Seljuk sultanate had destroyed the hopes on which al-Māwardī's exposition was built. Caliphate and sultanate were now and henceforth two separate institutions, and the only chance of salvaging something from the wreckage lay in an alliance between them (which was, for a time, actually realized) by which the caliphate retained its responsibility for, and supervision of, the Community's religious activities, and the sultanate conducted the temporal affairs of government. Hence the term sultān, signifying "temporal power," which had in earlier times been applied loosely to caliphs and temporal governors alike, now became an official title conferred by the caliph on sovereign princes in the temporal sphere.[15]

Satisfactory though the theory of a concordat or alliance might

[15] In the parallel case of the decline of the temporal power of the Fātimid (Shī'ī) caliphs at Cairo, a different solution was found. There the supreme military commander was officially appointed vizier to the Caliph, with the formal style of "the sultān" (cf. Abū Shāma, *Kitāb al-Rawdatayn* [Cairo, A. H., 1287], Vol. I, p. 130, line 13).

be for the jurists, the sultanate was too massive an institution and too closely associated with military power to be tied to any external definition of its status. For the independent power which it was already acquiring and exercising, an immediate religious authority was found in the old tradition, "The sultan is the shadow of God upon His earth, with whom all the oppressed find refuge," a maxim which never fails to make an appearance (though generally without the second clause) in all subsequent political writings and dedications.

The resulting duality of powers and functions was still more sharply emphasized by the emergence of a distinctive political theory of the sultanate, based, in Ibn Khaldūn's classification, on "rational statecraft and its principles," and in particular on the old Persian tradition. Its standard exposition was given in the "Book of Government" (*Siyāset-nāmah*) of the Nizām ul-Mulk, vizier of the Seljuk sultans Alp Arslān and Malikshah (d. 485/1092). Apart from a brief selection of old juristic traditions, this work (which was destined to become the textbook of all later generations of Persian and Turkish rulers) owes nothing to Islamic theory; its arguments are based on expediency, and its proofs are drawn from history and experience. The caliphate is scarcely mentioned, and the whole exposition is centered on the "monarch" (pādishāh) "whom God selects and adorns with kingly qualities, and to whom He entrusts the well-being and peace of His servants." Even in his injunctions to maintain the orthodox faith and respect the doctors of religion, the Nizām does not rise above the level of political advantage:

> The best thing which a pādishāh must possess is true religion, for sovereignty and religion are as two brothers. Whensoever the state is disturbed, religion also suffers, and evil men and sowers of discord appear. Likewise when religion is attacked by disorders the state also is thrown into confusion; the sowers of discord seize the power and destroy the prestige of pādishāhs, heresy raises its head, and insurgents incite to violence.

The century of warfare between the caliphs and sultans which followed the decline of the Seljuks inevitably brought a sharp conflict between the two claims to authority. With their recovery of a measure of temporal rule the caliphs again asserted their headship of the Islamic world, but though it was accepted by Nūr al-Dīn and Saladin in the west, the Turkish sultans in Persia continued to maintain the incompatibility of religious headship with temporal power:

It is the duty of the imām to concern himself with the khuṭba and the prayers, which the temporal rulers are engaged in protecting, and which are the best of works and the highest offices, but to commit the sovereignty (pādishāhī) to sultans and leave worldly rule to their authority.[16]

On the other hand, the caliph's vizier asserted that the sultans derived their authority by delegation from the caliph's diwān, and put forward the claim that all Islamic lands were the property of the caliph and that no other person had any rights of property in these lands whatsoever.[17]

All this bandying of claims, however, could not conceal the fact that the acquisition of a small temporal kingdom by the later caliphs was in no sense a re-establishment of the old caliphate, but only served to assimilate the caliphate to the contemporary sultanates. Although it remained a symbol of historic continuity, venerated often in proportion to distance from Baghdad, yet by its involvement in petty local conflicts it was fast losing its power to stand for the spiritual unity of Islam. Thus the blow inflicted by the Mongol conquest of Baghdad in 1258 was less decisive than it seemed, in their consternation, to the contemporary Islamic peoples. The political theory of the Sunnī jurists had in its evolution acquired, as has already been seen, a sufficient degree of flexibility to accommodate itself to new situations. The disappearance of the 'Abbāsid caliphate did little more than remove from the scene one element which, whatever sentimental associations might still cling to it, was no longer relevant to the circumstances of an Islamic world in which political unity was henceforth a manifest impossibility, and of which a large portion was actually ruled by infidel Mongols.

So vividly and universally was this recognized that the attempt of the Mamlūk sultans of Egypt to resuscitate the 'Abbāsid caliphate in Cairo was generally ignored. Though it might gratify the Mamlūks to receive a formal diploma of investiture from their pensioners whom they in turn invested with caliphial titles, there is scarcely a single jurist who so much as refers to them. Yet the conviction persisted amongst Muslims in general that temporal power in itself carried no authority; the sole authority was that of the sharī'a and temporal power could be validated only by association with the sharī'a. The problem which they now faced was to determine the nature of that association.

16 Rāwandī, *Rāḥat al-Ṣudūr* (London 1921), p. 384.
17 *Ibid.*, p. 381.

In the exposition of the leading Ḥanafī jurist of Egypt under the early Mamlūks,[18] this essential principle is obscured. Ibn Jamā'a simply transfers, without more ado, the whole apparatus of the Māwardīan theory to the sultans; if election or nomination of an imām is out of the question, then there remains only "usurpation":

> As for the third method of acquisition of the imāmate, that whereby the bay'a is contracted by force, this is when a person possessed of military power exercises compulsion. If the office of imām is vacant at the time, and there aspires to it one who does not possess the qualifications for it but who imposes himself on the people by his might and his armies without any bay'a or nomination by his predecessor, then his bay'a is lawfully contracted and obedience to him is compulsory, for the sake of restoring and preserving the unity of the Muslims. This is in no way invalidated by his being barbarous or an evil-doer, according to the most authoritative opinion. When the imāmate is thus contractually assumed by one person in virtue of his military power and conquest, and there subsequently rises up another who overcomes the first by his might and his armies, then the first is deposed and the second becomes imām, on the grounds which we have already stated, namely, the well-being and unity of the Muslims.

But this doctrine, which amounted in effect to a complete divorce of the imāmate from the sharī'a and the abandonment of the Law in favor of a secular absolutism, was a patent contradiction, which could not be accepted by the general Community of Muslims. Least of all could it be accepted outside the Mamlūk dominions, where it seemed to imply recognition of the claim of the Mamlūks to be the universal "sultans of Islam." There is little evidence, in fact, that it was taken seriously in any quarter; but at least it served to show that the whole theoretical structure from which it derived had to be rejected, and some other principle found for the association of the state with the sharī'a.

Among the most vigorous critics of this doctrine was Ibn Jamā'a's lifelong opponent, Ibn Taymiyya, who in his effort to cleanse Islam of its accretions of heresy, deviations, and abuses, and to preach a return to the purity of early doctrine and practice, inevitably attacked the web of juristic argument regarding the caliphate. There is no obligation, he argued, whether in the Qur'ān, the sunna, or the ijmā' of the Companions, upon all Muslims to recognize a single caliphate. The historic caliphate was a temporary institution, based upon the Prophet's testament, and limited to the four rāshidūn. Since that time there have been only

18 Ibn Jamā'a, chief Ḥanafī qāḍī (1291-94 and 1309-27). "Taḥrīr al-Aḥkām," *Islamica*, Bd. VI (Leipzig, 1934), p. 357.

imāmates; but there are no canonical limitations upon their number and all talk of election is fictitious. The only political chiefs known to Islamic history are the temporal princes; their authority as imāms is acquired by a mutual contract with the Community in general, whereby the temporal princes, in close collaboration with the 'ulamā', carry out their religious and political functions as the sharī'a directs, and receive in return loyal obedience from the people. There is no unitary Islamic state, and the unity of Islam is assured simply by the community of structure and cooperation of the existing Islamic states.[19]

In limiting the term "caliphate" to the first four successors of Muḥammad and distinguishing it from the continuing "imāmate," Ibn Taymiyya was reasserting a doctrine which had been held for several centuries by the orthodox school of al-Maturīdī (d. 333/944) and had begun to enjoy more general acceptance since the end of the 'Abbāsid caliphate. In his identification of the imāms with the temporal princes he seemed, it is true, to reach the same conclusions in practice as Ibn Jamā'a, but for the admission of an indefinite number of such imāms at any one time, and the somewhat idealizing stipulation of their close cooperation with the 'ulamā'. This last condition, however, saved the principle by supplying both the requisite link between the temporal power and the sharī'a and the moral and religious basis of authority which Ibn Jamā'a's exposition had discarded, or seemed to discard.

There was, indeed, no way open to a solution of the problem except along these lines. We may suppose that it was felt with special acuteness in the Persian lands of Eastern Islam, where a long struggle had to be waged to restore the supremacy of the sharī'a over the Mongol code. That a Mongol and a Muslim prince enjoyed the same authority and were entitled to the same obedience was passionately denied by the Muslims under Mongol rule; for them the distinction was fundamental between government in accordance with the sharī'a and government on any other principles. The author of the compendium of Islamic history called *al-Fakhrī,* writing in 1302 under the rule of the converted Mongol Khan Ghazan, expresses their impatience when, after enumerating the good qualities which a king should possess—intelligence, justice, knowledge, clemency, fear of God, dignity, power to maintain discipline, loyalty to his word, supervision of the affairs of his kingdom, and generosity—he adds:

[19] H. Laoust, *Essai sur les doctrines d'Ibn Taimiya* (Cairo 1939), pp. 278-317; the same, *Le traité de droit public d'Ibn Taimiya,* (Beyrouth, 1948).

Whosoever possesses these qualities is worthy of the supreme headship, and if those who maintain various opinions and doctrines were to see things as they are and abandon their arbitrary notions, these are the conditions which would be taken into consideration in determining fitness for the *imāmate*. As for all the other things, they are of no account.[20]

This current of ideas was, in the eastern Muslim world, reinforced by a tributary which, after running for some centuries on the margins of Islamic thought, now entered the mainstream of Persian literature. From the beginnings of their acquaintance with Greek philosophy, Muslim philosophers had been attracted to the Platonic ideal of the philosopher-king, and from the time of al-Fārābī (d. 339/950) they had attempted to translate it into Muslim terms.[21] The earlier expositions had been too strongly tinged with Shī'ī and mystical doctrines to gain much favor among the orthodox, but the philosopher Nasīr al-dīn Ṭūsī (d. 672/1274), in an influential ethical treatise, brought it into close accommodation with the history of the Muslim caliphate.[22] He wrote:

The supreme leadership in the Virtuous City has four states:

(i) When there is living among them a king in the absolute sense. The sign of this is the union of four things in him: (a) wisdom, which is the aim of all aims; (b) perfect reasoning power, which leads to the attainment of aims; (c) excellence of persuasion and imagination, which is of the conditions of bringing to perfection; (d) power of fighting, which is of the conditions of protection and defense. His leadership is called the leadership of wisdom.

(ii) When there is no manifest king, and these four qualities are not united in one person but exist in four persons, and they by cooperation with one another undertake the administration of the city like a single soul. This is called the leadership of the virtuous.

(iii) When both these leaderships are nonexistent, but there is present a leader who is acquainted with the precedents set by former leaders who were adorned with the characteristics described above, and who by the excellence of his discrimination is able to utilize each precedent in its proper place, and is capable of deducing that which is not found in explicit form in the precedents of his forerunners from that which is explicit, and who combines excellence of address and persuasion and power of fighting. His leadership is called the leadership of precedent (sunnat).

(iv) When these characters are not united in one person, but are to be found in a number of different individuals, and these in cooperation undertake the administration of the city. This is called the leadership of the followers of precedent (asḥāb-i sunnat).

20 Ibn al-Ṭiqṭaqa, *al-Fakhrī* (Cairo A. H. 1317), p. 21.
21 See T. W. Arnold, *The Caliphate* (Oxford 1924), Chap. X.
22 Ṭūsī, *Akhlāq-i Nāsirī*, lith. 1883, pp. 410-11.

Stripped of its rationalizing elements, this teaching came closely into line with the principle that the Sunnī leaders were endeavoring to establish, that the true caliphate is that form of government which safeguards the ordinances of the sharī'a and aims to apply them in practice. How universally this doctrine was coming to be held may be seen from the positive manner in which the North African Ibn Khaldūn postulates it in the passage already quoted (p. 13), and from the common ascription of the term khalīfa to Muslim princes in all parts of the world in the fourteenth and fifteenth centuries. It can be said with conviction that the "classical" juristic theory of al-Ash'arī and his school fell completely into disuse from this time.

One final step still remained to be taken, namely, the theoretical reconciliation of the khilāfa of the righteous king with the current Persian doctrines of kingship, as set out by the Nizām ul-Mulk. Much thought had doubtless gone into this problem before its final and most successful definition by the Persian qāḍī Jalāl ud-Dīn Dawwānī (d. 908/1502) in a reworking of Ṭūsī's treatise, which remained until recent times one of the most popular works of Persian literature.[23]

Sovereignty in this exposition is a gift divinely bestowed upon the most eminent men. God sets one of His chosen servants upon the throne of the khilāfa, and devolves upon him the apportionment of rights and duties, as it is said in the Qur'ān: "We have made thee, O David, Our vicegerent on earth, therefore judge between men righteously," that is, with equity. The righteous government, which "considers the subjects as children and friends" and labors for their temporal and spiritual welfare, is the imāmate; whereas unrighteous government is the rule of force, which treats its subjects as beasts of burden and slaves.

Equity demands that each class and every member in his class should be maintained in his proper station. These classes consist of four political and social orders:

(1) "men of the pen," i.e., men of religious learning and insight, preachers, poets, and scientists;
(2) "men of the sword," the guardians of the state;
(3) men of business, artisans and craftsmen;
(4) husbandmen and producers of food.

[23] Dawwānī, *Akhlāq-i Jalālī*, translated by W. F. Thompson under the title of *Practical Philosophy of the Muhammadan People* (London, 1830), Chap. III, pp. 365 ff.

The sovereign must therefore see to the equitable maintenance of these classes in their own stations and functions; so long as each retains its proper place and receives its due portion of provision and honor, the state is well-balanced and its affairs are well regulated.

If we compare this latest exposition of Islamic political thought with the terms in which Abū Yūsuf addressed Harūn al-Rashīd (p. 5 above), we cannot but be struck with the remarkable consistency and tenacity with which the Muslim thinkers had pursued their main objective. The historic caliphate had lost its power and had perished, military conquerors had imposed their rule over every Muslim people, a rigid class structure had replaced the fluid social order of the early days, but through all vicissitudes the principles of Muslim government remained unchanged. It was on these same principles that both the Ottoman and the Mughal sultans continued to organize their administrations in the centuries that followed, until internal weaknesses brought the intrusion of new social and political ideas based upon an alien philosophy.

CHAPTER II

Pre-Islamic Background and Early Development of Jurisprudence

ISLAMIC LAW is the epitome of the Islamic spirit, the most typical manifestation of the Islamic way of life, the kernel of Islam itself. For the majority of Muslims, the law has always been and still is of much greater practical importance than the dogma. Even today the law remains a decisive element in the struggle which is being fought in Islam between traditionalism and modernism under the impact of Western ideas. It is impossible to understand the present legal development in the Islamic countries of the Middle East without a correct appreciation of the past history of legal theory, of positive law, and of legal practice in Islam.

Islamic law was created by Islam, but the raw material out of which it was formed was to a great extent non-Islamic.[1] This raw material, itself of varied provenance, was tested by religious and ethical standards, and gained a uniform character in the process. The operation of these standards, however, did not affect all fields of law equally; hardly noticeable in some cases, it led to the creation of novel institutions in others. Thus, in early Islam, legal institutions were only incompletely assimilated to the body of Islamic religious and ethical duties, and retained some of their own distinctive qualities.

Arabian law in the time of Muḥammad was not altogether rudimentary. Primitive indeed was the customary law of the Bedouin, some traces of which have survived in pre-Islamic and early Islamic poetry, and in tales of the tribes. The comparable conditions existing among the Bedouin in modern times, enable us to verify the information of these literary sources. Mecca, however, was a trading city in close commercial relations with South Arabia, Byzantine Syria, and Sassanian 'Iraq; and Medina was an oasis of palm-trees with a strong colony of Jews, mostly Arab converts. It is likely that both cities possessed a law or laws, probably

[1] For the whole of this chapter and the beginning of Chapter III, see J. Schacht, *The Origins of Muhammadan Jurisprudence* (Oxford, 1950); the same, *G. Bergstr ässer's Grundzüge des islamischen Rechts* (Berlin and Leipzig, 1935), pp. 8 ff.

containing foreign elements, which was more highly developed than that of the Bedouin. We can form some idea of the character of commercial life in Mecca and of the kind of law which it presupposes. The customary commercial law of Mecca was enforced by the traders among themselves, in much the same way as was the Law Merchant in Western Europe. In the case of Medina and other settlements, it can be presumed that agricultural contracts and land law were of similar importance. The law of family relationships and of inheritance, and the whole of the penal law, however, both among the Bedouin and the sedentary population, was dominated by the ancient Arabian tribal system. This system implied the absence of legal protection for the individual outside his tribe, the absence of a developed concept of criminal justice and the subsumption of crimes under torts, the responsibility of the tribal group for the actions of its members, and therefore unlimited vengeance for homicide, mitigated by the institution of weregeld (blood money).

The absence of an organized political authority in Arab society, both Bedouin and sedentary, implied the absence of an organized judicial system.[2] This does not mean that private justice prevailed in settling litigation concerning property rights, succession, and torts other than homicide. In these cases, if protracted negotiation between the parties led to no result, recourse was normally had to an arbitrator (ḥakam). The arbitrator did not belong to a particular caste; the parties were free to appoint as ḥakam any person on whom they agreed, but he was hardly ever the chief of the tribe. A ḥakam was chosen for his personal qualities, his knowledge, his wisdom, his integrity, his reputation, and last but not least, his supernatural powers. As supernatural powers of divination were found most commonly among soothsayers (kāhin), they were most often resorted to as arbitrators. Certain families and tribes also gained the reputation of special competence in deciding lawsuits, and their members were often chosen as arbitrators. Besides choosing an arbitrator, the parties to a lawsuit had to agree on the cause in action, the question which they were to put before the ḥakam. In order to test his powers, the parties regularly made the ḥakam divine an agreed secret, for instance a hidden object and its hiding place. The ḥakam, on his part, was free to accept or to refuse to act in any particular litigation. If he agreed to act, each party had to give security, either property or hostages, as a guar-

[2] E. Tyan, *Histoire de l'organisation judiciaire en pays d'Islam* (Paris, 1938), Vol. I, pp. 30 ff.

antee that they would submit to his decision. The decision of the ḥakam, which was final, was not an enforceable judgment (the execution had indeed to be guaranteed by the security), but rather a statement of right on a disputed point. It therefore became easily an authoritative statement of what the law was, or ought to be; the function of the arbitrator merged into that of a lawmaker, an authoritative expounder of the normative legal custom or sunna. The arbitrators applied and at the same time developed the sunna; it was the sunna, with the force of public opinion behind it, which had in the first place insisted on the procedure of negotiation and arbitration. Though thoroughly changed by Islam, these conditions have left lasting traces in Islamic law.

Muḥammad emerged in Mecca as a religious reformer, and he protested strongly when his pagan countrymen regarded him as merely another soothsayer. Because of his personal authority, he was invited to Medina as an arbitrator in tribal disputes, and as the Prophet he became the ruler and the legal authority of the Muslim community. His rejection of the character of a kāhin brought with it the rejection of heathen arbitration, inasmuch as the arbitrators were often soothsayers.[3] Nevertheless, when he served as a judge in his community, the Prophet continued to act in the function of a ḥakam.[4] Whenever the Qur'ān speaks of the Prophet's judicial activity, the verb ḥakama and its derivatives are used, whereas the verb *qaḍa'*, from which the term qāḍī was to be derived, refers in the Qur'ān regularly not to the judgment of a judge, but to a sovereign ordinance, either of Allah or of the Prophet. (It also occurs in connection with the Day of Judgment, but this is a judgment only in a figurative sense.) In a single verse, both verbs occur side by side;[5] here, the first refers to the arbitrating aspect of the Prophet's activity, whereas the second emphasizes the authoritative character of his decision. This isolated instance is the first indication of the emergence of a new, Islamic idea of the administration of justice. Thus, the Prophet attached great importance to being appointed by the believers as a ḥakam in their disputes, though the insistence of the Qur'ān on this point shows that the ancient freedom in the choice of a ḥakam still prevailed; the Prophet, too, reserved to himself the right of the ḥakam to refuse to act. His position as a Prophet, however, backed in the later stages of his career in Medina by a considerable political and

[3] Qur'ān IV, 60 (Egyptian ed.)
[4] Tyan, *op. cit.*, Vol. I, 85 ff.
[5] Qur'ān IV, 65.

military power, gave him a much greater authority than could be claimed by an arbitrator; he became a "Prophet-Lawgiver." However, he wielded his almost absolute power not within but without the existing legal system; his authority was not legal, but for the believers, religious, and for the lukewarm, political.

The legislation of the Prophet, too, was an innovation in the law of Arabia. Generally speaking, Muḥammad had little reason to change the prevailing customary law. His aim as a Prophet was not to create a new system of law; it was to teach men how to act, what to do and what to avoid, in order to pass the reckoning on the Day of Judgment and to enter Paradise. This is why Islam in general, and Islamic law in particular, is a system of duties, comprising ritual, legal, and moral obligations on the same footing, and bringing them all under the authority of the same religious command. Had religious and ethical standards been comprehensively applied to all aspects of human behavior, and had they been consistently followed in practice, there would have been no room and no need for a legal system in the narrow meaning of the term. This was in fact the original ideal of Muḥammad, and traces of it, such as the recurrent insistence on the merits of forgiveness and of deferring or renouncing one's claims, are found in the Qur'ān; but the Prophet finally had to resign himself to applying religious and ethical principles to the legal problems and relationships as he found them.

Thus we find in the Qur'ān injunctions to arbitrate with justice, not to offer bribes, to give true evidence, and to give full weight and measure. Contracts are safeguarded by the demand to put them in writing, to give earnest-money, and to call witnesses (all of these are pre-Islamic practices which the Qur'ān endorses); or, in short, by the command to fulfill them, a command which is typical of the ethical attitude of the Qur'ān toward legal matters. Even the prohibitions of gambling and of taking interest, though directly concerned with certain types of contracts, are not meant to lay down legal rules regulating the form and effects of these contracts, but to establish moral norms under which they are allowed or prohibited. The idea that such contracts, if they are concluded notwithstanding the prohibition, are invalid and do not create obligations, does not yet appear in the Qur'ān. The same attitude governs the Qur'ānic law of war and booty and the whole complex of family law. The law of war and booty is primarily concerned with determining the enemies who must be fought or may be fought, how the booty is to be distributed (within the general framework of the rules laid down by pre-Islamic custom), and how the conquered are to be treated. Family law and the law of inheritance are the only legal subjects that are fairly exhaustively treated in the Qur'ān, albeit in a number of scattered passages; here again the main emphasis is laid on the problem of how one should act towards women and children, orphans and relatives, dependents and slaves. The effects of a lawful action are not mentioned and are as a rule self-evident; but the effects of an unlawful action, for instance, the question of civil responsibility, are hardly envisaged either. Technical legal statements attaching legal consequences to certain sets of relevant facts or acts are lacking almost completely, as far as the law of obligations and family relations are concerned. They exist, and are indeed almost indispensable, in the field of penal law. It is easy to understand that the normative legislation of the Qur'ān incorporated sanctions for transgressions, but again they are essentially moral and only incidentally penal; the prohibition is the essential element, the provision concerning the punishment is a rule of action either for the organs of the newly created Islamic state, or for the victim and his next of kin who, according to ancient Arab ideas, had the right of retaliation. The Qur'ān is content to prohibit wine-drinking, gambling, and taking of interest without fixing a penalty (unless it be punishment in Hell). There are provisions concerning retaliation and weregeld, theft, unchastity, and slanderous allegation of unchastity, as well as procedure in the last two cases.

The reasons for Qur'ānic legislation on all these matters were, generally speaking, dissatisfaction with prevailing conditions, the tendency to improve the position of women and of the weak in general, and the desire to mitigate the practice of vengeance and retaliation; the prohibition of wine-drinking, gambling, and taking of interest, too, constitute a break with ancient Arabian standards of behavior. Besides, it had become necessary to deal with new problems which had arisen in family law, in the law of retaliation, and in the law of war because of the main political aim of the Prophet, the dissolution of the ancient tribal organization and the creation of a community of believers in its stead. It is possible that some actual disputes made the need obvious. Such disputes, it seems, were mainly responsible for legislation on matters of inheritance, a subject which is farthest removed from the action of moral principles and most closely connected with the granting of individual rights. In this case, too, Qur'ānic legislation lays down primarily not basic principles of law but rules of action regarding the estates of deceased persons; the ethical element appears in the urgent injunction to act justly in making wills, and generally in the tendency to allot shares in the inheritance to persons who had no claim to succession under the old customary law. This feature of Qur'ānic legislation was preserved in the system of Islamic law, and the purely legal attitude, which attaches legal consequences to relevant acts, is often superseded by the tendency to establish ethical standards for the believer.

The first three generations after the death of the Prophet, or in other words, the first century of Islam (seventh-eighth century A.D.) are in many respects the most important, though because of the scarcity of contemporary evidence, the most obscure period in the history of Islamic law. In this period, many distinctive features of Islamic law came into being and the nascent Islamic society created its own legal institutions. What little authentic evidence is available shows that the ancient Arab system of arbitration, and Arab customary law in general, continued under the first successors of the Prophet, the caliphs of Medina (seventh century A.D.) The caliphs, it is true, were the political leaders of the Islamic community after the death of the Prophet, but they do not seem to have acted as its supreme arbitrators, and there still remained room at a slightly later period for the exhortation to choose one's arbitrators from the tribe of the Prophet, the Quraysh. In their function as the supreme rulers and administrators, though of course devoid of the religious authority of the Prophet, the caliphs acted to a great extent as law-givers of the community; during the whole of this first century, the administrative and legislative activities of the Islamic government cannot be separated. This administrative legislation, however, was hardly, if at all, concerned with modifying the existing customary law; its object was to provide for the need of organizing the newly conquered territories for the benefit of the Arabs. In the field of penal law, the first caliphs went beyond the penal sanctions enacted in the Qur'ān by punishing, for instance, the authors of satirical poems directed against rival tribes, a common form of poetic expression in ancient Arabia. The enforcement of the law of retaliation and weregeld continued to be the responsibility of the next of kin of the victim. That the first caliphs did not appoint qāḍīs and in general did not lay the foundations of what later became the Islamic system of administration of justice, is shown by the contradictions and inherent improbabilities of the stories which assert the contrary; the alleged instructions for judges given by the Caliph 'Umar, too, are a product of the third Islamic century.[6]

Towards the end of the period of the caliphs of Medina, about the middle of the first century of Islam, the Islamic community was rent by political schisms, and the two "sectarian" movements of the Khārijīs and of the Shī'a established themselves beside the "orthodox" or Sunnī majority. The doctrines of Islamic law as adopted by the Khārijīs and by the Shī'a do not vary greatly from those of the several orthodox schools of law. From this, it was once concluded that the essential features common to these several forms of Islamic law were worked out before the schism, i.e., earlier than the middle of the first Islamic century. But recent research has shown that the ancient sects of Islam, at the time they split from the orthodox community, could not have shared with the majority the essentials of a system of law which did not yet exist. Rather, they adopted the fully developed legal system of the orthodox community, making only superficial changes of their own, in the second half of the second century of Islam or even later.

At an early period, the ancient Arab idea of sunna, of precedent or tradition, reasserted itself in Islam.[7] The Arabs were, and are, bound by tradition and precedent. Whatever was customary was right and proper; whatever the forefathers had done deserved to be imitated. This was the golden rule of the Arabs whose existence on a narrow margin in an unpropitious environment did not leave them much room for experiments and innovations which might upset the balance of their lives. In this idea of precedent or sunna the whole conservatism of the Arabs found expression. They recognized, of course, that a sunna might have been laid down by an individual in the relatively recent past, but then that individual was considered the spokesman and representative of the whole group. The idea of sunna presented a formidable obstacle to every innovation, and in order to discredit anything it was, and still is, enough to call it an innovation. Islam, the greatest innovation that Arabia saw, had to overcome this opposition, and a hard fight it was. But once Islam had prevailed, even among one single group of Arabs, the old conservatism reasserted itself; what had shortly before been an innovation, now became the thing to do, a thing hallowed by precedent and tradi-

[6] Tyan, *op. cit.*, Vol. I, 98 ff.

[7] I. Goldziher, "The Principles of Law in Islam," in *The Historian's History of the World*, Vol. VIII (New York, 1904), pp. 294 ff.

tion, a sunna. This ancient Arab concept of sunna became one of the central concepts of Islamic law.

It would seem natural to suppose that the explicit precepts of the Qur'ān on legal matters were observed from the beginning, at least as far as turbulent Arab society in a time of revolutionary change was amenable to rules. There are, indeed, two early decisions concerning a problem of divorce, one of which is based on the authoritative version of the Qur'ān, and the other on a variant reading. As the variant readings were officially abolished during the reign of the Umayyad Caliph 'Abd al-Malik (A. H. 65-86), it can be concluded that the doctrine in question had been formulated not later than the middle of the first century of Islam. On the other hand, there are several cases in which the early doctrine of Islamic law diverged from the clear and explicit wording of the Qur'ān. One important example, which has remained typical of Islamic law, is the restriction of legal proof to the evidence of witnesses and the denial of validity to written documents. This contradicts an explicit ruling of the Qur'ān which endorsed the current practice of putting contracts into writing.[8] John of Damascus, who flourished between A.D. 700 and 750, mentions the insistence on witnesses as a characteristic custom of the Saracens, and this, too, was probably established about the middle of the first century of Islam. Nothing is known about its origin.

During the greater part of the first century, Islamic law in the technical meaning of the term did not yet exist. As had been the case in the time of the Prophet, law as such fell outside the sphere of religion, and as far as there were no religious or moral objections to specific transactions or modes of behavior, the technical aspects of law were a matter of indifference to the Muslims. This attitude of the early Muslims accounts for the widespread adoption of legal and administrative institutions of the conquered territories, drawing on Roman (including Roman provincial) law, Sassanian law, Talmudic law, and the canon law of the Eastern churches. Outstanding examples are the treatment of tolerated religions, the methods of taxation, and the institutions of emphyteusis and of pious endowments (waqf). The principle of the retention of pre-Islamic legal institutions under Islam was sometimes even explicitly acknowledged, as in the following passage by an author of the third Islamic century: "Abū Yūsuf held that if there exists in a country an ancient, non-Arab normative custom (sunna) which Islam has neither changed nor abolished,

[8] Q. II, 282.

and people complain to the caliph that it causes them hardship, he is not entitled to change it; but Mālik and al-Shāfiʿī held that he may change it even if it be ancient, because he ought to prohibit (in similar circumstances) every lawful normative custom which has been introduced by a Muslim, let alone those introduced by unbelievers."[9] Both opinions presuppose the retention of pre-Islamic legal practices as normal.

The influence exercised on early Islamic law by the legal systems of the conquered territories, however, was not restricted to legal customs and practices; it extended to the field of legal concepts and principles, and even to fundamental ideas of legal science, such as the methods of systematic reasoning, and the idea of the "consensus of the scholars." The legal concepts and maxims in question are of that general kind which would be familiar not only to lawyers but to all educated persons. We shall see later that Muḥammadan jurisprudence started about the year A. H. 100. It follows not only that the whole first century of Islam was available for the adoption of foreign legal elements by nascent Islamic society, but that Islamic legal science began at a time when the door of Islamic civilization had been opened to potential transmitters of these legal concepts, the educated non-Arab converts to Islam. Some of the doctrines in question, such as the responsibility of the thief for twice the value of the object stolen, or the erection of adultery into a permanent impediment to marriage between the two guilty parties, did not succeed in gaining general acceptance, and only survived as unsuccessful or isolated opinions. This process of infiltration of foreign legal concepts and maxims into Islamic society through the medium of educated non-Arab converts extended over the greater part of the first century of Islam, but its results became apparent only early in the second century, when Islamic legal science came into being. That early Muḥammadan lawyers should have adopted consciously any principle of foreign law is out of the question.

We must now return to the middle of the first Islamic century, when the rule of the first caliphs of Medina was supplanted by that of the Umayyad caliphs of Damascus. The Umayyads were not the adversaries of Islam that they were often made out to be; on the contrary, it was they and their governors who were responsible for developing a number of the essential features of Islamic cult and ritual, of which they had found only rudimentary ele-

9 Beladsori, *Liber expugnationis regionum,* ed. by de Goeje (Leiden, 1865), p. 448.

ments. Their main concern, it is true, was not with religion and religious law, but with political administration, and here they represented the organizing, centralizing and increasingly bureaucratic tendency of an orderly administration as against the Bedouin anarchy of the Arab way of life. Both Islamic religious ideal and Umayyad administration cooperated in creating a new framework for Arab Muslim society, which had been recruited indiscriminately from all Arab tribes and was spread thinly over the vast extent of the conquered territories. In many respects, Umayyad rule represents the consummation, after the turbulent interval of the Caliphate of Medina, of tendencies which were implied by the nature of the Islamic community under the Prophet. This is the background against which the emergence of Islamic law, of an Islamic administration of justice, and of Islamic jurisprudence must be viewed.

The administration of the Umayyads concentrated on waging war against the Byzantines and other external enemies, on collecting revenue from the subject population, and on paying subventions in money or in kind to the Arab beneficiaries; these were the essential functions of the Arab kingdom. We therefore find evidence of Umayyad regulations, or administrative law, particularly in the fields of the law of war and of fiscal law. The accountancy for payments of weregeld straddles the field of penal law, and whereas the Umayyads did not interfere with the working of retaliation as modified by the Qur'ān (all they did here was to try to prevent the recurrence of Arab tribal feuds which threatened the internal security of the state), they supervised the application of the purely Islamic penalties laid down in the Qur'ān and of similar punishments. They, or rather their governors, also took the important step of appointing Islamic judges or qāḍīs. The office of qāḍī was created in and for the new Islamic society which came into being, under the new conditions resulting from the Arab conquest, in the urban centers of the Arab kingdom. For this new society the arbitration of pre-Islamic Arabia and of the earliest period of Islam was no longer adequate.[10] The Arab ḥakam thus was supplanted by the Islamic qāḍī, who was a delegate of the governor. The governor, within the limits set for him by the caliph, had full authority over his province, administrative, legislative and judicial, without any conscious distinction of function, and he could, and in fact regularly did, delegate his judicial authority to his "legal secretary," the qāḍī. The governor retained,

[10] Tyan, *op. cit.* Vol. I. 114 ff.

however, the power of reserving for his own decision any lawsuit he wished, and, of course, the power of dismissing his qāḍī at will.

The jurisdiction of the qāḍī extended to Muslims only; the non-Muslim subject populations retained their own traditional legal institutions, including the ecclesiastical (and rabbinical) tribunals which in the last few centuries before the Muslim conquest had to a great extent duplicated the judicial organization of the Byzantine state. The Byzantine magistrates themselves, together with the other civil officers, had evacuated the lost provinces at the very beginning of the Muslim conquest; nevertheless, because of a fundamental similarity in general structure between late Byzantine and early Islamic organization of justice, it has been suggested that the latter was modeled on the former, a process which may have been part of the adoption by the Muslims of the administrative organization of their predecessors. One administrative office, of which the functions were partly judicial, was indeed taken over in this way: the office of the "inspector of the market" (*agoranomos*), who had a limited civil and criminal jurisdiction. But the early Muslims had not only the Byzantine example on which to model their earliest administration of justice: the "clerk of the court," whose services must have become indispensable at an early period, had the same function as the corresponding official in the Sassanian administration; this was well known to contemporary authors.

The earliest Islamic qāḍīs, officials of the Umayyad administration, by their decisions laid the basic foundations of what was to become Islamic law. We know their names, and there exists a considerable body of information on their lives and judgments, but it is difficult to separate the authentic from the fictitious. Legal doctrines that can be dated to the first century of the hijra are rare, but it is likely that some of the decisions which are attributed to those qāḍīs, and which are irregular by later standards, do indeed go back to that early period. In a slightly later period, we can actually see how the tendency to impose an oath on the plaintiff as a safeguard against the exclusive use of the evidence of witnesses grew out of the judicial practice at the beginning of the second century. The earliest Islamic qāḍīs gave judgment according to their own discretion, or "sound opinion" (ra'y) as it was called, basing themselves on customary practice, which in the nature of things incorporated administrative regulations, and took the letter and the spirit of the Qur'ānic legislation and of other recognized Islamic religious norms into account as much as they thought fit. The customary practice to which they referred was either that of the community under their jurisdiction or that of their own home district, and in this latter case conflicts were bound to arise. Though the legal subject matter had as yet not been Islamicized to any great extent beyond the stage reached in the Qur'ān, the office of qāḍī itself was an Islamic institution typical of the Umayyad period, in which administrative efficiency and the tendency to Islamicize went hand in hand. The Islamic character of the office of qāḍī is emphasized by a subsidiary appointment which was, during the Umayyad period, often combined with that of a qāḍī: the duty of qaṣaṣ, literally "story-telling," that is to say, the religious instruction and edification of the people. The scene was thus set for a more thorough process of Islamicizing the existing customary law.

The work of the qāḍīs inevitably became more and more specialized, and we may take it for granted that in the late Umayyad period (c. A. H. 100-130) appointments as a rule went to "specialists," by which are meant not technically trained professionals but persons sufficiently interested in the right administration of justice to have given the subject serious thought in their spare time, either individually or in discussion with like-minded friends. The main concern of these specialists, in the intellectual climate of the late Umayyad period, was naturally to know whether the customary law conformed to the Qur'ānic and generally Islamic norms; in other words: the specialists from whom the qāḍīs came increasingly to be recruited were found among those pious persons whose interest in religion caused them to elaborate, by individual reasoning, an Islamic way of life in all its aspects. These pious persons surveyed all fields of contemporary activities, including the field of law, not only administrative regulations but popular practice as well. In their theoretical contemplations they considered possible objections that could be made to recognized practices from the religious, and in particular, from the ritualistic or ethical point of view, and as a result endorsed, modified, or rejected them. They impregnated the sphere of law with religious and ethical ideas, subjected it to Islamic norms, and incorporated it into the body of duties incumbent on every Muslim. In doing this, they achieved on a much wider scale and in a vastly more detailed manner what the Prophet in the Qur'ān had tried to do for the early Islamic community of Medina. As a consequence, the popular and administrative practice of the late Umayyad period was transformed into Islamic law. The resulting theory still had to be translated into practice; this task was beyond the power of the pious specialists and had to be left to the interest and zeal of the caliphs, governors, qāḍīs, or individuals concerned. The origins of Islamic law then were such that it developed not in close connection with practice, but as the expression of a religious ideal in opposition to practice.

This process started from modest beginnings towards the end of the first century of the hijra; a specialist in religious law such as Ibrāhīm Nakha'ī of Kūfa (d. A. H. 95 or 96) did no more than give opinions on questions of ritual and perhaps on kindred problems of directly religious importance, cases of conscience concerning alms tax, marriage, divorce, and the like, but not on law proper. The pious specialists were private persons, or we might call them amateurs; they were animated by their personal interest in questions of right behavior, and they owed the respect, in which they were often and in an increasing measure held by the people and by some of the rulers, exclusively to their own single-minded concern with the ideals of a life according to the tenets of Islam. They often had occasion to criticize the actions and regulations of the government, just as they had to declare undesirable many popular practices, but they were not in political opposition to the Umayyads and to the established Islamic state; on the contrary, the whole of the Umayyad period, until the civil war which heralded the end of the dynasty, was sometimes reckoned as part of the "good old times," its practice was idealized and opposed to the realities of the actual administration.

As the groups of pious specialists grew in numbers and cohesion they developed, in the first few decades of the second century of the hijra, into what is known, for lack of a better name, as the "ancient schools of law." This term ought to imply neither any definite organization, nor a strict uniformity of doctrine within each school, nor any formal teaching, nor again any official status, nor even the existence of a body of law in our Western meaning of the term. The "scholars" or "lawyers," members of the ancient schools of law, continued to be private individuals, interested and therefore presumably knowledgeable in the Islamic ideals as they ought to prevail in all fields of life, including what we should call the field of law. These individuals were singled out from the great mass of the Muslims by the very fact of their special interest, the resultant reverence of the people, and the recognition as kindred spirits which they themselves accorded one another.

I have spoken of the ancient schools of law in the plural because, overlying the common Islamic background, there had developed in the several widely separated centers of the Islamic world during the first century of the hijra local practices, for example, those concerning details of ritual, or special transactions adapted to local conditions. Apart from these variations in subject-matter, the not inconsiderable difficulties of communication between their several centers made differences among the ancient schools of law unavoidable. These differences, however, were conditioned by geography rather than by any noticeable disagreement on principles or methods. The general attitude of all ancient schools of law towards Umayyad popular practice and Umayyad administrative regulations was essentially the same, whether they endorsed, modified, or rejected the practice which they found. Aside from this common basic attitude, however, there existed at the earliest stage of Islamic jurisprudence a considerable body of common doctrine which was subsequently reduced by increasing differentiation among the schools. This does not imply that Islamic jurisprudence in the earliest period was cultivated exclusively in one geographical center, but that one place nonetheless was the intellectual center of the first theoretizing and systematizing efforts which were to transform Umayyad popular and administrative practice into Islamic law. The ascendancy of a single center of Islamic jurisprudence must have been maintained over an appreciable period, because the common ancient element sometimes comprises several successive stages of doctrine. All indications go to prove that 'Iraq was this center. The ascendancy of 'Iraq in the development of religious law and jurisprudence in Islam continued during the whole of the second century.

The more important ancient schools of law of which we have knowledge are those of Kūfa and of Baṣra in 'Iraq, of Medina and of Mecca in Ḥijāz, and of Syria. Our information on the Kūfians and on the Medinese is incomparably more detailed than that concerning the Baṣrians and the Meccans, but the picture gained from the first two schools can be taken as typical. Egypt did not develop a school of law of its own, but fell under the influence of the other schools, particularly that of Medina.

An important aspect of the activity of the ancient schools of law was that they took the Qur'ānic norms seriously for the first time. Historically speaking, Islamic law did not derive directly from the Qur'ān; it developed out of a practice which often diverged from the Qur'ān's intentions and even from its explicit wording. It is true that a number of institutions, particularly in the law of family relations and of inheritance, not to mention cult and ritual, were based on the Qur'ān from the beginning. But apart from the most elementary rules, norms derived from the Qur'ān were introduced into Islamic law almost invariably at a secondary stage. In particular, at this stage, formal legal consequences were drawn from the essentially religious and ethical body of Qur'ānic maxims, and applied to those branches of law, such as contracts and torts, which were not covered in detail by the Qur'ānic legislation. The zenith of this introduction of Qur'ānic norms into early Islamic law coincides with the rise of the ancient schools at the beginning of the second century of the hijra.

The ancient schools of law shared not only a common attitude towards Umayyad practice and a considerable body of positive religious law, but the essentials of legal theory, not all of which were systematically self-evident. The central idea of this theory was that of the "living tradition of the school," as represented by the constant doctrine of its authoritative representatives. This idea dominated the development of legal doctrine in the ancient schools during the whole of the second century of the hijra. It presents itself under two aspects: retrospective and contemporaneous. Retrospectively, it appears as sunna or "practice" ('amal), or as "well-established precedent" (sunna maḍiya) or "ancient practice" (amr qadīm). This "practice" partly reflects the actual custom of the local community, but it also contains a theoretical or ideal element, so that it comes to mean normative sunna—the usage as it ought to be. This ideal practice, which was presumed constant though it in fact developed as Islamic ideas were imposed on the legal subject-matter, was found in the unanimous doctrine of the representative religious scholars of each center, in the teaching of those whom the people of every region recognized as their leading specialists in religious law, whose opinion they accepted and to whose decision they submitted. It is only the opinion of the majority that counts; small minorities of scholars are disregarded. The consensus of the scholars, representing the common denominator of doctrine achieved in each generation, expresses the contemporaneous aspect of the living tradition of each school. How this consensus works is described by an ancient scholar of Baṣra in the following terms: "Whenever I find a generation of scholars at a seat of knowledge, in their majority, holding the same opinion, I call this 'consensus,' whether their predecessors agreed or disagreed with it, because the majority would not agree on anything in ignorance of the doctrine of their predecessors, and would abandon the previous doctrine only on account of a repeal (for instance in the Qur'ān, which their predecessors had overlooked) or because they knew of some better argument, even if they did not mention it." In the result, the decision on what constitutes normative practice is left to the last generation of the representatives of each school of law.

The consensus of the scholars is different from the consensus of all Muslims on essentials. This last, in the nature of things, covers the whole of the Islamic world but is vague and general, whereas the consensus of the scholars is geographically limited to the seat of the school in question, is concrete and detailed, but also tolerant and not exclusive, recognizing as it does the existence of other doctrines in other centers. Both kinds of consensus count as final arguments in the ancient schools of law, though the consensus of the scholars is of much greater practical importance and is the real basis of their teaching. It is only natural that the consensus of all Muslims should be considered infallible; that the consensus of the scholars should be regarded as infallible, too, is not equally obvious and the whole highly organized concept seems to have been influenced from abroad.

Originally, the consensus of the scholars was anonymous, that is to say, it was the average opinion of the representatives of a school, and not the individual doctrines of the most prominent scholars. The living tradition of the ancient schools maintained its essentially anonymous character well into the second half of the second century of the hijra. Nevertheless, the idea of continuity inherent in the concept of sunna or idealized practice, together with the need of creating some kind of theoretical justification for what so far had been an instinctive reliance on the opinions of the majority led, from the first decades of the second century onwards, to the living tradition being projected backwards and to its being ascribed to some of the great figures of the past. The Kūfians were the first in attributing the doctrine of their school to the ancient Kūfian authority Ibrāhīm Nakha'ī, mentioned above, although this body of elementary legal doctrine had very little to do with the few authentic opinions of the historical Ibrāhīm. It rather represents the stage of legal teaching achieved in the time of Ḥammād ibn Abī Sulaymān (d. A. H. 120), the first Kūfian lawyer whose doctrine we can regard as fully historical. By a literary convention, which found particular favor in 'Iraq, it was customary for a scholar or author to put his own doctrine or work under the aegis of an ancient authority. The Medinese followed suit and projected their own teaching back to a number of ancient authorities who had died in the last years of the first or in the very first years of the second century of the hijra. At a later period, seven amongst them were chosen as representative; they are the so-called "Seven Lawyers of Medina," the most prominent of whom is Sa'īd ibn Musayyib. Hardly any of the doctrines ascribed to these ancient authorities can be considered authentic. The transmission of legal doctrine in Medina becomes historically ascertainable only at about the same time as in 'Iraq, with Zuhrī (d. A. H. 124) and with his younger contemporary Rabī'a ibn Abī 'Abd al-Raḥmān.

The process of going backwards for a theoretical foundation of Islamic religious law as it was being taught in the ancient schools did not stop with the choosing of these relatively late authorities. At the same time at which the doctrine of the school of Kūfa was retrospectively attributed to Ibrahīm Nakha'ī, and perhaps even slightly earlier, that doctrine and the local practice which in the last resort was its basis were directly connected with the very beginnings of Islam in Kūfa, beginnings associated with Ibn Mas'ūd, a Companion of the Prophet. It was, however, not to Ibn Mas'ūd himself that reference was made in the first place, but to an informal group of "Companions of Ibn Mas'ūd" who were, in some general way, taken to guarantee the authentic and uninterrupted transmission of the correct practice and doctrine in Kūfa. At a secondary stage, the general reference to the Companions of Ibn Mas'ūd gave rise to a formal and explicit reference to Ibn Mas'ūd himself, and a considerable body of early Kūfian doctrine was attributed to him. Though this body of doctrine differed in a number of details from the general teaching of the Kūfian school which went under the name of Ibrāhīm Nakha'ī, Ibrāhīm appears as the main transmitter from Ibn Mas'ūd, and many opinions were projected back from Ibrāhīm still farther to Ibn Mas'ūd. The historical Ibrāhīm had not had personal contact with the historical Ibn Mas'ūd, but some members of the originally anonymous Companions of Ibn Mas'ūd were later identified as older relatives of Ibrāhīm, and these formed a family link between the two authorities. Ibn Mas'ūd thus became the eponymy of the doctrine of the school of Kūfa. The corresponding eponymy of the Meccans was Ibn 'Abbās, another Companion of the Prophet, and references to him, too, alternate with references to the Companions of Ibn 'Abbās. The two main authorities of the Medinese among the Companions of the Prophet were the Caliph 'Umar and his son

Ibn 'Umar. Each ancient school of law, having projected its doctrine back to its own eponymy, who was invariably a local Companion of the Prophet, claimed his authority as the basis of its teaching. This association with Companions of the Prophet was called taqlīd.

Nor did the search for a solid theoretical foundation of the doctrine of the ancient schools of law stop at the Companions of the Prophet: there remained a further step. This step was taken in 'Iraq, perhaps in Baṣra, where not later than in the very first years of the second century of the hijra, the sunna, the practice of the local community and the doctrine of its scholars, were called "sunna of the Prophet." This term put the ideal practice of each community of Muslims directly under the authority of the Prophet. It expressed an axiom, but did not yet imply the existence of positive information in the form of "traditions" which became prevalent later, that the Prophet by his words or actions had in fact originated or approved that practice. This originally 'Iraqi concept of the sunna of the Prophet was taken over by the Syrians; their idea of living tradition was the uninterrupted practice of the Muslims, beginning with the Prophet, maintained by the first caliphs and by the later rulers, and verified by the scholars. The Medinese, on the other hand, hardly used this concept.

It was not long before various movements arose in opposition to the opinions held by the majorities in the ancient schools of law. In Kūfa, for instance, where the name of Ibn Mas'ūd had become attached to the main stream of legal doctrine, any opinions which were put forward in opposition to the traditional doctrine of the majority had to invoke an equally high, or possibly an even higher, authority, and for this purpose the name of the Caliph 'Alī, who had made Kūfa his headquarters, presented itself easily. The doctrines which in Kūfa go under the name of 'Alī do not embody the coherent teaching of any individual group; all we can say is that, generally speaking, they represent opinions advanced in opposition to the living tradition, that is, to the contemporary average teaching, of the school of Kūfa. One group of doctrines attributed to 'Alī represents crude and primitive analogies, early unsuccessful efforts to systematize; they reflect the opinions of groups or individuals who were ahead of the majority of their contemporaries in Kūfa in systematic legal thought. Another group of unsuccessful opinions ascribed to 'Alī shows a rigorous and meticulous tendency, and goes farther than the average doctrine of the Kūfians in taking religious and ethical considerations into account. Unscuccessful 'Iraqi opinions of this type, attributed to 'Alī, correspond almost regularly to doctrines attested in Medina, where most of them represent the common opinion. It is in keeping with the relatively later development of the Medinese school that a body of doctrines which remained unsuccessful in Kūfa, where it could not overcome the already established tradition of a school of law, succeeded to a considerable degree to gain recognition in Medina.

In contrast to the opposition in Kūfa, the opposition in Medina reflected the activity of the Traditionists. The movement of the Traditionists, the most important single event in the history of Islamic law in the second century of the hijra, was the natural outcome and continuation of a movement of religiously and ethically inspired opposition to the ancient schools of law. The schools of law themselves represented an Islamic opposition to popular and administrative practice under the later Umayyads, and the opposition group which developed into the Traditionist movement emphasized this tendency. The main thesis of the Traditionists, as opposed to the ancient schools of law, was that formal "traditions" deriving from the Prophet superseded the living tradition of the school. It was not enough for the ancient schools to claim that their doctrines as a whole were based on the teachings of Companions of the Prophet who were likely to know the intentions of their master best, or even that their living tradition represented the sunna of the Prophet. The Traditionists produced detailed statements or "traditions" which claimed to be the reports of ear or eyewitnesses on the words or actions of the Prophet, handed down orally by an uninterrupted chain of trustworthy persons. Hardly any of these traditions, as far as rules of law are concerned, can be considered authentic; they were put into circulation, no doubt from the loftiest of motives, by the Traditionists themselves from the first half of the second century onwards. Occasionally, the Traditionists acknowledged this activity more or less openly, as in the traditions which report the Prophet as having said: "Sayings attributed to me which agree with the Qur'ān go back to me, whether I actually said them or not," and "Whatever good sayings there are, I said them."

The Traditionists were not confined to Medina, but existed in other centers of Islam where they formed groups in opposition to, but nevertheless in contact with, the local schools of law. Their standards of reasoning were inferior to those of the ancient schools, and even Shāfi'ī, who at the end of the second century was to succeed in making their main thesis prevail in Islamic law, complained repeatedly that their superficial and uncritical adherence to traditions led them into error, and that their failure to reason systematically put them at a disadvantage. The Traditionists' own feeling of inferiority expressed itself in the following saying ascribed to the Prophet: "Luck to the man who hears my words, remembers them, guards them, and hands them on; many a transmitter of legal knowledge is no lawyer himself, and many a one transmits legal knowledge to persons who are more learned in it than he is."

The Traditionists disliked all human reasoning and personal opinion which had become an integral part of the living tradition of the ancient schools and which had, indeed, been a constituent element of Islamic legal thought from its very beginnings. They put into circulation a number of traditions in which they disparaged human reasoning in law. They were also presumably responsible for some of the traditions directed against Umayyad popular and administrative practice, although it is not always possible to determine whether a particular doctrine originated in Traditionist circles or within the ancient schools of law. The introduction of Islamic norms into all aspects of life, including the sphere of law, was by no means a distinctive interest of the Traditionists; they were preceded in this by the ancient schools of law themselves. The general tendency of the Traditionists was the same as that of the other opponents of the dominant schools in 'Iraq and in Medina: a certain inclination towards strictness and rigidity which was not, however, without exceptions. They were occasionally interested in purely legal issues, for reasons which now escape us, but their main concern was with subordinating the legal subject-matter to moral principles. There are, for instance, two traditions put into circulation by the Traditionists in Medina, according to which the Prophet had prohibited underbidding and overbidding, and certain practices which might create an artificial rise or fall in prices. Their aim was to make these practices illegal in the same way as, say, the taking of interest was illegal, so that contracts concluded in defiance of the prohibition would be invalid. These particular traditions did not prevail with the Medinese, who, in common with the 'Iraqis, minimized them by interpretation, and the effort of the Traditionists to change the doctrine of the ancient schools of law remained unsuccessful in this case.

Initially the ancient schools of law, Medinese as well as 'Iraqi, offered strong resistance to the disturbing element represented by the traditions from the Prophet. It has often been presumed that it was the most natural thing, from the first generation after the Prophet onwards, to refer in all cases to his real or alleged rulings. This was not the case. Traditions from the Prophet had to overcome strong opposition, and the arguments against them and in their favor extended over most of the second century of the hijra. At the same time it is obvious that once the authority of the Prophet, the highest in Islam, had been invoked, the thesis of the Traditionists, consciously formulated, was certain of success, and the ancient schools had no real defense against the rising tide of traditions from the Prophet. The best they could do was to minimize them by interpretation and to embody their own attitude and doctrines in other alleged traditions from the Prophet, but this meant that the Traditionists had gained their point. Though the ancient schools of law were brought to pay lip-service to the principle of the Traditionists, they did not, however, necessarily change their positive legal doctrine to the full extent desired by the latter group. The Traditionists were sometimes successful in bringing about a change of doctrine, and when this happened, the doctrine of the minority in opposition became indistinguishable from that of the majority of the school; but they often failed, and we find whole groups of "unsuccessful" Medinese and 'Iraqi doctrines expressed in traditions from the Prophet. It goes without saying that the interaction of legal doctrines and traditions must be regarded as a unitary process, the several aspects and phases of which can be separated only for the sake of analysis. All this introduced inconsistencies into the teachings of the ancient schools of law and these schools accepted traditions from the Prophet only as far as they agreed with their own living tradition or idealized "practice"—that is to say, the practice as it ought to be. The next step was to be taken by Shāfi'ī at the end of the second century of the hijra.

The discussion so far has been concerned mainly with the tendency of the early specialists to Islamicize, that is, to introduce Islamic norms into the sphere of the law. This endeavor was, however, accompanied by the parallel and complementary tendency to reason and to systematize. Reasoning was inherent in Islamic law from its very beginnings. It started with the exercise of personal opinion and of individual judgment on the part of the earliest specialists and qāḍīs. It would be a gratuitous assumption to regard the independent decision of the specialist or of the magistrate as anterior to rudimentary analogy and the striving after consistency. Both elements are found intimately connected in the earliest period which the sources allow us to discern. Nevertheless, this individual reasoning, whether completely independent and personal or inspired by an effort for consistency, started from vague beginnings, without direction or method, and moved towards an increasingly strict discipline.

The oldest stage of legal reasoning is represented by 'Iraqi traditions which show crude and primitive conclusions reached by analogy. An old conclusion of this kind, which prevailed in the 'Iraqi doctrine, was to demand a fourfold confession of the culprit before he incurred the punishment for unchastity, by analogy with the four witnesses prescribed for this case by the Qur'ān. This was originally merely the result of systematic reasoning. The 'Iraqi opposition groups exaggerated the underlying tendency towards caution, and put into circulation a tradition relating that 'Alī once turned away an offending woman four times and punished her only after her fifth confession; this opinion did not achieve recognition. The original 'Iraqi doctrine requiring four confessions spread into Ḥijāz, and was there incorporated in a group of traditions under the authority of the Prophet, the final result of which was a tradition concerning a man called Ma'iz who committed unchastity and confessed, but was turned away three times by the Prophet and punished only after his fourth confession. Although ultimately expressed in traditions from the Prophet, the doctrine did not prevail in the school of Medina and remained confined to 'Iraq. The underlying conclusion by analogy provoked another comparable opinion which held that the Qur'ānic punishment of mutilation for theft could be applied only after a twofold confession by the culprit, by analogy with the two witnesses demanded in this case. This doctrine was again expressed in a tradition from 'Alī, but was only partly successful in 'Iraq.

The minimum value of stolen goods, for the Qur'ānic punishment for theft to be applicable, was fixed by some 'Iraqis by a crude analogy with the five fingers, at five dirhams. The generally accepted doctrine in 'Iraq, however, fixed it arbitrarily at ten dirhams, and as a justification of this discretionary decision traditions from Ibn Mas'ūd, 'Alī, and even the Prophet were cited. This doctrine has to be regarded as the original opinion, and the analogical reasoning as a refinement which was finally unsuccessful. The minimum value of stolen goods provided the starting point for fixing, by a crude analogy, the minimum amount of the ṣadāq, the contractual payment made by the bridegroom to the bride which was an essential element of the contract of marriage. Here, too, the original 'Iraqi decision was arbitrary: "We think it shocking," they said, "that intercourse should become lawful for a trifling amount," and therefore Ibrāhīm Nakha'ī disapproved of a ṣadāq of less than forty, and once he said of less than ten dirhams." This discretionary decision was later modified, not for the better, by a crude analogy, according to which the use of a part of the body of the wife by the husband ought not to be made lawful for an amount less than that set for the loss of a limb through the punishment for theft, and the minimum amount of ṣadāq was fixed at ten dirhams. This reasoning was expressed in a tradition from 'Alī. The Medinese recognized originally no minimum amount of ṣadāq; only Mālik, followed by his personal disciples, adopted the 'Iraqi analogical reasoning, and starting from his own doctrine that the punishment of mutilation could be applied only in cases where the minimum value of the stolen goods was three dirhams, fixed the minimum ṣadāq at the same amount. At the same time, the 'Iraqis had found this crude analogy unsatisfactory, and fell back on the authority of traditions which had appeared in the meantime.

The results of this early systematic reasoning were not infrequently expressed in the form of legal "puzzles," or in the form of legal maxims or slogans, which were sometimes rhyming or alliterative. Some typical slogans are: "there is no divorce and no manumission under duress"; "the child belongs to the marriage bed"; "profit goes with responsibility"; "the security takes the place of that for which it is given" ('Iraqi); and, in favor of the opposite doctrine, "the security is not forfeited" (Medinese). These maxims became a favorite mode of expressing legal doctrines in 'Iraq and in Ḥijāz in the first half of the second century of the hijra, and reflect a stage when legal doctrines were not yet automatically expressed in traditions, though most of them gradually acquired the form of traditions. The element of personal discretion and individual opinion in Islamic law was prior to the growth of traditions, particularly of traditions from the Prophet, and it was due only to the essential success of the Traditionists that most of these originally independent decisions of scholars were put into the form of traditions.

The literary period in Islamic law begins about the year A. H. 150, and from then onwards the development of technical legal thought can be followed step by step from scholar to scholar. It tended, first, to become more and more perfected until it reached the zenith of its development at the end of the second century. There is secondly an increasing dependence on traditions, as a greater number of authoritative traditions came into being. Thirdly, considerations of a religious and ethical kind, which represented one aspect of the process of Islamicizing the legal subject-matter, tended to permeate systematic reasoning, and both tendencies became inextricably mixed in the result. All three tendencies culminated in the teachings of Shāfi'ī as will become evident from a short survey of the thought of some of the main representatives of Islamic law in the second century of Islam.

The opinions of the Syrian Awzā'ī (d. A. H. 157), for instance, represent the oldest solutions adopted by Islamic jurisprudence, whether he maintained the current practice, or regulated it, or Islamicized it as was usual with him, or gave a seemingly simple and natural decision as yet untouched by systematic refinements. The archaic character of Awzā'ī's doctrine makes it likely that he conserved the teaching of his predecessors in the generation before him. When the doctrine which goes under his name was formulated, the Islamicizing and systematizing tendencies of earliest Muḥammadan jurisprudence had, it is true, already started to operate, but they were still far from having penetrated the whole of the raw material offered by the practice. The doctrine as given by Awzā'ī therefore often appears inconsistent. His systematic reasoning, though appreciable in extent, is generally rudimentary, and his legal thought shows as a rule a rigid formalism.

The reasoning of the Medinese Mālik (d. A. H. 179), on the whole, is comparable to that of Awzā'ī, particularly in the dependence of both on the practice, the living tradition, the consensus of the scholars, rather than on systematic thought. The accepted doctrine of the Medinese school, which Mālik aimed to set forth, was itself to a great extent founded on the individual reasoning of the school's representatives. In combining extensive use of reasoning with dependence on the living tradition, Mālik seems typical of the Medinese. In the majority of cases, we find Mālik's reasoning inspired by material considerations, by practical expediency, and by the tendency to Islamicize. There are a fair number of cases where his technical legal thought shows itself to be sound and consistent.

In 'Iraq, the discussion of technical legal problems must have started slightly earlier than the time of Ibn Abī Layla, a qāḍī of Kūfa (d. A. H. 148). His doctrine, taken as a whole, shows a considerable amount of technical legal thought, but it is generally of a primitive kind, somewhat clumsy, shortsighted, and often unfortunate in its results. His loose and imperfect method is not incompatible with formalism and the stubborn drawing of consequences. A rigid formalism is perhaps the most persistent single typical feature of his legal thought. Nevertheless, his technical reasoning is far from rudimentary; the striving for systematic consistency, the action of general trends and principles pervade his whole doctrine. In a great number of cases, Ibn Abī Layla's doctrine represents seemingly natural and practical common sense, and rough-and-ready decisions. This practical, common sense reasoning of his often takes practical, and particularly Islamic-ethical considerations into account. Connected with these considerations is Ibn Abī Layla's regard for actual practice, a tendency reinforced by his being a qāḍī. There are numerous traces of his activity as a qāḍī in his doctrine, last but not least his conservatism, so that he represents an earlier stage in the development of Islamic jurisprudence than his contemporary Abū Ḥanīfa.

With respect to 'Iraqi legal reasoning as represented by Ibn Abī Layla, Abū Ḥanīfa (d. A. H. 150) seems to have played the part of a theoretical systematizer who achieved considerable progress in technical legal thought. Not being a qāḍī, Abū Ḥanīfa was less restricted than Ibn Abī Layla by considerations of practice. At the same time, he was less firmly guided by the needs of the administration of justice, and whereas Ibn Abī Layla's doctrine is often primitive but practical, Abū Ḥanīfa's, though more highly developed, is often tentative and, as it proved to be, unsatisfactory. In Abū Ḥanīfa's doctrine, systematic consistency has become normal. The emphasis shifts from the practical aspects of legal reasoning—Islamicizing, common-sense decisions, and other considerations which were still prevalent in Ibn Abī Layla's doctrine—to the technical and formal qualities of legal thought. Traces of primitive reasoning and systematic inconsistencies remain, but they are relatively few in number. More significant than these features are those numerous cases which show Abū Ḥanīfa's legal thought to be not only more broadly based and more thoroughly applied than that of his predecessors, but technically more highly developed, more circumspect, and more refined. Abū Ḥanīfa's legal thought was, however, not final, and his companions and disciples rejected an appreciable part of it as defective.

Of Abū Ḥanīfa's disciple Abū Yūsuf (d. A. H. 182) it need only be said that he was more dependent on traditions than his master, because there were a greater number of authoritative traditions in existence in his time, and that compared with his increasing dependence on traditions, other kinds of practical considerations are less prominent in his doctrine. Sometimes the contemporary sources state directly, and in other cases it is probable, that Abū Yūsuf's experience as a qāḍī caused him to change his opinions on matters of law. But these frequent changes of opinion also betray some uncertainty and immaturity, and his legal thought is on the whole of a lower standard than that of Abū Ḥanīfa. It is also less original and thoroughly dependent on that of his master. Abū Yūsuf represents the beginning of the process by which the ancient 'Iraqi school of Kūfa was replaced by that of the followers of Abū Ḥanīfa.

Shaybānī (d. A. H. 189), the great disciple both of Abū Ḥanīfa and of Abū Yūsuf, depends even more on traditions than Abū Yūsuf does. This shows itself not only in changes of doctrine under the influence of traditions, but in his habit of duplicating his systematic reasoning by arguments taken from traditions, and in the habitual formula "We follow this" by which he almost invariably rounds off his references to traditions from the Prophet and from other authorities, even when he does not, in fact, follow them. Shaybānī used independent personal opinion to the extent common in the ancient schools of law, but most of his reasoning that appears in the guise of personal opinion is in fact strict analogy or systematic reasoning. To this extent, Shaybānī prepared the way for Shāfi'ī's rejection, on principle, of discretionary decisions and insistence on strict analogical reasoning. Systematic reasoning is the feature most typical of Shaybānī's technical legal thought. It is by far superior to that of his predecessors in general and to that of Abū Yūsuf in particular; it is the most perfect of its kind to be achieved before Shāfi'ī. Shaybānī was the great systematizer of the Kūfian doctrine. He was also a prolific writer, and his voluminous works, which he put under the authority of his master, Abū Ḥanīfa, became the rallying point of the Ḥanafī school which emerged from the ancient school of Kūfa.

In Shāfi'ī (d. A. H. 204), who considered himself a member of the school of Medina though he made the essential thesis of the Traditionists prevail in Islamic law, legal reasoning reached its zenith; it hardly ever again approached and never surpassed the standard he set. When Shāfi'ī wrote, the process of Islamicizing the law, of impregnating it with religious and ethical ideas, had in the main been completed. We therefore find him hardly ever influenced in his conscious legal thought by practical considerations of a religious and ethical kind, such as played an important part in the doctrines of his predecessors. We also find him more consistent than the earlier jurists in separating the moral and the legal aspects, whenever both arise with regard to the same problem. In this respect, Shāfi'ī did not carry out the program of the Traditionists who had tried to identify the categories "forbidden" and "invalid."[11] The sphere of law retained a technical character of its own, and legal relationships were not completely reduced to or expressed in terms of religious and ethical duties. On the other hand, Shāfi'ī's fundamental dependence on formal traditions from the Prophet, in which he followed the Traditionists, implied a different, formal way of Islamicizing the legal doctrine. In theory, Shāfi'ī distinguished sharply between the argument taken from traditions and the result of systematic thought. In his actual reasoning, however, both aspects are closely interwoven; he shows himself tradition bound and systematic at the same time, and this new synthesis may be considered typical of his legal thought. Shāfi'ī's systematic reasoning has its limitations. It breaks down occasionally over irrational traditions or institutions which defy rationalizing. More serious are those faults which come from his polemical attitude towards the ancient schools of law, an attitude which in the case of the Medinese is mitigated by a sentimental attachment, but which in the case of the 'Iraqis is allowed full scope. His dependence upon traditions from the Prophet, too, by making it impossible for him to reject straightforwardly any traditions except on the authority of another, contrary, tradition from the Prophet, is responsible for inconclusive arguments and arbitrary interpretations. But the limitations and faults of Shāfi'ī's reasoning cannot detract from the unprecedentedly high quality of his technical legal thought, which stands out beyond doubt as the greatest individual achievement in Islamic jurisprudence.

Shāfi'ī recognized in principle only strict analogical and systematic reasoning, to the exclusion of arbitrary opinions and discretionary decisions such as had been customary amongst his predecessors. This is one of the important innovations by which his legal theory became utterly different from that of the ancient schools. His legal theory is much more logical and formally consistent than that of his predecessors, whom he blames continually for what appears to him as a mass of inconsistencies. It is based, as previously stated, on the thesis of the Traditionists that nothing

[11] For a discussion of these terms, see Chapter IV, p. 98.

can override the authority of a formal tradition from the Prophet. In accepting this, Shāfi'ī cut himself off from the natural and continuous development of doctrine in the ancient schools of law. For him, the sunna is no longer the approved practice as recognized by the representative scholars, it is identical with the content of formal traditions from the Prophet, even though such a tradition be transmitted by only one person in each generation. According to Shāfi'ī, one must not conclude that the Companions of the Prophet knew the intentions of their master best and would therefore not have held opinions incompatible with them. The opinions held and practices inaugurated by persons other than Companions of the Prophet were, of course, in Shāfi'ī's eyes, of no authority whatsoever. This new idea of the sunna as embodied in formal traditions from the Prophet disposed of the concept of living tradition of the ancient schools, even when the living tradition was loosely called "*sunna* of the Prophet." Traditions from the Prophet could not even be invalidated by reference to the Qur'ān. Shāfi'ī took it for granted that the Qur'ān did not contradict the traditions from the Prophet, and that the traditions explained the Qur'ān; the Qur'ān had therefore to be interpreted in the light of the traditions, and not vice versa. The consensus of the scholars, which expressed the living tradition of each ancient school, also became irrelevant for Shāfi'ī; he even denied its existence, and fell back on the general consensus of all Muslims on essentials. The thesis that "everything of which the Muslims approve or disapprove is good or bad in the sight of Allah" had been formulated shortly before Shāfi'ī. Shāfi'ī developed it further, but the principle, as he formulated it, that the community of Muslims would never agree on an error, was put into the form of a tradition from the Prophet only towards the middle of the third century of the hijra. This general consensus was sufficiently vague for it to allow Shāfi'ī to follow the traditions from the Prophet concerning all details. If detailed traditions from the Prophet were to have overriding authority, there was no room left for the exercise of personal opinion, and human reasoning had to be restricted to making correct inferences and drawing systematic conclusions from the traditions. Shāfi'ī was so serious in his main contention that he declared himself prepared to abandon any doctrine of his by which he might unwittingly have contradicted a tradition from the Prophet.

These, in short, were the principles of Shāfi'ī's legal theory. It was a ruthless innovation, and took him some time to elaborate, so that his writings contain numerous traces of the development of his ideas and some unsolved inconsistencies. But notwithstanding all this, Shāfi'ī's legal theory was a magnificently coherent system and superior by far to the theory of the ancient schools. It was the achievement of a powerful mind, and at the same time the logical outcome of a process which started when traditions from the Prophet were first adduced as arguments in law. The development of legal theory in the second century of Islam was dominated by the struggle between two concepts: that of the common doctrine of the community, and that of the authority of traditions from the Prophet. The doctrine of the ancient schools of law represented an uneasy compromise; Shāfi'ī vindicated the thesis of the Traditionists, and the later schools had no choice but to adopt the essentials of his legal theory.

CHAPTER III

The Schools of Law and Later Developments of Jurisprudence

WHEN THE Umayyads of Damascus were overthrown by the 'Abbāsids in A. H. 132 (A. D. 750), Islamic law as we know it had acquired its essential features; the need of Arab Muslim society for a new legal system had been filled. The early 'Abbāsids continued and reinforced the Islamicizing trend which had become more and more noticeable under the later Umayyads. For reasons of dynastic policy, in order to differentiate themselves and their revolution from the ruling house which they had superseded, the 'Abbāsids exaggerated the differences, and in conscious opposition to their predecessors made it their program to establish the rule of God on earth. As part of this policy, they set out to bridge the gulf that had opened from the beginning between the theoretical demands of the specialists and the practical necessities of administration. They made a point of consulting specialists in religious law on problems that might come within their competence, and a long treatise which Abū Yūsuf wrote at the request of the Caliph Hārūn on public finance, taxation, criminal justice, and connected subjects has come down to us.[1] But just as the pious specialists who had formed the vanguard of the Islamicizing tendency under the Umayyads had been ahead of realities, so now the early 'Abbāsids and their religious advisers were unable to carry the whole of society with them, particularly as the caliphs themselves were not always very sincere in their professed eagerness to translate the religious ideal into practice. It soon appeared that the rule of God on earth as preached by the early 'Abbāsids was but a polite formula to cover their own absolute despotism. They were thus unable to achieve a permanent fusion between theory and practice, and it was not long before their successors lacked not only the will but the power to continue the effort.

What the early 'Abbāsids did achieve was the permanent connection of the office of qāḍī with the sharī'a, the sacred law. This,

[1] Abū Yūsuf, *Le livre de l'impot foncier*, traduit et annoté par E. Fanan (Paris, 1921).

too, had been prepared under the Umayyads, but under the 'Abbāsids it became a fixed rule that a qāḍī had to be a specialist in the sharī'a. He was no more the legal secretary of the governor but was normally appointed from the center of the Empire. He was to apply nothing but the sacred law, without interference from the government, but this independence remained theoretical. With its increasing despotism, the temporal power became more and more unwilling to tolerate the existence of any truly independent institution; the qāḍīs were not only subject to dismissal at the whim of the central government, but had to depend on the political authorities for the execution of their judgments. This was particularly important for the administration of criminal justice. During the Umayyad period, when the qāḍīs were the legal secretaries of the governors, they or the governors themselves exercised whatever criminal justice came within the competence of the administrative authorities. But when, under the early 'Abbāsids, the office of qāḍī was separated from the general administration and became bound to Islamic law in substance and procedure, the formal rules of evidence of the latter made it impossible for the qāḍī to undertake a criminal investigation, and his inability to deal with criminal cases became apparent. Consequently, the political powers stepped in and transferred the administration of the greater part of criminal justice to the police.[2] Nevertheless, the office of qāḍī in its final form proved to be the most vigorous institution evolved by Islamic society.[3]

The centralizing tendency of the early 'Abbāsids which was responsible for the appointment of the qāḍī from the center, also led to the creation of the office of Chief Qāḍī. This appellation was originally an honorific title given to the qāḍī of the capital, whom the caliphs would normally consult on the administration of Islamic justice. The qāḍī Abū Yūsuf was the first to receive this title, and the Caliph Hārūn not only solicited his advice on financial policy and similar questions, as mentioned above, but used to consult him on the appointment of all qāḍīs in the Empire. Soon the Chief Qāḍī became one of the most important councillors of the caliph, and the appointment and dismissal of the other qāḍīs, under the authority of the caliph, was the main function of his office. It has been suggested that the office of Chief Qāḍī, which notwithstanding its historical importance has always been some-

[2] E. Tyan, *Histoire de l'organisation judiciaire en pays d'Islam* (Paris, 1938), Vol. II, pp. 360, 410 ff.

[3] H. F. Amedroz, in *Journal of the Royal Asiatic Society* (1910), 761 ff.

what neglected by the theorists of Islamic law, is of Persian origin and the translation, into an Islamic context, of the Zoroastrian *Mobedan-Mobed.* Its introduction by the early 'Abbāsids certainly coincides with the official adoption of many features of Sassanian administration, and ancient Arab writers themselves have pointed out the parallels between the two institutions.[4]

An institution which the early 'Abbāsids certainly borrowed from the administrative practice of the Sassanian kings was the "investigation of complaints." It was an attribute of the absolute monarch by which the caliphs themselves or, by delegation, ministers or special officials and later the sultans, heard complaints concerning miscarriage or denial of justice or other allegedly unlawful acts of the qāḍīs, difficulties in securing the execution of judgments, wrongs committed by government officials or by powerful individuals, and similar matters. Very soon, formal Courts of Complaints were set up. The more important lawsuits concerning property, which would in theory come within the jurisdiction of the qāḍī, tended to be brought before the Courts of Complaints, too, so that their jurisdiction became to a great extent concurrent with that of the qāḍīs' tribunals. The very existence of these administrative tribunals, which were established ostensibly to supplement the deficiencies of the qāḍīs, shows that at an early period, much of the administration of justice through the qāḍī had broken down.[5]

At the same time at which the qāḍī's tribunals found themselves superseded, to a considerable degree, by the Courts of Complaints, they had to accommodate themselves to the continued jurisdiction of the "inspector of the market" whose office, it may be recalled, had continued into the Umayyad period from Byzantine times. The early 'Abbāsids, while maintaining its functions, superficially Islamicized this office by appointing its holder so as to discharge the collective obligation, enjoined in the Qur'ān, of "encouraging the good and discouraging the evil," making him responsible for enforcing Islamic morals and behavior on the community of Muslims, and giving him the Islamic title of muḥtasib. In addition to his ancient police powers of enforcing traffic, building, sanitary, and trading regulations and deciding disputes arising therefrom, it was part of his duties to bring transgressors to justice and to impose summary punishments which came to include the flogging of the intemperate and the unchaste and even the amputation of

[4] Tyan, *op. cit.,* Vol. I, pp. 176 ff.

[5] Tyan, *op. cit.,* Vol. II, pp. 141 ff.; Amedroz, *op. cit.* (1911), pp. 635 ff.

the hands of thieves caught in the act. However, the sincere eagerness of the rulers to enforce these provisions of the sharī'a in practice commonly made them overlook the fact that the procedure of the muḥtasib did not always comply with the strict demands of Islamic law. The several aspects of the institution of the muḥtasib exemplify the nature and extent of the adoption of the ideal system of the sacred law under the early 'Abbāsids. The institution itself has survived, in some Islamic countries at least, into the present, and so has the right of every Muslim, notwithstanding the presence or the absence of an officially appointed muḥtasib, to come forth as a private prosecutor or "common informer."[6]

Under the Umayyads, the administration of justice had been left to the provincial governors and their qāḍīs, and the administrative and legislative activity of the central government, and of the provincial governors, too, had originally lain outside of, and was only gradually brought into, the orbit of nascent Islamic law. Under the 'Abbāsids, however, when the main features of the sharī'a had already been definitely established, when Islamic law had come to be recognized, in theory at least, as the only legitimate norm of behavior for Muslims, and when the qāḍīs, bound to apply this law, were being appointed under the direct authority of the caliph, the caliph himself had to be incorporated into the system. This was not done by ascribing to him the right to legislate: it would have been difficult to acknowledge this right of the ruler in a system of religious duties which had been formulated in opposition to the practice of the government and which was fast falling under the influence of the Traditionists, for whom only formal traditions from the Prophet carried authority. Even speaking of the Caliphs of Medina, themselves Companions of the Prophet, Shāfi'ī (who upheld the thesis of the Traditionists) could say: "A tradition from the Prophet must be accepted as soon as it becomes known, even if it is not supported by any corresponding action of a caliph. If there has been an action on the part of a caliph and a tradition from the Prophet to the contrary becomes known later, that action must be discarded in favor of the tradition from the Prophet." The solution which was adopted was to endow the caliph with the attributes of a religious scholar and lawyer, to bind him to the sacred law in the same way in which the qāḍīs were bound to it, and to give him the same right to the exercise of personal opinion as was customary in the ancient schools of law. The explicit theory of all this was formulated only

[6] Tyan, *op. cit.,* Vol. II, pp. 436 ff.; Amedroz, *op. cit.* (1916), pp. 77 ff., 287 ff.

much later, but the essentials were expressed in two traditions dating from the second century of the hijra, which put the doctrine into the mouth of the Umayyad Caliph 'Umar ibn 'Abd al-'Azīz in the following terms: "No one has the right to personal opinion on points settled in the Qur'ān; the personal opinion of the caliphs concerns those points on which there is no revelation in the Qur'ān and no past sunna from the Prophet; no one has the right to personal opinion on points settled in a sunna enacted by the Prophet." And: "There is no Prophet after ours, and no holy book after ours; what Allah has allowed or forbidden through our Prophet, remains so forever; I am not the one to decide but only to carry out, not an innovator but a follower."

According to this doctrine, which was consciously adopted very early under the 'Abbāsids, the caliph, though otherwise the absolute chief of the Islamic community, had not the right to legislate but only to make administrative regulations within the limits laid down by the sacred law. This doctrine was made retrospectively applicable to the preceding period. It effectively concealed the fact that what was actually legislation of the Caliphs of Medina, and particularly of the Umayyads of Damascus, had to a great extent, directly by being approved and indirectly by provoking contrary solutions, entered into the fabric of Islamic law. The adoption of the theory in question did not even lead to a clear division between legislation and administration for the future. The later caliphs and the other secular rulers often had occasion to legislate for their own administrative tribunals. But although this was in fact legislation, the rulers used to call it administration, and they maintained the fiction that their regulations served only to apply, to supplement, and to enforce the sharī'a and were well within the competence of the political authority. This fiction was maintained as much as possible, even in the face of contradictions with and encroachments on the sacred law. The most important examples of this kind of administrative legislation are the qānunnâmes of the Ottoman sultans.[7]

This was how Islamic law actually grew and, one might almost be tempted to say, was fated to grow out of seeds which had been sown well before 'Abbāsid times. In the first years of 'Abbāsid rule, however, an unsuccessful effort was made to introduce the idea of codification and legislation. The author of this proposal was the Secretary of State, Ibn Muqaffa', a Persian convert to Islam who was put to death about A. H. 140. In a treatise or

[7] J. Schacht, in *Der Islam*, Vol. XX (1932), pp. 211 ff.

memorandum which he wrote in the last few years of his life for the Caliph Manṣūr, he deplored the wide divergencies in jurisprudence and in administration of justice existing between the several great cities (and even their several quarters) and between the main schools of law. These divergencies, he said, either perpetuated different local precedents or came from systematic reasoning, which was sometimes faulty or pushed too far. He suggested therefore that the caliph should review the different doctrines, codify and enact his own decisions in the interest of uniformity, and make his code binding on the qāḍīs. This code ought to be revised by successive caliphs. The caliph, and the caliph alone, Ibn Muqaffa' asserted, had the right to decide at his discretion; he could give binding orders on military and civil administration, and generally on all matters on which there was no precedent, but he had to base himself on Qur'ān and sunna. The alleged sunna, however, Ibn Muqaffa' realized, was based not on authentic traditions from the Prophet and the Caliphs of Medina, but to a great extent on administrative regulations of the Umayyad government. Therefore, he concluded, the caliph was free to determine and codify the sunna as he thought fit.

Ibn Muqaffa' wrote at a time when the 'Abbāsid government was attempting to make Islamic law the law of the state, but when that law itself was still in its formative period. The revolutionary propaganda which had brought the 'Abbāsids to power had made extravagant claims for the divine kingship of the "cousins of the Prophet." Though the 'Abbāsids, once they had attained their goal, dissociated themselves quickly from the more extremist of their adherents, the plea of Ibn Muqaffa' for state control over law (and, incidentally, over religion, too) was in full accord with the tendencies prevailing at the very beginning of the 'Abbāsid era. But this was no more than a passing phase, and orthodox Islam refused to be drawn into too close a connection with the state. The result was that Islamic law became more and more removed from practice, but in the long run gained more in power over the minds than it lost in control over the bodies of the Muslims. The proposal of Ibn Muqaffa' marks a decisive turn in the history of Islamic law.[8] Hardly forty years after he wrote his memorandum for Manṣūr, Abū Yūsuf composed his treatise for Hārūn, and at that time Islamic law had already settled down into the essential shape which it was to retain in the future; this shows

[8] S. D. Goitein, in *Islamic Culture*, Vol. XXIII (1949), pp. 120 ff.

well the speed with which it developed during the second century of the hijra.

In the early 'Abbāsid period, too, the ancient schools of law, which had been based mainly on the teachings in one geographic center, transformed themselves into the later type of school, based on allegiance to an individual master. The religious specialists of each geographical unit in the central parts of the Islamic world began by developing a certain minimum agreement on their doctrines, and by the middle of the second century of the hijra many individuals, instead of working out independent doctrines of their own, started to follow the teaching of a recognized authority in its broad outlines, while reserving to themselves the right to differ from their master on any point of detail. This led in the first place to the forming of groups or circles within the ancient schools of law. Thus, there existed within the 'Iraqi of Kūfa the "followers of Abū Ḥanīfa,' a group which included Abū Yūsuf and Shaybānī; in addition, Abū Yūsuf had followers of his own. Similarly, within the school of Medina and particularly within Egypt, its dependency, there were "followers of Mālik" who regarded the book of their master as their authoritative work. They were originally only a fraction of the Medinese, just as the followers of Abū Ḥanīfa were only part of the Kūfians. But the extensive literary activity of the followers of Abū Ḥanīfa, particularly of Shaybānī, in 'Iraq, and of the followers of Mālik in North Africa, together with other factors, some of them accidental, brought it about that the ancient school of Kūfa survived only in the followers of Abū Ḥanīfa (or Ḥanafīs) and the ancient school of Medina only in the followers of Mālik (or Mālikīs). This transformation of the ancient schools of law into "personal" schools, which perpetuated not the living tradition of a city but the doctrine of a master and of his disciples, was completed about the middle of the third century of the hijra. It was the logical outcome of a process which had started within the ancient schools themselves, but was precipitated by the activity of Shāfi'ī.

Shāfi'ī, whose life spanned the second half of the second century, started as a member of the school of Medina, and continued to regard himself as one, even after he had adopted the essential thesis of the Traditionists and tried to convert to it the adherents of the ancient schools, particularly the Medinese, through vigorous polemics. He did his best to represent this new doctrine to them as one which followed naturally from their own premises and which, therefore, they ought to accept, but to adopt the thesis of Shāfi'ī meant, nevertheless, breaking with the school of Medina or, for that matter, with any of the ancient schools. It did not mean joining the ranks of the pure Traditionists because, as mentioned in the preceding chapter, their standards of reasoning were inferior to those of the ancient schools, quite apart from the fact that their interests were much less technically legal. Any legal specialist, therefore, who became converted to Shāfi'ī's thesis necessarily became a personal follower of Shāfi'ī, and in this way Shāfi'ī became the founder of the first school of law on an exclusively personal basis—certainly with a common doctrine, but a doctrine which had once and for all been formulated by the founder. Shāfi'ī might well protest that it was not his intention to found a school, that his opinions counted for nothing, and that he was prepared to amend them if he found himself unwittingly contradicting a reliable tradition from the Prophet; however, a direct disciple of his composed an "Extract from the doctrine of Shāfi'ī and from the implications of his opinions, for the benefit of those who might desire it," although Shāfi'ī forbade anyone to follow him or anyone else. The doctrinal movement started by the Shāfi'ī school of law was soon placed on a level of equality with the Mālikī and the Ḥanafī schools.

Shāfi'ī's effort to supersede the ancient schools of law by a new doctrine based on the thesis of the Traditionists failed, but he succeeded in making this thesis, which was indeed the logical outcome of the search for an irrefutable Islamic basis of the sharī'a, prevail in legal theory. Whereas the Ḥanafīs and Mālikīs, who continued the ancient Kūfian and Medinese schools, did not change their positive legal doctrine appreciably from what it had been when Shāfi'ī appeared, they finally adopted, together with the Shāfi'īs, a legal theory of traditionist inspiration. This "classical" theory of Islamic law, which was established during the third century of the hijra, was in many respects more elaborate than Shāfi'ī's own theory and differed from it in one essential aspect. Shāfi'ī, in order to be able to follow the traditions from the Prophet without reservation, rejected the principle of the consensus of the scholars, which embodied the living tradition of the ancient schools, and restricted his own idea of consensus to the unanimous doctrine of the community at large. The classical theory returned to the concept of the consensus of the scholars, which it considered infallible in the same way as the general consensus of the Muslims. However, it had to take into account the status which Shāfi'ī had meanwhile won for the traditions from the Prophet, and extended the sanction of the consensus of the scholars to Shāfi'ī's identification of sunna with the contents of traditions from the Prophet. The main result of Shāfi'ī's break with the principle of "living tradition" thus became itself part of the living tradition at a later stage. The price that had to be paid for this recognition was that the extent to which traditions from the Prophet were in fact accepted as a foundation of law was in the future to be determined by the consensus of the scholars, and Shāfi'ī's endeavor to erect the traditions from the Prophet, instead of the living tradition and the consensus, into the highest authority in law was short-lived. The fact that the Shāfi'ī school itself had to accept this modification of the legal theory of its founder shows the hold which the idea of consensus had gained over Islamic law.

Though the later schools of law shared the essentials of the "classical" legal theory, traces of the different doctrines of the ancient schools (their predecessors) have survived in some of them to a greater or lesser extent. The old unfettered use of personal opinion, for instance, continued to be recognized by the Ḥanafīs as legitimate under the name of personal "approval" or "preference," in cases where the strict application of analogy would have led to undesirable results. This does not mean that the followers of the Ḥanafī school are, or have been for more than a thousand years past, at liberty to use their own discretionary judgment, any more than the adherents of any of the other schools; it means only that the official doctrine of the school is in a number of cases based not on strict analogy, but on the free exercise of personal opinion on the part of the school's earliest authorities. Mālik, too, is known to have exercised his personal "preference" in a number of cases; the Mālikī school, however, prefers to use the method of "having regard for the public interest," a consideration which differs only in name, not in kind from the Ḥanafī practice. The Mālikīs accept the general idea of the consensus of the scholars, but above and beyond it they ascribe the same authority to the consensus of the scholars of Medina, the town of the Prophet and the true home of his sunna. This doctrine perpetuates the ancient idea of a local, geographical consensus. The Mālikīs also continue to give some theoretical importance to the "practice" of Medina concurrent with traditions.

In the later Middle Ages, when the active center of the Mālikī school had moved to the Maghrib or northwest Africa where it developed in relative isolation, a number of features became prominent there which were not shared by the other schools, and not even by Mālikī doctrine in other countries. Most of these particular features fall under the general heading of "legal practice," and are laid down in late works, recognized as authoritative, which bear titles such as *The General Practice, The Practice of Fez,* etc. Late Mālikī doctrine in the Maghrib takes more notice than do the other schools of law of the conditions prevailing in fact, not by changing the ideal doctrine of the law in any respect, but by recognizing that the prevailing conditions did not allow the strict theory to be translated into practice, and that it was better to try and control the practice as much as possible than to abandon it completely, thus maintaining a kind of protective zone around the sharī'a as far as necessary. Late Mālikī doctrine in the Maghrib upheld the principle that "legal practice prevails over the best attested opinion," and recognized a number of institutions unknown to "classical" Mālikī law.[9] If the late Mālikī doctrine, therefore, took limited notice of practice and custom, it remained nevertheless true that Islamic law, including the Mālikī school, ignored custom as an official source of law. As a point of historical fact, custom contributed a great deal to the formation of Islamic law, but classical Islamic theory was concerned not with the historical legal development but with the systematic foundation of the law, and the consensus of the scholars denied conscious recognition to custom.

The legal doctrine as it had been elaborated by Shāfi'ī did not satisfy the uncompromising Traditionists. It was derived, it is true, from traditions from the Prophet, but with the help of a highly developed method of analogical and systematic reasoning. The Traditionists, on their part, preferred not to use any human reasoning in law, and chose, as much as possible, to base every single item in their doctrine on a tradition from the Prophet, "preferring a weak tradition to a strong analogy," as their opponents put it pointedly. Although the number of individual traditions from the Prophet went on increasing, they did not by far cover every individual type of case, and the Traditionists were in fact unable to do without reasoning. However, the reasoning which they used was concerned with moral issues, and differed widely from the systematic legal thought which had been brought to

[9] L. Milliot, *Démembrements du Habous* (Paris 1918); O. Pesle, *Le contrat de Safqa au Maroc* (Rabat 1932); J. Berque, *Essai sur la méthode juridique maghrébine* (Rabat 1944).

technical perfection by Shāfi'ī, and which the Traditionists disliked. This becomes apparent in legal works inspired by Traditionists which contain the doctrines of the prominent Traditionist Ibn Ḥanbal (d. A. H. 241) and were compiled by his disciples about the middle of the third century. They mark the beginnings of the Ḥanbalī school which, it should be noted, never absorbed its parent movement as completely as the Ḥanafī and the Mālikī schools absorbed theirs. For some time, Ibn Ḥanbal and his adherents were regarded by the followers of the other schools of law not as real "lawyers" but as mere specialists on traditions. Nevertheless, the Ḥanbalīs became one of the recognized schools, and although they were never numerous, they counted among their adherents a surprisingly high proportion of first-class scholars of all branches. The Traditionists of the third century of the hijra do not seem to have shown much interest in legal theory except for the general idea of the authority of traditions, but when the scholars of the Ḥanbalī school came to elaborate a complete system of doctrine, they, too, had to adopt the "classical" legal theory which was based not on traditions but on consensus, and recognized analogical reasoning. It was left to the great independent Ḥanbalī thinker Ibn Taymiyya to reject the all-embracing function of consensus in law, and to affirm the necessity of analogical reasoning of an improved kind.[10]

About the same time that the movement of the Traditionists gave rise to the Ḥanbalī school, Dawud ibn Khalaf (d. A. H. 270) founded the Zāhirī school of law, the only school which owed its existence to and took its name from a principle of legal theory. It was their principle to rely exclusively on the literal meaning (zāhir) of the Qur'ān and the traditions from the Prophet and to reject as contrary to religion not only the free exercise of personal opinion which had been customary before Shāfi'ī, but also the use of analogical and systematic reasoning which Shāfi'ī had retained. For instance, the Qur'ān forbids "interest," and many traditions declare that the Prophet held that interest consists both in an excess quantity and in a delay on delivery accorded to a contracting party in the barter or sale of gold, silver, wheat, barley, and dates. The other schools extended this provision by analogy beyond the five commodities mentioned, either to all goods that were sold by weight or measure, or to all foodstuffs that could be pre-

[10] H. Laoust, *Essai sur les doctrines sociales et politiques de . . . B. Taimiya,* and *Contribution à une étude de la méthodologie canonique de . . . B. Taimiya* (Cairo 1939).

served, and so on. The Zāhirīs, however, refused to extend the ruling to commodities other than those mentioned in traditions. In this particular case, the Zāhirī school seems laxer, but in others it appears much stricter than the other schools; it applied an abstract principle without regard for the consequences. It was not so much abstract thought itself which the Zāhirīs rejected, but the technical methods of legal reasoning, which they considered subjective and arbitrary. In the last resort, they, too, were unable to do without deductions and conclusions, but they tried to represent them as implied in the texts themselves. Another axiom of the Zāhirīs was that the only legally valid consensus was the consensus of the Companions of the Prophet. (It was this Zāhirī thesis that Ibn Taymiyya took over in a mitigated form.) The legal thought of the Zāhirīs has certain points of resemblance with the doctrine of the Ḥanbalīs and of the Traditionists in general, but essentially it goes back to the uncompromising attitude which had been taken by some "puritan" movements (e.g., Khārijīs, Mu'tazila) as far back as the first century of the hijra.[11]

There were several other "personal" schools of law, not to mention a number of more or less independent scholars, particularly in the early period. But since about A.D. 1300 only four schools of law have survived in orthodox Islam. They are the Ḥanafī, the Mālikī, the Shāfi'ī, and the Ḥanbalī schools, and this historical account will be briefly interrupted in order to describe their present distribution and their attitude to one another.[12]

The Ḥanafī school started in 'Iraq and was favored by the early 'Abbāsid Caliphs. At a relatively early period, it spread as far as Afghanistan, where it is recognized in the constitution as the official doctrine, and to the Indian subcontinent (now Pakistan and India), where it is followed by the overwhelming majority of the Muslims, including Indian immigrants in other parts of the world; it is also followed by the majority of the Muslims in China. In the Arab countries it is well represented in 'Iraq and Syria. It further became the favorite school of the Turks, both in Central Asia and particularly in the Ottoman Empire, where it enjoyed the constant favor of the dynasty and exclusive official recognition; apart from Turkey proper, the Turkish Muslims in the Balkan countries, Cyprus, Rhodes, etc. are all Ḥanafīs. As a legacy of former Ottoman rule, the Ḥanafī doctrine has official status to this day in the tribunals where Islamic law is administered, even in those former

[11] I. Goldziher, *Die Zâhiriten* (Leipzig 1884).
[12] L. Massignon, *Annuaire du monde musulman* (Paris 1930).

provinces of the Ottoman Empire where the majority of the native population follows another school, e.g., in 'Iraq, Syria, Jordan, Israel, Egypt, the Anglo-Egyptian Sudan, and Libya.

The Mālikī school grew out of the school of Medina which had already gained a foothold in Egypt. It spread over practically the whole of Muslim Africa: Upper Egypt, the Anglo-Egyptian Sudan, parts of Eritrea and Somaliland, Libya, Tunisia, Algeria, Morocco, and the whole of Central and West Africa as far as it is Muslim, including French West (and parts of Equatorial) Africa, Gambia, and Northern Nigeria. The Mālikī school alone is recognized in the religious courts of Morocco and Algeria; in Tunisia, the Mālikī and Ḥanafī schools are on an equal footing. The Muslims of the eastern coastal territories of Arabia, bordering on the Persian Gulf (Kuwayt, the Saudi Arabian province of Ḥasa, Bahrayn, Trucial Uman), as far as they are not Ḥanbalīs (Wahhābīs) or Sectarians ('Ibāḍīs, Shī'īs), also follow the Mālikī school.

The Shāfi'ī school began in Cairo, where Shāfi'ī spent the last years of his life. It still prevails in Lower Egypt, in the Ḥijāz (including Mecca), and in parts of South Arabia (Aden, Haḍramaut, and parts of Yaman). It is further well represented in parts of Eritrea and Somaliland, and prevails among Muslims in Tanganyika and Kenya. There are also Shāfi'īs in some districts of Central Asia, and on the Malabar and Coromandel coasts of India. Finally, the Shāfi'ī school is followed by the overwhelming majority of Muslims in Indonesia, in Malaya and the rest of the British East Indies, and by the few hundred thousand Muslims in Siam, French Indo-China, and the Philippines (Sulu).

The Ḥanbalī school did not at once succeed, in the same way as the other surviving orthodox schools of law, in prevailing in any extensive territory, but it had followers in many parts of the Islamic world, including Persia (before it became Shī'ī). One of the great centers of the school for many centuries was Baghdad, where it was represented not only by a number of serious scholars, but by some of the most turbulent elements of the populace and their extremist leaders, whose revolts in the name of the sunna did the reputation of the Ḥanbalīs much harm. The Ḥanbalīs were numerous in Syria and Palestine, too, and Damascus became and remained for a long time another important center of the school, whose contribution to the intellectual climate of Syria in the thirteenth century after Christ was not negligible. It was against this background that the Ḥanbalī reformer Ibn Taymiyya (d. A.D. 1328) and his disciple Ibn Qayyim al-Jawziyya arose in Damascus; these two original scholars are, however, in their teaching not typical of the Ḥanbalī school as a whole. From the fourteenth century onwards, the school seemed on the verge of extinction, until the puritanical Wahhābī movement of the eighteenth century, and especially the Wahhābī revival at the beginning of the present century, gave it a new lease on life. The Wahhābī movement grew out of the alliance between the Ḥanbalī scholar Muḥammad ibn 'Abd al-Wahhāb, who had studied the works of Ibn Taymiyya, and the petty Arab chief Muḥammad ibn Sa'ūd. This is why the Wahhābīs have adopted the special doctrines of Ibn Taymiyya on Islamic theology and law, though as far as positive religious law is concerned, they follow the normal Ḥanbalī doctrine. Whereas the Ḥanbalī school had always been regarded as one of the legitimate schools of law in Islam, the intolerant attitude of the earlier Wahhābīs toward their fellow-Muslims caused them for a long time to be suspected as heretics, and they have come to be generally considered orthodox only since their political successes in the present generation. The Ḥanbalī school is officially recognized in Saudi Arabia, and the inhabitants of Najd, the eastern half of that country, are practically all Ḥanbalīs; there are also fairly considerable numbers of them in Ḥijāz, the western half of the realm, and in the adjoining principalities on the Persian Gulf.

In their relationship to one another, the orthodox schools of law have generally practiced mutual toleration. This attitude goes back to the time of the ancient schools of law, which had accepted the original geographical differences of doctrine as natural. The maxim that disagreements in the community of Muslims were a sign of divine favor, had already been formulated in the second century of the hijra, though it was put into the mouth of the Prophet only much later. This mutual recognition was not incompatible, and did indeed go together with vigorous polemics and the insistence on uniformity of doctrine within each geographical school. The opportunity for disagreements on questions of principle arose only from the time of Shāfi'ī's systematic innovation onwards. In this particular case, the several schools arrived, as we saw, at a compromise, and generally speaking the consensus, which acted as the integrating principle of Islam, has succeeded in making innocuous those differences of opinion that it could not eliminate. The four schools, then, are equally covered by consensus, they are all deemed to translate into individual legal rules the will of Allah as expressed in the Qur'ān and in the sunna of the Prophet, their alternative interpretations are all equally valid, their methods of reasoning equally legitimate; in short, they are equally orthodox. The same held true of the other schools of law as long as they existed; before about A.D. 1300, not four but up to seven schools were regarded as the equally legitimate interpretations of the sacred law; but once a school had ceased to exist, consensus became effective again, and it was no longer permissible to adhere to those schools which once had been on an absolutely equal footing with the others. This is a telling example of the way in which consensus acts in reducing differences progressively. The extinction of whole schools of law was brought about partly by the growing weight of consensus itself, and partly by external circumstances, such as the partiality of rulers for certain schools of law, or their more or less favorable geographical situation. Even within the individual schools and in their relationships to one another consensus acts as an integrating principle. Not only will the recognized doctrine of each school, through the elimination of stray opinions, become more and more uniform and settled down to the most minute details, as time goes on; it also happens not infrequently that a school which, from its own premises, would have to regard an act as indifferent or permissible, prefers in fact to classify it as commendable or reprehensible, so as not to diverge too much from those of other schools which regard it as obligatory or as forbidden. These peacefully competing legal doctrines, these alternative explanations of Allah's commands, are therefore far from being "sects."

On the other hand, there are sects in Islam, as opposed to the "orthodox" or Sunnī majority. Their origin was political, and due to differences concerning the succession to the caliphate. On the origins of their legal systems and their relationship to orthodox Islamic law, all that is necessary has been said in the preceding chapter; and the legal doctrines of the Shī'a, the numerically most important of the sects, will be discussed in Chapter V, below.

After this brief discussion of the present distribution and the mutual relationship of the schools of law in Islam, we must return to the early 'Abbāsid period. In the first few decades of 'Abbāsid rule, Islamic law, with the active help of the government, seemed at last on the point of capturing the practice. But it was denied this success: the administration of the state and religious law drew apart again, and the increasing rigidity of the sharī'a itself prevented it from keeping pace with the practice. This calls for two parallel surveys: one of the later development of Islamic law in itself, and the other of its attitude to the changing practice.

The early 'Abbāsid period saw not only the rise of the schools of law, but the end of the formative period of Islamic law, a process of which the formation of the schools was a symptom. The whole sphere of law had been permeated with the religious and ethical standards proper to Islam; Islamic law had been elaborated in detail; the principle of the infallibility of the consensus of the scholars worked in favor of a progressive narrowing and hardening of doctrine; legal theory was taking on its final form; and a little later, the doctrine which denied the further possibility of "independent reasoning" (ijtihād) sanctioned officially a state of things that had come to prevail in fact. To the earliest specialists in religious law, the search for legal rulings had been identical with the exercise of their personal opinion, of their own judgment on what the law ought to be, basing themselves on the rudimentary guidance available in the Qur'ān and in the practice of the local community of Muslims, and applying the standards so gained to the administrative practice and customary law prevailing in Arabia and in the recently conquered territories. The questions of who was a qualified scholar, and of who had the right to independent exercise of his own opinion, had not yet arisen. This personal judgment was open to anyone sufficiently interested to embark upon this kind of speculation on religious law. The freedom to exercise one's own judgment independently was progressively restricted by several factors, such as the achievement of a local, and later of a general, consensus, the formation of groups or circles within the ancient schools of law, the subjection of unfettered opinion to the increasingly strict discipline of systematic reasoning, and last but not least, the appearance of numerous traditions from the Prophet (and from his Companions), traditions which embodied in authoritative form what had originally been no more than private opinions. Thus the field of individual decision was continually narrowed down, but nevertheless, during the whole of the formative period of Islamic law, the first two and a half centuries of Islam, there was never any question of denying to any scholar or specialist in the sacred law the right to find his own solutions to legal problems. The sanction which kept ignoramuses at bay was the general disapproval of the recognized specialists. It was only after the formative period of Islamic law had come to an end, that the questions of "independent reasoning" and of who was qualified to undertake it were raised.

The first doubts that contemporary scholars enjoyed the same liberty of reasoning as their predecessors are noticeable in Shāfi'ī, and from about the middle of the third century of the hijra the idea began to gain ground that only the great scholars of the past who could not be equaled, and not the epigones, had the right to "independent reasoning." By this time, the term ijtihād had been separated from its old connection with the free use of personal opinion, and restricted to the drawing of valid conclusions from the Qur'ān, the sunna of the Prophet, and the consensus, by strict analogy or systematic reasoning. Shāfi'ī had been instrumental in bringing about this change, but he did not hesitate to affirm the duty of the individual scholars to use their own judgment in drawing these conclusions. By the beginning of the fourth century of Islam (about A.D. 900) the point had been reached, however, when the scholars of all surviving schools felt that all essential questions had been thoroughly discussed and finally settled, and a consensus gradually established itself to the effect that from that time onwards no one could be deemed to have the necessary qualifications for independent reasoning in law, and that all future activity would have to be confined to the explanation, application, and, at the most, interpretation of the doctrine as it had been laid down once and for all. It followed that from then on every Muslim had to belong to one of the recognized schools.

Since this "closing of the door of independent reasoning," as it was called, the doctrine had to be derived not independently from the Qur'ān, the sunna, and the consensus, but from the authoritative handbooks of the several schools. Again, the official doctrine of each school is contained not in the works of the old masters, though they might have been qualified to exercise ijtihād in the highest degree, but in those handbooks, usually of a late period, that the common opinion of the school has recognized as the authoritative exposition of its current doctrine. Even the most competent contemporary scholars are considered, and have been considered for more than a thousand years, imitators and copyists, unable to draw the appropriate conclusions from, or to apply intelligent criticism to, the often conflicting opinions of the old authorities, and bound to accept the latest stage of the doctrine as laid down by the most recent consensus. The final doctrine of a school sometimes differs from, and in any case goes far beyond, the opinions held by its founders. The details of the growth of doctrine within each school, though amply documented by the existing works, still remain a subject for scholarly investigation. The recognized handbooks contain the last stage of authoritative interpretation that has been reached in each school and has been ratified by consensus. They are not in the nature of codes: Islamic law is not a corpus of legislation, but the living result of legal science.

The consensus that declares that since the fourth century of Islam there have been no more scholars qualified to derive Islamic law independently from its sources, expresses only a statement of fact and not a logical necessity, and there have appeared from time to time scholars who claimed that they fulfilled the incredibly high demands which the theory lays down as a qualification for "independent reasoning." However, these claims, as far as positive law was concerned, have remained theoretical, and none of the scholars who made them has actually produced an independent interpretation of the sharīʿa since the "closing of the door of ijtihād." The denial of ijtihād brought with it the unquestioning acceptance of the doctrines of established schools and authorities. This opposite of ijtihād (in its later meaning) was called taqlīd, a term which had originally denoted the kind of reference to Companions of the Prophet that had been usual in the ancient schools. It was against this later concept of taqlīd rather than in favor of ijtihād that Dawūd ibn Khalaf, the founder of the Zāhirī school, and after him the eminent Ḥanbalī, Ibn Taymiyya, followed by his disciple Ibn Qayyim al-Jawziyya, made their protests of principle. They considered it unauthorized and dangerous to follow blindly the authority of any man, excepting only the Prophet, in matters of religion and religious law. (This applies, of course, only to scholars and not to laymen.) The theoretical rejection of taqlīd became one of the tenets of the Zāhirī school, though in practice it left its individual adherents hardly more freedom of doctrine than the other schools.

Ibn Taymiyya did not explicitly advocate the reopening of the "door of independent reasoning," let alone claim for himself the right of ijtihād; but as a consequence of his narrowly formulated idea of consensus he was able to reject taqlīd, to interpret the Qur'ān and traditions from the Prophet afresh, and to arrive at novel conclusions concerning many institutions of religious law. The Wahhābīs, who constitute the great majority of the present followers of the Ḥanbalī school, have adopted, together with Ibn Taymiyya's theological doctrines, the whole of his legal theory, including his rejection of taqlīd; but at the same time they have retained, unchanged, Ḥanbalī positive law as it had been developed in the school before Ibn Taymiyya, apparently without being troubled by the resultant discrepancy. Under the direct or indirect influence of the Wahhābīs, both the reformist movement of the Salafiyya and the various schools of thought that are known as Modernism, from the last decades of the nineteenth century onwards, reject taqlīd. Some Modernists, in particular, combine this with extravagant claims of a new, free ijtihād, but neither movement has produced any results worth mentioning in the field of positive religious law. The recent Modernist legislation in some Islamic countries concerning the sharī'a takes its inspiration from modern constitutional and social ideas rather than from the essentially traditional problem of the legitimacy of ijtihād and taqlīd.[13] (This legislation will be briefly discussed at the end of this chapter.)

Whatever the theory might say on ijtihād and taqlīd, the activity of the later jurists, after the "closing of the door of independent reasoning," was no less creative, within the limits set to it by the nature of the sharī'a, than that of their predecessors. New sets of facts constantly arose in life, and they had to be mastered and moulded with the traditional tools provided by legal science. This activity was carried out by the muftīs. A muftī is a specialist on law who can give an authoritative opinion on points of doctrine, and his considered legal opinion is called fatwa. The earliest specialists in Muḥammadan law, such as Ibrāhīm Nakha'ī, were essentially muftīs whose main function was to advise interested members of the public on what was, in their opinion, the correct course of action from the point of view of religious law. This precautionary and advisory element is still clearly discernible in the work of Mālik. From the beginning, the specialists had formed separate groups of like-minded amateurs, and in the time of Shāfi'ī a class of professionals was emerging. Shāfi'ī informs us that the knowledge of the details of religious law was beyond the reach of the general public, and not even found among all specialists. The members of the public had been in need of specialist guidance from the very beginning of Islamic law, and this need grew stronger as the law became more technical and its presentation more scholastic. The practical importance of the sacred law for the pious Muslim is much greater than that of any secular legal system for the ordinary law-abiding citizen. Islamic law does not only come into play when he has to go to the courts nor is it exclusively concerned with practical legal problems; it tells him what his religious duties are, what makes him ritually clean or unclean, what he may

[13] *Encyclopaedia of Islam*, s. v. *Idjtihād, Taklīd;* Laoust, *Essai*, 226 ff; the same, *Contribution, passim;* the same, *Le califat dans la doctrine de R. Rida* (Beyrouth 1938), pp. 134 ff; H. A. R. Gibb, *Modern Trends in Islam* (Chicago 1946).

eat or drink, how to dress and how to treat his family, and generally what he may with good conscience regard in the widest sense as lawful acts and possessions. There was thus a constant need of specialist guidance on these questions.

From the start, the function of the muftī was essentially private; his authority was based on his reputation as a scholar, his opinion had no official sanction, and a layman might resort to any scholar he knew and in whom he had confidence. In order, however, to provide the general public, and also government officials, with authoritative opinions on problems of sacred law, Islamic governments from some date after the final establishment of the schools of law have appointed scholars of recognized standing as official muftīs. (The chief muftī of a country is often called Shaykh al-Islam.) However, their appointment by the government does not add to the intrinsic value of their opinions, they have no monopoly of giving fatwas, and the practice of consulting private scholars of high reputation has never ceased. A qāḍī, too, may consult a scholar when he is in doubt, and official muftīs are often attached to qāḍīs' tribunals. Parties to a lawsuit before the qāḍī will arm themselves with fatwas as authoritative as possible, though the qāḍī is not bound to accept any of them.[14]

The doctrinal development of Islamic law owes much to the activity of the muftīs. Their fatwas were often collected in separate works, which have a considerable historical interest because they show us the most urgent problems which arose from the practice of a certain place and time. As soon as a decision reached by a muftī on a new kind of problem had been recognized by the common opinion of the scholars as correct, it was incorporated in the handbooks of the school and the fatwas of the authors of recognized handbooks soon acquired an authority only slightly less than that of the handbooks themselves. Compilations were also made of the fatwas of more than one scholar, covering the whole extent of the law, and serving as a kind of supplement to the handbooks. For a number of reasons, the judgments given by the qāḍīs had no comparable influence on the development of Islamic law after the end of its formative period in early 'Abbāsid times, essential though the contributions of the earlier qāḍīs had been to laying its foundations.

It will have become clear from the preceding paragraphs that Islamic law, which until the early 'Abbāsid period had been adaptable and growing, from then onwards became increasingly rigid

[14] Tyan, *op. cit.*, Vol. I, pp. 323 ff.

and set in its final mold. This essential rigidity of Islamic law helped it to maintain its stability over the centuries which saw the decay of the political institutions of Islam. It was not altogether immutable, but the changes which did take place were concerned more with legal theory and the systematic superstructure than with positive law. Most of these later developments of Islamic jurisprudence, which include interesting examples of the interaction of the various schools, still remain to be investigated. Taken as a whole, however, Islamic law reflects and fits the social and economic conditions of the early 'Abbāsid period, but has become more and more out of touch with later developments of state and society.

It has already been observed that the government took over the administration of criminal justice. As regards taxation, only lip-service was paid to the sharī'a and its moderate demands. Concerning constitutional law, the doctrine of the sharī'a is merely a fiction and retrospective abstraction. In the vast field of the law of contracts and obligations, the sharī'a had to resign an ever increasing sphere to practice and custom. We have seen that the theory ignored custom as an official source of law, but that the late Mālikī doctrine in northwest Africa, while maintaining this attitude in principle, to a degree took notice of the existence of customary practices and tried to cover existing conditions with the cloak of legality. This is a particular and explicit case of a situation that prevailed implicitly everywhere and at all times in the law of contracts and obligations. The theory of the sacred law did not fail to influence custom and practice considerably, albeit in varying degrees at different places and times, but it never succeeded in imposing itself on them completely. This resulted chiefly from the fact that the ideal theory, being essentially retrospective, was from the early 'Abbāsid period onwards unable to keep pace with the ever changing demands of society and commerce. The law of contracts and obligations stands in the middle between the law of family, inheritance, and pious endowments (waqf) on one side, and criminal, fiscal, and constitutional law on the other. On the first branches, the sharī'a (notwithstanding the existence of some customs derogatory to it) had the firmest hold; on the last, it had very little, if any, influence.[15]

The law of contracts and obligations, situated between those two extremes, was ruled by a customary law which respected the

[15] C. Snouck Hurgronje, *Verspreide Geschriften* (Bonn and Leipzig 1923 ff.), Vols. II and IV, *passim*.

main principles and institutions of the sharī'a, but showed a greater flexibility and adaptability. It was brought into agreement with the theory of the sharī'a by the ḥiyal or "legal devices," which were often legal fictions. They can be described in short as the use of legal means for achieving extralegal ends, ends that could not be achieved directly with the means provided by the sharī'a, whether such ends might or might not be in themselves illegal. The "legal devices" enabled persons who would otherwise have had to break the law, or under the pressure of circumstances would have had to act against its provisions, to arrive at the desired result while actually conforming to the letter of the law. For instance, the Qur'ān prohibited interest, and this religious prohibition was strong enough to make popular opinion unwilling to transgress it openly and directly, while at the same time there was an imperative demand for the giving and taking of interest in commercial life. In order to satisfy this need, and at the same time to observe the letter of the religious prohibition, a number of devices were developed. One of them consisted of the creditor buying from the debtor an object for the amount of the capital, payable in cash, and the debtor, immediately afterwards, buying the same object back from the creditor for a larger amount, representing capital and interest, and payable at some future date. There were hundreds of these devices, many of them highly technical, but all with a scrupulous regard for the letter of the law.

Circumventions and other devices are not unknown to other legal systems, and legal fictions in particular played a considerable part also in Roman law. But their function in Roman law was to provide the legal framework for new requirements of the practice with the minimum of innovation; in Islamic law it was to circumvent positive enactments. The giving and taking of interest corresponded indeed with a requirement of commercial practice, but a requirement that the Qur'ān, and Islamic law after it, had explicitly and positively banned. The "legal devices" represented a *modus vivendi* between theory and practice: the maximum that custom could give, and the minimum (that is to say, formal acknowledgment) that the theory had to demand. This voluntary quasi-abdication of theory from practically the whole field of commercial law in favor of custom was facilitated by the sacred and therefore inscrutable character of Islamic legal theory, which called for observance of the letter rather than of the spirit. Many religious lawyers and representatives of the sharī'a, starting with the great Ḥanafī authorities Abū Yūsuf and Shaybānī, elaborated such devices and put them at the disposal of the public. One such book, which is credited to Khaṣṣāf, a Ḥanafī lawyer of the third century, but was probably written in 'Iraq in the fourth century of the hijra, enables us to discern, through the thin veil of its legally unobjectionable forms, the realities of practice in that time and place.[16]

A further feature of customary commercial law was its reliance on written documents. As mentioned in the preceding chapter, Islamic law, at a very early period, diverged both from an explicit ruling of the Qur'ān and from current practice by denying the validity of documentary evidence and restricting legal proof to the testimony of witnesses. Written documents, however, proved so indispensable in practice that, notwithstanding their persistent neglect by the theory, they remained in constant use, became a normal accompaniment of every transaction of importance, and gave rise to a highly developed branch of practical law with a voluminous literature of its own. Theory continued to reason as if there were no documents but only the oral testimony of witnesses, possibly aided by private records of their own. Practice continued to act as if the documents were almost essential and the "witnessing" only a formality to make them fully valid; and the professional witnesses came in fact to exercise the functions of notaries public. Again, the authors of the practical books of legal formularies were themselves religious lawyers and specialists in the sharī'a, and they provided forms for all possible needs of the practice which had only to be "witnessed" in order to become legally valid. Finally, even strict theory deigned to recognize the existence of written documents and to admit them as valid evidence, the Mālikīs to the widest extent, the Ḥanafīs with more hesitation, whereas the Shāfi'īs continued to reject them on principle; but the actual use of written documents was equally extensive among the adherents of all schools of law.[17] In the modern period, during which the application of Islamic law and the organization of its tribunals has been increasingly modified by independent Islamic governments, written documents have been generally admitted as valid proof, and sometimes the competence of the qādīs has even been restricted to cases in which documentary evidence is produced.

Written documents often formed an essential element of ḥiyal.

[16] J. Schacht, in *Der Islam*, Vol. XV (1926), pp. 211 ff.; the same, editions of the ḥiyal books of Shaybānī (1930), Khaṣṣāf (1923), and Qazwīnī (1924).

[17] E. Tryan, *Le notariat et la régime de la preuve par écrit* (Beyrouth, 1945).

The more complicated ḥiyal often consisted of several transactions between the parties concerned, each of which was perfectly legal in itself, and the combined effect of which produced the desired result (which, it will be remembered, could not be directly reached by any single transaction under the rules of the sharī'a). Each transaction was recorded and attested in a written document as a matter of course. Taken in isolation, a document recording a single transaction or a declaration made by one of the parties might be used by the other party to its exclusive advantage and for a purpose contrary to the aim of the whole of the agreement. In order to prevent this from happening, the official documents were deposited in the hands of a trusted intermediary or umpire, together with an unofficial covering document which set out the real position of the parties to each other and the real purport of their agreement. The umpire then, acting on the contents of the covering document, handed to each party only those papers to which they were entitled at any given stage. He prevented an unauthorized use of any document by producing, if necessary, the document of a compensating transaction or declaration which had been prepared beforehand for the very purpose of guarding against the abuse of any of the documents. The whole phenomenon of customary commercial law is of considerable importance for the legal sociology of Islam in the Middle Ages.[18]

These and similar points of interaction between theory and practice form another vast field, still awaiting investigation, in the legal history of Islam. The examples which have been given show that the theory of the sharī'a possessed a great assimilating power, the power of imposing its spiritual supremacy even when it could not control the material conditions. A further consideration of the practice as such lies outside the scope of this survey of the development of Islamic jurisprudence; it should be mentioned, however, that the hostile references to the practice in treatises of Islamic law are one of our main sources for its investigation.

Thus, a balance gradually established itself in most Islamic countries between legal theory and legal practice; an uneasy truce between the specialists in religious law and the political authorities came into being. The sharī'a could not abandon its claim to absolute theoretical validity, but as long as it received formal recognition as a religious ideal from the Muslims, it did not insist on being carried out in practice. The laws that rule the lives of the Islamic peoples have never been coextensive with pure Islamic

[18] J. Schacht, in *Der Islam*, Vol. XXII (1935), p. 220.

law.[19] These general and normal conditions were occasionally disturbed by violent religious reform movements, such as that of the Almoravids in northwest Africa and Spain from about A.D. 1050 to 1146, that of the Fulānis or Fulbe in West Africa, including northern Nigeria, in the nineteenth century, and that of the Wahhābīs in Arabia, in the nineteenth and again in the present century. The Almoravids and the Fulānis were Mālikis, the Wahhābīs, as mentioned before, Ḥanbalīs. All these movements made it their aim, in the states which they set up, to enforce Islamic law exclusively, to abolish the double system of administration of justice, and to outlaw customary and administrative law. In the past, the effects of these religious reform movements on the observance of the sharīʿa usually tended to wear off, until a new equilibrium between theory and practice established itself.

Essentially of the same kind, though sensibly different in their effects, were the efforts of existing Islamic states (later than the early ʿAbbāsid period) to subject the actual practice to the rule of the sacred law. The most remarkable and, for a time, the most successful of these efforts was made in the Ottoman Empire under the sultans Muḥammad II, Bayazid II, Salim I, and Sulayman I, from the middle of the fifteenth to the end of the sixteenth century. These sultans were more serious in their desire to be pious rulers than the early ʿAbbāsids, and they endowed Islamic law in its Ḥanafī form with the highest degree of actual validity in a society of high material civilization that this law had possessed since early ʿAbbāsid times. With the abolition of the sharīʿa in Turkey in 1926, the history of Islamic law in that country came to an end.

Another important, though less lasting effort to apply the whole of Islamic law in practice was made in India under the Mogul Emperor ʿAlamgir (1658-1707), as part of the orthodox reaction after the ephemeral religious experiment of the Emperor Akbar. Here, too, the Ḥanafī doctrine was followed, and an enormous compilation of fatwas and extracts from earlier works was made by order of the Emperor, whose name it bears. This instance of a prince appearing officially as the sponsor of a work of religious law is well-nigh unique. The strong influence of the sharīʿa on the practice which ʿAlamgir inaugurated lasted well into the period of British control in India.

When the East India Company decided to assert sovereign rights in 1772, and British judges were called upon to administer

[19] J. H. Kramers, in *Archives de l'histoire du droit oriental,* Vol. I (1937), pp. 401 ff.

justice outside the "factories" of the company, they found not only civil but criminal law ruled by the sharī'a, and the sharī'a, though successively modified, remained the basis of criminal law in India until 1862. The Islamic law of evidence was not entirely abolished until 1872. As regards the law of family and inheritance and all other institutions sanctioned by religion, the continued validity of the sharī'a for Muslims was guaranteed by a regulation of 1772, which has substantially remained in force until this day. But the qādīs were at the same time replaced by British judges. It is true that the judges were originally given the assistance of Muslim "law officers," muftīs in fact, who had to expound for the benefit of the former the correct doctrine of the sacred law, and that subsequently judges in the Muslim parts of British India came to be increasingly recruited from among Indian Muslims. But the whole judiciary was trained in English law, and English legal concepts, such as the doctrine of precedent, and rules derived from English common law and equity inevitably invaded Islamic law as applied in India to an ever-increasing extent. The appellate jurisdiction of the Privy Council, too, much against its intentions, could not fail materially to affect the law. One of their decisions on waqf, applying English legal reasoning to an institution of Islamic law, had such grave consequences that it had to be corrected by the *Waqf Validating Act of 1913*, which in its turn had to be made retroactive in 1930. In this way, Anglo-Muḥammadan law, worked out in great part by English trained Indian Muslim lawyers themselves, has become an independent legal system, substantially different from the strict Islamic law of the sharī'a.[20] The most important single act in this field in the closing years of British rule in India was the *Sharī'at Act* of 1937, which abolished the legal authority of custom among the Muslims of India and imposed upon them the official doctrine of the sharī'a as modified by statute and interpreted by Anglo-Indian jurisdiction. To enforce the pure theory of the sharī'a as against custom in a country in which the sharī'a was in any case restricted in its validity and deeply anglicized even in its central chapters, was an act of deliberate archaism and purism.

In the Middle East, the Western influence on Islamic law was not technically legal, as it was in India, but exerted itself as a consequence, first of Westernizing tendencies, and later of the Modernist movement, both of which arose out of the contact of the world of Islam with modern Western civilization. Modernism aims at adapting Islam to modern conditions, by renovating those parts

[20] A. A. A. Fyzee, *Outlines of Muhammadan Law* (2nd ed., Oxford, 1954).

of its traditional equipment that are considered medieval and out of keeping with modern times. Islamic law in its traditional form, the only form in which it has existed so far, is subject to Modernist criticism in the first place, but such a change as the Modernists have in view would alter its character beyond recognition.

During the nineteenth century, the effects on Islamic law of the contact with the West were restricted to the adoption of the Western form of codes subdivided into articles, both in the official codification of the Ḥanafī law of contracts, obligations, and civil procedure in the Majalla (the Ottoman Civil Code), and in the private, though officially sponsored codifications of the Ḥanafī law of family and inheritance, property, and waqf, undertaken by Qadrī Pasha for Egypt. Only in the present generation has the ground been prepared for legislation by Islamic governments on family law, the law of inheritance, and the law of waqf, subjects which have always formed part of the central domain of the sharīʿa. This legislative interference with the sharīʿa itself (as opposed to the silent or explicit restriction of its sphere of application by custom or by legislation) presupposes the reception of Western political ideas. A modern sovereign, a modern government, and particularly a parliament are differently placed with regard to Islamic law than a traditional Muslim ruler and even the former Ottoman caliph. The legislative power is no more content with what the sharīʿa is prepared to leave to it officially or in fact, but wants itself to determine the sphere which is to be left to the sharīʿa, to restrict it, and to modify what remains according to its own requirements. This Modernist legislative interference with Islamic law started modestly with the Ottoman family law of 1917, which was later repealed in Turkey but remained valid in some of the Ottoman successor states. Then, from 1920 onwards, most of the Modernist legislative movement took place in Egypt, where its main milestones were Decree-Law No. 25 of 1929 on family law, Decree-Law No. 78 of 1931 on the organization of the sharīʿa tribunals, Law No. 77 of 1943 on inheritance, Law No. 48 of 1946 on waqf, and Law No. 71 of 1946 on legacies. Other Islamic countries in the Middle East followed suit. All branches of law in which the sharīʿa is still being applied in practice have been modified more or less deeply. This leads to an unprecedented relationship between religious and temporal law. The method used by the Modernist legislators savors of unrestrained eclecticism; the "independent reasoning" that they claim, goes far beyond any that was practiced in the formative period of Islamic law; any opinion held at some time in the past is likely to be taken out of its context and used as an argument. On the one hand, Modernist legislators are inclined to deny the religious character of the central chapters of the sharī'a; on the other, they are apt to use arbitrary and forced interpretations of the Qur'ān and traditions whenever it suits their purpose. Materially, they are bold innovators; formally, they try to avoid the semblance of unprecedented interference, and to justify modern innovations by traditional authorities. Legal Modernism in the Middle East is as much a departure from the strict Islamic law of the sharī'a as is Anglo-Muḥammadan law.[21]

Parallel with the tendency to modify the sharī'a is the desire to elaborate new laws on the foundations of the basic principles of the sharī'a. When the modern Egyptian secular codes were copied from French civil law, a few institutions and isolated rules were taken over from Islamic law, for instance, the institution of preemption and the rule that payment for alcoholic beverages could not be enforced in law. Now something much more ambitious is suggested: the taking of some general ideas from Islamic law and deriving from them a new, modern system. This is called "temporal Islamic legislation"—a contradiction *in adjecto* in the light of history. But it is significant that those who want to pervade modern secular law with an Islamic spirit are to a great extent the same persons who advocate modifying Islamic law in those fields in which it is still being applied in practice. They also uphold a unified jurisdiction, bridging the gulf between secular and sharī'a tribunals. This would amount to secularism, but is coupled with the demand of a return to the principles of Islamic law. The common aim underlying this program and the program of legal Modernism is to express modern ideas, which have been borrowed from the West, in a traditional medium.[22]

As a result of this development which has been very broadly sketched in the preceding paragraphs, the application of Islamic law at present varies widely in the several Islamic countries.[23] Whatever the future may bring, the sharī'a will always remain one of the most important, if not the most important, subject of study for the student of Islam.

[21] J. Schacht, in *Der Islam,* Vol. XX (1932), pp. 209 ff.; the same, in *Mélanges Maspéro,* Vol. III (Cairo 1935-40), pp. 323 ff.

[22] The problem of the modernization of the Sharī'a will be discussed in the second volume of this work (ed.).

[23] G.-H. Bousquet, *Du droit musulman et de son application effective dans le monde* (Algiers, 1949).

CHAPTER IV

Nature and Sources of the Sharī'a

ISLAM is not only a religion, it is a political system, and though in modern times devout Muslims have endeavored to separate the two aspects, Islam's whole classical literature is based upon the assumption that they are inseparable. Most legal systems have at one time or another in their history been intimately connected with religion; but the two great Semitic systems, the Jewish and the Islamic, are probably unique in the thoroughness with which they identify law with the personal command of a single Almighty God. This is the more remarkable in that Islam has never recognized a priesthood, and in the Jewish system the priesthood became extinct at an early stage in the elaboration of the law.[1]

To the Westerner, law is a system of commands enforced by the sanction of the state. This concept is wholly alien to Islamic theory. On the one hand, the state has from time to time enforced much which could not be called law; on the other hand, the law of God remains the law of God even though there is no one to enforce it, and even though in many of its details it is quite incapable of enforcement. Indeed, the law is reverenced for its divine character even by people who do not profess to obey it; and so we find communities living according to customs completely at variance with the divine command, yet on occasion imbued with religious fanaticism.

Law, then, in any sense in which a Western lawyer would recognize the term, is but a part of the whole Islamic system, or rather, it is not even a part but one of several inextricably combined elements thereof. Sharī'a, the Islamic term which is commonly rendered in English by "law" is, rather, the "Whole Duty of Man." Moral and pastoral theology and ethics; high spiritual aspiration and the detailed ritualistic and formal observance which to some minds is a vehicle for such aspiration and to others a substitute for it; all aspects of law; public and private hygiene; and even courtesy

[1] I.e., at the fall of the Temple, A.D. 72. For a century or more before that the development of the law had passed from the priests to the rabbis. The likenesses between Islamic and Rabbinical law, as well as their differences, deserve fuller investigation than they have yet received.

and good manners are all part and parcel of the sharī'a, a system which sometimes appears to be rigid and inflexible; at others to be imbued with that dislike of extremes, that spirit of reasonable compromise which was part of the Prophet's own character. The word sharī'a originally meant the path or track by which camels were taken to water, and so by transfer the path ordained of God by which men may achieve salvation. This conception of a path or way of life is very common in early Islam. It occurs again in the word sunna (see below) and in the name of the earliest Mālikī law book, the *Muwaṭṭa'* of Mālik himself.[2]

The scientific study and elucidation of the sharī'a is called fiqh, a word which today is commonly and aptly translated "dogma," but which in its origin means ratiocination, the use of the human reason, as opposed to 'ilm, knowledge based solely on revelation or intuition. But this early distinction has long since been obscured so that it is not uncommon to speak of 'ilm al-fiqh, the science of jurisprudence or dogma, 'ilm having become a general word for all knowledge. Fiqh is divided into two branches, 'uṣūl al-fiqh or the bases or roots of jurisprudence, and furū', the branches or the detailed applications.

One further observation of a general character must be made here. Sharī'a, being the whole duty of man, played an important role in the Islamic educational system. When a heroine of the Arabian Nights, reciting a list of her charms, says that she knows the rules of inheritance according to all the four schools, she is not claiming to be a professional lawyer but merely to have had the best university education available. It follows that the teachers of the law developed problems which in practice could never occur, merely for their educational value as exercises in logic, dialectics, and even arithmetic. The same phenomenon is also observable to some extent in other systems which have been developed in a scholastic atmosphere, notably in the Talmudic stage of Jewish law and among the later medieval Hindu lawyers. It is also worth emphasizing again that, as in Rabbinical law, the lawyers are theologians and the theologians lawyers. For example, the two most famous Islamic philosophers and theologians, al-Ghazzālī and Averroes,[3] wrote legal treatises of first-class importance.

[2] In the case of the word sharī'a, there may be some idea of divine direction: cf. the Jewish and Christian uses of the term "way." In the case of sunna, however, it is merely "the beaten track," i.e., custom, though theoretically connected with the Prophet.

[3] 'Abd al-Raḥmān ibn Rushd al-Qurtabī. The philosopher must be distinguished from his grandson of the same name, the lawyer. But in fact both grandfather and grandson wrote legal treatises still extant.

THE ROOTS OF JURISPRUDENCE

Islamic orthodoxy conceives of the sharī'a as having sprung from four principal roots, or, to use English legal terminology, sources. These are: (1) the Qur'ān (the Word of God); (2) the sunna (the Practice of the Prophet); (3) ijmā' (consensus); and (4) qiyās (analogy).

There are also certain minor sources to be considered later, but these four should be discussed first.

THE QUR'ĀN

Every word of the Qur'ān is regarded as the utterance of the Almighty communicated in His actual words by the angel Gabriel, the Holy Spirit, to the Prophet. The correct method of introducing a quotation from the Qur'ān is not (as in the case of the Old Testament) "It is written" but "God (be He exalted) said." The Qur'ān is not and does not profess to be a code of law or even a law book, nor was Muḥammad a lawgiver in any Western sense.[4] The Qur'ān is an eloquent appeal (to Muslim ears, "a miracle of eloquence") to mankind and to the Arabs in particular, to obey the law of God which, it is (in the main) implied, has already been revealed or is capable of being discovered. Nevertheless, it would be a grave mistake to overlook the influence of the Qur'ān in the creation of the Islamic legal system. That influence has been exercised in four different ways.

First, in the last years of his career the Prophet, as a ruling sovereign, was faced with a number of legal problems on which he sought divine guidance, and the answers which he uttered in trance form a definite legal element in the Qur'ān. There are commonly said to be five hundred such texts, but most of these deal with the ritual law, and there are no more than about eighty which deal with subjects which Western lawyers would regard as legal material. These eighty texts have been construed, by a method of statutory interpretation which Anglo-American lawyers might well find congenial, so as to extract the utmost ounce of meaning from them. For example, the Sunnī and the Shi'ī Ithna 'Asharī[5] systems of inheritance have alike been built up from about half a dozen verses of the Qur'ān and are unintelligible except by reference to them. The difference between the two is that the Sunnīs

[4] Goldziher wisely remarks that "Prophets are not theologians"; nor, it may be added, are they lawyers, though their message provides material both for theologians and lawyers.

[5] Twelvers, the Shī'ī sect recognizing a succession of twelve imāms. See Chap. V.

regard these revelations as amendments of the previous law, while the Ithna 'Asharīs endeavor (not always successfully) to treat them as abrogating it altogether.

Second, nonlegal texts in the Qur'ān, moral exhortations, and even divine promises have been construed by analogy to afford legal rules. Thus the texts, "Surely they say, usury is like sale. But God has made sale lawful and usury unlawful" (Q. II 276-277), and "They will ask thee concerning wine and gambling. Say, in both is sin and advantage to men. But the sin thereof is greater than the advantage" (Q. V. 216), have had an all pervading influence on the whole doctrine of contract and those unilateral acts (e.g., kafāla, iqrār) which in Islamic law resemble contract. The lawfulness of such acts is estimated in terms of their resemblance to sale, and the only appreciation of or attempt to define contract in general terms is normally to be found in discussions of sale. Usury, the taking of a "use" for money, and gambling (the idea being extended to cover almost any transaction which involved the transference of a risk) are regarded as the opposite types. It cannot be doubted that among a wealthy mercantile community such as that of Mecca these puritanical doctrines were a complete innovation; and it is equally beyond doubt that in spite of the abiding strength of devout Muslim sentiment against usury and gambling, these prohibitions have been consistently evaded throughout the history of Islam. Otherwise, commerce and finance, particularly the financing of agriculture, would have been brought to a standstill. Similarly, it has been argued with considerable plausibility that Qur'ānic texts proclaiming that God will not punish any man save for his own sins have been applied to the debts which he leaves unpaid at his death with far-reaching results in the law of administration of assets.[6] It is noteworthy, however, that other texts of the Qur'ān which one might naturally expect would become the basis of legal doctrines, for instance, those on the value of written evidence in relation to contracts and wills, appear from this point of view to have been completely neglected.

Third, it is explicitly stated in numerous texts of the Qur'ān that the law of God has been previously revealed to Jews and Christians, and in one text (Q. X, 94) the pious Muslim (or the Prophet himself) is expressly bidden if he have any doubt to consult those to whom the Scriptures have been revealed before him. Therefore, although as the gulf between Islam and the previous

[6] Professor 'Abd al-Ḥamīd Badawī in *L'Egypte contemporaine* (1914), pp. 14-51, especially p. 24. See Q. XVII, 16; XXXIV, 24; XXXIX, 9.

"peoples of the Book" grew wider, and the doctrine arose that preceding revelations had been corrupted and were unreliable, the founders of the Islamic legal system could hardly be blamed if they turned to proselytes from the earlier religions for assistance. So far as Christians were concerned there was at that date no body of Christian civil law claiming to derive its authority from revelation. Any influence which Roman law may have had on Islamic jurisprudence was not by the channels of direct or conscious borrowing and may for our present purpose be ruled out.[7] But the case was otherwise with Rabbinical law. Here, at any rate, was a system of law akin at many points to Arabian custom, founded on the same monotheistic principles and imbued with the same spirit as Islam. In other fields than law the impact of Rabbinical learning on Islam is well established. In law, the influences are still obscure; but 'Umar's instructions to the qāḍī,[8] if genuine, are by far the oldest Islamic legal documents outside the Qur'ān which we have, and even if not genuine they are interesting as early evidence of how Islamic lawyers believed their system to have been developed. Of those instructions it has been well said that the man who delivered them had a Jewish lawyer at his elbow. There is reason also to suppose (a point which will be discussed further in dealing with qiyās) that the logical and dialectical methods of Islamic lawyers owe something to the Rabbinical schools.

Finally and above all, the Qur'ān converted the heathen Arabs (whose pre-Islamic law had consisted entirely of ancestral and mercantile customs and apparently had had little or no connection with what passed for religion among them) to the idea that law is the direct command of God; and since it is the cardinal tenet of Islam that God is One, it follows that His law must be a single whole.[9] For that whole the devout builders of the Islamic system were bound to search.

[7] See S. G. Vesey-Fitzgerald, "The Alleged Debt of Islamic to Roman Law," *Law Quarterly Review*, Vol. LXVII (1951), pp. 81-102.

[8] D. S. Margoliouth, "Omar's Instructions to the Kadi," *Journal of the Royal Asiatic Society* (April 1910), pp. 307-26.

[9] It is important not to overlook this at the present day. Many parts of the sharī'a are obsolete either by reason of causes internal to Islam or owing to the influence of the West. Yet it is sometimes impossible fully to understand the doctrines which remain except by reference to those which have become obsolete. For instance, the law of nasab (commonly but not quite accurately rendered in English by "legitimacy") cannot be understood unless we realize that it has no necessary connection with lawful marriage. A woman's children (at least in the Sunnī schools) are all legitimate in their relation to her (compare the Roman-Dutch law maxim, "A mother makes no bastard"). A man's children are his legitimate children unless the intercourse by which they were begotten amounted to the crime of zinā', or at

All three of the other principal sources of law, but more particularly sunna and ijmā', are a necessary deduction from the Qur'ānic axiom of the unity of God's law.

THE SUNNA

The most obvious source of information concerning the law of God to which enquirers could turn was the path or practice of the Prophet himself, and of his companions so far as their practice could be taken as evidence of what he approved. Just as the Common Law is to be culled from the decisions of the judges recorded in the year books and law reports, so the sunna, the Common Law of Islam, is to be culled from the traditions which are for this purpose the Law Reports of early Islam.[10] We may add that just as in fact the Common Law is older than the Law Reports, so also the sunna is older than the traditions. Here we come to a curious point. The normal course of intellectual development in the humanities and the social sciences is that practice comes first and theory afterwards by a process of generalization from observed facts: logical thought comes before logic and society before the social sciences. Similarly religion, any great religion, is older than its theology, and law (*Recht*) is older than jurisprudence (*Rechtswissenschaft*). Yet according to orthodox Islamic exposition, which was in the main apparently accepted even by such great scholars as Sachau and Snouck Hurgronje, the theory came first and the practice was built upon it. This is certainly not true; much of the law is pre-Islamic and all of it had a history before being cast into the theoretical mold. Nevertheless, the theory profoundly influenced the whole structure of the law and is still a vital force. To put the same thing in other words: professors of law do not initiate law, but they classify, clarify, amplify, and sometimes correct it. This was the real function of the mujtahids or professors of legal sci-

---

any rate was in the category of zinā'. The fixed punishment for this was exceedingly severe, and accordingly just as the "pious perjury" of English judges and juries evaded the severity of the law against larceny by fine distinctions, so in like manner the humane instincts of the Islamic lawyers evaded the application of this penalty by accepting almost any excuse for finding that conduct, even though reprehensible and punishable by a ta'zīr or (lesser) discretionary penalty, was not zinā'. The Prophet himself may be said to have set the fashion in this respect by exacting an almost impossible standard of proof. This is a matter on which lawyers trained in English ideas have sometimes gone astray.

[10] Just as the sharī'a is a great deal more than law, so likewise, the traditions are a great deal more than merely law reports. For this reason they are a fascinating and varied field of study to many besides lawyers.

ence. Of the process by which ijtihād (independent reasoning) became atrophied we shall speak below.

From the very earliest days of Islam and throughout its history there has been a cleavage between the umarā' (amirs, military leaders, and civil governors) and the fuqahā' or lawyers. One may compare, omitting the hereditary aspect, the *noblesse de l'épée* and the *noblesse de la robe* of aristocratic France. The cleavage, like every other important fact in Islamic history, is consecrated by a forecast traditionally ascribed to the Prophet. It is as dangerously easy to exaggerate the importance of this cleavage as it is to ignore it. The lawyers on the one hand were bound by the Qur'ān itself to acknowledge the unity of the Islamic state and consequently the necessity for a head of the state, however distasteful an individual occupant of that office might be to them. The rulers on the other hand, however lightly religion may have sat on their consciences, were bound to make some outward deference to it, for it was to the religion of Islam that they owed their position. Nevertheless, the cleavage is there.

Islamic tradition is apt to emphasize the splendor of Islam by painting pre-Islamic Arabia in unduly gloomy colors. That the civilization of Mecca before Muḥammad was harsh and crude, degenerate in some respects and undeveloped in others, is probable. Nevertheless, it was a civilization: the complicated life of a great city, wealthy, prosperous, and with business connections of very long standing extending into the Roman Empire in one direction and in the other to Abyssinia, Arabia Felix, and directly or indirectly into India and perhaps beyond.[11] Such a civilization could not have existed without a legal system, particularly since there was no strong central authority. The use of the words qaḍā (judgment) and fatwa (legal opinion) in the Qur'ān shows that there was not only a body of substantive law but a system of courts and lawyers not unlike that which has since become familiar in Islam; and at least one famous rule of procedure ("Evidence is for him who claims, the oath is on him who denies"[12]) has been traced to a pre-Islamic source.

This pre-existing legal system of Mecca and the probably somewhat more primitive law of Medina are, as Goldziher has shown,

11 There is even a curious legend, which, of course, cannot be stressed, of a relative of the Prophet who went to China for trade before the Prophet's mission and returned to find Islam triumphant.

12 The same two principles are to be found in Rabbinical law, though laid down in different places; and the first, at least, in Roman law, although the application was probably somewhat different.

the main material of the sunna of Islam. Although it is true that the Qur'ān had called upon the Arabs to abandon the customs of their fathers in favor of the law of God (Q. II, 170; V, 104; etc.); they were and are an intensely conservative people. In any case it would have been quite impossible for them to abandon the existing law until they knew what the Law of God was, and the caliphs and their judges continued to administer the existing law except insofar as it had been clearly abrogated by the Qur'ān. The Qur'ān readers in the mosques who developed into the jurists (fuqahā') could not but deal with this same legal material subjecting it to the religious test: did the Prophet (who was born, brought up, and lived nearly all his life under this system) approve of this or that rule, or condemn it? But the fuqahā' were not working in a vacuum; they were testing and according to their lights refining an existing system.

Here, a suggestion may be very tentatively put forward. When the schools of law become definite, we find the school of Abū Ḥanīfa described as ahl al-ra'y, the people of opinion, and that of Mālik as ahl al-ḥadīth, the people of tradition. It is difficult, however, to fit these labels to the facts. Mālik frequently decided questions on the basis of his own personal opinion; on the other hand, the *Kitāb al-Kharāj* of Abū Yūsuf, the oldest Ḥanafī law text extant, is very definitely an attempt to build up law on a basis of tradition, though largely traditions of the Companions and their successors. May it not be that the term ahl al-ra'y was originally applied by the orthodox casuists (the puritans of their day) to the caliph's judges and lawyers and later used to describe Abū Ḥanīfa and his school when they allied themselves with the 'Abbāsid regime? The two jāmi's (collections) of Muḥammad al-Shaybānī, the third great Ḥanafī doctor who has been described by Sachau as the real founder of the Ḥanafī school, breathe an entirely different spirit. They rarely quote either Qur'ān or Tradition, and are concerned with the dialectical elaboration of a known and settled system.

The sunna is to be found in traditions, according to the accepted classification, traditions of what the Prophet said, did, or by his silence approved. Another possible division is into aḥadīth qudsiyya, traditions claiming to contain direct divine inspiration; traditions of the Prophet himself; and traditions which embody legal decisions of the first four caliphs or of other Companions of the Prophet. Of this division one can only say that the aḥadīth qudsiyya, if genuine, ought to have found a place in the Qur'ān, and the very fact that they have not is an argument against their authenticity. Muslim scholars have in the past been inclined to rank the authority of traditions of the caliphs and Companions below that of traditions which vouch the authority of the Prophet himself. But a modern scholar might well take a converse view, since fabricators, whether deliberate or self-deceiving, would naturally tend to claim the highest available authority.

That there has been wholesale fabrication of traditions is universally admitted by Muslim and Western scholars alike. Indeed, the existence and the danger of such fabrication was well known from almost the earliest period of Islam. At the first it may have been innocent enough. Many of the Companions were people who had known the Prophet intimately; and the psychological step from feeling confident of what the Prophet's view would probably have been to persuading oneself that he had in fact so decided is one which an honest mind might easily take without being conscious that it has crossed the border between opinion and fact. As time went on, many of the traditions were obviously attempts to read back the controversies, or the conditions of later ages, into that earlier period from which guidance was sought.[13] But the unreal clarity with which this process invests these traditions does not always preclude a foundation in fact. Take for instance the famous tradition of the interview between the Prophet and Mu'ādh. As it stands, the sequence of authority—Qur'ān, sunna, ra'y—proceeds with the well-drilled regularity of a church catechism or a code of law. This is unconvincing; yet, equally clearly, no ruler would have sent a lieutenant on so important a mission without first receiving him in private audience; nor would the Prophet have sent out a man if he had felt any doubt of his loyalty to Revelation or to his own policy, or of his capacity for the exercise of discretion. It is the formalism rather than the substance of the tradition which lays it open to suspicion, and also its attempt to create a legal theory out of what can hardly have been more than administrative advice.

Snouck Hurgronje, in reference primarily to the great mass of nonlegal tradition, held that the skepticism of Western scholars had perhaps been carried too far (*Mohammedanism,* p. 32). On the other hand, devout Muslim scholars from a very early date recognized that there was an immense amount of falsification, some of

13 The same phenomenon is traceable also in some of the alleged differences of opinion between the three founders of the Ḥanafī school, Abū Ḥanīfa, Abū Yūsuf, and Muḥammad al-Shaybānī.

it deliberate, going on. They set about, therefore, to sift the traditions with such critical apparatus as they possessed. Unfortunately, this apparatus suffered from the cardinal defect which is inherent, even to this day, in the Islamic theory of evidence—the presumption that a respectable man who would not willingly tell a lie is therefore necessarily telling the truth. Of faulty memory, wishful thinking, reading back the present into the past, casting the color of one's own opinions on the facts, and of the effect of leading questions—in fact, of all those psychological problems of which a judge, a cross-examining counsel, or a research student are aware today—they were in the main completely unconscious. Any wholesale condemnation of the personal good faith of the six classical collectors of traditions seems to involve an equally great and less pardonable ignorance of the principles of evidence. Schacht, however, has recently given very strong reasons for the view that at about the time of the founders of the great Sunnī law schools and before the time of the six great collections of traditions in the ninth century, there was deliberate forgery of traditions by responsible lawyers on such a scale that no purely legal tradition of the Prophet himself can be regarded as above suspicion. The new evidence revealed by Schacht's researches raises the strong suspicions of previous scholars to the level of proof.[14]

However, any attempt to sift the genuine from the false in the great mass of traditions is a hopeless task today. If a tradition is to be found in any of the six great collections which are universally accepted by Sunnī Islam, it has canonical authority. Unfortunately, the growth of spurious tradition was not stopped by the establishment of these canonical collections. Contradictory opinions habitually cite contradictory traditions, and one writer says frankly, "The ḥadīth is the form in which we state our conclusions."[15] Although few authors are as candid as this, it is impossible to read, for example, the *Hidāya,* the work of al-Marghinānī (d. A.D. 1197) which more than any other summarizes the development of the Ḥanafī school, without coming across numerous cases in which the dialectical development of the doctrine is obviously the main consideration with the author, the tradition, genuine or not, being added to give a cachet or hallmark to a conclusion reached on other grounds.

The Qur'ān and the sunna are sometimes spoken of as the roots

[14] J. Schacht, *Origins of Muhammadan Jurisprudence* (Oxford, 1950).

[15] Quoted by G. H. Bousquet, *Precis de droit musulman* (2nd ed., Alger, 1947), p. 31.

of the bases (uṣūl al-uṣūl), a phrase which implies that the other foundations of the law are merely subordinate to and dependent on them. There are, however, as we shall show, some independent elements in the other sources.

IJMĀ' OR CONSENSUS

It was a reasonable deduction from Qur'ānic teaching, duly consecrated by a ḥadīth, that God would not permit His people universally to be in error. *Quod semper, quod ubique, quod ab omnibus fidelibus* is no less a Muslim than it is a Catholic doctrine. Such consensus was reckoned to be of two kinds, ijmā' al-umma, consensus of the whole community of Islam, and ijmā' al-'a'imma, consensus of the imāms, or leaders of the people, which for this purpose means the great law teachers. Examples of the first sort are to be found in the details of the ritual of the Mecca pilgrimage, universally practiced by all pilgrims though it would be hard to find authority for them in any early legal text. In modern times the authors of the Ottoman Family Law of 1917, the first great work in the Modernist attempt to reform Islamic law from within,[16] cited the universal and longstanding practice of all respectable Muslims throughout the world, among other reasons, in support of their proposal to make the registration of Muslim marriages compulsory, although in fact no such provision will be found in any authoritative law book. Of the second sort of ijmā' we may distinguish two kinds. The first is agreement on the interpretation of a Qur'ānic text or tradition, such as for instance that Q. IV, 12 refers to the uterine, and Q. IV, 177 to the agnate, brothers and sisters, or that the payment of debts comes before the distribution of legacies though the Qur'ān three times over mentions them in the reverse order. Of this class of ijmā' one can only say that, quite apart from reverence for authority, any careful student would almost inevitably reach the same conclusion. They are in fact instances of universal qiyās. The second and more remarkable class consists of a number of pithy statements of legal principle which do not profess to be based on anything in the Qur'ān or in the Prophet's own practice, but which are, nonetheless, universally accepted as authoritative. Of these a striking instance is the rule that "the will of the wāqif (founder of a waqf) is as an express text

16 Previous Ottoman codes were either open importations of law codes from France (e.g., the Code de Commerce) or Germany (e.g., the Provisional Law of Mortgages), or violently conservative documents such as the Majalla. See below, Chap. XII.

of the lawgiver" (irādat al-wāqif ka naṣṣ al-shāri'); i.e., the founder of a waqf, creating, as he does, a perpetuity, may legislate for the devolution of the enjoyment of the waqf in perpetuity, probably a wider privilege than any other system of law concedes to the individual, and this within a system which in theory, at least, confines the legislative power of the State within the narrowest possible limits!

NAṢṢ AND QIYĀS

Authoritative texts of the Qur'ān, authoritative traditions, and the pithy statements of consensus above mentioned are commonly called naṣṣ, a word implying the highest degree of textual authority. They are contrasted with qiyās or reasoning by analogy, a source of less authority. It is said, for instance, that "custom can override a qiyās, it cannot override a naṣṣ." Qiyās is probably older, though of less authority, than ijmā'.

It is frequently said that the doctrine of qiyās is an importation of Rabbinical methods of legal exegesis into Islam, and it has been suggested that the word qiyās itself is of the same origin as its Rabbinical counterpart, *ha kasha*[17] and that the latter is merely a rendering into Hebrew of the Greek *symballein.* Such identifications have their dangers. All rational beings reason by analogy even if they are unconscious of it, just as Monsieur Jourdain spoke prose *sans le savoir.* There is nothing extraordinary or even noteworthy in the fact that the reasoning processes of two different communities are the same. It becomes remarkable when we find not only that they reason in the same way but that they consciously classify their own mental processes in similar categories. While the published researches of Margoliouth[18] and the recent work of Schacht[19] certainly tend to strengthen the likelihood of borrowing from Rabbinical sources, no one has yet traced the whole of Hillel's elaborate sevenfold classification of analogy into Islam, though the mental atmosphere is at least similar and borrowing not improbable. In time, however, qiyās in Islam acquired a meaning entirely different from any of Hillel's categories. When the author of the *Hidāya,* for instance, says that the testamentary power is lawful by istiḥsān (see below) but contrary to qiyās, he has obviously parted company with any conception of analogical deduction from divine revelation. The testamentary power is expressly provided for in

[17] Other philologists, however, deny this and the suggested Greek origin seems gratuitous.

[18] D. S. Margoliouth, *Early Development of Muhammedanism* (New York, 1914).

[19] J. Schacht, *op. cit.*

the Qur'ān itself, and no question of analogy in the sense in which Hillel used analogy arise. What the author means is, rather, that wills are contrary to the general theory of the law by which all of a man's earthly rights terminate at his death. This idea that the law is a single logical whole may, as we have shown, be regarded as an inevitable deduction from the Qur'ān, or it may be due to the influence of Greek philosophy. In theory the unity of the law may no doubt be held to be implicit in the Old Testament no less than in Islam. But it does not appear to have been developed in this direction by Rabbinical jurisprudence.

THE SHĪ'Ī SCHOOLS

A somewhat different view of the uṣūl al-fiqh is taken by the Shī'ī schools, for a full discussion of which see Chapter V. It is here sufficient to note that, while the Shī'a vie with the Sunnīs in devotion both to the Qur'ān and (subject to a divergence in criteria of ḥadīth) to the sunna, there is strictly speaking no room for ijmā', qiyās, istiḥsān, or istiṣlāḥ so long as a Shī'ī sect has a living and accessible imām to whom all legal questions can be referred as a final authority and who (in theory at least) possesses considerable power of legislation. Such an imām is the Agha Khan, the head of the Nizāris. But where the imām recognized by the sect has disappeared from worldly ken as in the case of the Ithna 'Asharī sect and of the Bohoras, reference to universal agreement (ijmā') and of intellect ('aql) to tackle new problems becomes inevitable and is openly acknowledged. It appears, however, that the dā'ī of the Daudi Bohoras claims and exercises some part of the pontifical powers of the occult imām whose representative he is. In Iran, legislation by the Parliament is expressed as being provisional pending the "return of the Lord of the Hour."

At this point, and before proceeding to the minor sources of law, it may be well to survey the system which has been built up on the foundations which have been discussed thus far. Dīn[20] (religion) is held to consist of two parts, imān or faith and islam or obedience, each of these being based on a list of pillars or essentials with which we are not here concerned. The word "islam" means literally absolute surrender, i.e., to the will of God; and the will of God is that men should pursue ḥusn (beauty) and avoid qubḥ (ugliness) of life and character. The ultimate guide to the will of God is, of course, revelation, from which alone one can discover what is right or wrong. The law being concerned

20 The original meaning of this word is "judgment."

first and last with the relation between God and the human soul, it follows that the individual is the paramount consideration; the law is strongly individualist and is primarily subjective in form. Men are to consider the value of each action in the sight of God; its earthly consequences are incidental. The Shāfi'ī jurist al-Nawawī, in the Preface of his work, *Minhāj al-Ṭalibīn,* well sums up the spirit of the system when he says that "the best way to manifest obedience to God and to make right use of precious time is assuredly to devote oneself to the study of the law."

THE FIVE VALUES

All human acts are, therefore, classified in five categories according to their value in the sight of God:[21] (1) farḍ or wājib—expressly commanded either in the Qur'ān or in the Traditions, or by ijmā'. (2) sunna, masnūn, mandūb, or mustaḥabb—recommended or desirable. (3) jā'iz or mubāḥ—permitted or indifferent. (4) makrūh—reprobated. (5) ḥarām—absolutely forbidden and abominable.

The first category is normally divided into farḍ 'ala al-'ayn, commands which are absolutely binding on every individual Muslim, and farḍ 'ala al-kifāya, those which are binding on the Islamic community as a whole but are sufficiently discharged so long as some portion of the community is obeying them. The outstanding instance of the latter is the jihād or holy war. This is binding on the Islamic community but not on individual Muslims save in a grave emergency in which the existence of Islam is threatened. Some Muslim moralists, however, distinguish between al-jihād al-kabīr, the greater warfare, i.e., the warfare of the human soul against the forces of evil which is farḍ 'ala al-'ayn (for which purpose the martial texts of the Qur'ān are construed in an allegorical sense[22]) and al-jihād al-ṣaghīr, the lesser warfare, which is farḍ 'ala al-kifāya.

It should be noted that even the absolute commands, farḍ, and prohibitions, ḥarām, of the sacred law do not necessarily imply the sanction of the state. Thus, it is an absolute command based upon well-authenticated tradition[23] that a bridegroom should give a marriage feast according to his means, and that the guests whom

[21] A somewhat similar classification occurs in Rabbinical law, but its rational basis is different.

[22] The allegorical interpretation of similar bellicose texts in the Bible is, of course, familiar to both Jews and Christians.

[23] Bukhārī, 87, 68; cf. Nawawī's *Minhāj al-Ṭalibīn,* p. 314 (Howard's translation).

he invites should not refuse to attend without lawful excuse.[24] But though absolutely binding in conscience these rules do not look to the state for enforcement, nor will their infraction affect the validity of the marriage.

While the absolute commands and prohibitions are not always matters of strict law, it is hardly too much to say that recommendation and disapproval (masnūn and makrūh) are never so. They belong rather to the spheres of morality, good manners, and pious zeal. As an instance of good manners, one may cite the rule that parties to a bargain should not separate without some interchange of courtesies, though by remaining together each of them, according to Shāfiʿī doctrine, exposes himself to the possibility of the other calling off the contract. Additional fasting (in the month of Muḥarram) and additional prayers (besides the daily five) are similarly recommended. And the Prophet (echoing in this the prophet Malachi) is reputed to have said that divorce is "in the sight of God the most detestable of all permitted things"—a tradition which, whether genuine or not, has proved totally powerless to limit capricious divorce.

Of the five values by which human acts are judged, the norm is ibāḥa, or permission. All human acts are permitted, or indifferent, unless and until some authority can be discovered in the sources of the law which either raises them to a higher or degrades them to a lower class. Permissible acts are of two classes, those for which express permission is to be found in an authoritative text (naṣṣ), e.g., permission to a free Muslim to have in his discretion as many as four wives, and those the permissibility of which is inferred from the fact that they are mentioned in legal sources. But whether express or implied, the doctrine of permissibility has been a protection (albeit flimsy at times) for the individual Muslim against irresponsible despotism and has also contributed to the immutability of the law. Who is the merely human ruler that he should dare to take away or to modify a liberty which is granted by God Himself? The individual Muslim need not avail himself of the divine permission; that is a matter which God has left to his discretion. But it would be presumptuous for him to endeavor to contract himself *altogether* out of a liberty which God has allowed. Nevertheless, on occasions in Islamic history, powerful rulers, or in recent years, legislative assemblies with public opinion behind them, have from time to time been able to amend the

24 Cf. Matthew, 22:2-9. In Islam as in Judaism, the bridal feast is given by the bridegroom; in Christianity and Hinduism it is given by the bride's parents.

law; and devices by which a man may restrict his liberty (e.g., of polygamy), even though he cannot completely abrogate it, were early invented by the lawyers.

THE RIGHTS OF GOD; THE RIGHTS OF MAN; AND MIXED RIGHTS

Islam divides the whole of human life and conduct into two categories: 'ibādāt, or ḥuqūq-allah, the service or rights of God, and mu'āmalāt or ḥuqūq al-'ibād, civil affairs, or the rights of God's servants. The former includes purification, prayer, fasting, pilgrimage, holy war, and lastly, the payment of taxes (for the commonwealth is a religious commonwealth with God at its head; and the zakāt, originally almsgiving, became a compulsory levy like a tithe, and eventually both income tax and death duties).[25] This dichotomy, however, is more apparent than real, for throughout the sphere of mu'āmalāt the question of the ethical value of acts is uppermost and colors everything. For example, waqf, whatever its historical origin may have been, is justified as a devotional practice of drawing near to God, Who is interested in the welfare of His creatures. A plea of guilty in a criminal case (distinguished from a confession of judgment in a civil suit) may, as in other systems, be withdrawn because punishment is regarded as belonging to God, and a plea of guilty is the acknowledgement (iqrār) of a debt due to Him. He knows the whole truth and will not be deceived whether the acknowledgement be true or false.

Islamic jurisprudence has been called a science of classification; and, truism though it be that all science involves classification, this observation embodies an important truth. The mujtahids distrusted abstractions; they never, for instance, had any clear theory of the juridical personality of a waqf or of the bayt al-māl (treasury). They never worked out any general theory of contract beyond the principles to which we have already referred; their list of contracts and of acts which resemble contract is restricted and based on sale. But they revelled in classification. We have already mentioned the five pillars of Islam and six pillars of imān, the four bases and the five values.

When, therefore, in the attempt to catalogue on a basis of origins the whole field of law, the Islamic jurists were forced to acknowledge or to invent doctrines which did not square with any of the four great sources, it was natural that they should seek a

[25] The zakāt, however, is a mixed right since the poor of Islam have an interest in it.

label for these left-overs. The first such label to appear is istiḥsān, which means literally "choosing for better." Although the earliest source where this term has been found is a Mālikī one, the idea is more congenial to the Ḥanafīs. The word has been variously translated into English as "preference" or "equity," in each case with or without the word "juristic." Either of these translations has its dangers. Istiḥsān is not equity in any sense in which Roman or English lawyers would recognize the word, for it is not a set of legal principles and certainly could not claim a higher sanctity than the law of God. As for "preference," the advocates of istiḥsān endeavored, not always very successfully, to meet the objection of their critics that they were basing the law on their personal preferences rather than following the law of God. Probably the best English translation is Hamilton's phrase, "favourable construction." For it would appear on an examination of specific cases of istiḥsān that it is applied in two main classes of cases: (1) where the application of a strict qiyās would lead to abolishing an already existing and salutary or at least harmless custom, as when Muḥammad al-Shaybānī pronounced in favor of the validity of waqf or anything which by custom could be the object of a waqf; or when with reference to the rule that only existing things can be sold, he pronounced valid the sale of a crop which gives several pickings in the season though only the first fruit was formed; and (2) when the application of a strict qiyās would lead to an unnecessarily harsh result. Of this, a good example occurs in the law of administration of assets of deceased persons. On strict principle, since legacies and inheritances may be calculated on the estate only after all debts have been paid, it would appear that no legatee or heir can take possession of anything till the debts have been duly discharged. But where the estate is clearly solvent, this would be unnecessarily harsh, so by istiḥsān it is permissible to proceed to distribution in such a case even before all the debts have been paid.

The next such label is istiṣlāḥ or maṣlaḥa. The root ṣ-l-ḥ implying "reconciliation" or "goodwill" embodies in various forms, active and passive, one of the key thoughts of the Qur'ān (see, e.g., Q. IV, 127 and Q. VI, 86). But the desiderative form has acquired a general meaning very similar to the English idea of "public policy" or "the policy of the law." Roman and Rabbinical parallels also have been suggested. Al-Ghazzālī defines maṣlaḥa as "consideration of what is aimed at for mankind in the law, that is, five things, namely, maintenance of religion, of life, of reason, of descendants, and property."[26] Here again the critics, notably al-Shāfi'ī himself (of whom al-Ghazzālī was a professed follower), had a telling criticism to make: if istiṣlāḥ is really based on the divine purpose, then it is simply a form of qiyās and there is no need for a separate category. If it is not, the law of God is being tampered with.[27]

Al-Shāfi'ī himself has a further category of this kind, istiṣḥāb, "the seeking for a link."[28] This is not nearly so elastic as istiḥsān or istiṣlāḥ, being rather a principle of evidence than of general law, namely, that an existing state of affairs shown to have existed may be presumed to have had a lawful origin and to continue in existence until the contrary is shown. The application of such a principle to substantive law is naturally restricted.

At this point a further source of law should be mentioned, namely, ḍurūra or necessity. This would perhaps be classed as a form of istiḥsān but for the fact that it professes to be based on a Qur'ānic text (Q. II, 239), in which the mounted soldier awaiting battle is allowed to say his prayers in the saddle instead of dismounting, as he should ordinarily do, to go through the prescribed ritual. A similar doctrine, of course, existed in Rabbinical law (see 1 Maccabees 2:41 and Matthew 12:3-5) and in each case it is the rights of God which are affected. If there were no other food to be had in a desert place (the next step in the argument ran) a starving Muslim might eat of forbidden things, since to eat of forbidden food, though a sin, is a lesser sin than to be party to the death of a true believer. After this, we are gravely told that the bay' bil-wafā', or mortgage by conditional sale, came into existence to meet the necessity of the heavily indebted people of Bukhara. The bay' bil-wafā' was, of course, an immense advance on rahn or pledge, since it permitted a debtor to remain in possession while giving the creditor adequate security by the transfer of title and also because it provided a means of evading the law against usury. But that it came into existence as a natural development

[26] See R. Paret in *Supplement* to the *Encyclopaedia of Islam,* pp. 103-105, for an excellent account of istiḥsān and istiṣlāḥ.

[27] About a century after al-Ghazzālī, the great poet and wit, Shaykh Sa'dī of Shirāz, coined the Persian proverb: *Durūgh i maṣlaḥat amiz bih az durūstī fitna angiz* (a politic lie is better than a tactless truth). Witticism, of course, must not be taken seriously. But it is worth noting that in the original context (Guhstan I.1.) the maṣlaḥa which the lie promoted fell strictly within al-Ghazzālī's definition, namely, the saving of life and submission by a monarch to the divine injuction to be merciful.

[28] The classical account for Western readers is Goldziher's article in *Wiener Zeitschrift für die Kunde des Morgenlandes,* Vol. I, pp. 128-236.

and not by reason of any juridical doctrine is obvious from the fact that it exists not only in the Ḥanafī system but in other systems of Islamic law, e.g., the Mālikī, under other names and with no suggestion of such an origin. The law did not come into existence by reason of the theory; the theory was applied afterwards to justify it.

It goes without saying that this doctrine of necessity has been but sparingly applied, and to the simple piety of the ordinary Muslim it is repugnant. To take the case of the starving man in the desert, he would say, "If it is the will of God that I die today, I shall die; if God wills, I shall live, and whether I commit the sin of eating forbidden food or not will not affect my earthly fate." Arnold in his *Islamic Faith* gives several recent instances in which this frame of mind might well be called heroic.

A discussion of the Majalla is not within the scope of this chapter, but Articles 2-100[29] of that Code are vital to any consideration of Islamic jurisprudence. They are a series of maxims intended to embody the underlying principles of the law and to illustrate the history of its development. One group of these maxims deals with questions of evidence, burden of proof, and presumptions, and another group with the validity of custom under the law. The remainder are principles of substantive law. All of them are epigrammatic in form and many of them are so brief and cryptic as to be unintelligible without either a commentary or copious examples. They are said to have been culled from the works of Ibn Nujaym, a writer of the tenth century of the hijra (d. A.D. 1563) and his followers, who attempted to extract the general principles underlying the law. But in fact most of them are much older, and several of them can be traced to Talmudic sources; e.g., citation Article 4, "Certainty is not dispelled by doubt" (Tal., "Certainty and doubt, certainty prevails") and Article 7, "Injury cannot exist from time immemorial" (Tal. B.B. 23a, "There is no hazakah to things causing injury"). Others again have parallels and perhaps sources in well-known Latin maxims. Most striking of all is Article 2, a saying attributed to the Prophet on the authority of 'Alī, "Actions are judged by intention (niyya)." To this we shall refer again.

In spite of all their ingenuity and religious zeal to reform the

[29] Originally a further twenty maxims were considered for inclusions by the drafters of the *Majalla,* but these were rejected as being implied in the ninety-nine which have survived. They may, however, be found as a footnote to an early Greek translation of the *Majalla.*

law, however, the mujtahids found themselves forced to admit the validity of a residuum of practices which they obviously disliked and which do not fit into any of their categories. An example of this is the so-called bidā' or bādī' divorce—divorce, that is to say, which is contrary to the sunna. The sunna rules of divorce were devised in order to ensure as far as possible that a husband should not exercise his prerogative of divorce save in a calm manner after due deliberation; and the very word bidā' (meaning heresy or innovation) connotes a measure of censure. Bidā' divorce was not really an innovation but a survival of pre-Islamic license which the Sunnī lawyers, generally speaking, found themselves powerless to prevent. The Ithnā 'Asharī lawyers to their credit ruled that all bidā' divorces were void and of no effect. It might perhaps be argued that shuf'a (often mistranslated "preemption"), the option of the co-owner to buy the share of one of the owners who wants to sell to a third person, is another instance of the same kind. It is not based on anything in the Qur'ān; the traditions quoted in support of it are of the flimsiest character and those few collected by al-Bukhārī obviously refer to something quite different. It is admittedly contrary to analogy, yet its place in the sunna is established. Although the lawyers accepted it as part of the sunna, they nevertheless endeavored to limit it by every means in their power.

The mujtahids are the early expounders and architects of the law; and ijtihād (the word literally means hard striving or strenuousness) is the mental discipline of their profession. The word connotes a power of making law, of deducing new principles and applying them to new facts. In theory, as we have already said, this mental discipline resulted in the discovery of the law of God on the basis of revelation according to the accepted categories of the uṣūl al-fiqh; but in reality, the part of the sharī'a which is deduced solely from revelation is small since many of the legislative commands even of the Qur'ān itself contain an element of custom which the command modifies but does not abolish. Rather, the sharī'a is a collection of laws derived from diverse origins which have been forced into a single religious mold and elaborated to the uttermost by immense labor and dialectical acumen. Throughout runs a striking contrast between archaic material and logical refinement.

But the sharī'a, whatever we may think of its origins, is universally accepted by Islam as the law of God. God, at any rate so far as human experience of Him may presume to go, is unchanging,[30] and to a pious mind this may appear to imply that His law is also unchangeable. Sir Henry Maine in a famous passage of his *Ancient Law* defined equity as a set of principles claiming on account of a higher sanction to supersede the ordinary law; he went on to point out with reference to both the Roman and the English systems that the principles derived from this higher sanction must sooner or later be carried to all their logical conclusions and become as sterile as the original law unless some further and external means of reform can be found. Now in Maine's sense the whole sharī'a is a system of equity, that is to say, it claims a divine sanction. It has not superseded the previous law; it has enfolded it and impressed it with the divine hallmark, and once the system had been logically worked out, no further reform or development was theoretically possible.

This fact has been recognized by Muslim lawyers who speak of the early expounders of the law as having in various degrees the right of ijtihād, that is to say, the right of enlarging and vivifying the law by their interpretation. Then came, according to these lawyers, "the closure of the gate of interpretation"[31] after which no lawyer might presume to express an opinion of his own; he must merely follow blindly the opinions of those who preceded him, having perhaps a limited power of choice where the opinions of the early jurists were contradictory. Ameer Ali, indeed,[32] quotes from Ibrāhīm Ḥalabī, a late medieval Ḥanafī writer, through Mouradjea d'Ohsson,[33] an elaborate classification of the Ḥanafī lawyers into seven grades of whom the first three have the power of ijtihād and the last four are mere copyists. Such elaboration is purely fanciful. Some development of the law is discernible even in comparatively modern times, for example, in the commentaries on the *Hidāya* which sometimes oppose istiḥsān to the dry formalism of that treatise. Moreover, cases without precedent do not cease to occur; and collections of fatwas given on such cases have continued to add to the law even to the present day. Nevertheless,

30 Theologians went so far as to hold that even God's own changelessness is subject to His Almighty will. But into flights of this kind the ordinary Muslim does not enter.

31 The simile is Jewish. Cf. Luke 11:52; cf. also the titles of the three most distinctively legal books of the Mishna and Talmud, the "Three Gates." But in Jewish law the gate, though sometimes closed, was burst open in successive ages.

32 Ameer Ali, *Mohammedan Law* (4th ed., Calcutta, 1912, 1917), 2 vols.

33 *Tableau Général de l'Empire Othoman* (Paris, 1787-1820), 3 vols.

the "closure of the gate" itself is a historical fact; the main outlines of the law were settled in the first three centuries of the hijra, and new principles have not been evolved since then.

Other causes also contributed to the rigidity of the law. We have already spoken of Arab conservatism, and of the value of the concept of divine law as a check on despotism. Although Islam never recognized the right of any human ruler to do anything except administer the law of God, and although its constitutional lawyers evolved a doctrine of the social contract by which the imām was supposed to have contracted with the people of Islam to do just that, yet it never evolved a constitutional theory capable of acting as a check on despotism. Such theory as it had was somewhat similar to the *defidatio* of feudal theory. If the people as represented by their leaders felt that the imām had broken his contract, they could denounce the contract and so depose him. But this was only theory. In practice, a capable and unscrupulous despot could always forestall and prevent any such denunciation. This being so, the rigidity and technicality of the law, the generally upright character of its expounders, and the respect which they consequently enjoyed were at any rate some protection to the common people.

A similar phenomenon occurs in the history of English law. At a time when the judges were wholly dependent on the royal pleasure they were, nevertheless, able to protect, to some extent, the liberty of the subject against the despotism of the Tudors and the still more fantastic despotism claimed by some of the Stuarts by wrapping themselves in the rigidity and technicality of the common law.

Technicality or formalism is the other outstanding characteristic which most people would have recognized in the sharī'a as it stood fifty years ago and to some extent even at the present day; and this in spite of the fact that one of the most famous traditions of Islam is that embodied in Article 2 of the Majalla: "I have heard the Messenger of God say actions are judged by their intentions."[34]

The same problem of formal and technical rules occurs in other systems of law. For instance, although the fully developed Roman law of Justinian lays great and confident emphasis on sub-

[34] This word "niyya" (intention) has a definite religious flavor, the practice of "directing the intention" before an act of prayer being common to Jewish, Christian, and Islamic devotional writers. It differs somewhat, therefore, from intention in English law.

jective mental states, it seems probable that earlier Roman law contented itself with outward objective tests, as indeed for a large part of its history did the English law. But the formalism of law in Islam has been carried to very great lengths, particularly in the Ḥanafī school. Formalism was, as we have said, something of a protection against irresponsible despotism. It sprang, however, from other origins: a rigid and archaic system of procedure which, like the old English system, tended to clarify the issues at the expense of completeness, and a still more archaic system of evidence in which cross-examination was unknown and formally perfect evidence from two witnesses of irreproachable character bound the Court. In the Ḥanafī system at any rate, formalism went beyond this. According to the Ḥanafī jurists, there were three words of such tremendous importance that a man who had uttered them could not plead that he did not intend them or even that he was drunk or acting under duress, namely, the words of marriage, divorce, or emancipation of a slave. Further, the doctrine of acknowledgement was such that when a man had once acknowledged a state of affairs to be true neither his denial nor that of his successors in interest could be admitted, even though that acknowledgement was made for the express purpose of defeating the claims of those successors. (To this, however, there were exceptions.) Thus it came about that a system which was professedly derived from the life and teachings of a great Reformer became in time an obstacle to reform.

What means of escape had the Islamic lawyers from the rigidity of their system? Maine, it will be remembered, spoke of "fictions, equity, legislation" in that order as the agencies by which the gap between stable law and changing society is narrowed. None of these three, in the sense in which Maine uses the words, was available to Islam. In place of equity, apart from the fact just mentioned that the whole of the sharī'a is in Maine's sense a system of equity, we have only the very limited scope of istiḥsān and istiṣlāḥ and a still more severely limited recognition of judicial discretion. For fictions we have rather what continental writers call "devices." For legislation we have what is in theory only administrative regulation.

First, the devices. Maine's definition of a fiction is "any assumption which conceals or affects to conceal the fact that a rule of law has undergone alteration, its letter remaining unchanged, its operation being modified," and his typical fiction is the institution of adoption. But the plentiful "devices" of Islamic law are not of this sweeping character, and their potentiality as instruments of legal reform is more limited, quite apart from the fact that the lawyers, even of a single school, are frequently at variance as to which devices are and are not admissible. Examples of laws of which the religious origin is unquestionable but which were nevertheless felt to be irksome are the sweeping prohibition of usury and the limitation of legacies to one-third of the inheritance; the rule that waqf property is forever inalienable (being *res nullius divini juris),* and the doctrine of shuf'a are two among many of which the religious origin is perhaps less directly obvious but which were equally felt to be irksome, and accordingly created a demand for evasive devices. But, indeed, devices have been recognized, or attempted, in every field of the law, and the more rigid and formal a legal system becomes the easier and more inevitable it becomes to use formality for the purpose of defeating formality.

To survey the whole of this vast field would take us beyond the permissible limits of such a chapter as this. A few instances only may be given. We have already mentioned the bay' bil-wafā'. In its most complete form (sometimes called bay' bil-istighāl) the borrower mortgages his land by conditional sale to the lender, who, having by this sale become the owner of the land leases it for the term of the mortagage at a rent to the mortgagor. Technically, the prohibition against usury is satisfied since what the mortgagee is receiving is not a payment for the use of his money, but rent for the use of his land, but obviously this is merely the same thing under another name. The devices by which attempts have been made, from time to time, to defeat the restrictions on legacies are more complicated, since generally speaking public opinion recognized the justice of those restrictions and was opposed to evasion, but to a limited extent evasion was possible by formal acknowledgement (even deathbed acknowledgement) of debt or deposit. The inalienable character of waqf, coupled with the rule against accumulations, if applied strictly, would have made it impossible for these foundations to raise funds for any sudden emergency, and accordingly the practice of leasing land in perpetuity at a premium which was practically the sale value, together with a peppercorn rent, was widely practiced throughout the late Ottoman Empire under the names of ḥikr, ijāratayn, and inzāl. The tenure so created was freely alienable. Shuf'a was more often defeated by an insistence on the petty technicalities of the law. One device may perhaps be mentioned, though it was only effective against a pre-emptor who claimed by right of neighborhood. This was to sell one's property to a stranger, reserving to oneself the ownership of a narrow margin all round the property. As contiguity was essential to the neighbor's claim, he had no rights, for his land did not border on that sold, nor had he any rights when, at a later date, the marginal strip was given to the purchaser of the central land, since pre-emption does not arise on gift in Ḥanafī law, the only system which recognizes the rights of neighbors.

Equity we have already discussed, and also, briefly, the field of legislation. Strictly speaking, Islamic theory does not recognize the possibility of human legislation; all that the human ruler can do is to make regulations for carrying the Divine Law into effect. The border line between legislation and regulation, however, is, as all lawyers of the present day throughout the world are painfully aware, extremely difficult to draw. There are a few instances of regulation near the border line in the time of the early caliphs, notably one in which the infliction of the divinely established (ḥadd) penalties for theft was temporarily suspended during a famine. The conquest of Constantinople put the Turkish sultans on the throne of the Roman Emperors, with a legislative tradition derived from Rome. Decree legislation in the form of qānūns and nizāmat-namés became increasingly frequent and the pretense that such legislation was merely for the purpose of carrying out the sacred law became increasingly hollow. Sulaymān the Magnificent (al-Qānūnī) codified a considerable portion of the law of his Empire and in particular made far-reaching reforms in the criminal law. The law of ijāratayn was embodied in a qānūn of A.D. 1607 and the legislation of the nineteenth and twentieth centuries almost completely threw overboard this pretense of subordination under the divine law. It was possible, too, to ordain that certain classes of claims should not be heard at all or should not be heard after the expiration of a period of time, and so to introduce, though imperfectly, a statute of limitations.

But, in fact, the sacred law of Islam has probably never, save for brief periods of extreme religious zeal, been enforced as a whole, though it has never been without powerful influence on the framework of Islamic society. Rules which are felt to be unduly irksome merely fall into desuetude in favor either of more enlightened or, it may be, of less enlightened practices. This brings us to a further potential source of reform, namely, custom. Both Ḥanafī and Mālikī law recognize within limits the validity of custom; Shāfi'ī law refuses to recognize it. In fact, however, it is mainly among Shāfi'ī communities that the gap is widest between the sharī'a and the law actually lived by the people. The 'ādat law (customary law) of Indonesia, the matrilineal system of the Moplahs, and the *kilemba* of the Swahili are instances. The Mālikī jurist, al-Wansharisī (d. A.D. 1508) says that ancient custom should, if possible, be brought within the realm of the Sacred Law, but that it is law whether it can be so brought or not. In Ḥanafī law the rule prevails that custom (resembling in this respect istiḥsān which, as above noted, is sometimes linked with it) can overrule a qiyās, but cannot abrogate a naṣṣ. There was also a maxim in this school that "custom is an arbitrator," i.e., that, just as an arbitrator, though he must follow the law, has a discretion in its detailed application and need not be too strictly bound by technicality, so also a similar latitude could be allowed to custom.

Finally, although the sharī'a professes to be a single logical whole, yet in practice there is still an immense diversity of opinion, not only between the different schools of law, but even between different teachers in the same school. The catholic spirit of Sunnī Islam refuses to call any long-standing opinion unorthodox, and allows to the individual Muslim a startling liberty of choice between conflicting doctrines. Accordingly, modern reformers have had recourse to the expedient of building up from the various conflicting opinions a composite law such as they deem more suitable to the modern world. It is recognized in Ḥanafī law that "the provisions of the law vary with the change of the times" and al-Zurqānī, a Mālikī writer, says that "new decisions can be given with regard to new conditions."

The relation of Islamic law and jurisprudence to the other legal and customary systems among which they grew up is still obscure. Parallels more or less close can be drawn not only from Roman and Talmudic law, but also from systems where there is no possibility of borrowing, as for instance English law (see above, *passim*) and medieval Teutonic law. At times during the Middle Ages the Islamic system appears to have marched on parallel lines with the canon law of the Christian Church, notably in such matters as usury, *lucrum cessans* (loss of profit), and *damnum emergens* (capital loss). Most of these parallels are due to what Santillana calls "L'identité essentielle de l'âme humaine." But whatever indebtedness there may be, the Islamic system remains unique and quite unlike any other. Its nearest approach to Roman law is, as might be expected, in the sphere of market law; it also shares with Roman law a doctrine of the indivisible nature of ownership and of a separation between *dominium* and *usufruct*. But English lawyers are apt to overlook the unique character of their own doctrine of estates; the doctrine of *dominium* and *usufruct* is surely simpler and more natural. Both, as regards contracts and land, however, the differences between the Roman and the Islamic systems are as pronounced as the similarities. In the law of marriage and divorce one cannot escape a feeling that the naturally reforming instincts of the Prophet himself have been balked of their fulfillment; at any rate, the result is unique, though the applications of these laws vary enormously in different Islamic communities. Perhaps the most characteristic branch of the law is that dealing with succession, in which the principle of arithmetical subdivision, aimed at satisfying the claims of competing relatives, is carried out with great precision, mathematical ingenuity, and detail. The system is quite unlike any other in the civilized world, but the peak of peculiarity is reached in the position assigned to grandparents. The grandfather and grandmother are nowhere mentioned in the texts on inheritance in the Qur'ān, and there is much conflict about them between the different Islamic schools. Yet all agree to the extent of allowing grandparents to compete with (or in the case of the paternal grandfather in Ḥanafī and Ḥanbalī law, totally to exclude) the brothers and sisters and their descendants. This contradicts the rule now widely accepted in fully developed legal systems, even some of those derived from Roman law, by which inheritance cannot ascend where it can descend; and though it is true that Justinian's Novella 118 does allow the grandparents to compete with and in some cases to exclude the collaterals, yet the principles on which it does so are different from those of the Islamic systems. The position assigned to the grandparents is one of those points which are beginning to be found unsuitable to the present day.

Nor would it be right to conclude such a survey as this without brief mention of the immense topic of waqf.[35] For this, partial parallels or prototypes may perhaps be found both in Roman and Rabbinical law, the Rabbinical analogies being still obscure but suggestive. It remains true that waqf is peculiar to Islamic law, and unlike anything in any other system. It fulfils the part played in other systems by the law of religious and charitable foundations, trade guilds, and corporations, and the contrivances, such as the English strict settlement, which have been elaborated by lawyers to maintain the stability of great families. Indeed, the rules of waqf are almost the exact opposite of those prevalent in other

[35] For a fuller discussion, see below, Chap. VIII.

fields of Islamic law, so that it has the appearance of a jurisprudence within a jurisprudence, a doctrine within a doctrine. It has enabled wealthy persons whose estates might otherwise have attracted the cupidity of the ruling power to provide for their dependents and descendants by placing their lands under the protection of religion, and even sultans have not disdained to use it for this purpose. But where practiced on a large scale, as in many parts of the Ottoman Empire, it has often produced the same economic stagnation which we associate with "the dead hand" in other systems. It is nonetheless characteristically Islamic both in its main principles and in its details and could not have occurred in any other system.

Enough has been said to show that whatever the materials may have been which the architects of the Islamic legal system used, the edifices which they erected (both the sharī'a and the fiqh, the law and the philosophy of the law) were entirely their own, products as Renan rightly says of the *propre genie* of the Arabs and indelibly stamped with the religion of Islam.

CHAPTER V

Shī'ī Legal Theories

WITHIN THE last two decades a great deal of research has been done on the Shī'a, but the earliest phase of their religion and law remains largely unexplored. Although Strothman wrote his article on the "Shī'a" in the *Encyclopaedia of Islam* twenty-five years ago, his statement, "There is no thorough account of the Shī'a," is still substantially correct. I hope that with the recent publication of Zāhid 'Alī's *History of the Fatimids of Egypt*[1] and Volume I of the *Da'ā'imu'l-Islam*,[2] scholars will once again turn their attention to the earliest phases of Shī'ism.

Shī'ism is no longer regarded as a "heresy," but as the logical development of certain definite tendencies and philosophical views held by one group of the Muslims after the death of the Prophet Muḥammad. When the caliphate came into the hands of the Umayyads after the death of the first four caliphs and religion itself was made the plaything of political ambitions, the murder of Ḥusayn, the Prophet's grandson, set the seal on official Shī'ism. This faith preserved the passionate remembrance of this tragedy at Karbalā,' created an "imām" who would be the focal point for the love normally showered on the Founder of Islam, and systematically formulated a theology (kalām) and a law (fiqh) in opposition to the Sunnī creed.

The real aims of Shī'ism can be briefly stated as (1) *political,* to entrust the caliphate to an 'Alīd; (2) *psychological,* to create a human focus for the concentration of that love and devotion (called walāya) which should normally be directed to the person of the Prophet himself; (3) *religious,* to create a central authority for the church of Islam, whose decrees would be infallible. In considering the historical development of theology in Islam and the early creation and development of the idea of the imāmate, it is well to remember that law, religion, and politics were closely interrelated in the Shī'ī doctrine, as they were in the Sunnī.

1 Zāhid 'Alī, *Tarīkh-i Fatimiyyin-i Miṣr* (Urdu). Osmania University Series No. 371 (Hyderabad-Deccan, 1948/1357).

2 The *Dā'ā'imu'l-Islam* of the Qāḍī an-Nu'mān b. Muḥammad, ed. by A. A. A. Fyzee (Cairo, 1951/1371), Vol. I.

IMĀMATE

Before we discuss the institution of the imāmate (the Shī'ī term for the caliphate) a word on the Shī'ī schools is in order. The term Shī'a means "party" and it refers specifically to the party of 'Alī, son-in-law of the Prophet, considering him the only rightful successor of the Prophet in temporal and religious matters, and denying this right to all who did not belong to the house of 'Alī. The Shī'a deny the principle of election by the people in the matter of the imāmate, and hold that the Prophet appointed 'Alī as his vicegerent in A.H. 10 (A.D. 632) at Ghadīr al-Khum on the outskirts of Medina. They assert that when the Prophet uttered the words: fa man kuntu mawlāhu, fa 'aliyyun mawlāhu, "Hence, he who recognizes me as his Master, for him 'Alī (too) is Master,"[3] the appointment (naṣṣ) of 'Alī as his vicegerent was completed and never revoked. In fact, later incidents mentioned by Shī'ī writers such as Kulaynī, Ṣadūq, and Nu'mān show that the Prophet confirmed and acted on the assumption that 'Alī was the heir apparent of the spiritual kingdom.

The Shī'a are divided into several schools of thought, the two most important are the Ithnā 'Asharī ("Twelvers") and the Ismā'-īlī, or "Seveners." The Zaydīs, who are concentrated in the Yaman, combine Shī'ī and Sunnī doctrines. The principal cause for the division of the Shī'a was the succession after the fourth imām, Zayn al-'Ābidīn. One of his sons, Zayd (died A. H. 122) was accepted as imām by a certain group who were called the Zaydīs. They recognize the principle of election as the basis of succession. The majority of the Shī'a followed Muḥammad al-Bāqir and after him Ja'far al-Ṣādiq. After the death of Ja'far, another split took place, the majority followed Mūsa al-Kāzim and six imāms after him, thus making twelve imāms in all (hence, their name, "Twelvers"). The last of these imāms is believed to have disappeared and to be returning as the Mahdī (Messiah). The minority of the Shī'a, after the death of Ja'far, did not acknowledge Mūsa al-Kāzim, but followed his elder brother, Ismā'īl, and are now known as Ismā'īlī or "Seveners." They are mostly to be found in India, but small groups of them live in Central Asia, Iran, Syria, and the Persian Gulf shaykhdoms.[4] The majority of the Shī'a belong to the Ithnā

[3] For a Fatimid version of the *ḥadīth,* see *Ibid.,* Vol. I, pp. 20-21.

[4] The Ismā'īlīs may be divided into two groups: the *Khojas* or Eastern Ismā'īlīs, who are the followers of Agha Khan, and the Western Ismā'īlīs, or the *Bohoras.* The latter are mostly to be found in the Persian Gulf, Southern Arabia, and Syria; the former in Central Asia, Iran, and the Frontier Provinces of India.

'Asharī school and are to be found in Iran and Iraq and in smaller groups in India.

How do we define the imām? What are his distinguishing characteristics? First, the imām is the ḥujja, the proof of God;[5] second, he is al-qā'im bi-amri'l-lah, the upholder of the Command of God;[6] third, he is the sāḥibu'l-zamān (or qā'imu'l-zamān), the Lord of the age.[7] As the deputy of God he is deathless, has miraculously remained alive since his ghayba (absence), and will return like a true Messiah to fill the earth with justice and equity. The Ithnā 'Asharīs (Twelvers) believe in ghayba, that is, the disappearance of the imām from the world;[8] not so the Ismā'īlīs. They believe that there can be no ghayba in this world. The imām cannot completely disappear, even if to the profane eyes of the people he is invisible, mastūr (veiled), hidden from the sight of those whose vision does not possess the penetration of the true adept.[9] If the imām were to disappear from the world, even for a moment, "verily, the earth would perish with all its inhabitants."[10]

The imām is the central figure in the Shī'ī world; on him are focussed the hopes of the world, the love and devotion due to the Prophet, the passion and tragedy of Karbalā'.[11] He is the "leader" (imām), not the khalīfa (successor of the Prophet). He is the Perfect Man (al-insānu'l-kāmil) and acts as a link between Man and God. He is the mysterious, logical and spiritual principle which binds the whole universe together and, therefore, the final authority in both law and religion.

What is his status relative to the Prophet? In classifying the position of the imām, Strothmann distinguishes three concepts: (1) the Zaydī; (2) the Ithnā 'Asharī; and (3) the Druze. The Zaydīs, nearest akin to the Sunnī, limit the manifestation of God in the

5 *A Shiite Creed,* translation of *Risālatu'l-I'tiqādāt* of Shaykh Ṣadūq Ibn Bābawayhī by A. A. A. Fyzee. Islamic Research Association Series No. 9 (Oxford 1942), SC 95; W. Ivanow, *Creed of the Fatimids* (Bombay, 1936), Article 38.

6 *A Shiite Creed, loc. cit.; Encyclopaedia of Islam* (Leiden-London, 1913-1934), Vol. IV, p. 351.

7 *A Shiite Creed, loc. cit.; Encyclopaedia of Islam,* II, 642.

8 D. M. Donaldson, *The Shiite Religion* (London, 1933), pp. 226 ff., especially 235; *Encyclopaedia of Islam,* Vol. II, p. 135.

9 Zāhid 'Ali, *op. cit.,* 469 ff.; Ivanow, *op. cit.,* Article 37.

10 *Agar khali shawad jahan az imam-i zaman yak lahza wa yak lam'a (lamha?) wa yak sa'at wa yak chashm zadan, jahan wa ahl-i jahan nist wa halak shawand. Kalami Pir.* Persian text, edited and translated by W. Ivanow. Islamic Research Association Series, No. 4 (Bombay, 1935), text 26, lines 3-4.

11 A. A. A. Fyzee, *Outlines of Muhammadan Law* (2nd, edition, Oxford, 1954), p. 31; Donaldson, *op. cit., index.*

imām to "right guidance" (huda) only, and deny that the substance of God entered into the human body of 'Alī. Among the Ithnā 'Asharīs, on the other hand, the deathlessness, evanescence, and final appearance of the living imām imply a being which, although not God and by no means the equal of the Prophet, yet possesses certain miraculous or supernatural attributes. The ghulāt (extremists) seem to equate the imām with God Himself. An example of this belief in the divinity of the imām is found in the Druze faith, which proclaims al-Ḥākim as God incarnate.[12]

A simpler classification would consider the person of the imām from the strictly Muslim point of view. Although this constitutes over-simplification, one may ask whether the Shī'a consider the imām to be (a) *lower* in status than the Prophet; (b) *equal* to the Prophet; or (c) *higher* than the Prophet. The weakness of such a classification is that, even within a particular group of Shī'a, different authorities hold slightly divergent views. For example, a few of the Ithnā 'Asharī authorities assert the equality of the imām with the Prophet. Moreover, actual belief does not always correspond to dogma; a substantial number of the Ismā'īlī Khojas (Eastern Ismā'īlīs) hesitate to subscribe to the dogma that the spiritual head of the community, the Agha Khan, is the veritable incarnation of the Hindu god, Vishnu.[13] In spite of these limitations, a general analysis on this basis may prove useful.

The vast majority of the Shī'a hold the imām inferior to the Prophet. It is impossible to give accurate figures, but out of the three hundred and sixty-five million adherents to Islam in the world,[14] perhaps fifteen to twenty million are Shī'a. Of these, the majority, twelve to thirteen million, are Ithnā 'Asharī; and these, the "Shī'a" of common parlance, state in unmistakable terms that the twelve imāms are the proofs of Allah "after the Prophet."[15] 'Alī, having been appointed by the Prophet to be his vicegerent (waṣī, imām), cannot claim equality with the Messenger of God. *A fortiori,* the question of comparison with God, does not arise; for it is God who has given the imām certain supernatural powers, such as ghayba and 'iṣma (infallibility), and it is by His will that

[12] Zāhid 'Alī, *op. cit.,* pp. 218 ff.; *Encyclopaedia of Islam,* Vol. IV, p. 352.

[13] Fyzee, *Outlines of Muhammadan Law,* p. 4 (a).

[14] Hazard, *Atlas of Islamic History* (Princeton, 1951), p. 5.

[15] Fyzee, *A Shiite Creed,* p. 95; *al-Bābu'l-Ḥādi 'Ashar* by Ḥasan b. Yūsuf al-Ḥillī, with commentary by Miqdād-i Faḍil, trans. by W. M. Miller (London, 1928) p. 69, Articles 191 and 193. 'Alī ranks *after* the Prophet by reason of naṣṣ, the appointing authority being the Founder of Islam.

the imām will return to the earth as the Messiah and fill it with justice and equity.[16]

The Zaydīs, often designated as the most practical and the most catholic of the Shī'a, do not claim for their imām anything more than "right guidance." An imām before recognition must be elected by the people, and the qualifications for eligibility are clearly laid down. Exhibiting a practical amalgamation of Sunnī and Shī'ī principles, they affirm (1) that the imām must be a descendant of the Prophet (ahl al-bayt) through Ḥasan or Ḥusayn; (2) that he must be able to defend his community and must therefore be sovereign; and (3) that he must possess the necessary character, piety, and learning.[17]

The Western Ismā'īlī (Musta'lian or Fāṭimid) concept of the imām is that he ranks definitely below the Prophet. Although he is a direct descendent of 'Alī, he is a human being who eats, drinks, and leads a normal life. He is mastūr (hidden from the sight of ordinary men) but not ghā'ib (absent).[18]

Next comes the question of equality. Few have claimed that 'Alī or his progeny were equal to the Prophet. Al-Ḥillī, the author of *al-Bābu'l-Ḥādi'Ashar,* claims that the imām is equal to the Prophet.[19] On a closer examination of the Arabic text, it may appear to be a rhetorical turn of phrase not intended to be understood literally.[20] Among the Shī'ī the imām is usually placed higher or lower than the Prophet, but seldom as his equal.

We now come to those interesting groups who place the imām above the Prophet. The Nizārī Ismā'īlīs consider the imāmate higher than the nubuwwa (Prophethood). Because the imāmate is a permanent, deathless institution, the world would perish if the imām were to withdraw even for a moment. The nubuwwa is not a permanent instrument of religion; God sends his messenger only as a mouthpiece of the imām.[21] The Khojas (Indian followers

16 The later form of the doctrine of *imāmate,* with colorful additions by Muḥammad Bāqir-i Majlisī and others of equal faith and imagination, will be found in E. G. Browne, *A Literary History of Persia,* Vol. IV, p. 353, esp. 381 ff., and Donaldson, *op. cit.,* p. 305.

17 Strothmann, "al-Zaidīya," *Encyclopaedia of Islam,* Vol. IV, pp. 1197, 352.

18 A. A. A. Fyzee, *Outlines of Muhammadan Law,* pp. 32 and 4 (B); Zāhid 'Alī, *op. cit.,* 538 ff., esp. 549; Ivanow, *Creed of the Fatimids, op. cit.,* Arts. 31-37. The essential doctrine is in the *Da'ā'imu'l-Islam,* I, Chap. I, read with II, Book of Wills.

19 Ḥillī, *op. cit.,* p. 71.

20 [Ḥillī] *Al-Nāfi'yawmi'l-Ḥashr fī sharḥ Bābu'l-Ḥādī 'Ashar.* (Bombay: Naṣirī Press, A. H. 1319), p. 51.

21 *Kalami Pir, op. cit.,* xli, xxxviii; the references are so numerous that it is needless to multiply them. A good general introduction to Ismā'īlīsm is W. Ivanow,

of the Agha Khan), who call their imām "Mawlāna Hazar Imām,"[22] went a step further and, under the instruction of Pir Ṣadru'd dīn, declared the imām to be an incarnation of the God Vishnu. This is embodied in the authoritative doctrinal text, the *Das-Avatar* (Ten Incarnations):

"God has incarnated Himself as the glorious Tenth Avatar.
He manifested Himself in the person of Shah Mawla Murtada 'Alī.
We welcome Thy incarnation for the sake of love for the Truth!
The Lord will ride his horse, bestowing love and benevolence (and scattering devils).
O, Thou, save Thy devotees!
O, Thou, scatter the devils!
O, Thou, punish the demons!
O, Thou, save the jamats [colloquial for *jama'at*] of the believers!
O, Thou, grant what they wish!
O, Thou, fulfill Thy promises!"

. . . .

"O, my Lord, Thou art my God in the Tenth Incarnation,
Thou hast incarnated as the glorious Tenth Avatar in the person of Naklanki, whose glorious name is Shah Mawla Murtada 'Ali!"

And finally the Khoja Shahāda:

"I testify there is no deity except One God,
I testify that Muḥammad is the apostle of God,
I testify that Amīru'l-Mu'minīn 'Alī is surely Divine."[23]

The Agha Khan case, Advocate-General vs. Muḥammad Ḥusen Ḥuseni (otherwise called Agha Khan), 1866 Bombay High Court Reports 323, establishes that this is the official doctrine of the Ismā'īlī Khojas, but certainly most of the Ismā'īlī Khojas would not subscribe to this creed in its literal sense, and are aligning

---

Brief Survey of the Evolution of Ismailism, Ismaili Society Series B-7 (Bombay, 1952). On the imamate, see 54 ff.

22 This is the Indian Khoja pronunciation of the Arabic *ḥāḍir,* "present," to distinguish it from *ghā'ib,* "absent or evanescent." The Begum Agha Khan is designated as *mata salāmat,* an interesting Indo-Persian compound. *Mata* is Hindi for "mother" and *salāmat* is a contraction of *salāmat bashid,* which means "may you remain safe" in Persian. The news of the Ismā'īlī mission will be found in their official weekly published in Bombay, *The Ismā'īlī,* in Gujarati and English. Publishers: The Ismailia Association, Dongri Street, Bhimpura, Bombay 9, India. The present publisher is V. N. Hooda and the Honorary Editor is P. L. Mody.

23 *Collectanea,* I. Being a collection of studies on Ismā'īlī subjects by W. Ivanow, M. Kamil Ḥusain, and others Ismā'īlī Society Series No. 2. (Leiden, 1948). The passages cited will be found on pp. 112-15.

themselves increasingly with the orthodox Muslim faith.[24] They assert that these are mystical statements, proclaiming the greatness of Mawla ʿAlī, and we must not probe further into such sacred mysteries. The fact is that the majority know little of their own faith and are rapidly coming within the periphery of orthodox Islam.

Among the so-called ghulāt, the Druzes equate the Fāṭimid Caliph al-Ḥākim with the Divine Being, and although their doctrine is kept a guarded secret, we can certainly say that they have accepted the Christian ideas of incarnation and divinity, including the Immaculate Conception.[25] The ʿAlī-Ilāhis deify ʿAlī and believe in the theory of incarnations.[26] The Nuṣayrīs are more influenced by the Christian doctrine of the Trinity and believe that ʿAlī, Muḥammad, and Salmān al-Fārisī constitute together the Divine Being.[27] Deriving their belief from the doctrine of walāya (which we shall discuss later), the Mutawalīs, Lovers of ʿAlī, also deify ʿAlī b. Abī Ṭālib. The generic term " ʿAlawīs" is in common use, but it is not clear whether it embraces both Nuṣayrīs and Mutawalīs, or only the former, as suggested by H. C. Holme.[28] Probably it is a term loosely embracing all those who in their excessive love (walāya) of ʿAlī tend to equate him with God. Before we leave the subject, another tiny sect, the Tā'usis, may also be mentioned. It is not certain whether it is an off-shoot of the Nuṣayrīs or is more closely related to the Babi faith, with heterodox Shīʿī syncretism. At any rate their imām, if not God Himself, is a combination of the Ithnā ʿAsharī imām, the Messiah, the Nabī, and the Quṭb.[29]

After this brief survey, it is possible to say that the large majority of the Shīʿa believe that Muḥammad, the Prophet of God, was higher in rank than his vicegerent, ʿAlī b. Abī Ṭālib; that the ghulāt (extremists) believe ʿAlī to be an incarnation of the Divine Being and thus place him above the Prophet; and that a small minority believe him to be the equal of the Prophet. G. M. Wickens suggests that the nearest equivalent of the Shīʿī imām is

24 Fyzee, *Outlines of Muhammadan Law*, p. 4(A). A good general introduction is by W. Ivanow, "Isma'iliya," *Encyclopaedia of Islam, Supplement*, 98-102.

25 Ivanow, *Brief Survey . . . Ismailism*, pp. 22, 60; the account in *Encyclopaedia of Islam* (I, 1075) is somewhat outdated.

26 The latest account is by W. Ivanow in *Truth-Worshippers of Kurdistan*, Ismaili Society Series No. A-7 (Leiden, 1953). Also *Encyclopaedia of Islam*, Supplement s.v. "Ahl-i-Haqq", and Vol. I, p. 292, s. v. " ' Ali Ilahi."

27 *Encyclopaedia of Islam*, Vol. II, 473-74; and Vol. IV, p. 117, s. v. "Salmān."

28 *The Middle East, a Political and Economic Survey* (London, 1950), p. 53.

29 J. Nikitine in *Encyclopaedia of Islam, Supplement*, p. 246.

not the Catholic Pope but the Nestorian Christ.[30] This is plausible generalization, but on careful examination it is unsatisfactory. Our present knowledge of Shī'ī sects in general and of the doctrine of imāmate in particular does not warrant the identification of the Shī'ī imām with the God-Man of the Nestorians, for only a fractional minority of the Shī'a, the Druzes, Ahl-i-ḥaqq, and the Nuṣayrīs identify the imām with the Divine Being.[31]

The legal significance of the imāmate can only be understood in terms of the dogmas of walāya and 'iṣma. Because the imām is the leader of the community and the Lawgiver by Command of God, it is necessary for man to be truly devoted to him. This love and devotion is known as walāya.[32] To create a human focus for that love and affection which was directed towards the person of the Prophet, the Shī'a conceived this interesting theological dogma. The Fāṭimid doctrine is that Islam is based upon seven pillars—walāya, ṭahāra, ṣalāt, zakāt, ṣawm, ḥajj, jihād—and of these walāya is the most excellent. Through it and a knowledge of the walī (imām) a man attains his destination of spiritual consummation.[33] The Ithnā 'Asharī ḥadīth, on the authority of Shaykh Ṣaduq Ibn Babawayhi, is: "The friendship of 'Alī is my stronghold (ḥiṣn), and whoever enters my stronghold is safe from my punishment."[34] This ḥadīth implies the following legal and moral principles: (1) love of and devotion to the People of the Family (ahlu'l-bayt), the imāms, (2) obedience to their commands, (3) imitation of their actions and conduct, and (4) recognition of their rights and belief in the institution of the imāmate.[35] Further, "he who dies without recognizing the imām of the time, dies the death of a kafir."[36] Consequently, absolute obedience is required of the common man (mukallaf).

[30] In his recent article on Persian Religion in the *Legacy of Persia* (Oxford, 1953), p. 153.

[31] Dr. Zāhid 'Alī is of the opinion that the total number of Ismā'īlīs, including the Druzes, the Khojas and the Bohoras, cannot exceed 500,000. The present writer entirely agrees with him and does not subscribe to the inflated figures commonly given by pious sectarians. To these, a few more thousands have to be added, who hold the beliefs of the Ahl-i-Ḥaqq, Nuṣayrīs and Mutawalīs. In the aggregate, a figure of one million would be a fairly liberal estimate (Zāhid 'Alī, *op. cit.* p. 579).

[32] Not *wilāya,* a common mistake. See Fyzee, *A Shiite Creed,* p. 96, footnote 6; and the *Da'ā'imu'l-Islam,* Vol. I, Chap. I.

[33] *Ibid.,* Vol. I, p. 3; Ivanow, *Creed of the Faṭimids,* p. 9; and A. A. A. Fyzee, *Ismaili Law of Wills* (Oxford, 1933), p. 9.

[34] Donaldson, *op. cit.,* p. 347.

[35] Fyzee, *A Shiite Creed,* p. 97.

[36] *Da'ā'imu'l-Islam,* Vol. I, pp. 31 and 34; *Kalami Pir,* pp. 27, 48, 61, 69; Donaldson, *op. cit.,* p. 351.

As man has to obey the imām, he must of necessity be sinless, infallible, and incapable of error. The Roman Catholic church asserts that the Pope in his official acts (as distinguished from his private life) is infallible. The Shī'ī Creed asserts, however, the principle of infallibility ('iṣma) extends not only to public acts, but also to the most trivial and private ones.[37] Although the Fāṭimids accept the principle of infallibility, there is not so much insistence on it in their books, and a lesser amount of space is devoted to it. This is so presumably because the Nizārī imām partakes of the nature of God; while, in the Musta'lian creed, sinlessness is implicit in their philosophical concept of the imām.

CALIPH, IMĀM

If one is to understand Shī'ī legal theories, a clear distinction must be made between him who imposes the law (mukallif) and him who is required to obey it (mukallaf). The doctrine of taklīf has been dealt with by Shaykh Ṣaduq in his *I'tiqādāt.*[38] Taklīf is the obligation to obey the law. As the fountain head of law, God is the mukallif and imposes his law upon man, the mukallaf. But God enforces his law through the imām, who in turn is served by the mujtahids for the interpretation of the law and by the heads of Shī'ī temporal states, who ordinarily have the sanctions for enforcement. Thus, the man in the street is the mukallaf or 'abd.

An essential part of the doctrine of taklīf is the justice of God. The Shī'a call themselves the ahlu'-l'adl wa'l-tawhid[39] to distinguish themselves from the Sunnīs, the ahlu'l-sunna wa'l-jamā'a. This 'adl consists of His kindness (luṭf) in not imposing upon human beings a burden greater than their strength, for, "Allah burdens not a soul beyond its capacity" (Q. II, 286).

We must now deal with the fundamental difference between the Sunnī caliph and the Shī'ī imām. First, the caliph (khalīfa) is a servant of the law; the imām is its interpreter and master. Secondly, the caliph is elected by the people; the imām is appointed by the previous imām. The appointment of the caliph depends upon the wish of the people; it is, or at least in theory it can be, a

[37] Fyzee, *A Shiite Creed,* p. 100; Goldziher on 'iṣma in *Encyclopaedia of Islam,* 543, is somewhat meager; Donaldson, *op. cit.,* Chaps. 29, 30, 31; Fyzee, *A Shiite Creed,* p. 99; Ḥillī, *op. cit.,* p. 64, Art. 179 and index "ma'ṣum." The Faṭimids do not stress 'iṣma to a great extent, Ivanow, *Creed of the Faṭimids,* pp. 46, 47; but it is a dogma of their faith, Zāhid 'Ali, *op. cit.,* p. 554.

[38] Fyzee, *A Shiite Creed,* p. 31; Ḥilli, *op. cit.,* Arts. 131 ff.

[39] Shaykh Ṣaduq, *Kitābu'l-Tawḥīd* (Tehran, 1285/1869), p. 61; Ḥilli, *op. cit.,* 40 ff.

democratic choice. The appointment of an imām is an "Act of God," an ordinance promulgated by the previous imām, called naṣṣ. Thirdly, the caliph is removable for sinful acts; the imām appointed by God cannot be deposed by man. Fourthly, the caliph is removable for committing sinful acts; the imām is sinless and infallible. And finally—legally the most important constitutional issue—there may or may not be a caliph in the world; religion does not die; the world does not collapse if there is no one who possesses the attributes of a Sunnī caliph. But the Shī'ī imām is always present, necessarily functioning, whether ghā'ib (Ithnā 'Asharī), mastūr (Fāṭimid); ḥādir (Nizārī), or in the shape of a divine incarnation (Druzes, Nuṣayrīs, 'Alī-Ilāhis).

A Sunnī Muslim obeys the law even if there is no head of Islam; but the Shī'ī Muslim has the spiritual satisfaction of having his imām always with him. The idea of the imām gives psychological solace to a follower, and creates a central and infallible authority to provide moral and legal sanctions.[40]

QIYĀS

Qiyās, the fourth source of Sunnī law, is rejected or ignored by the Shī'ī groups with the exception of the Zaydīs who accept it. The Fāṭimids and the Ithnā 'Asharīs emphatically reject qiyās, the Nizārī Ismā'īlīs ignore it because they have no definite system of jurisprudence, and the Ibādīs have recourse to ra'y rather than to qiyās.

Although it is known that qiyās is not acceptable to the majority of the Shī'a, the reasons for their denunciation of this doctrine, the theory which they developed at the earliest times and the ultimate solution they offer are imperfectly known. The Qur'ān and sunna do not, and cannot, solve all the difficulties that have arisen in succeeding centuries. It was therefore possible to bridge the gulf by convenient ḥadīth made up for the occasion; this, however, would also fail because the individual mulla or mujtahid may not have the learning, ingenuity, or originality to rise to every occasion. It is my conjecture that the word ijtihād (hence, mujtahid)

[40] On *khalīfa* the main authority is V. Bartold's essay, summarized by C. H. Becker in *Der Islam,* VI, p. 35. See also *Encyclopaedia of Islam,* Vol. II, p. 881, which gives a bibliography, and T. Arnold, *The Caliphate* (Oxford, 1924). The relation between caliph and imām has not been exhaustively treated, but the following may be consulted: On the Ithnā 'Asharī concept, Donaldson, *op. cit.,* pp. 305-56; on the Fāṭimid doctrine, Zāhid 'Alī, *op. cit.,* 538 ff.; for general considerations and the Nizārī view, Ivanow, *Brief Survey of . . . Ismailism,* 54-63. The value of an imām in concealment is discussed by Imām 'Alī Zaynu'l-'Abidīn even *before* the event (Donaldson, *op. cit.,* p. 310). See Chap. I, above.

has a somewhat different connotation among the Ithnā 'Asharīs than among the Sunnīs, and it would be interesting to pursue this line of investigation to its logical conclusion. It may therefore be safe to assume that they rejected qiyās in opposition to the Sunnī because it would impair the foundation of the imāmate. Man cannot interfere with this divine institution; the principle of election cannot be accepted, naṣṣ or the designation of 'Alī by the Prophet, the "divine right" of the ahl al-bayt, the mysterious connection between the nūr (light) of imāmate and legitimate descent from 'Alī—all these would be meaningless if by the process of qiyās human beings could interfere with the law as laid down by divine ordinances contained in *direct* revelation (Qur'ān) or *indirect* revelation (the rules laid down by the Prophet or the imām.)[41]

Apart from psychological and doctrinal factors, a study of the ikhtilāf uṣul al-madhāhib indicates clearly the possibility that during the Fāṭimid period, that is, the earliest epoch when a regular Shī'ī dynasty had the problem of ruling a large country, the creation of one central authority for the interpretation and enforcement of the law was clearly contemplated. Dr. Zāhid 'Alī has shown, with sufficiently cogent evidence, that the Ismā'īlīs in the early days named their ḥudūd (religious hierarchy) on the analogy of Christian priesthood.[42] It is, therefore, not impossible that the early Shī'a wished to create a Church of Islam somewhat on the lines of the Papacy. This now is still in the realm of hypothesis—a hypothesis which I hope will be further investigated by those who have access both to the literature of the early Fāṭimids and to the literature of the Catholic Church.

The term qiyās in law means "deduction by analogy,"[43] but in logic and philosophy it also means "syllogism, deduction." Qiyās, as a method of reasoning by which the human mind proceeds from the known to the unknown, is said to occupy a central position in

[41] On the Shī'a and its problems, see a little known but valuable work by Professor Mirza Muḥammad Sa'īd, *Madhhab awr Baṭinī Ta'līm* (Lahore, 1937). Being in Urdu its value is to a large extent lost to Western scholars, but his analysis of psychology and the deeper motives of the Ismā'īlīs is extremely valuable.

[42] In a note written by his own hand in my [A.A.A. Fyzee] copy, Zāhid 'Alī, *op. cit.*, p. 513.

[43] *Encyclopaedia of Islam,* Vol. II, p. 1051, s. v. "Kiyās." 'Abdur Rahim says that the root meaning is "measuring," "accord," "equality" *(Muhammadan Jurisprudence,* Madras, 1911, pp. 138); he also collects a number of Sunnī definitions. The authoritative Ithnā 'Asharī lexicon of sharī'a terms, *Majma'u'l-Bahrayn,* a Shī'ī lexicon by Fakhru'd-din b. Muḥammad b. Aḥmad al-Najafi (Tehran, 1321) defines it as taqdīr, and goes on to explain, "I deduced (qistu) a thing from another thing and know it (qaddartuhu) by comparison," see *q-y-s,* 347.

the logic of Muslim philosophers. If the premises are correct, the possibility of human knowledge increases vastly. We can now see the importance of qiyās in law; from a simple word meaning "measurement or comparison," and its application in deductive logic, a doctrine has developed in which the possibilities of deduction give the individual judge a great measure of freedom. "Individual reasoning in general is called ra'y, 'opinion'. When it is directed towards achieving systematic consistency . . . it is called qiyās."[44] The logical implications are (1) that human beings have the right to deduce new principles from the ancient rules, and (2) that juristic opinion will necessarily vary.

These principles were not accepted by the Fāṭimids and the Ithnā 'Asharīs. They were specifically denied by the Fāṭimid Qāḍī 'Abdu'l-'Aziz, grandson of Qāḍī Nu'man in his *Ikhtilāf uṣuli'l-madhāhib,*[45] and by the Ithnā 'Asharī doctor, Haṣan b. Zaynu'l-dīn b. 'Ali b. Aḥmad al-'Āmilī, known as *"Shāhid-i Thānī,"* in his *Ma'ālimu'd-dīn fi'l-uṣūl.*[46]

The Qāḍī 'Abdu'l-'Azīz was a judge during the times of the Caliphs al-'Azīz bi'l-lah and al-Ḥākim bi-amri'l-lah, and was ultimately killed by al-Ḥākim in 410/1011.[47] 'Abdu'l-'Azīz was the grandson of the renowned Nu'mān, "the Abū Ḥanīfa of the Shī'a," who was a jurist, author, and dā'i (propagandist) of the first four Fātimid caliphs.[48] Ḥasan-i 'Āmilī, better known as "Shāhid-i Thānī," was a learned theologian and his *Ma'ālim* is the most widely used textbook on uṣūl.[49]

[44] J. Schacht, *Origins of Muhammadan Jurisprudence* (Oxford, 1950), p. 98.

[45] See A. A. A. Fyzee on Nu'mān in *Journal of the Royal Asiatic Society* (London, 1934), Vol. 16, No. 18, read with page 27; Ivanow, *Guide to Ismaili Literature,* No. 79. After twenty years of study and reflection, I cannot sustain my opinion then expressed; and feel that *Ikhtilāf* is a useful work on Fāṭimid jurisprudence and deserves to be studied and edited.

My [A. A. A. Fyzee] own copy of *Ikhtilāf uṣūli'l-madhāhib* is a poor manuscript, machine-made thin paper, 140 folios, 5½ by 8½ inches, 16 lines to the page. "Vile Indian *naskh,"* (when you complain of the handwriting of a manuscript), the Bohoro shaykhs are accustomed to say with a significant and apologetic smile—"al-khatt ma yuqra" (sic). It is surprising how badly the generality of scribes of the Western Ismā'īlīs write. Full of mistakes, but fairly intelligible, as the language is not abstruse. Copyist, Ḥamud Yaḥya Ismā'īl (probably a poor Yemenite student writing for miserly wages; not a Bohora); copied at Surat, in the well-known madrasa of Sir Adamji Peerbhoy (Arabicized, Firbha'i) dated 1335/1917. My copy was acquired in 1932 in Bombay.

[46] Published 'Abdur-Rahim (Tehran, 1312/1894).

[47] De Lacy O'Leary, *History of the Fatimid Caliphate,* p. 163.

[48] Fyzee, in *Journal of the Royal Asiatic Society,* 1934, 1-32; *Encyclopaedia of Islam,* II, 953; *Da'ā'imu'l-Islam,* Vol. I, Introduction; Ivanow, *Guide to Ismaili Literature,* p. 37.

[49] Ṭūsī's List, No. 2989, p. 532; and Kantūri, *Kashfu'l-Ḥujub wa'l-Astār* (Calcutta, 1935).

The *Ikhtilāf* is a comparatively slight volume of 140 folios. A brief note on its contents will prove useful:

(1) On the traditions that are preserved (ma'thūr) .... Folios 1-7.
(2) On various traditionists and a confutation (radd) of the methods of those that differ (mukhtalifūn) .... Folios 8-19.
(3) On those who believe in taqlīd and their confutation Folios 19-49.
(4) On the consensus (ijmā') and the madhhab of jamā'a (Sunnīs) .... Folios 49-73.
(5) On the qiyās .... Folios 73-113.
(6) On those who affirm the validity of Istiḥsān (Ḥanafīs) and their confutation .... Folios 113-117.
(7) On those who affirm the validity of Istidlāl (Mālikīs) and their confutation .... Folios 117-123.
(8) On those who affirm the validity of Ijtihād and Ra'y and their confutation .... Folios 123-140.

The author explains that he wrote this book on the authority derived from his father, the Qāḍī Muḥammad, who in turn related it on the authority of his father, the Qāḍī Abū Ḥanīfa Nu'mān b. Muḥammad, author of *Da'ā' imu'l-Islam.* Nu'mān had obtained the permission of the Caliph-Imām al-Mu'izz Muḥammad, from al-'Azīz bi'llah, and the author 'Abdu'l-'Azīz, from al-Ḥākim, who put *by his own hand* the seal of approval on the book (Folio 2).[50]

After explaining, with reference to various traditions, the error of the common Muslims in permitting divergent opinions, he describes the services to society and religion of al-Mahdī bi'l-lah, the Founder of the Fāṭimid Dynasty, and reports from him the following ḥadīth: "by us [imāms], God has opened (the gates of) religion; by us, has He sealed them" (Folio 6). Here is one of the many foundations for the creation of one single authority, inerrant and infallible, for matters concerning religion and law. Later, he describes the action of the 'āmma (as distinguished from the khāṣṣa, the true believers, that is, the Fāṭimid Ismā'īlīs), as regards Qur'ān, sunna, and ijmā'. The Sunnīs derive new rules by the methods of ra'y, qiyās, and even ijmā'. But all these are based on one fundamental error (aṣl wāḥid), namely, the following of passion (hawa) and conjecture (ẓann) (Folios 7-8).

50 Among the Bohoras (Musta'lian Ismā'īlīs of India), it is still customary for a book to be written and presented to the dā'i for his approval, which is expressed, after perusal or official examination, by inserting the basmala in the handwriting of the regnant dā'i.

It is probable that an additional reason for centralization was that the state wanted to conserve and channel the increasing power of the 'ulamā in different spheres of life.

The earlier portion, as far as Folio 70, is full of the usual praises of 'Alī both by himself—such as, "ask me before you lose me" (Folio 33) and by the Prophet, who always places 'Alī and the Household very high in his own personal estimation and affection. The book is full of barbs and stories against the Sunnī Imām Abū Ḥanīfa Nu'mān b. Thābit al-Kūfī (Folio 63).[51]

In Folio 70, we have an important statement of what jamā'a should mean, how it is misinterpreted by the Sunnī, and how people have fallen into error by following legal rules based on opinion and conjecture instead of following the single, infallible source of knowledge, the imām. "After the Prophet, the designation of jamā'a can only be applied to those that are united in obedience to the imām (ijtama'a 'ala ṭā'ati'l-imām)." "How can we call people by the name of ahlu'l-sunna wa'l-jamā'a, when they oppose the *sunna* of the Messenger and disagree with those who confirm the authority of the same?" (Folio 71). Jamā'a is therefore explained, in the Shī'ī sense, as those who are united in their obedience to the single authority, the imām. The author strenuously opposes ijtihād, nazar (speculation), ra'y (opinion), qiyās (analogy), and related concepts (Folio 77 ff.).

His special confutation of qiyās commences in Folio 73. Following the direct statement that qiyās "destroys the very foundation of religion" (Folios 90-91), there is an interesting account of an encounter between Imām Ja'far al-Ṣādiq (the Veracious) and Abū Ḥanīfa al-Nu'mān b. Thābit Kūfī, the Sunnī Imām.

"Imām Ja'far asked him: 'How do you give decisions?' And he (Abū Ḥanīfa) said: 'according to the Book of God. And what I do not find in the Book of God, I seek in the Practice (sunna) of His Prophet. And what I do not find in the Book of God and the Practice of His Prophet, I deduce (qistuhu) on the basis of the two sources' " (Folio 92). Whereupon, the Imām tells him that the first of those who used their own powers of reasoning in preference to revealed authority was Iblīs (Satan), and how wrong he was! There are various other stories similar to these in the works of the Ithnā 'Asharī legists, Kulaynī, Ṣadūq, Ṭūsī, and others.

The author 'Abdu'l-'Azīz says that the isnād has been omitted in his book for the sake of brevity (Folio 95) and because when an

[51] To distinguish him from Abū Ḥanīfa of the Shī'a the Qāḍī al-Nu'mān b. Muḥammad b. Aḥmad b. Manṣūr b. Ḥayyun al-Tamīmī al-Maghribī al-Fāṭimī.

imām relates a tradition from the Prophet, no authority is necessary. The Imām Muḥammad al-Bāqir was asked by Ṣadir al-Ṣayrafī why the Shīʿa ʿulamā differed amongst themselves. Some of them said that the imām whispered in his ear, that he (the jurist) was inspired, that he gave judgments in accordance with the books of his ancestors; or that he decided in accordance with what he dreamed. And the imām said: "Do not take anything from them, O Ṣadir; we are the Proofs of God and the trusted ones (umanā') among men. The opinion we give as to lawful (ḥalāl) and unlawful (ḥarām) things are all from the Qur'ān (Folio 97.)" The doctrine is (1) that only the word of God is binding, and (2) that the imām is the sole interpreter of the ordinances of God.

Istiḥsān is dealt with in Folio 98 and istidlāl in Folio 119. Different kinds of errant qāḍīs are criticized (Folio 129), and ijtihād is refuted (Folio 140).

Finally, he says that there are only three foundations of the law: (1) Qur'ān, (2) Sunna, and (3) what comes to us from the imāms (ma jā'a mina'l-a'imma); there is no other source. On the very last page he says that this book, the *Ikhtilāf,* is specially directed against qiyās. It is thus clear that this book is written mainly to support the doctrine of one central authority for all true believers in matters of religion and law, and to refute the Sunnī doctrine of qiyās.

Next we come to the Ithnā ʿAsharī doctrine. The *Maʿālim* states that ijmāʿ among the Ithnā ʿAsharī jurists means "agreement of those who interpret in their religious judgments (fatāwa sharʿiyya) the commands of the imāms on a particular question" (p. 174). The mujtahids therefore cannot create law, or deduce new rules; theirs is merely the duty to interpret. This is to be compared with the doctrine of precedent in the Common Law. The judge has to interpret and follow the law; he cannot make law. That is the legislative function of Parliament, not part of the judicial function of the judiciary.

The imām is never absent: "Verily, The Time of Obligation (zamānu'l-taklif) is never without an imām who is Infallible (maʿṣūm), who is the Guardian of the law (ḥāfiz li'sh-sharʿ), a reference to whose word is obligatory,"[52] And further, the *ijmāʿ* is the pronouncement (kāshif) of the saying of the imām.[53] Later on, a whole section is devoted to the refutation of qiyās and istiṣḥāb.[54]

[52] *Maʿālim,* p. 175.
[53] *Loc. cit.*
[54] *Ibid.,* p. 223.

POSITIVE LAW—MUT'A, WILLS, INHERITANCE

We shall now deal with a few rules of positive law to show the application of these general principles. Temporary marriage (mut'a), wills (waṣāya), and inheritance (farā'iḍ) will be discussed briefly with a consideration of the differences between the Ḥanafī and Ithnā 'Asharī schools of law. The historical, political, and social reasons why these differences exist are not thoroughly known, but a few points can be mentioned.

The word mut'a means "enjoyment, use," and in its legal context it may be rendered "marriage for pleasure."[55] It is a marriage for a fixed period with a stipulated payment to the wife. During the Prophet's time, it was fairly common in Arabia. The old Arabian custom of mut'a, a useful type of legalized prostitution (especially during a military campaign), was later forbidden by the Prophet. After a confirmation of this prohibition by 'Umar, it was given up by the Sunnī, but the practice persisted among the Ithnā 'Asharī Shī'ī.

At present, all the schools of the Sunnī, and of the Shī'a, including the Zaydīs and the Fāṭimids,[56] consider it illegal. The Ithnā 'Asharis, probably because of its firm suppression by the second caliph, 'Umar, consider it lawful, and their theologian, al-Ḥurr al-'Āmilī, goes so far as to say: "The believer is only perfect when he has experienced a mut'a!"[57] On the other hand, the *'Uyūnu'l-Akhbār* of Sayyidu-na Idris 'Imādu'l-dīn, a Musta'lian dā'i (propagandist) contains an interesting tradition of the Fāṭimids. "Someone asked him [the Imām al-Mu'izz li-dīni'l-lah] about the mut'a marriage, and the Imām asked in turn: 'Do you wish that a mut'a may be performed with one of your close relatives [literally, the prohibited ones]?' And the man said: 'No, God is my witness!' And the Imām said: 'This should be sufficient for you; do not choose a rule for others which you would not for yourself.' "[58]

[55] Fyzee, *Outlines of Muhammadan Law*, p. 11; Schacht, *op. cit.*, pp. 266-67.

[56] [Faiz Badruddin] Tyabji, *Muhammadan Law* (3rd. ed., Bombay, 1940), p. 25, notes; *Bombay Law Reporter*, Vol. 33 (1931). I [A. A. A. Fyzee] edited the text of the *Da'ā'im* and three other legal works in the "Ismaili Law of Mut'a," *Journal of the Bombay Branch of the Royal Asiatic Society*, 1932, 85-92.

[57] Fyzee, *Outlines of Muhammadan Law*, p. 100. The subject is interesting but unfortunately there is no exhaustive monograph on it.

[58] Idrīs 'Imādu'l-dīn (19th dā'i of the Yaman, died 872/1468), *Journal Bombay Branch of the Royal Asiatic Society*, 1934, 12; *'Uyūnu'l-Akhbār*, Vol. VI. This historical work is in seven volumes and is still unpublished although the Osmania University, Hyderabad, possesses a complete copy. Zāhid 'Alī, *op. cit.*, 602, No. 38; Ivanow, *Guide to Ismaili Literature*, p. 62, No. 258.

The next question I wish to deal with is the law of wills (waṣāya). The word waṣiyya has at least four different meanings which I have explained and illustrated in my *Ismā'īlī Law of Wills,* namely (1) a will, oral or written, (2) a specific legacy, (3) the capacity of an executor, executorship, and (4) a moral exhortation. In India a written will is often called waṣiyyat-nama, a Persian compound.[59]

A peculiarity of the Islamic law of wills is this: a man may, during his own lifetime, give away the whole of his property under the rules of hiba; but after his death, he cannot bequeath more than one-third of his property.[60] Now, it is this one-third, "the bequeathable third," about which there is a controversy between Ḥanafīs and Ithna 'Asharī authorities.

CONSENT OF HEIRS

If a man wishes to bequeath more than one-third of his property, he can do so only with the consent of his heirs. Such consent must be obtained in Ḥanafī law, *after* the testator's death, whereas in Ithnā 'Asharī law the requisite consent may be obtained *either before or after* the testator's death.[61]

BEQUESTS TO HEIRS

Here again, there is a very real difference between the Ithnā 'Asharī and Ḥanafī rules. Among the Sunnī, generally, the tradition accepted as binding is: There shall be no bequest to an heir (la waṣiyyata li-wārithin),[62] and therefore if a will contains a bequest to one who, at the testator's death, would receive a share of inheritance under the law applicable, such heir is not entitled to the legacy. The Fāṭimids agree with the Sunnī rule. [63]

The Ithnā 'Asharīs, however, basing their opinion on a Qur'ānic verse (2, 180), hold that a legacy, which is otherwise lawful and does not infringe the one-third rule, can certainly go to an heir.[64]

These two rules are of extreme practical importance and we shall consider each of them by a simple illustration.

A testator who is dying has two sons X and Y, and a great

[59] A. A. A. Fyzee, *Ismaili Law of Wills* (Oxford, 1933), pp. 8-9.

[60] Fyzee, *Outlines of Muhammadan Law,* p. 87. "Property" means the net assets, that is, what remains after paying debts and funeral charges, *Ibid.,* pp. 306-7.

[61] Fyzee, *Outlines of Muhammadan Law,* p. 187.

[62] *Ibid.,* 310-11.

[63] Fyzee, *Ismaili Law of Wills,* Arts. 19-21 give the text of the *Da'ā'im.*

[64] For a full discussion, see Tyabji, *op. cit.,* 789.

friend Z. X and Y are well placed in life, but Z is badly off, and the testator wishes to provide for him. Suppose X and Y agree in the testator's lifetime to a bequest exceeding the one-third to Z. Is the bequest valid? Yes, if the testator is an Ithnā 'Asharī; no, if he is a Ḥanafī. But consider the complications that can arise; the father may be an overbearing man, able to coerce his sons; one of the sons may agree to the arrangement during the father's lifetime, but withdraw from it at the instance of a capricious wife after the father's death; or the sons, dutiful and normal, may agree in the father's lifetime, but become poor while the crafty Z becomes rich, powerful and greedy. Hence, X and Y have no sympathy left for him. In all such cases, the school of law to which the father belonged *at his death* is of great importance.

The same story can be repeated with variations in the case of a bequest to an heir. A son Yūsuf is poor, and the will provides for him, in addition, of course, to his share of inheritance. Harūn, his brother, agrees during the lifetime of his father. But later, on account of greed, poverty, ill-will, or the insinuation of friends, retracts and files a suit for his full share. Here again it is of the utmost importance to determine the school of law to which the deceased belonged when he died. Although a bequest to an heir, limited to the one-third, is valid among the Ithnā 'Asharīs, with or without consent, it is not among the Sunnī, where no bequest can ever be taken by an heir, whose share has been immutably fixed by the Qur'ān. The rule of law is that the madhhab by which the rules of wills, administration of estates, and inheritance are determined is the madhhab of a man at his death.[65]

In the law of inheritance, the divergence between the Ḥanafī law and its Ithnā 'Asharī counterpart is so extreme and so remarkable that it seems strange that no one except Tyabji should have dealt with the question.[66] His treatment of the *Islamic Law of Inheritance* is so detailed, so systematic, and so meticulously accurate, that it has met with universal appreciation. He approaches the question as a lawyer and a judge, but neglects the historical and other aspects.

The main principles laid down by Tyabji may be briefly summarized. First, the Sunnī Law of Inheritance is a mixture of the old Arabian tribal law and the Qur'ānic reform. The two streams

[65] Fyzee, *Outlines of Muhammadan Law,* p. 336. A man in India may freely change his madhhab, *ibid.,* 62-64; and apart from the case of Shiblī Nu'mānī, p. 63, footnote (b), there are many cases in India where a man has changed his school or sub-school more than once.

[66] Tyabji, *op. cit.,* p. 926.

flow in the same channel, but their waters do not mix freely.[67] The Shi'ī Ithnā 'Asharī law developed later and extended considerably the application of Qur'ānic principles. Second, the principle of ta'ṣib is accepted in Sunnī law, but not among the Shī'īs. Third, the classification of heirs is entirely different. Among the Ḥanafīs it is Qur'ānic heirs, Tribal heirs, Uterine heirs; among the Ithnā 'Asharīs, it is Class I, Class II, Class III, on entirely different principles. Fourth, stirpital succession[68] was adopted more systematically, and occasionally even regardless of sex, among the Shī'īs; whereas the Sunnīs say that stirpital succession is of limited application. Fifth, among the Shī'īs, females, however remote, inherit on the analogy of the shares of the daughter or sister; while in the Sunnī interpretation, the males predominate.

This is a very cursory, superficial summary of a subject of fascinating complexity and importance, which, unhappily, has so far not been treated either historically or exhaustively.[69]

[67] Fyzee, *Outlines of Muhammadan Law*, p. 332.

[68] This term has been defined by Blackstone as follows:

"In the law of descents and distribution, this term denotes that method of dividing an intestate estate where a class or group of distributees take the share which their deceased would have been entitled to, taking thus by their right of representing such ancestor, and not as so many individuals."

[69] Fyzee, *Outlines of Muhammadan Law*, pp. 403-06.

CHAPTER VI

Family Law

"FAMILY LAW," as used here, means those laws upon which the Muslim family is founded and which govern the relationships among its members. It includes laws relating to marriage, to the rights of children and relatives, and to the finances of the family, including expenses, the distribution of inheritances, bequests, waqfs, and related matters.

Although the Muslim countries derive their family law from Islamic law, they have adopted varying schools of interpretation whose differences, however, are slight and confined to minor rather than major matters. Pakistan, Syria, and most of 'Iraq adhere to the Ḥanafī, as do the Muslims of India, China, and Japan. This school was formerly predominant in Egypt and continues to be the basis of that family legislation which has not been changed since 1920, when the country began to borrow from other sources of Islamic law. Certain provisions of the marriage laws of 1920 and 1929 were taken over from other schools. Such borrowings were comparatively unimportant in the case of the legislation on inheritance enacted in 1943, since Muslim jurists differ little on this subject. The laws of 1946 on waqf and bequests, on the other hand, were composites of several schools, and did not reflect any one body of opinion. The Mālikī school prevails in North Africa, the Ḥanbalī school in Saudi Arabia, and the Zaydī school in the Yaman. In Iran and parts of 'Iraq the school of the Twelver Shī'īs is followed.

MARRIAGE

THE DRAWING-UP OF THE MARRIAGE CONTRACT

The conclusion of the marriage contract, i.e., the act of marriage itself, is preceded by the betrothal, in which each of the contracting parties seeks to determine if the other is free to marry and in which the man expresses his desire for marriage. The betrothal is not a contract but a promise to make a contract. Therefore, it is permissible for either of the parties to withdraw from it in order that there may be complete freedom of choice in the marriage. This is sanctioned even by certain Mālikī jurists who, although they consider a promise to make a contract as binding, make an exception in the case of a betrothal. The other party has no right to demand compensation for such withdrawal ('udūl) if he suffers damage only through the betrothal or the withdrawal. However, compensation may be claimed for damage caused by deception. If one of the betrothed has presented any gifts, he has the right to demand their return if they are in existence, but no right to demand their price if they have been consumed. Mālik held that if the giver is the withdrawing party, he cannot demand the return of any gifts, whether they are in existence or not; but that if the receiver withdraws, then he must return the gifts if they are in existence and their price if they are not.

The marriage contract is concluded by an offer (ijāb) and acceptance (qabūl), both of these must be made on the same occasion (fī majlis wāḥid) by two qualified parties. Three conditions are required to make the marriage valid: (1) there must be nothing in the form of the marriage contract indicating that it is intended to be of limited duration; (2) the contract must be published and made known; and (3) there must be no impediment of relationship or religion which would interdict the marriage.

The requirement that there must be no intention of limiting the duration of the marriage contract is based on the principle that marriage should be upheld, and should not come to an end except as the result of an unforeseen event which prevents it from continuing. A marriage cannot be concluded if the form of the contract stipulates a fixed period for which it is to be valid or, in the opinion of the great majority of jurists, if a time limitation is implied. The condition that the marriage must be made known is fulfilled by the presence of two witnesses—the number specified by the Prophet—providing that they have not entered into an agreement with the parties to keep the marriage secret.

If a marriage has been contracted by competent persons in the presence of two witnesses and has been adequately publicized, it has been concluded in a valid fashion and is complete and binding. It requires no religious or other rites or ceremonies, since in Islamic law formalities have no value insofar as contracts are concerned and are carried out only if the two parties are willing. The marriage contract must be made public in order to be completed, for, as the Prophet is reported to have said, it is the publicizing which makes the difference between that which is permitted and that which is forbidden. There are no other formalities apart from this.

However, the Egyptian Government in 1931 decided that a case concerning the validity of a marriage would not be heard unless the plaintiff were in possession of an official document in case the other party denied the marriage. But if he should acknowledge the marriage and deny anything resulting therefrom which might be a subject of complaint, then the complaint is to be heard. The Egyptian law is based on the condition laid down by the jurists that the contract should be given publicity and that the way in which publicity is given is by registering the contract, which is to be done by means of an official document.

IMPEDIMENTS TO MARRIAGE

Under certain circumstances, a valid marriage cannot be concluded. Marriage is permanently prohibited to persons between whom there exist certain specified relationships which cannot be terminated; and is temporarily interdicted by certain relationships or conditions which are susceptible of termination, the prohibition obtaining only so long as the relationship or condition exists. The relationships which entail permanent prohibition of marriage are those of blood (qarāba), marriage ties (muṣāhara), and milk. Under the prohibition established by blood kinship (nasab), marriage with persons in any of the following categories are invalid: (1) Female ascendants, e.g., mother, mother's mother, and so on; and father's mother and so on. Marriage with any mother or grandmother is forbidden. (2) Female lineal descendants, e.g., daughter, daughter's daughter, and so on; and son's daughter, and so on. (3) Offspring of one's parents, e.g., full sisters or half-sisters, whether on the father's side or the mother's side, and their offspring; and female offspring of one's brothers. (4) Offspring of one's male and female grandparents, if they are one degree removed, e.g., paternal and maternal aunts of whatever category; the paternal aunt, who is one's father's sister, is forbidden, as is the paternal [great-] aunt, who is the sister of one's grandfather. But their children and the children of paternal and maternal uncles of whatever degree are permitted and one may enter into marriage with them. One's maternal aunt is forbidden but the daughter of one's mother's maternal aunt is permitted, for she is more than one degree removed.

In the case of kinship by marriage, the prohibition of marriage is determined by the existence of marriage between a male person and one of his prospective wife's relatives or between her and one of the prospective husband's relatives. Those females who are prohibited because of such relationship are: (1) The wife's female ascendants of all degrees, e.g., the mother of a woman whom one has married by a valid contract and her female grandparents of whatever degree. If the marriage which created this relationship has been contracted but not consummated, the mother of the man's wife is nevertheless forbidden to him since the contract alone is sufficient to establish prohibition. (2) The wife of a man's male ascendants of whatever degree, even though the marriage may not have been consummated. (3) The wife of one's offspring, to whatever degree. If a person married a woman and the two separated either before or after consummation of the marriage, the woman is not permitted either to his brother or to a male ancestor, even though he should be far enough removed to be permitted to marry her, for the contract alone suffices to establish the prohibited relationship.

The concept of milk relationship is peculiar to Islamic law, since other legal systems do not regard suckling as establishing a legal relationship between the infant who is suckled on the one hand, and the woman who gives suck and her husband on the other. Muslim jurists, however, hold that since the infant takes nourishment from the body of the woman who nurses it, its body becomes part of hers, just as it is part of the body of the woman who nourished it in the womb; and that the woman who gives such thus becomes a mother of the child. Similarly, her husband is considered a father of the child, since he was responsible for the pregnancy which created the milk. The relatives of both are related to the child in the same degree that they would be if the milk parents were the actual parents.

A Muslim is forbidden to marry persons in any of the eight following categories of suckling kin: (1) His mother by suckling and all of her ascendants. (2) His children by suckling, and their descendants. (3) The children of his parents by suckling, and their descendants. (4) The descendants of his grandparents by suckling if they are of the first degree. These include the children of a maternal grandmother by suckling, and maternal and paternal aunts by suckling. However, the daughters of paternal and maternal aunts are not prohibited. (5) His wife's ascendants by suckling, if the man has separated from his wife, whether before or after consummating the marriage. (6) The descendants by suckling of whomever marries such a wife if he leaves her after consummating the marriage. However, if the separation has taken place before the consummation of the marriage, then such female descendants are permitted to a man. (7) The wife of an ascendant by suckling, to whatever degree, whether her husband had been separated from her before or after consummating the marriage. (8) The wife of a descendant by suckling, to whatever degree, whether or not the marriage has been consummated.

Certain relationships and conditions act as a temporary bar to marriage. It is not permissible to conclude a marriage contract with the wife of another man, or with a woman who is in 'idda following the death of, or her divorce from, her husband. The length of the 'idda is about three months for a divorced woman and four months and ten days for a woman whose husband has died. When this period has passed she may marry, since the relationship which had caused the prohibition of marriage, i.e., the claim of the former husband, has come to an end.

The conclusion of a marriage contract with a person who does not follow one of the revealed religions (i.e., Judaism, Christianity, and Islam) is not valid. However, a Muslim woman may not marry a non-Muslim man unless he accepts Islam.

The basic reason for the distinction which is made in Islamic law between revealed religions and other religions is that the customs of Islam are close to the spirit of the other revealed religions but are very far removed from that of paganism. It is therefore possible for a Muslim husband and his Christian or Jewish wife to live together in harmony, with each one following his religion. This is not possible between a Muslim man and a pagan woman owing to the lack of a common spirit between the two religions; she might worship a cow while he was sacrificing one or preparing to do so.

A woman who has been divorced three times by the same husband is prohibited to him until she has been married to another man. If a man divorces his wife three times it is an indication that there is a deep-seated incompatibility between them, and he may not marry her again until she and another man have married, lived together as husband and wife, and then separated for one reason or another. Remarriage to the former husband is then permitted, because it is possible that the woman may have improved her conduct by association with another man if the cause of the incompatibility was on her side, or because the man may have improved his conduct by long absence from her, if the cause of the incompatibility had been on his side.

Simultaneous marriage to two wives who are closely related,

viz., sisters or an aunt and her niece, is not permitted, for their both being married to the same man breaks the bond of kinship between them and gives rise to hostility, for which reason such a marriage is not allowed. Likewise, for example, a man is not allowed to marry his wife's paternal aunt while he is still married to his wife. Neither may he marry her if he has divorced his wife and her ʻidda has not been completed; he must wait until the ʻidda has expired, a period of about three months.

A Muslim who has four wives—the maximum permitted at any one time, despite the practice of some Shīʻī sects and certain of the Zāhirīs—cannot contract a valid marriage with a fifth woman until he has separated himself from one of the other four and her period of ʻidda has expired.

WOMAN'S FREEDOM TO CHOOSE A HUSBAND AND THE QUESTION OF SUITABILITY

An adult and mentally sound male has complete freedom of choice in connection with marriage. Most jurists consider the age of adulthood to be fifteen years; but in various Muslim countries this age is increased if requisite financial and other conditions are not present, so that there is variation from one government to another. But does a woman who is adult and of sound mind have full freedom to choose a husband and contract a marriage as a man can? The jurists are agreed that nobody can force an adult and mentally sound woman into a marriage to which she does not consent. The only dissent on this point comes from al-Shāfiʻī, who allows the forcing of a virgin into marriage, but the majority of the Muslim jurists do not agree with him.

Although the majority of jurists are agreed that a woman cannot be compelled to choose a particular husband, they have held that she alone should not make the choice, but should be assisted in this by the relative who is her guardian, i.e., her father, grandfather, brother, paternal uncle, or paternal cousin, or any other blood relatives on her father's but not on her mother's side. If she has no guardian she can ask the qāḍī's permission to marry. Also, if she has a guardian and disagrees with him on the subject, such as by choosing a person to whom he does not agree, she can take her case to the qāḍī and seek his permission to marry. The qāḍī listens to her petition and the objection of her guardian; if the qāḍī thinks that the guardian's objection is in her interest he rejects her petition, and if he does not think that the objection is sound then her marriage can take place. In the event that she and her guardian see eye to eye, the latter undertakes to draw up the marriage contract on her behalf.

Such is the opinion of the majority of jurists. But according to Abū Ḥanīfa a woman has complete freedom to choose her husband and conclude the marriage contract herself. No one can force her to accept her guardian as an associate in making her choice so long as she is of age and of sound mind and on condition that she makes a suitable choice. For if she chooses someone who according to popular opinion and estimation is inferior to her, her guardian can petition for the nullification of the contract by the qāḍī; the guardian can do the same if the contract is invalidated by misrepresentation. The school of Abū Ḥanīfa is supported by many ḥadīths from the Prophet and is still followed on this question in Egypt, the Sudan, Syria, Lebanon, 'Iraq, Pakistan, and by the Muslims of India, China, and Japan. In these countries a woman has complete freedom to choose her husband so long as he is suitable.

Abū Ḥanīfa was just as severe regarding the conditions with respect to suitability (kifā'a) as he was liberal in granting freedom to a woman to choose her husband. More than any other jurist he adhered stringently to the conditions surrounding the suitability of the husband for his wife with respect to equality of the man's family to that of the woman in those aspects of reputation and esteem in which families are apt to differ. All other jurists are less exacting than Abū Ḥanīfa in this respect. Mālik considered suitability only on the grounds of religious affiliation, piety, and freedom of the man from bodily defects. The Mālikī school approximates the Ḥanbalī in one of the two authorities it cites on this subject; another authority cited on this subject adds to this requirement suitability of descent. The Shāfi'ī school on the whole takes a position similar to that of the Ḥanafīs; even though the Ḥanafī is stricter and judges suitability on the basis of reputation ('urf). The Ḥanafīs claim that the basis for this is found in certain ḥadīths, but some of the 'ulamā say that there are no traditions of the Prophet which are applicable to the question of suitability but that there are six considerations which determine it: (1) lineage (nasab); (2) Islam; (3) free status; (4) financial suitability; (5) suitability in rectitude and piety; and (6) occupation.

The question of lineage was a consideration only among the Arabs, since it was they who prided themselves on their lineage and safeguarded it. Only a man of Quraysh was suitable for a woman of that tribe, but some non-Qurayshīs were suitable for others. Most of the Shāfi'īs say that if there are non-Arabs who pride themselves on their lineage, then suitability of lineage is to be taken into consideration in their case, i.e., a man whose family is of a lineage inferior to that of a woman is not suitable for her. The consideration of Islam means that a Muslim whose father was a non-Muslim is not suitable for a woman whose parents are Muslims; that a man whose parents only were Muslims is not suitable for a woman whose grandfather was a Muslim; and that a man one of whose grandfathers was a Muslim is suitable for a woman whose grandparents were Muslims. This type of suitability is taken into consideration only among peoples who are other than Arab in origin, such as the Egyptians and other non-Arab peoples who accepted Islam. Among those peoples of Arab origin, on the other hand, a Muslim man is *ipso facto* suitable for a woman whose grandparents were Muslims. This is the practice which is current in Egypt. Free status is applicable only to non-Arabs. A man who is free but whose father was a slave is not suitable for a woman whose father was free, but since slavery has long since disappeared it has no validity today. Financial suitability means that the husband should be capable of meeting the expenditures and the bride-price (mahr) appropriate to the status of the intended bride. If he can do this, he is regarded as having satisfied this criterion and nothing further is required of him. This, however, is without prejudice to the question of equality (kifā'a) in wealth, which requires that there should not be a great difference in wealth between the husband and the wife's father. Within the Ḥanafī school there is a difference of opinion with regard to this criterion, but the prevailing opinion does not consider this difference as an impediment to marriage. A man who is known to be irreligious is not considered to be suitable for a pious woman who is the daughter of a pious father. Within the Ḥanafī school there is a difference of opinion regarding this type of suitability. The prevailing view, however, is that a man is not unsuitable unless he makes a public show of his impiety in such a manner as to make a laughing stock of himself. The occupation of the husband should be similar to that of the wife's father and not one of which he should be ashamed. There is a difference of opinion of this type of suitability, but the prevailing view is that occupation is a bar if the difference between the two is a great one.

These are the factors which are taken into consideration by

Abū Ḥanīfa in determining suitability, and the views of al-Shāfi'ī are very similar. Mālik and Aḥmad ibn Ḥanbal, on the other hand, differ from him. They consider the question of suitability as applicable only to the man, and not to the woman. They lay down the condition that the status of the man must be equal to that of the woman's family, but they do not make the condition that the woman should be equal to the man. This question of suitability is taken into consideration at the time the marriage is performed. If the woman contracts a marriage without the consent of her guardian, the latter has the right to raise the question of the husband's suitability, but he does not have this right if she marries with her guardian's consent. If she marries a man who is unsuitable without having received her guardian's consent, then the contract is invalid, according to the prevalent opinion of the Ḥanafī school.

The Ḥanafī school lays great stress on suitability and is very strict with respect to it. There are two reasons for this. In the first place, marriage is a relationship between two families and there must be the greatest possible degree of agreement between them. Custom ('urf) does not prohibit a woman of low status from marrying a man of noble origin, since he raises her position. But a woman of noble origin does not improve the low status of her husband. Secondly, since the woman is granted freedom to marry whom she will, her guardians must have the reserved right to make suitability a condition to the marriage in order to safeguard the rights of both parties.

PROVISIONS REFERRING TO THE MARRIAGE CONTRACT

First there is the essential provision that none of the contracting parties is permitted to make conditions which contradict Islamic marriage laws; if conditions are made which contradict the provisions of the law, then such conditions are invalid and cannot be enforced. But can one of the contracting parties make additional conditions which do not run counter to already existing provisions, even though they introduce additional stipulations for which no previous provision has been made?

The opinion of the jurists differs on this question. The Ḥanbalīs require the fulfillment of all conditions not already provided for by the law so long as they are not contrary to those provisions which have already been made. For example, a woman can stipulate in the contract that the man shall not take her on his travels or marry any other wife. According to Aḥmad ibn Ḥanbal, such a condition would have to be fulfilled because otherwise the woman would have the right to break the contract.

Most jurists say that conditions which are made in the contract in excess of those provided by the principles of the law are invalid; they are to be disregarded and do not affect the validity of the contract. Such conditions do not have to be fulfilled; moreover, in a marriage contract no conditions should be made which are different from those prescribed by the law unless they confirm what the latter already has produced. For example, a woman can make the condition that surety must be provided for expenditures or the bride-price; such a condition would be valid since it confirms conditions which already existed.

The duties imposed by the law do not impose any financial duty on a wife with respect to her marital life. There is no expenditure or groom-price which she must meet and her husband has no authority over her property. Indeed, she has full freedom to manage her own property whatsoever. Her property is entirely independent of his. Marriage restricts her financial freedom only to a small degree, for Mālik says that if a woman is married she cannot give away more than a third of her property; otherwise she is completely free to do what she likes with her property.

The most important of the legal rights which marriage creates between the two spouses is firstly, that of mutual inheritance (tawarruth); each inherits from the other when he dies. (We shall speak of this right when we discuss inheritance). The second right is that of the bride-price, while the third is that of support (nafaqa) and the fourth is obedience.

THE BRIDE-PRICE

The bride-price (mahr) is a due which the husband must pay to the wife in accordance with the marriage contract, but it is not a condition which affects the validity of the contract nor is it an essential requisite. Therefore, if the bride-price is not mentioned in the contract, the contract is still valid. The bride-price must be on a par with that received by other women of equal status in the bride's family, such as her sister, her paternal aunt, or the daughter of her paternal uncle. There is no upper limit to the bride-price, but whatever sum is mentioned in the contract must be paid. The Ḥanafīs and the Mālikīs set a minimum limit to the bride-price.

Many jurists, including al-Shāfi'ī, do not do this, but hold that everything that can be considered as goods or benefit is property which may constitute the bride-price.[1]

It is not necessary to pay the entire bride-price at the time the contract is made. It may be deferred either in whole or in part. Whatever the two parties agree upon with reference to immediate or deferred payment is binding upon these parties. If they do not agree on any particular arrangement, then the customary usage of the locality in which the contract is made is to be followed. Should the locality have no customary usage in this matter, the principle to be followed is that of full payment at the time the contract is concluded.

In certain Muslim countries there has grown up a tendency to reduce the sum paid upon the conclusion of the contract and to increase the amount the payment of which is deferred. For example, the amount which is paid down is one dollar and that which is deferred is $5,000 as compensation to the woman in the event of divorce, since payment of the deferred sum is postponed until either the woman is divorced or one of the two spouses dies. The sharī'a permits this; indeed, this procedure is based on its logic and fundamental principles. The woman can refuse to move to her husband's house until he has paid her that portion of the bride-price (sidaq) which was due upon the conclusion of the contract.

The existence of a valid marriage contract in itself makes necessary the payment of the bride-price, which is a right of the wife. If there is a bride-price agreed upon in the contract, then the agreement shall be in force if such bride-price is commensurate with the status of the wife or the bride-price of a woman of similar status of the family of her father. If it is less than the bride-price of a woman of her status and her guardian is satisfied with it, then it is equally acceptable. But if the guardian is not satisfied with it, then, according to Abū Ḥanīfa, it is necessary to raise the bride-price to that of a woman of equal status; otherwise the qāḍī can cancel the contract.

If there is no definitely indicated bride-price, then the bride-price of a woman of similar status must be paid.

When the bride-price has been established it is not rigidly fixed and incapable of reduction simply because of the contract. On the

[1] The term "bride-price" rather than "dowry" is used here to avoid confusion with the common meaning of "dowry" and to stay closer to the original conotation of mahr.

contrary, when necessary, it can be either reduced in part or eliminated entirely; it can also be confirmed *in toto*.

It is confirmed *in toto* upon the consummation of the marriage and upon the death of one of the spouses. If the wife has moved into the husband's house and he has consummated the marriage, the bride-price is confirmed *in toto* and is not liable to diminution, either in whole or in part, under any circumstances.

The bride-price is reduced by half if the husband divorces his wife before consummating the marriage or if he separates himself from her for any other of the various causes for separation if the causes for the separation lie on the man's side and the wife has had nothing to do with the matter.

All of the bride-price is cancelled if the wife, for reasons of her own, separates herself from the husband before the marriage has been consummated and the husband has had nothing to do with the matter, such as repudiating her. In such a case the bride-price is cancelled *in toto* so long as the marriage has not yet been consummated.

It is noted that Abū Ḥanīfa thought cause for the confirmation (ta'ākkud) of the bride-price exists when the man secludes himself with his wife in a place where they are safe from observation by others; this is equivalent to actual consummation of the marriage and confirms the bride-price *in toto*. Mālik considers such seclusion as equivalent to actual consummation of the marriage if the woman has moved to her husband's domicile and has remained there for a year. Aḥmad ibn Ḥanbal's view on seclusion is similar to that of Abū Ḥanīfa, but he adds that such things as kissing and embracing are to be reckoned as actual consummation of the marriage in confirming the bride-price *in toto*. Al-Shāfi'ī holds that only actual consummation of the marriage confirms the bride-price and does not consider seclusion, etc., as equivalent to consummation in this respect.

If no bride-price has been named but the bride-price of a woman of similar status is called for, and if divorce takes place before the marriage is consummated without anything having taken place which would confirm the bride-price, then the equivalent of half the bride-price must be given to the bride as a present. This present should be one proper for a woman of her status and within the capability of the husband to pay.

If the bride-price must be paid, either in whole or in part, then it becomes a right of the woman similar to any right due to one person from another. She may release the husband from it or cancel all or part of it according to the relation between the two. However, such a case should be carefully investigated lest the woman has released him under compulsion. For this reason some of the successors of the Companions of the Prophet permit the woman to revoke such a release made by her. It is related that Caliph 'Umar instructed his qāḍīs that "the desires and fears of women are to be given consideration; so even if a woman has given away property and then wants to take it back, she may do so."

The bride-price is a right of the woman and she is not obliged to give anything in return for it. It is not she but the man who is responsible for furnishing the house. However, it is customary in the Muslim countries for the woman to furnish the house, and her family goes to considerable expense to do this. Nevertheless, this is a practice of custom and is not required by law.

The requirement of the bride-price for the woman is in the nature of a gift, for which reason the Qur'ān calls it a niḥla, or present (hadiyya). This gift was required of the man, but not the woman, because it was essentially the man who did the working and earning in life, while a woman's working for gain was something exceptional. When the woman comes to her husband she needs clothing, jewelry, and other things appropriate to her wedded life. It, therefore, was the man's duty to aid her in this from his financial resources, and this aid was the bride-price.

SUPPORT (NAFAQA)

It is the husband's duty to support his wife as soon as she moves into his house or prepares to move into it. If he requests her to move and she refuses to do so, then she has no claim to being supported by him unless her refusal is for a legal cause such as his failure to make the required advance on the bride-price to her; the house is not up to that prescribed by law as fitting to one of her status; or the fact that his house is inhabited by his family and that it would not be to her advantage to live with them. All such cases would be legal causes for her refusal and would not relieve the husband of the necessity of supporting her.

It is the opinion of the majority of jurists that the wife should be supported in a style which is in conformity with the husband's status. Even though she might be of a wealthy family, if the husband is one who works for a living then he is expected to support his wife in the manner becoming to a worker and more than this cannot be required of him.

By support is meant paying for necessary food, clothing, and shelter. If a woman of her status is accustomed to having servants, he shall be obliged to pay the expenses of a servant for her. The amount of money alloted to the wife's support is determined by referral of the matter to the qāḍī each month, each week, or each year, according to the manner in which the husband gains his living. For example, the practice in Egypt is to determine it each month.

In the event that the husband refuses to support his wife, the Ḥanafī school permits his imprisonment until he does so. The majority of jurists hold that she can also request a separation on the grounds of such refusal and that the qāḍī can grant her a divorce from the husband if such grounds are established.

If the husband has fallen into financial difficulties and is unable to support his wife, the Ḥanafī school does not release him from the obligation to support her, but it provides that she shall be supported by one of her relatives who would have been obliged to support her if she were not married, such as her father, her brother, her mother, or her grandfather. Such support becomes a claim against the husband, the payment of which can be demanded if his financial condition improves. Abū Ḥanīfa does not permit either separation or release from responsibility for support on the grounds of financial incapacity.

If a woman's husband is in financial straits and cannot provide her with necessary food, clothing, and shelter, then the majority of jurists permit her to request a separation on these grounds and allow the qāḍī to grant such a separation if the grounds are established.

The only jurists who state that the husband is not responsible for supporting his wife if he is incapable of doing so are those who belong to the Ẓāhirī school. They maintain that the husband is not responsible for supporting his wife if he is in financial straits and unable to do so. They go even further and say that if the wife is wealthy she must support her husband, but this is a view which is unusual among Muslim jurists.

OBEDIENCE

Obedience is a right which the husband can demand of his wife. By obedience is meant that she should transfer herself to his domicile, live with him, and that they should live together in harmony. She can refuse to move to his domicile only for the reasons already stated.

If he goes on a journey and requests her to accompany him, it is her duty to do so. She cannot refuse to accompany him unless it has been established that she cannot trust him or if his object in getting her to travel is to injure her. For example, he might have a domicile in the city and take her to his domicile in the country for purposes of deceit or injury and not merely for harmonious companionship. In these two circumstances she would have the right to refuse to accompany him, since being obliged to accompany a husband whom she did not trust or who sought to injure her would be a cause of damage and harm to her; for Islam does not countenance harm or injury.

TERMINATING THE MARRIAGE CONTRACT

The marriage contract is automatically terminated if anything happens which makes its continuation incompatible with the established precepts of Islam. For example, one of the two spouses might abandon Islam; or in the case of two non-Muslim spouses, either the wife might embrace Islam, or in the case of a pagan couple, the husband might become a Muslim. In these and similar cases, the marriage contract is legally dissolved without being voided by one of the contracting parties.

The marriage contract is terminated by divorce, which is a legal action undertaken either by the husband or the qāḍī by which the contract is terminated. It is necessary here to explain briefly the reason for this.

It is decreed that the fundamental principle of the marriage contract is that it is permanent and is to endure as long as the spouses live. But in order for it to continue it is not alone sufficient for the sharī'a to lay down the law that it is permanent; the love which binds the two spouses together must continue also, for it is the tie on which the continuation of true married life depends. But the spouses might develop a strong aversion to each other, thus making love difficult. In such a case one of three choices must be made: (1) To continue the marriage despite this strong aversion, thus giving rise to ill-will and rancor. The continuation of this situation would not be to the interest of the family; (2) Physical separation while preserving the married state. This would be an offense against morality and might drive the two parties to vice. (3) Divorce, which breaks the marriage bond and makes an act of ill-will out of what had originally been an act of blessing. This is the soundest way, even though it means the destruction of the family.

If, then, there must be divorce when aversion is strong, in whose hands shall the decision regarding divorce lie? Shall both parties decide it jointly, shall the law decide it, or shall one of the two parties decide it?

There is no doubt but that if the two parties agree on divorce it must be carried out. It is only necessary to see that this agreement has not taken place in a momentary fit of anger which might quickly pass away; Islam has made provision for such an eventuality as we shall make clear.

There remain the other two cases, namely whether the judge (qāḍī) is to determine when divorce can take place or whether this can be done by one of the two parties.

If the woman wants a divorce it can take place only by decision of the qāḍī, because the husband has undertaken financial responsibilities with regard to this marriage; he has made an advance payment on the bride-price and is to pay the balance upon divorce; he has furnished the house and has incurred many expenses. If the wife could divorce him on her own responsibility he would lose all that he had spent on her. It is therefore necessary for the qāḍī to intervene in order to ascertain that she has requested a divorce because she has been wronged. If such is the case, then the husband bears the consequences and loses the money which he has spent on her. If it is established that the aversion is on her part and that it is the cause of her seeking a divorce, then the qāḍī divorces them on condition that she reimburse the husband for all that he has spent on his marriage. This is the procedure of the school of Mālik which was the practice also of some of the Companions of the Prophet and their successors. The intervention of the qāḍī was for the purpose of preventing the husband from being wronged if it were she who bore the aversion to him, so that the husband would not lose the money which he had spent on her.

The wife can divorce herself from her husband without the intervention of the qāḍī if when the contract is drawn up a condition to that effect is made accompanied by what in the technical terminology of the jurists is called *tafwīḍ* (authorization), or giving the wife the right to divorce herself from her husband whenever she chooses. Since the husband has previously agreed to this, the divorce can be executed against him even though it involves an injustice to him. Just as such authorization can be made by a provision at the time the contract is drawn up, so can it be done during the course of married life, and the husband can grant his wife this right whenever he chooses. If he does so, she can exercise it without the intervention of the law; she divorces her husband with his own consent, since she has been empowered to do so by him. The practice of authorization has been established by Mālik, Abū Ḥanīfa, and many of the Prophet's Companions and their successors.

We conclude, then, that the husband can divorce his wife without the intervention of the qāḍī, and that the wife can divorce her husband either by a qāḍī, by a provision made at the time the contract is drawn up, or by being empowered to do so by her husband during the course of married life.

But we have not set forth the reservation made by Islam in order that divorce should be resorted to only in case of strong and serious aversion. Islam, in principle, has made the strictest reservations on this subject with regard to wives with whom the husbands have consummated the marriage. In their case they must be divorced not only once, but three times. The reason for this is that if the man wished to divorce his wife with whom he has consummated the marriage he does so; however, the marriage relationship does not cease solely because of the divorce, for he retains the right to take her back during the period of the 'idda. During this time he may take her back merely by making a verbal declaration to that effect and without making a new contract or paying a new bride-price. If he takes her back during this period, married life between them continues as if nothing had happened. However, this divorce is charged against his account as a caution against his divorcing her a second time. If the allotted time of at least three months passes without his taking his wife back, the marriage relationship is severed, for his failure to take her back during this long period and the fact that such action would cost him nothing while divorce would cost him much, indicated that he strongly detests her and that no proper wedded life is possible between them so long as such detestation exists.

Even so, they may take up a new married life by concluding a new contract and by his paying a new bride-price. If he divorces her after having taken her back during the 'idda, or by having made a marriage contract with her if the 'idda has expired, it is counted as a second divorce and the regulations which govern it are exactly the same as those governing the first divorce. But if he divorces her for the third time, the marriage relationship is severed by the divorce itself. He is not permitted to marry her again until she has taken another husband and has lived with him as a wife. If she and her new husband then part for any reason, the first husband may then re-marry her.

The above are restrictions on divorce in cases of strong aversion. There are also temporary restrictions to divorce on the same grounds. A husband may not divorce his wife during her menstrual period, since the husband usually does not have intercourse with his wife at that time. He can divorce her only after she has finished menstruating, and on condition that he has not subsequently had intercourse with her before the following menstrual period, for his failure to have intercourse with her while she is clean indicates that an aversion exists, while his having intercourse with her indicates that he accepts her and thus divorce cannot take place.

Divorce exists in three degrees. The first is revocable divorce (al-ṭalāq al-raj'ī), which means that the husband can take his wife back during the period of the 'idda. The first and the second divorce apply to a wife who has had intercourse with her husband; these two divorces do not terminate married life but are a warning of severance. The second degree, clear divorce of the lesser separation (*al-ṭalāq al-bā'in baynūnatan ṣughra*), applies to the divorce of a wife with whom the husband has not had intercourse; to the divorce of a wife with whom the husband has had intercourse if the divorce takes place in consideration of a payment by which he redeems himself from her; and to the type of revocable divorce in which the 'idda has expired. In the case of this type of divorce the two parties can take up married life anew by concluding a new contract and by the husband's paying a new bride-price.

The third category of divorce is manifest divorce of the greater separation (al-bā'in baynūnatan kubra). This is divorce which is fulfilled by three repudiations. In this case the husband can marry the wife again only after she has lived as a wife with another man under a valid contract which has stipulated that the union was to be permanent at the time the contract was made.

A divorce granted by the qāḍī at the request of the woman belongs to the first category if it is granted for non-support; such is the view of the school of Mālik. This is contrary to the opinion of al-Shāfi'ī and Aḥmad ibn Ḥanbal, who hold that it belongs to the second category: (1) if it is due to a deep-seated and long-standing or permanent defect in the husband and if the woman cannot live with him without injury, as in the case of his being insane or suffering from elephantiasis, leprosy, or impotence; (2) if it is because of injury done by the husband to his wife, such as injuring her by treating her in a way not proper to one of her status, or by remaining absent from her for a year or more even though he leaves her money sufficient for her expenses. In such a case, if she seeks a divorce and the qāḍī grants it, it is a clear divorce (ṭalāq bā'in).

THE 'IDDA

This is the period for which the woman must wait before marrying again whether in the event of divorce or death. The reason in the case of divorce is to ascertain whether the woman is pregnant and to provide an opportunity for him who has divorced his wife to take her back. In the case of death, it is both to ascertain whether the woman is pregnant and to provide a period of mourning for the deceased husband.

In the event of divorce the 'idda is necessary only if intercourse has taken place or its equivalent, such as the woman's having been secluded with someone who could make it the equivalent of intercourse. In case of the death of the husband, the 'idda is necessary whether or not intercourse has taken place, since the mourning makes such a period of waiting mandatory.

The 'idda comes to an end with the termination of pregnancy if the wife was pregnant at the time of her divorce or her husband's death. If she was not pregnant, then the 'idda, in case of death, is four months and ten days. The period has been given this length of time because in such a time pregnancy would become perceptible; if it has not appeared when this period of time has passed then the 'idda is considered to be terminated. It is also the period of time which is sufficient for the mourning. In the event of divorce, the 'idda, according to some jurists, runs for three menstrual periods. This applies to women who are in the age of menstruation. The period of time is so fixed in order that it can be ascertained whether the wife is pregnant, one menstrual period not being sufficient; and in the case of revocable divorce, both to give the husband sufficient opportunity to take the wife back and to ascertain whether she is pregnant.

If the divorced woman is not of such an age as to be menstruating, then her 'idda lasts for three months, since most women menstruate monthly and a month is equivalent to one menstrual period.

Whether the 'idda is reckoned according to the menstrual periods or the intervals between them, it is the woman who announces the end of the 'idda and her word must be accepted. Some women deny having menstruated in order to extend the period of the 'idda if during it they are being supported by the husbands who had divorced them. Therefore, some of the imāms have dealt with the situation and some jurists have set the maximum length of the 'idda at one lunar year, while the Mālikīs have made it a solar year (sana bayḍā'). If she sees him again she waits another year; the upper limit is three years, but the term can be extended beyond that to five years. This is because the period of suckling is reckoned only if the woman was nursing at the time of her divorce; the limit to the period of suckling is two years.

The wife in a state of 'idda has a claim to being supported by him who is divorcing her if she is in 'idda because of divorce. The cost of support is determined in exactly the same manner as during marriage, whether it is a case of revocable or irrevocable divorce. The Shāfi'īs, on the other hand, do not provide for the support of a woman in 'idda following irrevocable divorce unless she is pregnant.

A woman who is in 'idda following the death of her husband does not receive support, for support was the duty of the husband who died. If he has left some property, then she inherits a part of it, as we shall explain.

THE RIGHTS OF CHILDREN

The rights of children are fixed from the time of birth. Some of these are related to the father, some to both parents, and some to the mother. The first right is the establishment of the child's paternity, followed by the right to food, upbringing, care for the child and his possessions, and, finally, support.

THE ESTABLISHMENT OF KINSHIP

In Islamic law the provisions governing the establishment of paternity are based on four principles. The first principle is that a valid marriage contract in itself establishes the paternity of the child. If the wife bears a child and if it is uncertain whether she was carrying the child before the marriage contract was made, then its paternity is established as belonging to the husband. The Ḥanafīs do not make it a condition that the two spouses must have come together after the marriage, but hold that a child's paternity is fixed even though the two spouses have never come together and even if such coming-together had been impossible. But Aḥmad ibn Ḥanbal, al-Shāfi'ī, and Mālik have voiced the opinion that a valid marriage contract is a cause for the fixing of paternity if a coming-together had been possible; if it is established that a coming-together was not possible, then the paternity is not fixed. Ibn Taymiyya stated a view, which is also said to be one handed down from Aḥmad ibn Ḥanbal, that the existence of the marriage contract is cause for the determination of paternity only in the event that the marriage has actually been consummated; in this view a mere coming together or the possibility thereof is not sufficient.

As a second principle, the jurists consider that the minimum age for a child to be born alive and properly formed, so that it may inherit, be inherited from, and be possessed of rights, is six lunar months. If a married woman bears a child less than six months after her marriage, then its paternity is not attributed to the husband, since she was undoubtedly carrying the child before her marriage. However, the husband may claim the child and declare that it is his, on condition that he does not state that it was the product of fornication.

The jurists differ regarding the maximum period of pregnancy. Some of them say that it is two years, some four years, and some five years. The Zāhirīs say that it is nine months; some of the Mālikīs say that it is a year, which is perhaps the median figure. It is noted that it is necessary to exercise as much care as possible to fix the legitimacy of the child; this is in the child's interest in order that its paternity may not be denied while the marriage is in force, unless the wife gives birth to the child within a period shorter than that which is accepted. In the event that the paternity of the child is repudiated during 'idda, the safeguard is taken that it can be repudiated only if the wife has borne the child after the maximum period accepted for pregnancy. In the case of a child born to a wife in 'idda, the attribution of its paternity to the husband who divorced her or to her dead husband can be denied only if she has given birth to the child more than one year after the date of the divorce or the death of the husband; this is applicable among those who consider the maximum period of pregnancy to be a year.

The third principle concerns attribution of paternity. In the event of adultery, there is no attribution of paternity, for the Prophet said, "A child is to be attributed to the marriage bed; the adulterer is to be stoned." If a married woman has committed adultery the paternity of the child is not attributed to her partner in adultery; it is attributed to her husband unless he repudiates it, but the acceptance of such repudiation is hedged about with many restrictions and reservations.

The fourth principle is that acknowledgment fixes paternity. A husband who acknowledges a child to be his fixes his paternal relationship to the child on condition that: the paternity of the child is not already certain; the characteristics of the child are such that the husband could be its father; the child accepts him as his father, if the child is capable of forming an opinion, and does not state that he is illegitimate. If the child holds that he is illegitimate, then his paternity is not attributed to the husband since we have already said that adultery does not create an attribution of paternity; it requires the penalty of stoning.

Mālik adds another condition, namely, that kinship (qarīna) cannot be established on the basis of a false statement in an acknowledgment made by him who does the acknowledging, or his failure to state clearly a reasonable basis for his relationship to the child, such as the fact that he was a foundling; that the child's mother had been married to another man and that the child's paternity had not been established with regard to the previous husband; or that the child had been brought from a certain place and that the man making the acknowledgement had not been known to have been in that place.

SUCKLING

Suckling is the first feeding of the infant after it is born and for this reason it is one of the infant's primary rights; it is a right due him from his father and his mother. It is his mother's duty to suckle him, while it is his father's duty to provide the mother with the food, clothing, and shelter which she needs. The money which the husband spends on his wife for her support or which he gives her if she is in 'idda is sufficient for this purpose; but if the mother is not receiving such support owing to the interruption of the marriage relationship between her and the father, then it shall be the duty of the father to pay her a suckling allowance sufficient to meet all her aforementioned needs.

If the mother refuses to suckle her infant she is not forced to do so; the law cannot compel her unless the child will take no breast but hers, unless no other woman can be found to suckle him, or unless the child and the father are so poor that they cannot pay anyone else and there is no one to donate the money for this purpose. Mālik says that the mother can be compelled to suckle her child if she belongs to a class the women of which suckle their children; but if she belongs to a class the women of which do not suckle their children, then she does not have to suckle her child.

The father under any circumstances can give the child out to a wet-nurse who is not the child's mother. If a woman can be found who will nurse the child voluntarily, even though she is not a relative of the child, she is more suitable than the mother if the mother refuses to suckle the child except for payment.

The cost of suckling an infant is part of the expenses of its support. The expenses of a living child may be taken from its property. If the infant possesses property through gift, bequest, inheritance, or waqf, then the cost of suckling him, like all expenditure on him, may be taken from his property. If the infant has no property, then the cost of suckling him shall be borne by him whose duty it is to support the infant, namely, the father. If he has no father or if his father is unable to pay, then the infant shall be supported first by his grandfather and then by his other relatives, as we shall explain in the section dealing with the support of relatives.

UPBRINGING

There are three types of guardianship (wilāya) which are fixed for a child from the time of its birth: (1) the guardianship of upbringing (tarbiya), (2) the guardianship of education or the spiritual guardianship, and (3) the guardianship of its property if it has any.

The first phase of the first guardianship, which is called that of dependence (ḥiḍāna), is overseen by women and not by men. This is because at this stage of its life the child needs to be cared for by women and cannot do without them; it is therefore up to the mother to care for the child during the period of dependence. If the child has no mother or if it has one who is unfit to carry out this duty, the duty shall devolve upon those female relatives of the child whom it is forbidden to the child to marry. The relatives on the mother's side have priority over those on the father's side; the mother's mother is preferable to the father's mother, the mother's sister is preferable to the father's sister, and the maternal aunt has priority over the paternal aunt. In sum, any relative on the mother's side has preference over her opposite number on the father's side, since the right originally belongs to the mother and so her relatives have priority over those of the father if they are of the same degree.

The condition is made that the woman who takes care of the child during the period of dependency shall be of sound mind, trustworthy, capable of looking after the child, that she shall not be distracted by other activity from caring for the child and looking after its upbringing, and that she should not take the child to live with one who is of a different religion (ajnabī) from the child. If the mother has been married to someone of a different religion than the child, then she is not fit to care for the child. Identity of religion between the child and the woman who takes care of it while it is dependent is a condition only if the child has reached the age of religious understanding or if she has tried to instruct the child in her religion in such a way as to give rise to fear for the religion of the child.

If the woman who is caring for the child during the period of dependence is not its mother, she shall not leave the town in which the child's father is living so that he can look after the child's upbringing and see it from time to time without difficulty. If the woman who is looking after the child during its period of dependence is the mother, then she is either living in the conjugal house if the marriage is being maintained or is supported by the father. Otherwise, the woman may take the child to her own town where she was married to the father, because since he chose this place where her family resided for the marriage it signifies that he is agreeable to her residing in it with his child.

The woman who is looking after the child during its period of dependence has the right to remuneration for her services except if the father has been supporting the mother either during the period of marriage or of 'idda. If a woman is found who will donate her services and the mother will be satisfied only with remuneration, the former shall not have priority over the mother unless the remuneration would be made from the child's property or if the father is unable to pay the remuneration while she who donates her services is one of those relatives who are qualified to take care of the child during the period of its dependence.

Remuneration for taking care of the child during the period of its dependence is to be paid from the child's property if he has any. If he has none, then the remuneration shall be paid either from the father's property or from that of those relatives whose duty it is to pay it in case the child's father is unable to pay or is dead.

The age at which the period of dependence terminates has been fixed by some jurists at seven years for a male child and nine years for a female child. Other jurists have fixed it at nine years for a boy and eleven years for a girl. Certain jurists have not set any age limit, but have left it at the age when the child can do without women's help, dress and feed himself, and look after his household affairs himself.

Care during the period of dependence is a right which belongs to the child, and the father and the mother may not agree to abrogate it. If they do so the agreement is invalid, and if the woman should agree to relinquish her right and then should demand it back, her request would be granted.

However, if the father and mother have agreed that a girl should remain in her mother's hands until she is fifteen years of age, the agreement is permissible and binding, since certain jurists have decreed that the period of dependence extends up to that age; furthermore, there is no harm done to the girl if she remains in her mother's care until puberty so that she can learn what it is customary for women to know. But this kind of an agreement cannot be made in the case of a male child, for after the age of dependence he needs to learn what it is customary for men to know.

THE SPIRITUAL AND PROPERTY GUARDIANSHIP OF THE CHILD

When the child has passed the age of dependence his spiritual guardianship is exercised by his spiritual guardian. This is a relative on his father's side and may be his father, his father's father and his ascendants, and then the grandfather's full brothers; or it may descend either from the father to his sons and then to his full paternal uncles, or go from a father to his sons and their sons, and in this way to every male relative who in descent is not separated from the child by the interposition of a female relative.

The spiritual guardian of the child looks after his upbringing until the age of puberty. If a male child reaches this age sound in mind the spiritual guardianship is terminated and the child becomes free unless when he reaches puberty he is not responsible for himself. For example, if it is observed that he conducts himself in such a way that it would give rise to fear if he were given his freedom.

In the case of a female child, she remains under the guardian as long as she remains a virgin, except if she either gets to be an old maid (i.e., if she reaches the age of say thirty years and is still a virgin) or acquires a mind of her own and understanding, when she may manage her own affairs. If she marries, the spiritual guardianship over her ceases completely; if she is subsequently divorced her guardian can take charge of her to ward off dishonor from himself and his family, except in cases where it is feared that she might be the cause of trouble after her divorce.

The age of puberty in Muslim law is generally considered to be fifteen lunar years in the case of both boys and girls.

The guardianship over the child's property cannot be exercised by all of those who can exercise the spiritual guardianship.

The former is assigned to the father and then to whomever the father appoints as guardian thereof after himself; then to whomever the grandfather appoints thereto after himself; and then to the qāḍī, who appoints someone to be responsible for the property of orphans.

If the property guardianship devolves upon the father, then no one exercises any check on him unless his actions reveal lack of foresight, bad conduct, and untrustworthiness. In such a case the qāḍī intervenes either by dismissing the father if he gives rise to fears for the child's property, or by restraining his behavior to bring it in line with the child's interests.

In the case of guardians other than the father, their authority is restricted to whatever is in the child's interest. The qāḍī may intervene at any time to check the expenditures made by such persons.

The age at which the guardianship over a child's property ends is the aforementioned age of puberty. But this guardianship over the property does not terminate solely because of the child's attaining this age; he must also give evidence of his maturity, i.e., the appearance of financial sense and his ability to manage his property. For there is a Qur'ānic provision which says: "If you have perceived that they are of mature understanding, then hand their property over to them."[1] Because of the complexity of business affairs in this day and age, because of the long period taken up by schooling, and because of the wide range of economic systems, some of the Muslim countries, such as Egypt, have deemed it advisable that the termination of the property trusteeship should take place when the child has reached the age of twenty-one solar years, for in this day and age mature financial sense is not attained before this age; even so, the condition was made that this did not apply to a mentally deficient person who might squander his property.

It is noted that there is no difference between a girl and a boy so far as property guardianship is concerned. A girl must manage her property just as a boy does if she reaches the age of discretion and has no one to supervise her.

THE SUPPORT OF MINORS

A minor is to be supported from his own property if he has any. If a child has property which has come to him by gift, inheritance, bequest, or endowment, then he shall be supported from this property. If he has no property, then he shall be supported by his father; no one, not even the child's mother, even though she be

[1] Q. IV, 5.

wealthy, may assist the father in supporting the child; for the mother's property is entirely separate from that of her husband and marriage is not a financial partnership between the two. If the child has no father then he is to be supported by his relatives. We shall explain this when we deal with the support of relatives under the financial organization of the family.

THE FINANCIAL ORGANIZATION OF THE FAMILY

In Islam, the term "family" (usra) includes the husband and wife, the children, the ascendants of the married pair, and all relatives, including the collateral ones (ḥawāshī), in addition to brothers and sisters. Paternal uncles and aunts are reckoned as belonging to the family, likewise maternal uncles and their children, since even though they are connected through the female side of the family they have moral and material rights and therefore belong to the family.

Within the family in this broad and general meaning, Islam created property relationships which make the family a cooperative economic and social unit. This mutual financial assistance may be summarized under three headings:

(1) If a member of the family commits a crime expiable by an appropriate financial penalty, the latter is to be paid by the blood-related members of the family ('āqila). These are a person's relatives who belong to the same clan ('aṣaba), i.e., the relatives who are related to him on the male side, such as sons and fathers, paternal uncles and full brothers or brothers by the same father, children of paternal uncles, and children of brothers. The initial responsibility for this duty falls upon the closest of these relatives, which means the one who stands closest in line of inheritance, as we shall explain later.

(2) The duty of supporting a poor relative falls upon his wealthy relative, no matter what his degree of relationship may be. The closest relative, however, has priority, i.e., the closest one in the line of inheritance as we shall explain below.

(3) Inheritance devolves upon all relatives, although priority goes to those who are closest in degree and strength of relationship, save that priority cannot be transferred from the closest relative to someone else unless the former does not exist.

The first of these headings is connected with penal law. We shall therefore give a summary explanation only of the other two headings.

THE SUPPORT OF RELATIVES

The jurists are agreed that relationship is one of the grounds which makes it encumbent on a wealthy or income-earning relative to support a relative who is unable to earn his living. The jurists, however, differ on the limits of the degree of relationship which requires support of a relative. Mālik and al-Shāfiʿī restrict it, while Abū Ḥanīfa and Aḥmad ibn Ḥanbal have made it broader. Mālik holds that the support of relatives refers only to one's children without extending to their descendants, and to one's parents but not including their ascendants. Al-Shāfiʿī opens the door a little wider and makes the support of relatives cover all descendants whatsoever if they are poor and unable to earn their living; according to him, this applies also to ascendants on both the father's and the mother's side, of whatever degree, if they are poor.

Abū Ḥanīfa is much more liberal. According to him, the relatives whom one must support include those whom one is prohibited from marrying, i.e., if one of the two relatives were a female the other would be prohibited from marrying her. This applies to ascendants, descendants, and collateral relatives and there is no difference between the relatives on the father's side and those on the mother's side. The order of preference goes according to the order of inheritance when there are a number of persons who are obliged to provide support.

However, Abū Ḥanīfa and his followers make a distinction between relationship by birth, or the relationship of descendants and ascendants, and collateral relationship. In the case of the latter, the necessity of providing support is conditional by identity of religion; but the father's supporting his son and the grandfather's supporting his grandson and vice-versa must be carried out when needed even though there may be a difference in religion; a non-Muslim father must be supported by his Muslim son.

The Ḥanbalī school maintains that support devolves according to the order of inheritance; he who inherits from another when he dies must support him if he is in need of it in accordance with the principle of law that "loss is according to gain," and that benefits are mutual. It does not provide that it is necessary to support relatives whom one is prohibited from marrying; according to Aḥmad ibn Ḥanbal one cousin must support another since they inherit from each other. But according to Abū Ḥanīfa, this is not obligatory, since even though they inherit from each other there is no prohibited degree of marriage between them, for a male cousin may marry his female cousin, and if one of the two relatives involved is a female she is not prohibited from marrying the other.

In the case of one relative's supporting another, the condition is made that he who seeks such support must be in need. Since it is the duty of descendants to support their ascendants, it is sufficient for the ascendant to be poor. This applies also even if the ascendant is able to earn his livelihood but does not do so in fact, since the kindness to one's father and mother which Islam demands makes it incumbent upon the descendant to make every effort on their behalf; also, whatever he earns is a gain for them also. In the case of relatives other than these, they must not only be poor but unable to earn their livelihood.

The condition is made that he to whom a request for support is addressed must be earning his living and must have something left over from his own needs. However, if he who requests support is one of a son's parents, the son is obliged to take him into his own household if he does not have a surplus sufficient to support the two of them separately.

THE DISTRIBUTION OF THE ESTATE AFTER DEATH

The property which a person owns in life reverts to his family after his death. This is because the life of the family is considered to be an extension of his life, because the benefits in the family are mutual, and because cooperation between the members is an established thing which is made a duty by Islam.

Ownership of property resulting from death is called "ownership by succession" (al-milkiyya bil-khilāfa). In Islamic law succession is of two kinds: optional succession (khilāfa ikhtiyāriyya) and compulsory succession (khilāfa ijbāriyya).

Optional succession may stem from the bequest (waṣiyya); it is optional on the part of both him who makes the bequest and him who is the beneficiary. He who makes the bequest can make it or not as he pleases, while the beneficiary is free either to accept or reject it. The amount of the bequest is limited to one-third of the property owned by a person when he dies.

Compulsory succession is that which follows from inheritance prescribed by law. This is because if there has been a bequest, the law allotted fixed proportions of two-thirds of the property to the spouse and the relatives and fixed proportions of the whole if no bequest was made. Everything is established according to a known proportion and by fixed degrees. Property ownership which occurs through this type of successorship is compulsory; no one has any choice in the matter, for the owner cannot choose one inheritor in preference to another nor can he alter the shares of two-thirds of his property after payment of the dues connected with the estate.

The ownership of the property is compulsorily added to the property of the inheritor and does not depend on his acceptance thereof. For this reason the Muslim jurists maintain that nothing accrues to a person's property compulsorily except an inheritance, for one cannot refuse it.

According to the sharīʿa, property ownership by inheritance does not entail any obligations, since the debts which were owed by him who left the inheritance are not passed on to him who inherits from him but devolve upon the former's property. If there are any prior commitments they must be fulfilled; if there are none, then there is no obligation upon the inheritor. There is therefore no need for him to accept it since there is no loss which would impel him to refuse it; indeed, an inheritance is profit in which there is no loss.

The law provides that two-thirds of the property should be distributed among the family and not left to one inheritor in order that the unity of the family might be maintained. For if he who left the inheritance were charged with the distribution he would tend to favor him whom he liked most and hostility might result; furthermore, whatever he might give, even though it might be just, might not be well received by him who was given nothing. Such hostility might break up the unity of the family. But if the division is prescribed by law, then no one can resent it even though his share might be a small one.

CLAIMS CONNECTED WITH THE ESTATE

There are three categories of claims against the estate: (1) the obligations contracted by the deceased, particularly the obligations connected with certain portions of his property; (2) his preparation for burial and putting him in a winding-sheet; and (3) the successorship to his property by bequest and inheritance.

According to the majority of jurists, the expenses of preparing the deceased for burial and winding the body in a sheet have precedence over any debts which the deceased may have contracted, since it is similar to the expense of supporting him; it therefore takes precedence over debts relating to property, such as pledged property, property which has a lien against it (thubita ʿalayha haqq ikhtiṣāṣ), and the like. But the Ḥanbalī school gives preparation of the body and winding it in its sheet precedence over all other claims.

The other two claims are the claim of creditors for personal debts and the claim of the successors by compulsory successorship. These two claims are related to the estate not merely from the time of death, but from the time of the illness which leads to death or which is connected with death. In the terminology of the Muslim jurists this is called the "death sickness" (maraḍ al-mawt); it is the illness which it is generally feared will lead to death and which is connected with death in fact.

From the time of the last illness these claims are attached to the property and not only to the conscience of the individual. This is because of the fear that the ill person might dispose of his property in such a way as to injure the creditors, who might not be able to recover their claims after his death if their claims are attached to his conscience and not to his property; it is because of the fear also that he might injure the heirs by giving his property away to others, thereby depriving the heirs of all or part of their inheritance.

For this reason the creditors and heirs may prevent the execution of actions which are injurious to them if the person who has undertaken such injurious action dies from his illness.

An action is deemed to be injurious to the creditors if it affects his capital. Any gift which might result in non-satisfaction of the creditors' claims can be made contingent on release from or payment of the debt. Likewise, any sale at a loss, however small, can be voided by the creditors if its execution would result in the loss of some of their rights; this is self-evident in the case of an estate heavily burdened with debt. In the case of property which is not so burdened the creditors have a right only to the payment of their claims. Any remaining dispositions are to be carried out as long as they do not affect the right which stands next to that of the creditors, namely, the right of those who by compulsory succession succeed to two-thirds of the property remaining after the payment of debts.

All gifts, whether open or made by a disposition of capital, such as sale at an excessively low price, can be paid only from the third set aside for bequests, with which they compete. This is to prevent the two-thirds of the property reserved for the heirs from being given away.

Dispositions which are subject to restriction are those in which there is involved a loss, of whatever size; this applies to estates burdened with debt. As for dispositions involving excessive loss, even if the estate is not so burdened and gifts made from it are only token ones, they still are related to the substance of the property. But dispositions made from the increase from such property is under no restriction and they cannot be challenged after a person's death.

It is noted, however, that the contracting of a debt is subject to restriction. If an ill person contracts a debt, such debt can be collected following his death only after the satisfaction of other debts which were either contracted before his illness or were contracted during his illness without its being understood that he was in his last illness. Such debts contracted only with the recognition that a person is ill are called debts of illness, while the others are called debts of health; the former are not paid until the latter have been satisfied.

Such is the relationship of claims to death sickness. The purpose here is to safeguard what is due to the creditors and the heirs after death and it does not interfere with any disposition which the ill person makes before his death. Protest is made after death if it is decided that the deceased's dispositions were made during his death sickness and were actually injurious to the right of the creditors to collect their claims and to the right of the heirs to two-thirds of the balance of the estate after payment of debts.

After death, debts secured by parts of the property and contracted before death, such as a debt secured by a pledge, are paid by selling the part of the property in question and settling the obligation. Whatever portion of the property is left is devoted to those debts which are not capable of being settled in this fashion; from it are paid first the debts contracted before the deceased's last illness (duyūn al-siḥḥa) and then those contracted during his death sickness (duyūn al-maraḍ).

It is noted that debts of the deceased which had been deferred become due upon death. Most jurists hold that the deferment is terminated since it was a personal right of the deceased and has terminated with the extinction of his person; it is also because of the fear that the property might be distributed and the debt become uncollectable. Also, they hold that the deferment becomes an injury to the heirs if they are prevented from profiting by their right until the debts are satisfied.

The Ḥanbalī jurists maintain that if the heirs so request, deferred debts do not fall due at the time of death provided that the heirs provide security to guarantee satisfaction of the debt when it falls due. If they do not provide such security, deferred debts become due by necessity.

COMPULSORY SUCCESSION

We have said that the right to compulsory succession begins from the onset of the death sickness. But ownership begins only from the time of death; does it, then, begin with death itself? If the property is not subject to debt, ownership of the total property begins with death itself if there have not been any bequests (waṣāyā) or in case provisions other than bequests have been made, if they fall within the scope of the third reserved for this purpose. Anything in excess of this third cannot be executed.

There are two schools of thought regarding the matter of estates which are subject to debt. The Ḥanafī and Mālikī jurists hold that the ownership of the heirs is confirmed with regard to that part of the estate not under debt. If the estate is burdened with debt they have no ownership at all over it; its ownership remains an obligation upon the deceased, for the latter's obligation persists until his debts are paid and his bequests have been executed. If the property is under debt but not burdened with it, the heirs' ownership is confirmed over that portion which is in excess of the amount of the debt and which is held in common ('ala al-shuyū'). The other school is that of Shāfi'ī and Aḥmad ibn Ḥanbal, which holds that even if the estate is burdened with debt, the ownership of the estate passes to the heirs. The debts, however, remain attached to the property and the creditors can request that it be sold to satisfy their claims.

As a consequence of this difference between these two schools there has arisen a difference in practice. According to the second school the increment goes to the heirs, but they are also responsible for the expenditures, since increment is the benefit derived from ownership and expenditures are the responsibility of the owner. According to the first school, increase is a consequence of ownership. If the ownership is divided between the deceased and the heirs, the increase forms part of the whole estate; likewise, if the entire ownership was in the hands of the deceased, as in the event that the estate is burdened with debt the increase belongs to the estate and the expenditures of the estate must be met from the estate itself.

The liquidation of claims against an estate is carried out by the executor (al-waṣī) appointed by the testator (mūrith). If there is no executor and the property is burdened with debt, an executor is appointed by the qāḍī. If the qāḍī appoints one of the heirs, the latter cannot refuse to serve. If the estate is not burdened with debt and there is no executor, the liquidation of claims against the property is carried out by the heirs themselves. In case the heirs refuse to pay the claims, the qāḍī may appoint someone to assist the creditors.

When the claims against the estate have been paid, the heirs can then either divide the property among themselves or, if they wish, leave it to be held in common as a property held in joint tenancy (ka-sha'n kull al-shurakā'). If some of them injure the others, the wronged party can have recourse to the courts and either appoint someone to divide the property or take over his share himself.

CONDITIONS OF INHERITANCE

There are three conditions attached to the transmittal of property by inheritance (tawrīth): (1) The death of the decedent either in fact or by legal decision. In the latter case, if a person disappears the qāḍī issues a decision declaring him to be dead according to the available evidence, and his property passes to his heirs. (2) It must be established that the inheritor is alive after the decedent has died. If this has not been ascertained, the majority of jurists hold that the inheritance is not confirmed. Therefore, if a father and his son both die accidentally by drowning, fire, destruction, or the like, neither inherits from the other, according to the opinion of most Muslim jurists, since there is no assurance that one of them survived the other. (3) There must be no barrier to inheritance, for the existence of such a barrier makes the inheritor ineligible for an inheritance.

There are two impediments to inheritance upon which all jurists are agreed: (1) homicide and (2) difference in religion. A third impediment, not agreed upon by all, is difference in nationality or country of residence.

The jurists are agreed that the killing of the decedent by the inheritor deprives the latter from inheritance, on the basis of a ḥadīth which says that "the killer shall not inherit"; however, there is a difference of opinion on this matter. Al-Shāfi'ī regards all killing as an impediment, even if it is justified by self-defense or is a punishment carried out by order of a court. Aḥmad ibn Ḥanbal decreed that the killing which acts as an impediment is that which is punishable either by fine or otherwise, for the punishment is evidence of blame; therefore, a judicial ('qaḍā'iyya) punishment is added to the legal (qānūniyya) punishment, and this is deprivation of inheritance. Abū Ḥanīfa held that the killing which constitutes an impediment is direct killing, either intentional or accidental. If it is not direct then it is not an impediment.

Mālik holds that the homicide which is regarded as an impediment must be a premeditated attack, whether it is carried out in partnership with someone else, caused by any means, or done by a false witness whose testimony leads to the decedent's being sentenced to death.

The majority of Muslim jurists hold that a Muslim cannot inherit from a non-Muslim and vice-versa. Even though a Muslim be married to a Christian woman, she cannot inherit from him if he dies and he cannot inherit from her if she dies. Each of them, however, can leave a bequest to the other; under such circumstances optional succession takes the place of compulsory succession. However, according to the provisions of Islam a Jew can inherit from a Christian; difference in religion is a barrier only if one of the parties leaving or receiving the inheritance is a Muslim.

At the present day difference in country of residence is called difference in nationality. Difference in nationality does not affect inheritance among Muslims, for one Muslim inherits from another Muslim no matter what their nationalities may be. If a Muslim is an American citizen he can inherit from a Muslim who is an Egyptian citizen.

In the case of inheritance between non-Muslims, if both the inheritor and the decedent are citizens of a state which is Muslim or largely Muslim then one can inherit from the other. Even if a Christian were a Turkish citizen and a Christian relative of his who was an Egyptian citizen died, he would inherit from him; for even though the two states are under different control they are considered as one state in Islamic law, as the Islamic State is a universal state.

Difference in nationality is a barrier only if one of the parties owes allegiance to a non-Muslim state. In case of difference of nationality one of the parties can inherit from the other only if both are non-Muslims.

INHERITANCE BETWEEN SPOUSES

Inheritance by marital status is the inheriting of a husband from his wife and vice-versa. The wife is entitled to a quarter of what her husband leaves if he has no descendants between whom and the husband there is no intervening female relative, e.g., a son, the son of a son, or the daughter of a son. If the husband has descendants of the aforementioned type who inherit from him, then the wife receives an eighth of the inheritance.

The husband is entitled to half of what his wife leaves if there are no descendants as just mentioned who inherit from her. If she has such descendants who inherit, then he gets a quarter.

The inheritance of spouses is provided by the Qur'ān. This inheritance is the share of the two spouses if there are relatives who are descendants or of the collateral category. If there are no relatives, the preferred view, according to Islamic law, is that all of the property goes to one of the spouses. Against this is the opinion that the inheritance goes to the public treasury, or the general treasury of the state.

THE INHERITANCE OF RELATIVES

Relatives are of three categories so far as inheritance is concerned: (1) Relatives who possess the right to an assured share (aṣḥāb al-furūḍ). These are those who have shares, such as a third or a sixth, assured by the Qur'ān just as it has assured the share of the two spouses. (2) Agnate relatives, who are a man's male relatives and under certain circumstances their womenfolk as well, between whom and the deceased there does not intervene a female of any degree of relationship. These do not take a fixed amount, but receive what is left over after those who have a right to an assured share have taken it. (3) Cognate relatives include paternal aunts, maternal aunts and uncles, the daughters of a brother, and the daughters of a paternal uncle.

Those entitled to an assured share, including one of the two spouses, take theirs first; then the agnate relatives take their share, and finally the cognate relatives. The last receive something only if there are no relatives entitled to an assured share or no agnate relatives, for they stand at the bottom of the list.

The precedence of those entitled to an assured share over the agnate relatives is not an inherent one, since logical procedure requires that the assured shares should be given out first. However, certain agnate relatives come before some of those who are entitled to an assured share: a son comes before full sisters either of the father or of the mother, and certain of those entitled to an assured share may also be agnate relatives under certain circumstances. Sometimes one inheritor may be entitled both to an assured share and at the same time the share of an agnate relative, in which case he takes what is due to both.

Those Entitled to an Assured Share (aṣḥāb al-furūḍ)

Those relatives who are entitled to an assured share are the father; the mother; the daughter; the daughter of the son; the full sister; sisters of the father or the mother; and the grandfather who in line of relationship is not separated from the deceased by a female; the grandmother on that basis; and the mother's brother.

The daughter. An only daughter takes half if there is no son or daughter beside her. Two or more daughters take two-thirds if there are no sons. If there are one or more sons in addition to the daughter or daughters, then all of them are agnates who get what is left over, each male getting twice as much as each female. The daughter or daughters then become agnates who are not entitled to an assured share. This manner of inheriting is fixed by the Qur'ān.

The daughter of a son. Here there are various categories. The closest are the daughters of the son, followed by the daughters of the son's son and those who are further removed. They are all called "daughters of the son"provided that no female intervenes in their relationship to the deceased. Thus, the daughter of a daughter of the son is not considered as a daughter of the son.

The only daughter of the son is entitled to half if there is no daughter of the father (bint ṣulbiyya) or daughter of the son or no son or son of a son who is more closely related than she.

If there is more than the daughter of a son in one category and if there is no daughter or daughter of a son or no son who is more closely related, then they take two-thirds regardless of how many of them there may be.

The above holds true if they have no son's son in their category. If they do, then they are not entitled to an assured share; they are agnates and the male receives as much as two females. In this case and in the two preceding cases the inheritance of the daughter is fixed by analogy, or on the basis that the daughter of the son is considered as a daughter since the daughter does not exist.

If there is an only daughter she is entitled to a half. If there is the daughter of a son, she takes a sixth, since the share of the daughters as a whole is two-thirds, the daughter takes half of the two-thirds and the rest of the two-thirds is taken by the daughter of the son. This is confirmed by a tradition of the Prophet.

The daughter of the son might not receive any of the inheritance. This could happen if there were a son, for he would cut her out; the same would happen if there were the son of a son more closely related than she. Again, she might not receive anything if there were two daughters taking the two-thirds and if there were no son's son in the same category as she or in one lower than hers. In the latter case she would be an agnate of his because of her need of him.

Inheritance by the father. The father takes one-sixth if there are sons or sons of sons not separated from the deceased by a female in line of descent. He also takes a sixth along with any surplus by virtue of being an agnate ('aṣaba), if the deceased has a female descendant who inherits and who in line of descent is not separated from the deceased by a female. He takes a sixth at first since he is one of those entitled to an assured share; then as an agnate he receives what is left over from the share of the daughters or the son's daughters.

If the deceased has no offspring who is an heir and who in descent is not separated from the deceased by a female, then the father is only an agnate who takes what is left; he is not among those who are entitled to an assured share. This position of the father is fixed by the Qur'ān, either explicitly in the text or by deduction from it.

Inheritance by the mother. The mother takes a third if the deceased has no offspring who in descent is not separated from the deceased by a female, if there are not two or more full sisters or brothers either of the father or the mother, and if inheritance between the father and the mother and one of the spouses is not restricted. But if the inheritance between the father, the mother, and one of the spouses is restricted and if there exist none of the other relatives mentioned in the preceding sentence, then the mother gets a third of what is left after one of the two spouses has taken his share. If the heirs are a mother, a father, and a wife, then the wife gets a quarter, the mother gets a third of three-quarters, and the father gets the remainder.

The mother gets a sixth if the deceased has offspring not separated from him in descent by a female, or if there are two or more brothers or sisters. The portion of the inheritance which goes to the mother is clearly fixed by the Qur'ān and by deduction from the text.

Inheritance by a mother's brother or sister. An only brother or sister of a mother gets a sixth. If there are two or more, whether they are all males, all females, or mixed, they get a third provided that the female is on exactly the same level with the male.

In the case of a brother or sister of a mother, it is provided individually and collectively that there must exist no male ascendant who in descent is not separated from the deceased by a female and no descendant who in descent is not separated from the deceased by a female. If there are children, parents, or grandparents existing then they do not inherit.

Inheritance by a full sister. A full sister is entitled to a half if she has no other full sister or full brother and if she fulfills the conditions governing her title to the inheritance. If there are two or more full sisters and they have no full brother they get two-thirds. If there are one or more full brothers who have one or more full sisters, then all are agnates and the male gets as much as two females. If one or more full sisters have no full brothers, but if there is a daughter or the daughter of a son, then they are treated like agnates after the daughter or the daughter of the son has received the assured share to which she is entitled.

In the case of inheritance by full sisters, the condition is made that the father shall not be in existence and that there must be no male descendant not separated in descent by a female. Most of the subject of inheritance by full sisters is covered by the Qur'ān; the rules governing their inheriting along with a daughter and a son's daughter are derived from the Prophet as transmitted by 'Abd-Allah ibn Mas'ūd.

Inheritance by a father's sisters. They inherit on condition that there should exist no father, no male descendant who is an heir and who in descent is not separated from the deceased by a female, and no full brother. If there are no full sisters, then the father's sisters take their place and assume the position of full sisters so far as matters of inheritance are concerned. If a full sister is entitled to half, then a father's sister gets a sixth as long as there is no father's brother with whom she must share the remainder, the male receiving twice as much as the female. If there are two or more full sisters, then the father's sister is not entitled to anything unless there is a father's brother with whom she is an agnate.

Inheritance by a father's sister has been fixed by consensus of the Prophet's Companions. Brothers and sisters of a father, however, receive the share of the full brothers if the latter do not exist.

Inheritance by a grandfather. The grandfather who is reckoned among those entitled to a fixed share and among the agnates is called the "true grandfather" (al-jidd al-ṣaḥīḥ). Between him and the deceased no female is interposed in the line of descent as we have already described it. He inherits only if there is no father or grandfather more closely related than he. If there are no full brothers or full sisters or none of these by the same father, he assumes the position and all the attributes of the father. However, in the event that the inheritance is limited between him and the mother and one of the two spouses, the mother does not share with him in taking a third of what remains: she takes a third of the whole and not a third of the remainder.

In the case of a grandfather surviving with full brothers and sisters or brothers and sisters by the same father, the jurists are divided owing to the difference of opinion among the Companions of the Prophet. Abū Bakr considered him to be like a father in this respect, and that he cut the others out just as the father did; Abū Ḥanīfa was of the same opinion. Zayd ibn Thābit, who of all the Companions was the one best versed in the precepts of Islam, did not consider that the grandfather, like the father, cut out either full brothers and sisters or those by the same father; he held that they inherit together with the grandfather, except that he shared with them on the same basis as a full brother or a brother by the same father and that his share could not be reduced below a third. The same view is held by al-Shāfi'ī, Aḥmad ibn Ḥanbal, and Mālik, by Abū Yūsuf and Shaybānī from among the followers of Abū Ḥanīfa, as well as by many others. According to 'Alī ibn Abī Ṭālib, the son of the Prophet's paternal uncle, such brothers and sisters inherit on the same basis as the grandfather and he considers the latter to be like a brother when the brothers are agnate, on condition that his share should not be less than a sixth. Inheritance by the grandfather has been established by analogy, hence this difference of opinion.

Inheriting by the grandmother. The grandmother who inherits is the true grandmother, i.e., she who in descent is not separated from the deceased by a mother's father. She inherits on condition that there is no mother or no grandmother more closely related than she. She receives a sixth. If there is only one grandmother she takes all of the sixth; if there is more than one grandmother they share the sixth if they are of the same degree, such as the mother of a mother or the mother of a father, both of whom share in the sixth. Inheritance by the grandmother is determined by the interpretation (ijtihād) of the Companions of the Prophet. This was based on a tradition of the Prophet regarding her inheritance.

Such is the inheritance of those entitled to an assured share. They receive fixed shares on condition that there is no one who cuts them out. It is possible for these shares to become so numerous that they exceed the whole unity, in which case each share is diminished in accordance with its size. In order to ensure this the Muslim jurists employ a device known as 'awl (provision), according to which the fractions indicating the size of the shares are replaced by the common denominator of the smallest figure capable of being apportioned. They have divided each portion into shares, and if the number of shares exceeds the common denominator, then the portions are in excess of the amount in question. In such a case the estate is divided up according to the number of shares, and not according to the original division, each portion being diminished in proportion to its size.

For example, if the heirs are a husband, a mother, a full sister, and a sister by the same father and if the estate consisted of seventy-two units, then the portions would be: husband, one-half; full sister, one-half; sister by the same father, one-sixth; and mother, one-sixth. The common denominator is six; the husband gets three shares, the full sister three shares, the sister by the same father one share, and the mother one share. The total of this is eight, so the estate of seventy-two units is then divided into eight parts instead of six and each portion is decreased according to its size; thus one-sixth becomes one-eighth and one-half becomes three-eighths. If those entitled to an assured share do not take the whole estate and if there are no agnates, then the remainder reverts to those relatives entitled to an assured share according to the size of the share to which they are entitled.

Agnate Relatives

Agnates, who are male relatives of the deceased who in descent are not separated from him by a female, inherit what remains after those entitled to an assured share have received their due. Their inheritance has been fixed in a general way by the Prophet's saying, "What is left over from fixed commitments belongs to a man's relatives in the male line."

The jurists have divided agnates into four classes: (1) that of filiation, or descendants whose relationship is not broken by the interposition of a female; (2) that of fatherhood, or the father, the true grandfather and so on ascending; (3) that of fraternity, or male descendants of the father in whose line of relationship to him no female intervenes; and (4) that of the uncle, or similar descendants of the true grandfather.

If only one of these exists, he alone is entitled to the remainder. If there are a number of them, those belonging to the most closely related type have precedence. The filial type has precedence over the paternal type, which in turn has priority over the fraternal type except in the case of brothers inheriting along with the grandfather. The brothers have precedence over the paternal uncles; if there are a number of them of the same type then those who are of the closest degree of relationship have precedence. If they are all of the same degree and type then precedence is given to those who have the strongest bonds of kinship: the full brother has priority over a brother by the same father because of the strength of his relationship, which is on the side of both the father and the mother, while the other is on the side of the father only.

The basis of agnate relationship is that it runs in the male line. The only females who can be agnates are: (1) full sisters or sisters by the same father if there are either brothers or female descendants who inherit; (2) daughters and daughters of a son who have sons or sons of sons to give them agnate status.

Cognate Relatives (dhawū al-arḥām)

These are relatives who are not considered to be among those previously mentioned who have a title to an assured share; neither are they agnates. In their case the male gets twice the share of the female. Like the agnates they are of four classes: (1) Descendants of the deceased who are not among those entitled to an assured share and who are not agnates, such as a daughter's daughter or a daughter's son. (2) Ascendants of the deceased who are neither agnates nor among those entitled to an assured share, such as the father of the mother and the mother of the father of the mother. (3) Descendants of the parents who are neither agnates nor among those entitled to an assured share, such as the son of a mother's brother, the daughter of a full brother, and the son of a full sister. (4) Descendants of the grandparents who likewise are neither agnates nor of those entitled to an assured share as previously mentioned, such as a maternal aunt, a paternal aunt, the daughter of a paternal uncle and the daughter of a maternal uncle.

In the case of cognates, the male inherits twice as much as the female if the male and the female are in the same class and degree of relationship and if there is no preference between them; if there is such preference then one or the other of them takes it all.

When there are a number of them who are of varying types and degrees of relationship, the first class has precedence over the second, which then precedes the third, while the third has precedence over the fourth. When they are all of the same class, those who are closest in degree of relationship have precedence. If they are all of the same degree of relationship then precedence goes to him whose father is entitled to an assured share or whose father is an agnate as set forth in detail under the fourth class. If they are all equal in this respect they share alike, save that a male gets twice as much as a female.

It is to be noted that if there are no relatives whatsoever, the entire estate is disposed of through optional succession or by bequest. If there is no will then the property goes to the bayt al-māl, i.e., the public treasury.

OBSERVATIONS MADE BY ISLAM ON THE DISTRIBUTION OF THE ESTATE

(1) Islamic law provided that two-thirds of the estate of the deceased be reserved for purposes of inheritance, whether it is so desired by those involved or not. Also, the meaning of the term "family" has been enlarged to include both near and distant relatives, though the nearer relatives have been given preference over the more distant ones. (2) The law-maker observed the principle of distributing the property, not concentrating it, for only rarely is an heir found who is entitled to the entire property. (3) In the matter of the difference in the size of the portions, the law-maker has observed the principle of the heir's need of the property. For this reason the male is granted in most cases twice as much as the female, for the financial burdens of the family fall upon the men, not the women, since it is the man who works and toils to supply sustenance for his wife and children. Similarly, the children receive a larger share of the inheritance than the parents when they inherit together, for the children are usually helpless offspring whose life lies in the future while the parents are well along in it; the children's need for the property is therefore greater, for they are facing life and its obligations. (4) Islam puts relationship through the mother on the same level as relationship through the father, though the portions which they receive are different.

Hence, inheriting by uterine brothers was in the same degree as that by full brothers or brothers by the same father.

The amount of the property subject to optional succession is one-third of the estate after payment of debts. It is taken from the property after such debts have been paid and before the property is distributed to the heirs, even though they are actually of the same category.

The remaining third does not go entirely to bequests (waṣiyya), but gifts made during the last illness are subtracted from it as we have already mentioned. Even though such gifts are not bequests according to the law, they are governed by the same provisions as are bequests and so are payable only from the third of the estate set aside for such purposes. Such gifts are different in character from bequests, for the latter are disbursements made in addition to those occurring after death, while the former are disbursements which by their very nature must be made while a person is alive.

The making of a bequest is an optional act which a person may perform during his lifetime. He may revoke, change, or replace it until he dies and only those parts of it can be executed which he has continued to preserve up to the time of his death. The majority of jurists are agreed that the beneficiary is not compelled to take over property bequeathed to him and that he may refuse it.

In the event of acceptance, title to the property begins from the time of death, not from the time of acceptance. Therefore, from the time of the testator's death the increase of the property goes to the legatee as long as it is the increase of property belonging to him, though there is a slight difference of opinion on this point. Also, all expenses connected with the property are charged to the legatee in accordance with the principle that "loss goes with gain."

INVALID AND LIMITED BEQUESTS

Every bequest made by a person during his lifetime is valid and is executable after his death unless the motive behind his making the bequest was contrary to the law. Examples would be a bequest made by a man to his mistress in order to get her to continue to live with him in a state of sin, or a bequest dedicated solely to an object contrary to the spirit of religion, such as to a gambling house, a dance hall, etc. Otherwise bequests are valid. Bequests can be made to any relatives whether or not they are relatives in the eyes of Islam, so long as a non-Muslim person making the bequest considers them to be such.

All conditions laid down by the person making the bequest

are valid and binding so long as they do not lay any restriction on the legatee with regard to marriage or so long as they do not contain anything which is not in the legatee's interest, such as a condition that he should not marry a particular woman. Such a condition would be invalid; the bequest could be valid and executable, but the enforcement of such a condition would not be obligatory.

BEQUESTS TO HEIRS

Most of the jurists hold that a bequest may not be made to any of the heirs we have previously mentioned, if they are heirs in fact and are not cut off from the inheritance by the existence of someone who has priority over him, unless the other heirs give their permission. This is because it would be contrary to the division established by the law and it might create discord and hatred among the heirs. The Shī'ī jurists, however, or at any rate a good many of them, permit a bequest to an heir and consider it to be the same as one made to an outsider. For they hold that God has given to him who makes the bequest a third of his possessions to dispose of as he wishes after his death and that some of the heirs might be infirm and need more goods either because of their poverty, youth, or total incapacity to earn their own living. They therefore maintain that it is up to him who makes the bequest to bequeath such a person a portion of the third to be added to his share of the inheritance.

OBSTACLES TO THE EXECUTION OF A BEQUEST

Even though a bequest is valid, it cannot be executed and becomes invalid if the recipient of the bequest kills him who has made it, for in doing so he is bringing something about prematurely and is punished by being deprived of it. Some jurists hold that the bequest nevertheless may be sanctioned if the heirs so permit. However, Abū Yūsuf of the Ḥanafī School, maintained that the bequest is invalid, and that even if the heirs allow it it is essentially a gift and is subject to the same conditions as outright gifts.

Neither can a bequest be executed if there is involved a difference of nationality of the kind which acts as an impediment to inheritance.

A bequest can be executed even though a difference of religion is involved. A Muslim married to a Christian woman may leave her a bequest. If a person is a Muslim and has non-Muslim parents, he can leave them a bequest. Such a bequest would be executed since it is an act of piety, which is permissible under any circumstances without restriction.

CONFLICT OF BEQUESTS

If there are a number of bequests, one does not abrogate another unless it contains something which indicates a retraction of a preceding one and a modification of the bequest in accordance with the most recent one.

It is possible also that there might be so many bequests that they exceed the third of the estate set aside for such purposes. If the heirs do not agree to all of them, then the third is prorated among bequests. If one person has been bequeathed 1,000, another 500, and a third person a like amount, making a total of 2,000 while the value of the property is only 1,000, the 1,000 is divided in proportion to the amounts bequeathed to each one. Thus the person who had been bequeathed 1,000 would get 500 and each of the other two would receive 250.

Such is the procedure when the bequests have not been made for religious rites. If they have been made for religious rites performed during a person's lifetime, such as the payment of obligatory alms or requital for religious shortcomings, and the third of the estate is insufficient to cover them all, then the most necessary ones from a religious standpoint have precedence over the others.

MANDATORY BEQUESTS

We have said that all bequests belong to the category of optional succession, which depends on both the option of the original owner and on the option of him who succeeds to part of his property. However, if a person has poor relatives who are not heirs of his, Islamic law makes it mandatory for such a person to use his option to bequeath them some of his property. Islamic law holds that this is a religious obligation and that like all such obligations it should be performed by free choice. The necessity of this religious obligation is mentioned in the Qur'ān, which also indicates that the courts may intervene to rectify anything contrary to religion, in the event that unjust bequests have been made while others which are necessary have been neglected. Some of the 'ulamā interpret this to mean that if a bequest has been made to an outsider while there are relatives who are more deserving of the bequest, the qāḍī may transfer the bequest from the outsider to the former poor and infirm persons. Ibn Ḥazm, of the Ẓāhirī school, goes so far as to say that if a person has left no bequests and has infirm relatives who are not heirs, the qāḍī may take something from the estate after such person's death and give it to those of his poor relatives who need it most. This would be a bequest by supererogation for he had neglected something which was an obligation, thereby causing an injustice to someone who had a claim on him; the qāḍī would then have acted in his stead to remove the injustice from the injured party. Only daughters' children who belong to the first category have any claim to a bequest.

The share due if the claimant is deceased will go to his descendants, of whom the males receive twice as much as the females. The share which is due to each person in the first category goes to his descendants.

Whatever is given out in this way is given as a bequest, not as an inheritance. Therefore the mandatory amount must not exceed the third. If there are other bequests and the third is inadequate to cover both these and the mandatory bequest, the mandatory bequest is executed first and the remainder belongs to the recipients of optional bequests.

CHAPTER VII

Transactions in the Sharī'a

THIS CHAPTER discusses the rules governing transactions which are set forth in the sharī'a. A detailed treatment is not possible within the limited space of one chapter, particularly if the views of the various schools were given detailed treatment. Therefore, this discussion is confined to general principles relating to ownership, contracts, and procedure as laid down by the majority of Muslim jurists. Important controversial points, however, will be alluded to briefly. This chapter is arranged in several subdivisions which cover the various aspects of transactions in the following order: property and ownership, legal obligations in general, torts or unlawful acts, contracts, discharge of obligations, transfer of obligations, procedure, and evidence.

PROPERTY AND OWNERSHIP

The rules governing transactions and the dispositions and rights derived therefrom are concerned primarily with property and wealth. It is therefore necessary to define and classify property.

There are three attributes of property in Islamic law: (1) it must have some value; (2) it must be a thing the benefit of which is permitted; and (3) it must be possessed. The Ḥanafī jurists have added a fourth attribute of property, namely, capability of being held in reserve. It follows that not all things may be classified as property. Whatever is not possessed of value, such as a corpse or a free man, falls outside the definition of property. To Muslims, wine and pigs are not property with intrinsic value because their use is forbidden.[1] Things which are not amenable to possession, such as air, sun, and sea, are precluded from the definition of property, because they are freely permitted to all. Similarly, a fish while

1 Some jurists, such as Abū Ḥanīfa and Mālik, though not Shāfi'ī and Ibn Ḥanbal, consider that alcoholic drinks and pork are property to non-Muslims. See Sarakhsī, *al-Mabsūṭ*, Vol. 11, pp. 102-105; Ibn Ḥazm, *al-Muḥalla*, Vol. 8, no. 1288; Kharashī's commentary on Sidi Khalīl, Vol. 4, p. 351; Ṭabarī, *Ikhtilāf al-Fuqahā'*, p. 160; Ibn Qudāma al-Maqdisī, *al-Mughnī*, Vol. 5, p. 442.

in the sea is not of value, but when it is caught it becomes property as a result of possession.[2]

Article 126 of the Majalla embodies the fourth attribute of property prescribed by the Ḥanafī jurists. It reads: "Property consists of something for which human nature has a penchant, and which can be held in reserve until it is needed." Since they cannot be held in reserve, services are excluded from this definition. However, both al-Shāfi'ī and Ibn Ḥanbal differed from the Ḥanafī jurists in this regard, maintaining that services are property inasmuch as they possess monetary value,[3] and this view was adopted in Article 64 of the Ottoman Civil Procedure Code, which contained some amendments to the Majalla in this respect.

THE CLASSIFICATION OF PROPERTY

The following are the major categories of property as classified by Muslim jurists:

(1) Measurable and non-measurable. Measurable property is that which is measured in terms of volume, weight, number, or length. Non-measurable includes property of all other kinds.

(2) Fungible and infungible. Fungible property is that which can be readily purchased in the market at a generally uniform price, such as printed books. Infungible property cannot be substituted easily or at all and, if it can be found in the market, varies in price. Examples are manuscripts, cattle, and horses. The practical importance of this distinction is illustrated by the restitution of property which has been wrongfully appropriated. Under such circumstances, fungible property must be replaced, while compensation must be paid for infungible property at the value obtaining at the time of the wrongful appropriation.

(3) Tangible and intangible property (al-a'yān wa al-manāfi'). Tangible property is that which can be discerned by the ordinary senses, such as sight and touch. Intangible property is that which can be perceived only by thought and meaning. There is controversy among the various schools concerning the question of intangible property and whether or not it may be regarded as measurable property.

(4) Movable and immovable (al-manqūlāt wa ghayr al-man-

[2] See Articles 127 and 1334 ff. of the *Majalla* and Ṣubḥī Maḥmaṣānī's work on the general theory of obligations and contracts in the sharī'a, (*al-Nazariyya al 'Āmma lil-Mawjibāt w-al-'Uqūd fī al-Sharī'a al-Islamiyya* [Vol. 1, pp. 8 ff]).

[3] Sarakhsī, *op. cit.* Vol. 11, pp. 78 ff.; Ibn Qudāma al-Maqdisī, *al-Sharḥ al-Kabīr,* in the appendix of *al-Mughnī,* Vol. 5, p. 429; Ibn 'Abd al-Salām, *Qawā'id al-Aḥkām,* Vol. 1, p. 172.

qūlāt). Movable property is that which can be transferred from one place to another. Immovable, also called real, property is that which cannot be transported, such as dwellings and land, or which cannot be transferred to another place without damage or loss, such as trees before they have been uprooted or cut down.

CLASSIFICATION OF REAL PROPERTY AND WAQFS

The sharī'a classifies real property into many types, of which the most important are: that which is held in absolute ownership (mamlūka); state-owned (amīriyya); common land (matrūka); dead land (mawāt); and waqfs.

Mamlūka, or real property held in mulk (ownership), is that which a person owns and the entity and usufruct of which he can dispose of as he sees fit. Amīriyya is that in which control is vested in the state and the utilization of which is granted to him who requests it against payment of compensation.[4] Common land is "that which is near an inhabited place and which is left as a public pasture, threshing ground, and wood lot." Dead land is "land which is owned by no one, which is neither a pasture nor a wood lot for a town or village, and which is far from the remotest settlement, i.e., in a place where the voice of a person shouting from the outskirts of a town or village cannot be heard." Ownership of dead land can be acquired by cultivating it with the permission of the state.[5]

Waqf property is that the owners of which have dedicated it in perpetuity and the usufruct of which is devoted to the particular purposes for which the waqf was established. Thus such property may not be sold, bought, granted as a gift, or inherited, and its title is inalienable. If the proceeds are assigned to a permanent charitable institution, such as a mosque or a hospital, it is called a waqf khayrī (charitable waqf). If they are assigned first to a non-permanent purpose, as when the maker allocates the proceeds to himself during his lifetime and then to his children upon his death, but directs them to a charitable purpose after the last beneficiary has died, it is called a waqf dhurrī (descendants' waqf).[6]

OWNERSHIP

Ibn Rajab al-Ḥanbali says of ownership:

The owner of all things is their creator, God. Man possesses only the benefit of them in the manner permitted by the law. He who pos-

[4] In the Ottoman code this was called rasm al-ṭapū (title deed fee).
[5] *Majalla,* Articles 1270-1272.
[6] For further discussion on waqf, see Chap. VIII, below.

sesses all benefits is therefore the absolute owner. He who enjoys partial possession has limited ownership and hence is designated by a special name, such as tenant or borrower.[7]

The Majalla defines property as follows: "That which one owns, whether an entity or its usufruct" (Article 125). This definition focuses upon that which is subject to ownership, i.e., the thing or the usufruct owned. What is important, however, is not the thing or the usufruct, but the legal right or rule which governs them. Therefore, the definition quoted by al-Suyūṭī from Ibn al-Subkī is clearer and more complete in this respect. According to him ownership is "a legal interest vested in a thing itself or in its usufruct, giving its beneficiary the right to profit from it or receive compensation for it according to the attribution which he possesses."[8]

Ownership, then, is applied to a thing itself or to its "manfa'a" (usufruct). If it is applied to the thing itself it is ownership in the sense of full and absolute right, *dominium,* or the real right which includes that of use, exploitation, and disposal *(ius utendi, fruendi, abutendi*). If it is ownership of "manfa'a" (use, usufruct), it includes real rights or interests existing in another person's property, i.e., life interest, and the various kinds of easements, such as the right of way over the property of another and the right of using water from the property of another person.[9]

It is a prerequisite of the Islamic concept of absolute ownership that it be basically all-embracing and unrestricted in principle. This absolute right, however, is subject to the following limitations: (1) The right of others. For example, a person who has built a house on his land may not extend its construction unto his neighbor's land.[10] (2) Public interest. The legal maxim that a private injury is tolerated in order to avoid a public injury[11] entitles the state to restrict the right of private ownership in the public interest. An example is the requisitioning of private land for the construction of public roads and the like. (3) Non-abuse of rights. This is a limitation according to some schools of Islamic law, as explained below.

As ownership is the right granted by law to an owner to bene-

[7] Ibn Rajab, *Kitāb al-Qawā'id,* p. 195.

[8] Quoted in Suyūṭī, *al-Ashbāh wa'l-Naẓā'ir,* p. 191.

[9] Maḥmaṣānī, *op. cit.,* Vol. 1, pp. 20-25; *Majalla,* Article 142; and Sarakhsī, *op. cit.,* Vol. 14, p. 170.

[10] *Majalla,* Article 1195.

[11] *Ibid.,* Article 26.

fit from a thing or usufruct legally owned, so is the overt use of the benefits of property called possession. Possession is rightful if it is exercised by a person who has a legal title. It is invalid if it is exercised by one who has no legal title, such as a usurper.

Possession is of considerable practical importance. For example, if two persons are involved in a dispute over the ownership of a thing and one of them has the object in his possession, the burden of proof falls upon the other person, since possession is an outward indication of ownership until the contrary is proved. This stems from the principle that the *status quo ante* is the basis upon which the case is judged.[12]

HOW OWNERSHIP IS ACQUIRED

The Majalla (Article 1248), quoting Ḥanafī works on jurisprudence, recognizes three principal means of acquiring ownership. The first is the transfer of property from one owner to another by such means as sale or gift. The second is by succession, such as inheritance. The third consists of occupying or coming into possession of a permissible thing which has no owner. The last can be either by direct means, as where possession is actually taken of a thing, or by indirect means, as where a vessel is put out to collect rainwater or a trap is set to catch game. The prerequisites to *occupatio* are: (1) possession, (2) intention to acquire the ownership, (3) the thing in question must be ownerless, (4) no damage should result to others or to the public.

There are other means of acquiring ownership. Of these the most important is through *accessio*, i.e., the incorporation or juncture, or mingling of two things belonging to two different persons in such a manner that they cannot be distinguished or separated without serious damage. The most important examples of incorporation are the dyeing of something belonging to another person, the construction of a building, the planting of trees on the land of another person, or the unintentional loss of control over property, as when a mountain falls on a garden, a camel or a hen swallows a pearl, etc. The interpretation of incorporation centers on the fundamental principle that "an accessory follows the principal." This can result in the transfer of ownership from one person to another, and under certain conditions the payment of compensation by the receiver. There have been numerous controversies among jurists with regard to the ramifications of such

[12] *Ibid.*, Articles 4, 5, 10, 1683, 1680, and 1757.

cases, but the detailed discussion of them is beyond the scope of this study.[13]

Finally, it is necessary to discuss briefly the attitude of the sharī'a towards prescription, or the lapse of time, insofar as it affects acquisition of ownership. The sharī'a does not accept prescription as leading to ownership, but the Ḥanafī and the Mālikī schools have accepted limitation solely as an estoppel against the owner's claim.

Under the Majalla, which followed the equity of the Ḥanafī school, the action relating to a claim of ownership shall not be entertained if the owner has abandoned his property for a period of fifteen years or more without legal excuse and then claims it from the possessor. The period of limitation has been set at ten years for amīriyya (state domain) land and thirty-six years in cases involving waqfs and real rights therein. No period of limitation applies to claims concerning property appropriated to the use of the public such as public highways.[14]

According to the Mālikī school, if a person possesses a thing for a specified period and controls it as an owner would control his own property without challenge in the presence of, with the knowledge of, and without protest from the original claimant and without legal excuse or hindrance, it is evidence that such a person owns it. The predominant view of this school fixes the period of limitation for real property at ten years, and at one, two, or three years for movable property. The period of limitation is reduced to only ten months for both real and movable property if the possessor is unaware of the original ownership. The Mālikīs cite the following tradition of the Prophet in support of their thesis: "He who possesses a thing for ten years is its owner." Their view is that possession alone does not bestow ownership, and hence limitation is not considered as a cause of ownership, since there is a tradition of the Prophet which says: "The right of a Muslim is not invalidated even by the passage of time."[15] Possession, however, is evidence of the transfer of ownership and constitutes an estoppel against the claims and evidence of the owner.[16]

[13] *Majalla,* Articles 47, 49, 898, 902, 1060, and 1061; Maḥmaṣānī, *op. cit.,* Vol. 1, pp. 102-104; Ibn Qudāma, *al-Mughnī,* Vol. 5, pp. 379-81 and 431; Ibn Rushd, *Bidāyat al-Mujtahid,* Vol. 2, p. 265, Shāfi'ī, *Kitāb al-Umm,* Vol. 3, p. 222; Shīrāzī, *al-Muhadhdhib,* Vol. 1, p. 275; Ḥaṭṭāb, *Sharḥ Mawahib al-Jalīl,* Vol. 5, p. 282.

[14] *Majalla,* Articles 1660-1675.

[15] Cf. *Majalla,* Article 1674.

[16] See the commentaries of al-Ḥaṭṭāb (Vol. 6, pp. 221-28) and Kharashī (Vol. 5, pp. 242-44); Maḥmaṣānī, *op. cit.,* Vol. 2, pp. 312-14.

INDIVIDUAL AND JOINT OWNERSHIP

Ownership may be vested in an individual or in several persons jointly. The definition of common (mushā') property is given in Articles 138 and 139 of the Majalla as that which contains undivided shares. An undivided share is one which extends to every part of the common property.

Article 1060 defines joint ownership as:

> A thing is being shared between or ascribed to two or more persons on the basis of any cause of ownership, such as purchase, gift, bequest, or inheritance, or by the pooling and amalgamating of their property in such a way that it cannot be distinguished or separated.

Joint ownership of property is divided into voluntary and compulsory categories in Articles 1062-1064 of the Majalla. The first is brought about by the partnership resulting from the act of the participants themselves, as in purchase, acceptance of gifts and bequests, or pooling of properties. The second is a partnership brought about by some cause other than the act of the participants or beyond their control, as through inheritance or the blending of individual properties. Joint ownership is regulated by special rules pertaining to division of the property and the control exercised by the partners.[17]

LEGAL DISPOSITIONS IN GENERAL

THE MEANING OF LEGAL DISPOSITIONS

The method pursued by Muslim jurists in working out the rules of the sharī'a was on the whole inductive. They studied both questions which were submitted to them or hypothetical ones which they posed as practical ones and on the basis of these constructed general principles. Hence, they did not approach obligations and contracts from the viewpoint of general theory, although it is possible to abstract and categorize a general theory from their writings.[18] The jurists discussed the sources of obligations under the title of "legal dispositions" (al-taṣarrufāt al-shar'iyya), which in their view consisted of acts which give rise to obligation and legal consequence. These are of two categories: verbal dispositions (qawlīyya) and dispositions of commission (fi'liyya). The former include all types of contracts and other similar dispositions such as waqfs, vows, and sometimes unauthorized agency. The latter are

[17] See Articles 1069-1090 and 1162-1191 of the *Majalla.*

[18] Maḥmaṣānī, *op. cit.,* Vol. 1, pp. 30-34.

prohibited actions which give rise to liability, such as the destruction or wrongful appropriation of the property of others.[19] Therefore, we shall briefly and in due order consider the sources of obligation as well as the exercise of rights, and how in certain situations the latter can be a cause of liability.

EXERCISE OF RIGHTS

It is a fundamental legal principle that when a person exercises a right which belongs to him, he exercises a right which has been permitted to him by law. It is obvious that when a person exercises his right within its legal bounds this permission releases him in principle from all consequences with regard to others that may arise therefrom. This is the meaning of the universal rule adopted from the *Kitāb al-Majamī'* in Article 91 of the Majalla:[20] "Legal permissibility negates liability." For example, if an animal belonging to one person perishes by falling into a well which another person has dug on his own property, the latter is not liable.[21] In English law the same principle is expressed as *damnum sine iniuria.*

Thus it is a basic principle that the exercise of a right does not in itself entail liability. However, it may cause serious injury to others, and may even be solely motivated by the desire to inflict such injury. There is no unanimity among the Muslim schools or modern legal codes as to whether the injurious exercise of rights is prohibited and can give rise to liability.

Abū Ḥanīfa and al-Shāfi'ī answered these questions in the negative, on the assumption that rights are absolute. Mālik, Abū Yūsuf (a disciple of Abū Ḥanīfa), and later Ḥanafī jurists held, however, that exercise of a right is to be prohibited if it should cause serious injury. This interpretation was adopted in Article 1197 of the Majalla, which provides that: "No person may be prevented from doing as he wishes with his property unless in so doing he should cause grave damage to other persons."[22] This approach focuses upon the result rather than upon the intention of the person exercising the right. If the result is fraught with grave danger, the exercise of the right is prohibited regardless of the intention.

[19] Kāsanī, *al-Bada'i'*, Vol. 7, p. 171; Nawawī, *al-Majmū'*, Vol. 9, p. 159; *Majalla,* Article 1007.

[20] See the *Kitāb al-Majāmu'* and its commentary *al-Manāfi'*, by Khādimī, p. 318.

[21] *Majalla,* Article 91.

[22] *Majalla,* Articles 19, 30, 1198, and 1200; Saḥnūn, *al-Mudawwama al-Kubra,* Vol. 15, p. 197; commentary of Zayla'ī on *al-Kanz,* Vol. 4, p. 196; and Ibn 'Ābidīn, *Tanqi'h al-Fatawī al-Ḥamīdiyya,* Vol. 1, p. 362.

A Mālikī jurist of the fourteenth century A.D., Ibrāhīm Mūsa al-Lakhmī, better known as Abū Isḥāq al-Shāṭibī, did not follow the objective approach used in the Majalla but followed the modern subjective approach, which directs itself to the intent of the person exercising the right. In his treatise *al-Muwāfaqāt fī uṣūl al-Sharī'a,*[23] al-Shāṭibī maintained that if an act which is legal in itself is committed with the sole intent of inflicting injury upon others *(animus nocendi)*, it is legally prohibited and must be prevented. He also held the converse, that the injurious exercise of a right is permissible if the intent is to achieve a lawful result and not to cause injury.[24]

THE NEGOTIORUM GESTOR AND UNAUTHORIZED DEALING IN THE PROPERTY OF OTHERS

One of the general maxims of the sharī'a is that "no person may deal with the property of another person unless by his permission or acting as his trustee." A person who deals with the property of another without legal permission is called an unauthorized agent (*negotiorum gestor* or fuḍūlī).[25] Agency, hire, or loan, however, permit the use of property of him who contracts such agreements. Trusteeship entails legal permission delegated to the trustee by law to manage the affairs of his ward, as when a father administers the property of his minor son.

Muslim jurists are not agreed on the validity of the acts of unauthorized agent. Some of them, including al-Shāfi'ī, hold that such acts are invalid even though accepted by the owner of the property.[26] The majority of jurists, including Abū Ḥanīfa and Mālik, have taken a different view, namely, that the validity of the acts of the unauthorized agent is dependent upon the ratification of the owner of the property. If he ratifies them, they become valid and effective, in accord with the principle that "Subsequent ratification has the same effect as a previous authorization to act as agent."[27] If the owner of the property refuses to ratify such acts, they become void except with certain necessary exceptions.[28] A third view, similar to that laid down in a number of modern

[23] Cairo: Raḥmāniyya Press, Vol. 2, pp. 348-64.

[24] These theories are discussed in detail in Maḥmaṣānī, *op. cit.*, Vol. 1, pp. 35-55.

[25] *Majalla,* Article 112.

[26] al-Shāfi'ī, *op. cit.*, Vol. 3, p. 13; Nawawi, *op. cit.*, Vol. 9, pp. 261 ff.

[27] *Ratihabitio mandato aequiparatur.* See Marghinānī, *op. cit.*, Vol. 3, p. 55; Ibn Qudāma, *al-Mughnī,* Vol. 3, p. 16; Rāfi'ī, *Fatḥ al-'Azīz* (in the appendix to *al-Majmū'*, Vol. 8, p. 122); Ibn Rushd, *op. cit.*, Vol. 3, p. 141; *Majalla,* Articles 111, 447, 857(1126, 1453, and 1544.

[28] Maḥmaṣānī *op. cit.*, Vol. 1, pp. 76-78.

codes, validates unauthorized dealings even if they are not accepted by the owner of the property, if such actions are to the latter's advantage and were carried out with the intention of asking refund for them from him. This view was expounded particularly by the Ḥanbalī jurist Ibn Qayyim al-Jawziyya.

UNLAWFUL ENRICHMENT

If it is illegal to deal in the property of others without permission or trusteeship, it follows that "no one may take another's property without legal cause." This principle is based upon divine-evidence, the most important of which is the Qur'ānic verse (IV, 33): "Do not appropriate unlawfully one another's property." This general principle is restated in Article 97 of the Majalla. Thus there must be some lawful cause for taking the property of others. When it is taken without cause, it must be returned regardless of whether it was taken by theft, as a prank, or in error.

On the basis of this the jurists have laid down the principle that a sum paid without obligation should be restored to the payer, regardless of whether payment had been made in error, for prohibited purposes, or for a purpose which has not been fulfilled. They likewise formulated the rule of *quantum meruit*, i.e., that compensation must be commensurate with the act or thing for which compensation is claimed. This applies in cases where a prior contract does not exist, has expired, has been invalidated, is silent on the amount of compensation, and in cases where gain results from the pooling and amalgamation of property.

Nevertheless, while recognizing the existence of obligation in cases of unlawful gain, such as the above, the Muslim jurists did not develop from them a general principle of obligation based on unlawful enrichment as some modern codes have done.[29]

TRANSGRESSIONS OR FORBIDDEN ACTS

Transgressions, which the jurists call "dispositions of commission," are those forbidden acts which result in the liability of him who commits them. They include the wrongful appropriation and the destruction of other people's property and involve questions of liability arising from misdemeanors and felonies. Since the misdemeanors and felonies are treated in the chapter on penal law, they are not discussed here.

[29] Maḥmaṣānī, *op. cit.*, Vol. 1, pp. 88-107.

WRONGFUL APPROPRIATION

There was no agreed definition of wrongful appropriation among the Muslim schools of law. The definition preferred by the Ḥanafī school is:

Wrongful appropriation is suppression of the possession of the rightful owner and the establishment of an invalid possession by the unauthorized and open seizure of property which has value, is respected, and which is movable.

This definition precludes the wrongful appropriation of real estate, contrary to the opinions of Shaybānī, a student of Abū Ḥanīfa, and of other jurists of the school. Wrongful appropriation is differentiated from theft in that it takes place openly, whereas theft is a clandestine act.[30]

A person who wrongfully appropriates property must restore the same. If it has been consumed, destroyed, or lost, whether as a result of his transgression or otherwise, he must replace it if it is replaceable property or pay the value prevailing at the time and place of the wrongful appropriation if it is infungible property, i.e., if it cannot be replaced in the market. According to the Ḥanafī and the Mālikī schools, in establishing the value of property, the time and place at which wrongful appropriation occurred must be taken into account; according to the Ḥanbalī school, it is the time at which the wrongfully appropriated property was destroyed; while with the Shāfi'ī school it is the maximum value of the property between the date of the wrongful appropriation to the time of destruction.[31] Furthermore, any increase accruing to wrongfully appropriated property must be returned to the owner, along with the property, and compensation must be paid for any diminution resulting from the acts of him who has wrongfully appropriated the property or from his use of it.[32]

Compensation for the loss of use or profit sustained as a result of wrongful appropriation is a disputed question among jurists. Al-Shāfi'ī maintained that in all cases there is liability for loss of use, while Abū Ḥanīfa held that it should be limited to certain exceptional cases. Mālik held that liability is present if it appears

[30] See Sarakhsī, *op. cit.*, Vol. 11, p. 54; Kāsānī, *op. cit.*, Vol. 7, p. 143; Ibn Nujaym, *al-Baḥr al-Rā'iq*, Vol. 8, p. 108; Rifā'ī, *op. cit.*, Kharashī *op. cit.*, Vol. 4, pp. 345, 347; Ibn Qudāma, *al-Sharḥ al-Kabīr*, Vol. 5, p. 375; and Maḥmaṣānī, *op. cit.*, Vol. 1, pp. 156-164.

[31] *Majalla*, Articles 890-891; Ghazzālī, *al-Wajīz*, Vol. 1, p. 209; Kharashī, *op. cit.*, Vol. 4, p. 351; Buhutī, *al-Rawd al-Murbi'*, Vol. 2, p. 115.

[32] *Majalla*, Articles 900 and 903.

that the person wrongfully appropriating the property has profited from it.

DESTRUCTION OF PROPERTY

In Islamic law, every injurious act wrongfully committed against the property of others makes the aggressor liable. This principle, which was especially applied to the destruction of property, was gradually broadened by the jurists to include all injuries, whether to property or persons, so that every injury was called "destruction."[33] This culminated in the emergence of a comprehensive theory of liability and its causes and conditions, based upon general legal maxims and embracing most illegal acts.

Liability is the obligation to replace destroyed property, if it is fungible, or to pay indemnification for it if it is infungible.[34] Liability of this type is called "liability for destruction," to distinguish it from contractual liability. It is similar to the modern distinction between delictual (i.e., arising from torts) and contractual responsibility. The following conditions must be present in order to give rise to liability for destruction:[35]

(1) The act must be injurious. "Act" is construed here in the widest sense, and includes physical acts, words, behavior, and negligence. Injury connotes material injury only. Moral injury was not recognized by the majority opinion. However, a number of Abū Ḥanīfa's companions are said to have held that in cases of pain resulting from physical assault or wounds the perpetrator is to pay an indemnity to be assessed by the judge in proportion to the suffering inflicted upon the victim *(pretium doloris)*.[36]

(2) The injury must be unlawful, that is, without legal right or sanction. Injury resulting from a permissible act or from the exercise of a right does not require compensation, save in exceptional cases which have been briefly cited in the preceding discussion of the misuse of rights.

(3) The injury must be either the direct or indirect result of the aggression. Direct destruction is the destruction of a thing itself without the intervention of any cause between the act and the result. Indirect destruction is doing something to one thing which would ordinarily lead to the destruction of something else; the

[33] See, for example, Kāsānī *op. cit.*, Vol. 6, p. 283.
[34] *Majalla,* Article 416.
[35] For details, see Maḥmaṣānī, *op. cit.*, Vol. 1, pp. 165-254.
[36] Sarakhsī, *op. cit.*, Vol. 26, p. 81; the *al-Ikhtiyār* commentary on *al-Mukhtār* by Mawṣilī, Vol. 3, p. 175; Zayla'ī, *op. cit.*, Vol. 6, p. 138.

destruction would then be the ordinary and patent result of the act. For example:

A person who causes a hanging lamp to fall and break by cutting the rope from which it is suspended is the direct cause of the destruction of the cord and the indirect cause of the destruction of the lamp; or, a person who splits a vessel filled with ghee so that the contents are lost is the direct cause of the destruction of the vessel and the indirect cause of the destruction of the ghee.[37]

(4) An illegal act resulting in indirect destruction must have been done intentionally, which applies also to cases where the destruction is caused by animals or inanimate objects. "Intentionally" is used by the jurists also to cover cases of neglect or carelessness. In acts of direct destruction, intent is not a condition. This is exemplified in the juridical rule that:

A person who is the direct cause [of injury], even though not intentionally, is liable. But a person who is the indirect cause [of an injury] is not liable unless he has acted intentionally.[38]

LAWFUL ACTS AND CONTRACTS

Having considered in the preceding pages unlawful acts or torts as a source of obligation, we shall now briefly discuss lawful acts (al-taṣarrufāt al-qawliyya). These legal acts are carried out with the intention of creating legal consequences. They fall into two categories: (1) legal acts arising from the will of one party, of which the most important are acts of unauthorized persons *(negotiorium gestio),* waqf dedications, bequests under certain circumstances, and the like; and (2) contracts, which are unquestionably the most important of legal acts. Therefore, the present discussion will be confined to a brief consideration of the rules of this second category.

Contract has been defined in Articles 103 and 104 of the Majalla as "the obligation and engagement of two contracting parties with reference to a particular matter. It expresses the combination of offer and acceptance. In the conclusion of the contract, both the offer and the acceptance are interrelated in a legal manner, the result of which is seen in their mutual relationship." Contract is a source of obligation and its faithful fulfillment is a duty in accordance with Sūra 5, Verse 1 of the Qur'ān: "Oh ye who believe, fulfill your pledges."

[37] *Majalla,* Article 888; see also Article 887 and Ḥamawī, *Sharḥ al-Ashbāh,* Vol. 1, p. 196; Ghazzālī, *op. cit.,* Vol. 1, p. 206; Qurāfī, *al-Furūq,* Vol. 4, p. 27.

[38] Ibn Nujaym, *al-Ashbāh wa'l-Naẓā'ir,* p. 113; *Majalla,* Articles 92 and 93; Maḥmaṣānī, *op. cit.,* Vol. 1, p. 198.

The required conditions for the valid conclusion of a contract are: (1) consent of the contracting parties; (2) legal competence on the part of the parties; (3) a subject matter; (4) a consideration; (5) a special form in certain cases. In the absence of a general theory of contract in Islamic law, we find rules and general conditions of contract scattered throughout the various categories of contracts.

Obligations originate from agreement and not from the observance of specific forms or technicalities. Acceptance, therefore, is sufficient for the consummation of a contract without its embodiment in any specific form. Article 3 of the Majalla states, *inter alia:* "In contracts effect is given to intention and meaning and not to words and phrases." The two most important exceptions to this are contracts of marriage, which must be attested to by witnesses, and of waqf dedication, which require specific expressions of consent.

CONSENT

The consent of the two contracting parties is the main pillar in the conclusion of a contract. It is the combination of offer and acceptance. The Majalla (Articles 101 and 102) has defined these in the following way:

> The offer consists of the initial utterance of one of the contracting parties with a view to making a disposition; he thereby makes the offer and fixes the disposition. Acceptance is the utterance made by one of the contracting parties in the second instance with a view to making the disposition, thereby completing the contract.

One of the conditions of acceptance is that it should correspond to the offer and should be tendered while the offer is still outstanding. Offer and acceptance may take place by word, act, gesture, or writing. If offer and acceptance are made by correspondence, the contract is considered to have been concluded at the place and time of the acceptance.

Silence is not ordinarily regarded as tantamount to acceptance except in situations where a person is required to indicate his position explicitly, his silence being taken as a tacit expression of that which he is bound to declare. This is the sense of the principle that "No statement is imputed to a man who keeps silence, but silence is tantamount to a declaration where one is necessary."[39]

[39] Ibn Nujaym, *al-Ashbāh wa'l-Naẓā'ir,* p. 61; Khadimī, *al-Manāfi'* commentary on *al-Majāmū',* p. 321; *Majalla,* Article 67.

IMPEDIMENTS TO CONSENT

Consent must be free of the impediments of error, misrepresentation, fraud, and coercion; this is briefly summarized as follows:[40]

(1) Ignorance or error constitutes an impediment to consent and a cause for voiding the contract if it concerns the nature of the subject matter of the contract or its fundamental attributes.

(2) Fraudulent misrepresentation, i.e., deceit, by one of the contracting parties which results in influencing the other party and leading him to conclude the contract likewise is an impediment to consent. If misrepresentation is accomplished by an act, as when someone dyes an old garment and claims that it is new, it is an impediment to consent in the opinion of most jurists. If the misrepresentation is solely verbal, it is not regarded as a cause for voiding the contract unless it is accompanied by undue disproportion between the mutual obligations *(laesio enormis)*.

(3) According to the Ḥanafī and the Shāfi'ī schools, disproportion between the mutual contractual obligation is a cause for voiding a contract only if it is gross[41] and accompanied by fraud. In exceptional cases, foremost of which are those involving waqf property, orphan's property, and the public treasury, gross disproportion without fraud is a sufficient cause for rescinding a contract. The Mālikī and the Ḥanbalī schools, however, hold that cause for voiding a contract of sale exists if the disproportion is excessive and if the victim is inexperienced.[42]

(4) A person exercising duress must be capable of implementing his threats. Furthermore, the person subject to duress must be sufficiently frightened to agree against his will and decide that the contract must take place under the influence of this fear. Muslim jurists of all schools have followed the "subjective" theory in determining the criterion of fear in duress. This theory holds that duress differs according to people's circumstances, the ways and means by which it is exercised, and the actions which are sought for. Thus duress may not only be physical, but may stem from verbal threats as well.

40 See Maḥmaṣānī, *op. cit.*, Vol. 2, pp. 164-199.

41 On the meaning of "gross fraud," see *Majalla*, Article 165, and Ibn Nujaym, *al-Baḥr al-Rā'iq*, Vol. 7, p. 169.

42 This closely approaches modern theories. See Article 138 of the German civil code; Article 21 of the Swiss code of obligations; and Article 214 of the Lebanese code of obligations and contracts.

THE OBJECT OF THE CONTRACT

Every contract must have an object (maḥall al-'aqd), which must fulfill the following conditions:

(1) The object must be capable of delivery. Thus, the sale of a sunken ship which cannot be salvaged or of a runaway animal which cannot be caught and delivered, is void.[43]

(2) The object must be specific and sufficiently known to the contracting parties.[44]

(3) The object must be in existence. A contract for future delivery is generally void. The most important exceptions are contracts of sale by advance or down payment ('aqd al-salam or al-salaf) against future delivery and contracts for the fabrication of something or for the sale of fruits. The Ḥanafī equitable view in this regard is stated in Article 207 of the Majalla:

> The sale at one and the same time of dependent parts coming successively into existence with those already existent is valid. For example, in the case of fruit, flowers, leaves, and vegetables, which do not arrive at maturity simultaneously, a portion thereof only having come out, that portion which has not arrived at maturity may be sold together with the rest.

However, a contract having as its object a future estate or an inheritance which has not fallen due is forbidden in the sharī'a because the right of inheritance vests only upon the death of the testator. Thus, any such contract would be applicable to a non-existent object.

(4) The object must be permissible in law; otherwise the contract is void.

Freedom of contract is fundamental in the sharī'a. This principle was expounded particularly by Ibn Qayyim al-Jawziyya, who demonstrated that in the view of the majority of jurists the basic principle in contracts is freedom and validity while illegality should be based on a clear provision of the law.[45] The exceptions are those provided for in the sharī'a. The jurists, however, are in disagreement on the application of this principle to subsidiary cases and questions. Some of them have interpreted it broadly, while others adopted a narrower approach, with yet a third group holding a balance between the two extremes.[46]

[43] *Majalla,* Articles 198 and 209.
[44] *Ibid.,* Articles 200, 238, 449-451, 630, 688, 709, 811, 858, and 1547.
[45] Ibn Qayyim al-Jawziyya, *I'lām al-Mawaqi'īn,* Vol. 1, p. 299.
[46] Maḥmaṣānī, *op. cit.,* Vol. 2, pp. 78-81.

THE CONSIDERATION IN A CONTRACT

Muslim jurists have disagreed over the question of consideration in a contract, including the meaning of the term and the extent of its effect on the contract. They have not investigated this problem as a general theory in contracts, but it is possible to deduce from the totality of their writings a theory similar to the modern continental theory of consideration (cause).

Among the general maxims of Islamic law are those that "Every sound-minded and voluntary doer acts with some end in view"; that "The purpose in a contract must be taken into account, because it may affect its validity, invalidity, dissolution, or inviolability"; and that "any consideration whose object cannot be attained is not legal."[47]

Thus, there must be a purpose or consideration for every contract which will differ according to the type of contract. The purpose or consideration in a contract of marriage is mutual love and begetting of children; in a contract of gift, the desire to do good for its own sake; and in a contract of mutual obligation, the exchange of the benefits or property from one of the contracting parties to the other.[48] The consideration or purpose must be in existence, permissible, and valid. On this basis the majority of jurists have declared mere promises, or contracts whose purpose was either nonexistent or illicit, null and void. For example, the Ḥanbalī, Mālikī, and the Ẓāhirī schools held invalid sales of juices, dates, or grapes for the purpose of making fermented drinks, or of weapons to seditious persons or brigands.[49]

The jurists also held that the continuance of the purpose or consideration was necessary to the validity of the contract. For example, Article 443 of the Majalla states:

> If anything happens to prevent the carrying out of the primary objective in a contract of service, the contract is cancelled. For example, if a cook is hired for a wedding celebration, and one of the persons to be married dies, the hire is cancelled. Likewise, if a person who has engaged a wet nurse dies the contract of hire remains valid, but if either the child or the wet nurse dies, the contract is cancelled."

[47] Shāṭibī, *al-Muwāfaqāt,* Vol. 2, p. 327; Ibn Qayyim, *op. cit.,* Vol. 3, p. 96; Qurāfī, *op. cit.,* Vol. 3, p. 171.

[48] Qurāfī, *ibid.,* pp. 171 and 238; Ḥasqafī, *al-Durr al-Mukhtār,* Vol. 2, p. 471.

[49] Ibn Qudāma, *al-Mughnī* and *al-Sharḥ al-Kabīr,* Vol. 4, pp. 40-41, 283-284; Ibn Ḥazm, *op. cit.,* Vol. 9, No. 1542; Haṭṭāb, *op. cit.,* Vol. 4, p. 267. For details see Maḥmaṣānī, *op. cit.,* Vol. 2, pp. 89-99.

CAPACITY

The parties to a contract must have legal capacity to enter into contractual obligations if a contract is to be valid. They must have the capacity to possess and exercise legal rights. The former is present from birth while the latter is only attained when a person reaches the age of discrimination. Incapacity, therefore, is restricted to a category of people called "interdicted" persons. The most important causes of interdiction are: slavery, minority, lunacy, imbecility, prodigality, debt, death-illness; according to some jurists, women and drunkards are included also. These causes of interdiction are briefly surveyed below.

(1) Slavery. This was widespread in the early days of Islam and remained so until it was gradually abolished. Nowadays it is rare. The abolition of slavery is consonant with the spirit of the Islamic sharī'a, which ordered that slaves be well treated and urged their liberation in many situations. Therefore, no useful purpose would be served by elaborating on this point.[50]

(2) Minority. A minor who is incapable of discriminating is not competent to enter into a contract of any sort. A minor of sufficient discrimination may be a party to a contract which is entirely for his own benefit, such as the acceptance of a gift; but he is not competent to enter into a contract which is entirely to his own disadvantage, such as the making of a gift. If it is not clear whether a contract, such as one of sale, is to the benefit or disadvantage of a minor, it may be concluded subject to the approval of the guardian. Muslim jurists have not been able to agree as to when a minor becomes of age, but the majority of them have held that it is when the child reaches the age of puberty. If no signs of puberty are discerned the coming of age is presumed to take place with the completion of the fifteenth year. However, a judge may hold the boy's property in custody even after he becomes of age until he shows maturity and understanding. The jurists also permitted a judge or a guardian to permit a boy endowed with discrimination to engage in business and make contracts.

(3) Lunacy and imbecility. A lunatic is one who is lacking in reason, while an imbecile is one who has deficient reason. The jurists classified the former in the category of a minor unable to discriminate and completely denied him competency to enter into contractual obligations. The imbecile they likened to a minor

50 Maḥmaṣānī, *ibid.*, Vol. 2, pp. 159-163.

capable of discriminating and regarded him as deficient in capacity as previously described.

(4) Prodigality. This included wastefulness, excess, and heedlessness. Abū Ḥanīfa and others declared against the interdiction of prodigals on the ground that an interdiction of a free man is invalid since "interdiction is control over the soul, and that a soul is of greater concern than property." The majority of jurists, however, and the Majalla authorized a judge to interdict a prodigal and to make public his decision. The capacity of an interdicted prodigal is incomplete and is similar to that accorded to a minor who possesses discrimination.[51]

(5) Debt. The majority of Muslim jurists, contrary to the opinion of Abū Ḥanīfa, have maintained that a judge may interdict a bankrupt debtor at the request of his creditors. The Majalla[52] accepted this view. The effect of interdiction is to prevent a debtor from carrying out transactions detrimental to his creditors.

(6) Last illness. There is no agreed definition of last illness or of its effects on the behavior of the sick person. The majority view, however, defines it as that state of helplessness in which death becomes imminent, and in which it may be feared that a person might conduct himself in a manner detrimental to his heirs and creditors. In such a case, the majority of jurists and the Majalla have held that a person does not possess unrestricted capacity to enter into contractual obligations. He is considered as partially interdicted from concluding certain prejudicial agreements, particularly those affecting the interests of his heirs and creditors, such as contracts of gift, or of sale on unfavorable terms, that is, at less than the true value. Such contracts are considered the equivalent of a bequest and their validity is contingent upon the agreement of the heirs or the creditors.[53]

(7) Womanhood or wifehood. The predominant view of the sharī'a is that a woman, whether married or unmarried, is fully as competent as a man and may dispose of her property as she wishes without let or hindrance. Only a few jurists took exception to the predominant view. Among them was Mālik, who opined that marriage should be considered a partial restriction on

[51] Kāsānī, *op. cit.*, Vol. 1, p. 170; Sarakhsī, *op. cit.*, Vol. 24, pp. 156-163; Saḥnūn, *op. cit.*, Vol. 13, p. 74; Shāfi'ī, *op. cit.*, Vol. 3, p. 194; Ibn Qudama, *op. cit.*, Vol. 4, pp. 524 ff.; *Majalla*, Articles 946, 961, 962, and 984 ff.

[52] *Ibid.*, Articles 959, 998 ff. See also Sarakhsī, *op. cit.*, Vol. 24, p. 163; Kāsānī, *op. cit.*, Vol. 7, p. 169; Saḥnūn, *op. cit.*, Vol. 13, p. 83; Kharashī *op. cit.*, Vol. 4, p. 173; Shāfi'ī, *op. cit.*, Vol. 3, pp. 189-191; Shirazi, *op. cit.*, Vol. 1, p. 320; Ibn Qudāma, *op. cit.*, Vol. 4, p. 455; Maḥmaṣānī, *op. cit.*, Vol. 2, pp. 148-154.

[53] *Majalla*, Articles 393 ff. and 1595 ff.; Maḥmaṣānī, *op. cit.*, Vol. 2, pp. 135-47.

a woman's capacity, particularly with regard to contracts of gift, which require for their validity the permission of the husband.[54]

(8) Drunkenness. The validity of contracts concluded by a drunken person was a controversial question. Some, such as the Ḥanafīs, accepted the engagements of a drunken person as valid and enforceable. Others, such as al-Shāfi'ī, regarded them as not binding on the ground that reason is a condition in transactions and that a drunken person is bereft of the faculties of reasoning.[55]

THE FORM OF A CONTRACT

The fundamental principle in Islamic law is that consent is sufficient to conclude a contract without the latter's having to be in any particular form. Hence, no conditions are made as to special wording or other formalities. The Majalla (Article 3) expresses this in the following words: "In contracts effect is given to intention and meaning, and not to words and phrases."[56] However, there are certain exceptions to this principle, which were made by the jurists because of their importance. Among these are contracts of marriage, waqf, and the like. Most jurists have held that a marriage contract is valid only if there are two witnesses, while a contract of waqf, in order to be valid, requires certain special phrases which convey the meaning of making it perpetual.[57]

THE MOST IMPORTANT TYPES OF SPECIAL CONTRACTS

(1) Sale is a contract which conveys ownership of property against remuneration. The Majalla, in Article 105, has defined it as: "The exchange of property for property." Sale is divided into four categories: (a) sale of property for a price (absolute sale), which is the best-known type of sale; (b) exchange, or sale, of cash for cash; (c) sale by barter; (d) sale by immediate payment against future delivery. A contract of sale is concluded by offer and acceptance and need not await delivery or payment.[58]

(2) Hire is the letting of a thing or service against remunera-

[54] *Ibid.*, Vol. 2, pp. 128-34.

[55] Ibn al-Humām, *Fatḥ al-Qadīr*, Vol. 3, pp. 40-42; Da'ūd Effendi, *Majma' al-Anḥur*, Vol. 2, p. 290; Shāfi'ī, *op. cit.*, Vol. 3, p. 209; Gazzālī, *op. cit.*, pp. 1 and 51; al-Haṭṭab, *op. cit.*, Vol. 4, p. 43; Ibn Qudāma, *op. cit.*, Vol. 8, pp. 254-57.

[56] See also Ibn Qayyim *op. cit.*, Vol. 3, pp. 82, 83, and 96.

[57] Maḥmaṣānī, *op. cit.*, Vol. 2, pp. 25-34.

[58] *Majalla*, Articles 105, 120-23, and 262; Sarakhsī, *op. cit.*, Vol. 12, p. 108; Marghinānī, *op. cit.*, Vol. 3, p. 17; Ibn Nujaym, *al-Baḥr al-Rā'iq*, Vol. 5, p. 256 and Vol. 6, p. 2; Saḥnūn, *op. cit.*, Vol. 9, p. 145 and Vol. 10, p. 2; Shāfi'ī, *op. cit.*, Vol. 3, p. 2; Buhūtī, *op. cit.*, Vol. 2, p. 1.

tion. The Majalla has defined it as: "The sale of given usufruct in exchange for a given remuneration." There are three types of hire as far as the subject of the contract is concerned: (a) hire affecting the usufruct of the substance, whether it be of real property, of goods, or of animals; (b) hire of labor, as in the hire of a servant; and (c) hire of a skill, as when one gives cloth to a tailor in order that he may tailor it into a garment.

(3) In a contract of gift, the donor makes over the ownership of his property to the recipient without remuneration. A condition for compensation may be made, but in this case the contract becomes subject to the rules of sale.[59] The jurists have disagreed as to whether delivery is a condition for the conclusion of a contract of gift. Mālik held that it was not necessary and that a contract of gift was concluded by offer and acceptance. Certain other jurists, including Ḥanafīs and Shāfiʻis, held that a gift becomes effective only upon delivery[60] and this view was adopted in the Majalla (Article 837): "A contract of gift is concluded by offer and acceptance and is fulfilled when the gift is taken possession of." This is on the basis of the general principle in Article 57 that: "A gift is fulfilled only when possession thereof is taken."

(4) A loan for use grants the ownership of the usufruct of something gratis. Like other contracts of gift, it is not completed until the borrower takes possession. Either of the contracting parties may rescind the contract at will and terminate the loan. The object of the loan is held on trust by the borrower, who is therefore not liable for its destruction, loss, or the diminution of its value, unless caused by his fault or negligence. The borrower is entitled to make use of the loan without compensation in accordance with the conditions of the contract or custom. He must meet the maintenance expenses of the property while it is in his possession and must return it in substance at the termination of the loan.[61]

(5) Loan of certain commodities, which may be determined by any measure of capacity, weight, or number, to the borrower who undertakes to return the like of that which he has received is also regarded as a contract of gift and is concluded only by actual delivery. This contract must not entail any interest on the prop-

[59] Cf. Marghinānī, *op. cit.*, Vol. 3, p. 185.

[60] Sarakhī, *op. cit.*, Vol. 12, p. 48; Maḥmaṣānī, *op. cit.* Vol. 2, pp. 18-26; al-Haṭṭāb, *op. cit.*, Vol. 6, p. 54; Ghazzālī, *op. cit.*, Vol. 1, p. 249; Ibn Qudāma, *op. cit.*, Vol. 6, pp. 246, 251.

[61] *Majalla,* Articles 765, 766, 810, 812-820, and 825.

erty to the creditor, because all increase which is provided for is regarded as a kind of usury, which is forbidden.[62]

(6) Deposit is an owner's placing his property in the custody of another person for safekeeping. The contract may be terminated at the will of either party. The property deposited is on trust in the possession of the person receiving it, and consequently the latter is not liable if it is destroyed or lost unless he is guilty of fault, wrongful action, or negligence. But if such deposit has been made for safekeeping in consideration of payment of a fee and the thing deposited has been destroyed or lost for some preventable cause, the trustee must be liable for it.[63]

(7) Guarantee is defined by the Majalla (Article 612) as "the joining of one obligation to another obligation with regard to a claim on something." That is to say, it consists of one person's joining his obligation to that of another person, and binding himself also to meet any claim attached thereto. According to the principle that "if the trunk falls, the branch falls with it," it follows that "if the principal is released from liability, the guarantor must also be released." The creditor, according to the Majalla,[64] has the option of demanding repayment from either the principal or the guarantor as he sees fit, i.e., he is not obliged to make his claim on the former first, as provided in a number of codes.[65]

(8) Pledge is a contract whereby the pledgor assigns property to the pledgee, who keeps it as security for a claim. A contract of pledge, according to the Majalla, is concluded by the agreement of the two contracting parties, but it is not complete and binding until the property pledged is taken possession of by the pledgee. A pledge may be cancelled either by agreement of both contracting parties or at the will of the pledgee alone, but the pledgor alone cannot cancel the contract. The pledgee may retain the property pledged until his debt has been paid. A pledgee may not make use of a property pledge without the permission of the pledgor, but he has priority over all other creditors in securing payment of his claim from such property.[66]

(9) Agency is a contract by which one person empowers another to act in his place in some matter. An agency may be general or limited, absolute or restricted. In general, a person may appoint

[62] Kāsānī *op. cit.*, Vol. 7, pp. 394-396.
[63] *Majalla,* Articles 763, 764, 773, 774, and 777.
[64] Articles 612, 618, 644, 650, and 662.
[65] E.g., Article 1072 of the Lebanese code of obligations and contracts.
[66] *Majalla,* Articles 701, 702, 718, 729, and 750.

an agent to perform any particular thing which he himself can perform, or pay or collect any claim arising from his dealings.[67]

(10) Settlement is a contract settling a dispute by mutual agreement. Arbitration is a contract in which the parties agree to select a third person to resolve their dispute and claims. Arbitration may be resorted to in property claims relating to the rights of individuals.[68]

(11) Partnership is a contract between two or more persons for the joint sharing of capital and profits. Partnerships, whether of equal or unequal shares, fall into three categories: (a) partnership in a specified amount of capital; (b) partnership in labor, in which the partners undertake to contribute labor or skill; and (c) partnership in credit, in which no capital is contributed and the partners buy and sell on credit on the understanding that they shall divide the profits.[69] Partnerships also may be of mixed character, involving capital and labor, agricultural fields and labor, and fruit orchards and labor. In the first case (muḍāraba), one party supplies the capital and the other the labor. A partnership involving agricultural fields and labor (muzāra'a) is one in which one party provides land and the other labor, the produce being divided between them. In a partnership involving fruit orchards and labor (mughārasa), the trees are provided by one party and are tended by the other, the fruit being shared between them.[70]

TERMINATION AND TRANSFER OF OBLIGATIONS

Contracts are terminated by mutual consent, by their own terms, or in consequence of the legal principles which govern contracts in general or specific types of contracts. Contracts which may not be terminated unilaterally may be terminated by agreement of the parties. Certain contracts, such as deposit, may be terminated by either one of the parties. In a contract of pledge, the pledgee, but not the pledgor, has the right of unilateral cancellation. Impediments, such as absence of one of the conditions of the contract or a defect in agreement, such as duress, give rise to an option to cancel a contract (see above). There are also cer-

[67] *Ibid., Articles* 1449, 1459, 1478, 1479, 1494, and 1498.

[68] *Ibid.,* Articles 1531, 1790, and 1841.

[69] For the various opinions as to which types of partnership are permissible, see: *Majalla,* Articles 1329-1332; Sarakhsī, *op. cit.,* Vol. 11, p. 174; Ibn al-Humām, *op. cit.,* Vol. 5, pp. 6, 28; Ibn Qudāma, *op. cit.,* Vol. 5, pp. 111-122; Kharashī, *op. cit.,* Vol. 5, pp. 258-270; Ghazzālī, *op. cit.,* pp. 186-187; Shīrāzī, *op. cit.,* Vol. 1, pp. 347-348; Ibn Juzay, *al-Qawanīn al Fiqhiyya,* pp. 283-284; Maḥmaṣānī, *op. cit.,* Vol. 2, p. 361.

[70] For the detailed rules governing each of these types of partnership, see *Majalla,* Articles 1404-1448.

tain general causes for termination of contracts and other obligations, such as settlement of debt, release, and expiration of the period of limitation.

A creditor may transfer his claim by sale or gift to a person other than the debtor and a debtor may transfer his obligation to another person.[71] The jurists have disagreed on the legality of the first type of transfer. Some of them, including Mālik, gave it unconditional sanction; others, including Shāfi'ī and Ibn Ḥanbal, were unequivocally opposed to it. The Ḥanafīs opposed it in principle but approved of its application in exceptional cases by means of legal fictions.

Transfer of debt was not permissible in Roman law, but the Muslim jurists of all schools sanctioned it and carried it to Europe through Spain and also through Sicily during the Crusades of the twelfth century A.D. The French word *aval,* derived from the Arabic ḥawāla, is evidence of this borrowing.[72] A transfer is concluded by agreement of the transferor, the transferee, and the person on behalf of whom the transfer is made; or of the transferee and the person on behalf of whom the transfer is made; or of the transferor and the transferee; or of the transferor and the person on behalf of whom the transfer is made. In the last case, the transfer, according to the Ḥanafī school, would be contingent upon the approval of the creditor and of the person on behalf of whom the transfer is made.

[71] Transfer of obligations by inheritance is not discussed here, since it falls under the law of personal status.

[72] D. Huvelin, *Annales de droit commercial* (Paris, 1901), pp. 22-26.

CHAPTER VIII

The Law of Waqf

THIS CHAPTER is intended as an introduction to the basic principles of the law of waqf, including its analogy to the English law of trusts and its more recent evolution in the Arab countries. The vastness and complexity of this field preclude a detailed exposition of the law of waqf, a full historical survey of its development, or a study of waqf in those areas outside the Middle East, such as India, Pakistan, and North Africa, where Islamic law is applied.

DEFINITION OF WAQF

More than one thousand years ago, long before the birth of the doctrine of uses and trusts in English law, Islamic law recognized and developed a legal expedient under the name of waqf (plural, awqāf) which permitted an owner to settle his property to the use of beneficiaries in perpetuity, his intentions as to the devolution of the benefits, the determination of beneficiaries, and all other matters relating to the trust being observed and respected in the same manner as a legal enactment. The accepted definition of waqf according to the Ḥanafī school is "the detention of the corpus from the ownership of any person and the gift of its income or usufruct either presently or in the future, to some charitable purpose."

Property becomes waqf upon a declaration by its owner (the wāqif) permanently reserving its income for a specific purpose. Ownership is thereupon "arrested" or "detained": the wāqif ceases to be the owner of the property; it cannot be transferred or alienated by him, the administrator of the waqf, or the beneficiaries; and it does not devolve upon the owner's heirs. While waqf property must be dedicated to a charitable use, this purpose may be ultimate rather than immediate, as when the wāqif reserves the income to his children and their descendants in perpetuity, with a provision that upon the extinction of his descendants, the income shall be used for the relief of the poor or some other charitable object. The Ḥanafī school holds that the wāqif may constitute himself the first beneficiary for life, but other schools do not concede to the original owner the right of being a beneficiary under the waqf. The beneficiaries need not be the wāqif's descendants, though this is generally the case; they may be strangers. Provided the first beneficiary is in existence, any number of persons may be designated to take successively the benefit of a waqf, whether they are in existence at the time of the dedication or not. This kind of waqf, being primarily destined for the benefit of the settlor's descendants, is called a family waqf or waqf dhurrī, thus distinguishing it from the waqf khayrī or charitable waqf in which the income is from the beginning devoted to a charitable purpose. There may be a combination of the two kinds of waqf from the outset, part of the usufruct being appropriated to children, relatives, or descendants, and the other part to a charitable use. Apart from certain differences in the manner of their administration, there is no difference in the nature of the two kinds of waqf or in the legal rules applied to them.

A waqf is administered by a trustee—the mutawallī or nāzir. The waqf instrument may name the original mutawallī and provide for the manner of appointment of his successors, for example, on the basis of primogeniture. In the absence of any such provision, the qāḍī will designate the trustee, usually giving preference in appointment to the wāqif's descendants. The duties of the mutawallī are to administer the waqf in accordance with the conditions of the waqf instrument, to protect the corpus of the waqf, and to receive and distribute the proceeds among the beneficiaries. The qāḍī always retains general supervisory powers over the mutawallī.

The concept of waqf involves, in addition to the immobilization of ownership, the definition and regulation of the rights, interests, and duties of various persons or classes of persons in relation to the property and its usufruct: the wāqif, whose intentions and directions must be observed; the mutawallī who is charged with the care, protection, and administration of the waqf; the present beneficiaries who are entitled to the income of the waqf; and the future beneficiaries whose rights will arise after those of the present beneficiaries have ceased.

ORIGINS OF WAQF

Charity is at the root of the development and extension of waqfs. The Qur'ān contains no reference to waqf, though it abounds with charitable injunctions:

They will ask thee what they shall bestow in alms. Say: let the good which ye bestow be for parents, and kindred, and orphans and the poor, and the stranger; and whatsoever good ye do, of a truth God knoweth.[1]

The true measure of charity is indicated in the following Qur'ānic verse: "Ye shall never attain to goodness till ye give alms of that which ye love; and whatever ye give, of a truth God knoweth."[2]

The institution of waqf has developed with Islam, and there is no doubt that credit must go to the jurists for having developed the legal theory of waqf. The separation of ownership from usufruct was not a new legal concept, but the settlement of the usufruct of property on successive generations in perpetuity for an immediate or ultimate charitable purpose is an institution created by the jurists during the first three centuries of Islam. There is no evidence that such a complex system of appropriating usufruct as a life interest to varying and successive classes of beneficiaries existed prior to Islam.

CONDITIONS OF VALIDITY

The conditions required for the validity of a waqf are as follows:

(1) The settlor (wāqif) must possess the capacity requisite for a valid alienation of property. He must, therefore, be of age and sound mind and must own the property that he intends to make waqf.

(2) The property to be made waqf must be tangible. An incorporeal right cannot be dedicated as waqf. With regard to movable property, there are differences of opinion, although the prevailing view is that movables, because they do not usually possess the quality of permanency, cannot be made waqf. To this rule, however, there are three exceptions established by custom. A waqf may validly be made of (a) movables permanently attached to immovable property; (b) animals, such as horses and camels; and (c) books and furniture. Money, valuables, and shares cannot be the subject of a waqf. This interpretation has had the result of narrowing the application of waqf mainly to real property.

(3) The property must be declared waqf by the owner. No particular form is necessary and the declaration may be either oral or written. It is sufficient for the settlor to indicate his intention to make the property waqf and to specify the charitable purpose to which it is to be devoted. It is generally accepted that this declaration is sufficient in itself for the creation of a waqf and that

[1] Q. II, 211.
[2] Q. III, 86.

delivery of possession to the mutawallī is not an essential condition of validity. The declaration may also be testamentary, but in this case it is subject to the rules governing testamentary dispositions, which do not permit a testator to dispose of more than one-third of his estate to a stranger, or to make any disposition to an heir unless ratified by the other heirs.

(4) The dedication of a waqf must be irrevocable, unconditional, and permanent. Moreover, save in the case of a testamentary waqf which takes effect only upon the death of the wāqif, the declaration must be intended to take effect immediately.

(5) The object of the waqf must be charitable in the general sense. The charitable object need not necessarily be the immediate beneficiary. Thus, the benefits of the waqf may first be reserved for the maintenance of the wāqif's children and descendants, or for that of strangers, with a provision that after extinction of the beneficiaries, the benefits of the waqf shall be appropriated to a charitable or pious purpose, such as the relief of the poor, the support of a mosque, or the advancement of education or religion.

The underlying and ultimate object of both kinds of waqf, whether family or charitable, is, therefore, an act of charity that gains favor with the Almighty. Although in many cases, men have dedicated their properties as waqf to escape taxation, as happened in Egypt at the time of the Mamluk rulers (A.D. 1254-1517), or out of fear of the prodigality of their children, or for reasons unconnected with charity—yet the waqf has in legal theory at least maintained its connection with the religious precept of charity. The charitable purpose of the waqf serves as its legal justification and constitutes the basic condition of its validity.

LEGAL RULES OF WAQF

A waqf is subject to three basic rules: irrevocability, perpetuity, and inalienability. Abū Ḥanīfa held a waqf to be revocable by its maker unless the declaration had been confirmed by a court decree. He suggested, therefore, in order to make a waqf irrevocable, that the wāqif deliver the property to the mutawallī and then claim it back from him on the ground that the declaration was not binding; this fictitious dispute would then be submitted to a qāḍī who would render a judgment establishing the irrevocable character of the waqf. The only exceptions recognized by Abū Ḥanīfa were a waqf made in favor of a mosque and a testamentary waqf coming into effect by reason of the death of the testator, both of which he held to be binding in themselves. However, Abū Yūsuf and Shaybānī, Abū Ḥanīfa's disciples, took the contrary view and held that a declaration of waqf is, in its nature, irrevocable. It is this latter opinion which has prevailed in practice under the Ḥanafī school. A waqf cannot be revoked after the declaration has been made, nor can the power to revoke be validly reserved.

The general Ḥanafī rule is that a waqf must be perpetual in order to be valid. If it purports to be made for a limited period or for a temporary purpose, it is void. According to the Mālikī school, however, a waqf may be limited as to time or as to a life or series of lives, and after the expiration of the time or the extinction of the life or lives specified, it reverts in full ownership to the wāqif or his heirs.

The perpetuity of the waqf does not imply the perpetuity of its objects. It merely means that the appropriation of the income of the waqf to charity must be intended to be perpetual, even though the specific object of charity has not a character of permanency or perpetuity. If a waqf is made for purposes which may fail or which are not perpetual, the view of Abū Yūsuf is that the waqf is valid, and that its benefits will accrue to the poor after the named objects cease. This is the accepted Ḥanafī view, although others have held that where the objects of the waqf are not permanent in character, and a general charitable intention cannot be inferred, the waqf is invalid.

There is, however, full agreement about the nonextinction of a valid waqf by reason of the extinction or disappearance of the charitable object specified in the declaration. In such a case, the benefit of the waqf is applied to another charitable or pious purpose. It has been stated that the rule obtaining in Islamic law in this respect is analogous to the doctrine of *cy pres* under the English law of trusts. Abdur Raḥīm says:

> If, however, the specified objects be limited or happen to fail, but a general charitable intention is to be inferred from the words of the grant, the *waqf* will be good and the income or profit will be devoted for the benefit of the poor, and in some cases, to objects as near to the objects which failed as possible. This rule is analogous to the doctrine of *cy pres* of the English Law.[3]

This is generally true subject to one observation. The *cy pres* doctrine aims at a judicial determination of a particular purpose to which the trust fund shall be applied which is as near to the settlor's intention as possible. Under Islamic law, there is no provision or

[3] Abdur Raḥīm, *The Principles of Muhammadan Jurisprudence* (Madras, 1911), p. 305.

machinery for such determination. It is assumed as a basic principle that the ultimate purpose of a waqf is charitable and, therefore, that the appropriation of the benefit of the waqf to the poor is a fulfilment of this purpose. Since the benefit of the poor is considered to be a residuary charitable object of a waqf, there is no necessity for a close scrutiny of the settlor's intention and careful construction of the trust instrument, as is required under the *cy pres* doctrine.

The effect of dedication of property as waqf is a relinquishment of ownership by the wāqif without any resultant acquisition of ownership by another person. Neither the wāqif nor his heirs after him have any proprietary interest in the corpus of the property. Moreover, the beneficiaries of a waqf have merely an interest in the usufruct, but none in the ownership of the waqf property. The mutawallī is vested not with ownership but only with the right of administration.

Certain jurists have advanced the view that ownership of waqf property is vested in God. More recently and under the influence of Western ideas, some modern writers have argued that the waqf is a juristic person, and that ownership is vested in the juristic person so created. Legal fictions, such as these, are weak and undesirable explanations. Is it not possible to say that the ownership is appropriated to the permanent object of the waqf and for that reason is immobilized and cannot be exercised by any one? Whatever formula is adopted to explain the vesting of ownership, it is certain that the corpus of waqf property becomes inalienable, as a natural consequence of the divestment of personal ownership of the waqf property.

The effect of inalienability is that property made waqf cannot be the subject of any sale, disposition, mortgage, gift, inheritance, attachment, or any alienation whatsoever. It can, as will be seen later, be leased because a lease implies the grant to the lessee of the right of user in consideration of a benefit without affecting ownership. There is, however, one exception to the general rule of inalienability. Waqf property may be exchanged for equivalent property; or it may be sold, subject to compulsory reinvestment of the price in another property, if the right of exchange or sale was originally reserved by the wāqif in the waqf instrument or, failing such reservation, if the original property falls into ruins or ceases to produce any benefit, so that the objects of the waqf cannot be fulfilled. In such cases, the sale is considered to be incidental to an exchange and the qāḍī grants authority for exchange or sale. The power to sell or exchange is very strictly exercised and waqf property may not, generally speaking, be sold in exchange for another property merely because the resulting increase of the corpus would be beneficial to the waqf. New property acquired, either by direct exchange or investment of the proceeds of sale, becomes waqf subject to the same terms and conditions as the original waqf. This exception to the rule of inalienability is, therefore, more apparent than real since a new corpus is substituted for the old one and the continuity of the waqf is maintained.

LEASE OF WAQF PROPERTY

As a general rule, in the absence of more liberal powers granted by the waqf instrument, waqf property may not be leased for more than one year. There is, however, some authority in the law to the effect that the limitation as to a yearly lease applies to buildings, whereas agricultural land may be leased for up to three years. The qāḍī may authorize a lease of longer duration where the waqf property is dilapidated and does not produce enough income to permit its repair; the lease permitted under these circumstances would be of a duration sufficient to yield an income which would cover the cost of repairs. In essence, the law thus prohibits any long leasing of the property which would be tantamount to a disposition of its ownership.

The inconvenience arising from the inalienability of waqf property led jurists during the period of the Ottoman Empire to create ingenious devices for evading the strictness of the rule. Under a device called ijāratayn, waqf property was, with the permission of the qāḍī, permanently leased to a person who undertook to pay (1) an advance rent which was used for the repair and improvement of the corpus, and (2) a postponed rent, payable annually, which was equivalent to three percent of the assessed value of the property. The lessee thereby acquired a perpetual right of enjoyment of the waqf property, his right having become by an Ottoman statute assignable and inheritable. For all practical purposes, the holder of ijāratayn on waqf property became its owner, subject to the payment of what was, in fact, a rent charge to the mutawallī of the waqf. If the lessee should die without heirs, the property would revert to the waqf. Another device adopted to defeat the rule of inalienability was an arrangement made by the lessee and the mutawallī, with the authorization of the qāḍī, by virtue of which the lessee acquired the permanent right, subject to the payment of an annual rent, to erect buildings, or plant trees upon waqf property. The holder became the owner of the buildings or the trees while the land remained waqf. Those two devices, which ostensibly were intended only to extend the time of possession of the tenant of waqf properties, became disguised means for the disposition of waqfs. Notwithstanding that they were clear deviations from the established doctrine of waqf, they were statutorily recognized and regulated in the Ottoman Empire and continue to exist in the Arab countries which were formed from the Ottoman Empire. These and other similar devices could minimize in part the undesirable economic aspects resulting from the immobilization of waqf but could not, and did not, remove the unsatisfactory features of a rigid inalienability of waqf property.

CONDITIONS OF THE WAQF

The waqf is administered in all respects in accordance with the conditions laid down in the waqf instrument. The wishes of the wāqif are carried out in perpetuity with a force equal to that of a legal enactment. The wāqif has full latitude regarding the conditions that he may prescribe for the operation of the waqf. In fact, so long as the wāqif casts the transaction in the form prescribed by law, that is, irrevocably appropriates the income in perpetuity either presently or ultimately to a charitable object, he has the right without any limitation or restriction to impose any conditions that he desires with regard to the administration of the waqf, the appointment of mutawallīs, the designation of beneficiaries, the application of income, the exchange of the corpus of the waqf, and generally all matters relating to the waqf. The waqf instrument may also reserve power to the wāqif alone, or to the wāqif and subsequent mutawallīs, to make alterations and amendments in the designation of beneficiaries or application of the income. The conditions which the wāqif may prescribe include the power to increase or diminish the shares of beneficiaries, to deprive any beneficiary of his share, and to add or exclude beneficiaries.

A waqf being a settlement in perpetuity, circumstances which could not have been anticipated by the wāqif may arise in course of time and necessitate a modification of the original terms of the waqf instrument. The reservation of the power to alter and modify conditions relating to designation of beneficiaries was a valuable means of adapting the waqf to new situations and adjusting it to changing circumstances. Here we have an example of legal ingenuity exercised with a view to saving the institution from the rigidity that it was bound to develop by reason of its permanent character. The reservation of the power to alter and modify the conditions of waqf has not, however, succeeded in protecting it from many criticisms which will be considered later.

It is interesting to observe in connection with the reservation of a right to alter the conditions of a waqf, the development of a rule of judicial construction that such a right may be exercised only once unless the waqf instrument specifically provides that it may be exercised on repeated occasions. The reasoning behind this judicial doctrine is that this reservation amounts to the right to exercise a discretion and that once the discretion is exercised, it is exhausted.

The wide latitude accorded the wāqif in the choice of the conditions that he may impose has, by reason of the unpopularity of certain conditions, become one of the causes of dissatisfaction with the institution of waqf. For example, the forfeiture of the right of a beneficiary upon contracting debts or upon marriage, or upon marriage into other than a designated family, the exclusion of female descendants from the benefit of a waqf, and like conditions that may be imposed by a wāqif have created dissatisfaction with the family waqf. The Ḥanbalī and Mālikī schools, while recognizing a wide latitude of the wāqif in the conditions that he may impose, do not recognize as legitimate conditions which arbitrarily deprive beneficiaries of their rights. The Ḥanafī school, however, does not invalidate such conditions.

DETERMINATION OF BENEFICIARIES

Complex questions may arise in relation to family waqfs regarding the exact determination of beneficiaries. One may refer, by way of illustration, to the usual provision made by a settlor that the property is reserved to the use of himself and, after him, of his descendants in perpetuity until failure of issue with a reversion of the benefits to the poor. Let us suppose that the wāqif leaves three sons who, being members of the same generation, share equally the income of the waqf. If one of the sons dies leaving issue, and his two brothers survive him, then the children of the deceased son, in the absence of a provision in the waqf instrument, do not share in the income until all the members of the previous generation have died, whereupon the second generation becomes entitled to the benefits of the waqf. Now, what happens to the share of the deceased son pending the entitlement of the second generation? Does it pass until the entitlement of the next generation to the surviving members of the first generation or does it pass to the residuary charity by way of a temporary reversion? These problems must be solved by reference to the terms of the waqf instrument.

COMPARISON WITH TRUSTS

It may not be without interest to compare the waqf with the analogous institution of trust developed under the English common law. The similarity between the Islamic institution of waqf and the early English conception of a trust is striking. Under both concepts, property is reserved, and its usufruct appropriated, for the benefit of specific individuals, or for a general charitable purpose; the corpus becomes inalienable; estates for life in favor of successive beneficiaries can be created at the will of the original owner without regard to the law of inheritance or the rights of the heirs; and continuity is secured by the successive appointment of trustees or mutawallīs.

Waqf and trust differ in certain respects but an analysis of these differences merely confirms the close similarity of the two concepts. It is commonly held that one of the most important differences is that under English law, the "legal estate" is vested in the trustee and he is consequently the "owner" of the trust, whereas the mutawallī is not considered to be owner of the waqf. In reality, the trustee is no more the owner of a trust than a mutawallī could be the owner of a waqf; the main function of both is to administer the property for the benefit, not of themselves, but of the object of the trust or waqf. Another difference between waqf and trust relates to duration; a waqf must, as a condition of its validity under the prevailing view, be perpetual, while a trust, except a charitable one, cannot be perpetual. It must not be forgotten, however, that trusts could originally be made in perpetuity until the rule against perpetuities came into force. It is not suggested that differences between the two institutions do not exist. In fact, the most important difference concerns the object. A trust may be made for any lawful object; a waqf is primarily intended for charity and even where it has as its object a family settlement, it is nonetheless required as a condition *sine qua non* that the ultimate object, after extinction of the designated beneficiaries, be charitable. In comparing trusts and waqf, however, what is of importance is the similarity based upon the same legal device of divestment or renunciation of ownership of property and the appropriation of its usufruct for a time or in perpetuity, in favor of successive beneficiaries, not all of whom are in existence at the time of the original settlement, but who are designated by or are capable of identification according to the wishes of the settlor.

A THEORY AS TO THE ORIGIN OF TRUSTS

The close resemblance between trust and awqāf naturally leads to an inquiry as to whether the English trust was derived from the Islamic waqf. There is no doubt that the waqf is the earlier of the two institutions. The legal theory of waqf was developed during the eighth and ninth centuries and there are awqāf today that were established more than one thousand years ago.

The origin of English trusts or uses, as they were first called, is of a later date. It is stated that the Franciscan Friars first introduced uses in England during the thirteenth century. One of the earliest recorded cases is referred to by Bracton as being of A.D. 1224, in which a man, before starting for the Holy Land, committed land to his brother to be kept for the use of his children. In the second quarter of the thirteenth century, several cases of land held for the use of the Franciscan Friars in England are to be found. For the view that the Franciscan Friars were largely responsible for the introduction of uses in England, we have the authority of Pollock and Maitland who observe:

> Lastly, in the early years of the thirteenth century the Franciscan Friars came hither. . . . We should be nearer the truth if we said that to all seeming the first persons who in England employed the "use" on a large scale were, not the clergy, nor the monks, but the Friars of St. Francis.[4]

It is significant to observe, at this stage, that when uses made their appearance in England, they were almost simultaneously utilized to effect settlement for family purposes as well as settlement for charitable purposes.

It is also interesting to examine the early applications of uses and compare them with the practice of family and charitable awqāf in Islamic law. Professor Holdsworth states:

> By means of directions given to feoffees to use, land owners could charge their land with annuities in favour of their relatives or dependents or with portions to their wives and younger children, and they could found charitable institutions and provide for their management.

He also observes that land

> . . . could be given to executors for a term of years and after its determination it could be given to the testator's son in tail. It could be made to

[4] Sir Frederick Pollock and Frederic W. Maitland, *History of English Law* (2nd ed., Cambridge, 1952), Vol. II, p. 229.

go over from one beneficiary to another on the happening of an event; thus, by means of these springing and shifting uses, landowners acquired a large and a certain control over the future of their property. There was no doubt a danger that this large control might be used to its own destruction if the property were so settled that it was vested in perpetuity in a succession of limited owners. But it would seem that this danger did not clearly arise during this period.[5]

It will have been observed that the three main features of waqf are first, the separation of ownership and usufruct; second, the vesting in beneficiaries of a right of enjoyment of the usufruct only; and third, the right of the settlor to vest the usufruct, excluding cases where a charity was directly the object of the settlement, in a succession of beneficiaries, present and future. These characteristics are also to be found in the early English use. Moreover, the several persons involved or concerned in a waqf correspond exactly to the various persons involved or concerned in the early English use. The wāqif of waqf property is analogous to the person making the feoffment to uses, subsequently named the settlor; the mutawallī is the same as the feoffee to uses, subsequently known as the trustee; finally, there are the beneficiaries, present and future, who exist in both institutions. The only substantial difference between a family waqf and an English use is that in the case of a waqf in favor of descendants or other private persons, there is an express or implied reversion of the usufruct to a charitable purpose. It will be remembered, however, that under Islamic jurisprudence this was the legal justification for the reversion in favor of the charity not taking effect until failure of posterity.

The analogy between waqf and use is therefore almost unquestionable. The chronology also, as we have seen, is favorable in support of the derivation of uses from waqf, since the theory and practice of the latter were fully developed in Islamic countries prior to the introduction of uses in England. The opportunities for such derivation also existed because there were at that time several points of contact between the Western world and Islam which may have helped to familiarize the West with the institution of waqf. There were the pilgrimages to the Holy Land which became both important and frequent during the eleventh and twelfth centuries. St. Francis himself went to Egypt in A.D. 1219; and there were the Crusades which, particularly during the twelfth century, sent tens of thousands of people from Europe to Asia Minor and the Holy Land. The device and conception of the waqf would surely at that

[5] Sir William Searle Holdsworth, *A History of English Law* (1st ed., London, 1903 to 1938), Vol. IV, p. 440.

time answer an urgent need in a country where, as remarked by Bacon, the lands were not "testamentary or devisable."

It may not be out of place to refer here to a general appreciation of the influence which the knowledge gained by the Crusaders had on Western culture:

> The coincidence of the thirteenth century "Renaissance" with the period of the Crusades is striking, and it would be rash to deny any share in the outburst of intellectual energy which marks the thirteenth century to the new ideas and broadened outlook of those who, having gone on crusade, have seen the world of men and things in a way to which the society of the tenth and eleventh centuries was unaccustomed. . . .[6]

It, therefore, seems reasonable to suggest that the early English uses may have been derived from the Islamic system of awqāf. This conclusion is further supported by the fact that the various theories so far advanced to explain the historical origin of uses appear to be questionable. One such theory is that the English use was derived from the Roman *fideicommissum*. This explanation, however, has been discredited and entirely rejected. Apart from other arguments, it is sufficient to quote one reason given by Pollock and Maitland: "The English use in its earliest stage is seldom, if ever, the outcome of a last will, while the *fideicommissum* belongs essentially to the law of testaments."[7] The other theory is that put forward by Mr. Justice Holmes and now currently accepted:

> Mr. Justice Holmes was the first to point out that the root idea underlying the conception of the use is to be found among the Germanic tribes. That root idea consists in the recognition of the duty of a person to whom property has been conveyed for certain purposes to carry out those purposes. The fact that one man trusts another in this way naturally appears in any sort of society which has progressed so far as to possess even the most rudimentary system of law. A very small amount of legal development will necessitate some sort of institution by which effect can be given to create trusts of this kind. That institution early Germanic law found in the *Salman* or *Treuhand*. He was, as we have seen, a person to whom property has been transferred for certain purposes, to be carried out either in the lifetime or after the death of the person conveying it.
>
> It is to this institution that we must look for the beginnings of the law as to bailment and agency. And it is to the same quarter that we must look for the origin of the earliest conveyances to uses.[8]

[6] E. J. Passant, "The Effects of the Crusades upon Western Europe," *Cambridge Medieval History* (Cambridge, 1926), Vol. V, p. 331.

[7] Pollock and Maitland, *op. cit.*, Vol. II, p. 239.

[8] Holdsworth, *op. cit.*, Vol. IV, pp. 410-11.

If one examines, however, the basis of this theory, it will be found that it proceeds merely on a vague analogy in the fiduciary position of the feoffee to uses and the *Salman*. It might be better to quote Mr. Justice Holmes:

The feoffee to uses of the early English law corresponds point by point to the *Salman* of the early German law, as described by Besseler fifty years ago. The *Salman*, like the feoffee, was a person to whom land was transferred in order that he might make a conveyance according to his grantor's directions. Most frequently the conveyance was to be made after the grantor's death, the grantor reserving the use of the land to himself during his life.[9]

The view of Mr. Justice Holmes, endorsed by Professor Holdsworth, as to the Germanic origin of the use is therefore exclusively based on an apparent similarity between the position of the *Salman* and that of the feoffee to uses and does not extend further so as to establish any resemblance in the nature of the two concepts such as has already been observed in the case of the waqf and trust. It appears that this view fails to take sufficiently into account the fact that the *Salman* was substantially an intermediary for a conveyance while the feoffee to uses was more in the nature of a trustee and possessed a closer resemblance to the mutawallī of the waqf. Moreover, the various aspects of the concept of a trust, involving the separation of usufruct from ownership, the creation of life estates, and the power of the original owner or settler to direct the passing of the usufruct from one beneficiary to another—all found with a striking similarity in the use and the waqf—are totally unknown to Germanic theory or practice and are strongly indicative of the relationship between use and waqf.

In concluding, it may be of interest to survey and compare very briefly the subsequent evolution of each institution. As is well known, uses developed into the modern forms of trusts and played an important part in the progress and evolution of Western communities; their position is summarized by Professor Holdsworth as follows:

Both the trust and the doctrine of consideration are peculiar to English Law, and to the law of those countries which have come under its influence. Both have their roots in the Middle Ages . . . both have had very large effects upon the development not only of our private but also of our public law. . . . Trusts likewise have, from the sixteenth century onwards, played a part in the development of our public law,

[9] O. W. Holmes, "Early English Equity," *Law Quarterly Review*, Vol. I, p. 163. For a critical appraisal of Holmes' theory, see Max Radin, *Handbook of Anglo-American Legal History* (St. Paul, Minn., 1936), pp. 430-33.

larger and more direct than that played by contract. They have peopled our state with groups and associations which have enabled the individual persons who have created or composed them, to accomplish much more than any single individual composing them could have accomplished. Students of these entities, if they have not attempted to deify them, have at least worked hard to personify them. And, whatever may be the nature of their personality, it is, as we shall see, quite clear that they have exercised a large influence over our commercial, religious, political and social life.[10]

In the case of waqf, there was, generally speaking, no evolution until the present time. It retained the rigidity of its original concept as devised more than a thousand years ago. One particular condition that contributed most to this rigidity was the requirement that a waqf must be established in perpetuity. Muslim jurists, we have seen, have held different views as to the duration of the waqf, some holding that being a charitable disposition, it must by its nature be perpetual, others contending that it could be limited as to time. The prevalent view, supported by practice, has tended towards the creation of perpetual waqf. The perpetuity of waqfs has naturally led to increasingly injurious consequences, both to the beneficiaries and to the objects of the waqf. A waqf dhurrī, it has been observed, prevents the alienation, economic exploitation, and improvement of the waqf property. Where the beneficiaries of the waqf are the descendants of the wāqif, they are likely to multiply, the ensuing result being that the income of the waqf, instead of being distributed among a small and limited number of persons as was the case at the time of the declaration, would after some generations have to be distributed in diminutive shares among several scores or even hundreds of beneficiaries. The benefits thus become so small as to be illusory. In consequence, the beneficiaries lose interest in the income of the property and the mutawallī loses interest in its care or upkeep. Again, waqf properties, being immobilized in perpetuity, cannot be sold or freely leased or exchanged, thereby impeding and stultifying their economic exploitation. Neither the mutawallī nor the beneficiaries present or future have any real incentive to improve waqf properties. Finally, the mutawallī of the waqf may neglect its administration or misuse his powers, thereby leading to endless disputes and litigation with the beneficiaries.

It is obvious that there are two basic reasons for the difference in evolution of the two systems, waqf and trust: on the one hand, English jurists checked at an early period the inconveniences and

[10] Holdsworth, *op. cit.*, Vol. IV, pp. 407-8.

dangers resulting from the perpetuity of a trust by developing a rule against perpetuities; on the other hand, the Anglo-Saxon peoples have adapted and expanded the trust system to serve various social and commercial objects, while the Arabs did not alter the rules of waqf so as to adopt them to changing conditions or to extend the concept to fields other than charity and family settlements.

RECENT EVOLUTION OF THE LAW OF WAQF IN THE MIDDLE EAST

The widespread dissatisfaction with the waqf dhurrī has led some Arab countries in recent times to amend the law of waqf so as to remove some of its unsatisfactory features or, as happened recently in Syria and Egypt, to suppress family awqāf altogether. The earliest movement for reform of the law of waqf manifested itself in Egypt.

EGYPT

In 1946, the Egyptian Parliament enacted a law regulating waqf which was a compromise between opposing tendencies as to abolition or maintenance of awqāf.[11] The committee charged with considering the revision of the law of waqf reported that the institution of waqf had existed for some thirteen centuries during which it had been a source of income for various charities and had helped many families to survive the vicissitudes of fortune. It was also stated that the dissolution of family waqf could have a serious impact upon real estate resulting in grave financial difficulties and complications. For these reasons, the family waqf was maintained but certain major amendments were introduced into the law. The condition of perpetuity was removed, the law providing that a charitable waqf may, at the option of the wāqif, be perpetual or temporary, but that a family waqf must be limited to not more than two generations, or if made for a term of years, to a period not exceeding sixty years from the date of the wāqif's death. The irrevocability of a waqf also was abolished and the wāqif was given the right to revoke the waqf wholly or in part and to alter its conditions. The law also contained various provisions relating to the partition or the termination of waqf, the entitlement of beneficiaries, and the administration of the waqf. This enactment is now merely of historical interest, since one of

[11] Law No. 48 of June 12, 1946.

the first acts of the new regime which assumed power in Egypt in the summer of 1952 was to abolish noncharitable waqfs. It is now provided that no waqf can be created except for a charitable purpose and any existing waqf that is not presently and exclusively devoted to a charitable object is dissolved.[12] The ownership of a waqf dissolved under the law reverts to the wāqif, if alive, and if he has reserved the right of revocation of the waqf; if not, the ownership vests in the beneficiaries of the waqf in accordance with their shares under the waqf instrument. In cases where the waqf instrument provides for the apportionment of the income between a charitable object and a noncharitable object, the waqf is nonetheless dissolved, except for the share belonging to the charitable object. The income of such share is set aside for such charitable object until sale or partition of the property.

LEBANON

The law of waqf in Lebanon conformed to the Ḥanafī school until the enactment of the law of March 12, 1947, regulating the waqf dhurrī, which was patterned after the Egyptian legislation of the preceding year. The changes effected by the Lebanese Statute may be summarized as follows:

(1) The rule of irrevocability of waqf is discarded (Article 7). This provision is based upon the view of Abū Ḥanīfa.

(2) The duration of a waqf dhurrī is limited to two generations (Article 8), after which ownership of the waqf reverts to the wāqif or his heirs (Article 9). These amendments are in accord with the teachings of the Mālikī and Ḥanbalī schools which allow the creation of a waqf for a limited period of time and the reversion of ownership to the wāqif and his heirs.

(3) Any condition in the waqf restricting the liberty of a beneficiary in relation to marriage, residence, or the contracting of debts is deemed to be null and void (Article 13). This amendment is based upon the views of the Ḥanbalī and Mālikī schools.

(4) Provisions are laid down for partition of the corpus of a waqf so that each beneficiary may administer his share (Articles 17-30), as well as for the dissolution of a waqf in cases where the property is dilapidated and incapable of repair, or if the income becomes insignificant (Articles 32-34). These amendments reflect the opinions of the Ḥanbalī and Mālikī schools.

(5) In the case of partition or dissolution of a waqf under the preceding provisions, a share equivalent to fifteen percent of the

[12] Law No. 180 of September 1952.

value of the property is appropriated to the eventual charitable object for which provision is made in the waqf instrument.

(6) Where the waqf is limited to specific generations—which may not exceed two as provided in Article 8—the descendants of a deceased member of one generation represent the decedent and take his share.

(7) Mutawallīs are made accountable for the administration of awqāf and liable for negligence.

(8) Movable property and shares of stock may be made waqf.

This Law thus sought to remove several aspects of the law of waqf that had proved to be unpopular or harmful to the economy of the country. It is noteworthy, however, that although this was a statutory regulation, the modifications or amendments to the law were based upon, and traced to, interpretations of the sharī'a according to one or more of its four schools. The practical value of the differences in views between Islamic jurists and between the various schools of law may not always have been fully realized, but became apparent when the attempt was made to amend the law of waqf upon principles that were not foreign to the sharī'a.

SYRIA

In 1949 Syria took the drastic step of abolishing the waqf dhurrī. The charitable waqf was not affected. By Legislative Decree No. 76, dated May 16, 1949,[13] the creation of a waqf dhurrī after the date of the decree is prohibited and any registration of such waqf dhurrī is deemed to be legally void (Article 1). Moreover, all awqāf dhurriyya which were established prior to that date are dissolved and must be liquidated in accordance with the provisions of the decree (Article 2). A special court is established to supervise the dissolution of awqāf dhurriyya and given jurisdiction to decide all disputes and matters relating thereto. The following provisions relating to liquidation may be of interest: If the corpus of the waqf is capable of partition, it shall be divided among the beneficiaries; if the waqf is partly dhurrī and partly charitable, it is partitioned among the beneficiaries themselves. If the waqf is not capable of partition, it shall be sold by public auction and the proceeds distributed in accordance with the following provisions:

(1) In the case of a waqf dhurrī, where the right of the chari-

[13] Published in the Syrian *Official Gazette* (1949), p. 1317. Leg. Decree No. 76 was amended by Legislative Decree No. 97 of Nov. 26, 1949, published in the Syrian *Official Gazette* (1949), p. 3379.

table object is contingent upon the extinction of the wāqif's descendants, five percent of the proceeds shall be appropriated to such charitable object, ten percent is allocated to national defense, and the remainder distributed among the beneficiaries.

(2) In the case of a waqf partly dhurrī and partly charitable, if the wāqif has indicated the share belonging to the charity, then such share shall be allocated to it; if the wāqif has omitted to mention the share that should be allocated to charity, then such portion of the proceeds shall be appropriated to the charitable object as would be sufficient to fulfil the wāqif's intention, provided that such appropriation shall not be less than five percent nor in excess of twenty percent of the proceeds.

As from the date of the decree, the office of mutawallī of a waqf dhurrī is suppressed. The administration of any property or proceeds appropriated to a charitable object as a result of the dissolution of a waqf under the law is henceforth vested in the Waqf Administration, a state agency.

The beneficiaries entitled to share in the corpus of the waqf or alternatively in the proceeds of sale are those existing at the date of promulgation of the Legislative Decree. Their shares are determined by the conditions laid down by the wāqif. If the waqf is limited to specific generations, the corpus of the waqf or its proceeds are divided among the existing beneficiaries in accordance with the conditions of the waqf, provided that the shares of any deceased members of the same generation as that of the existing beneficiaries shall be distributed to their children. Any condition imposed by the wāqif as to forfeiture of a beneficiary's interest shall be void unless it is for a cause that would prevent legal inheritance.

The Syrian enactment thus departed radically from established principles and eradicated an archaic and uneconomic institution that had remained rigid and unimproved through the centuries. The Syrian enactment set a precedent that was to be followed three years later in Egypt as we have already seen.

OTHER ARAB COUNTRIES

The law applicable to waqf in Saudi Arabia is the general law of the country, that is, the sharī'a law interpreted in accordance with the doctrine of Aḥmad ibn Ḥanbal.[14] However, if the judges find that any rule of Ḥanbalī doctrine may in its application to any particular case cause hardship and be opposed to public interest, they may apply an interpretation prevailing in the other

[14] Decision of Judicial Council, dated A.H. 7/1/1347 approved on 24/3/1347.

schools of law.[15] Apart from the legal provisions prescribing the application of sharīʿa law in all courts according to the doctrine of Aḥmad ibn Ḥanbal, there is practically no statutory legislation relating to waqf, except certain minor provisions that do not affect the substantive law of waqf. An example of these provisions is the prohibition of the leasing of waqf property for more than five years without the qāḍī's permission,[16] another is the permission granted to foreigners to acquire land in Saudi Arabia if it is to be made waqf in favor of a permanent charitable object.[17] The benefit of such waqf, however, cannot be assigned to foreigners residing outside Saudi Arabia or to purposes which must be fulfilled outside the country.

In ʿIraq and Jordan, no changes have taken place in the law of waqf, which continues to be applied in accordance with the principles of the sharīʿa law.

In concluding this discussion of the law of waqf and its recent evolution in the Middle East, it may be observed that the soundness and durability of a legal institution lie in its ability to survive changing circumstances and adapt itself to new needs and conditions. The rigidity that has encompassed the law of waqf for centuries made it impossible for this institution to withstand the impact of modern trends and recent developments in the Middle East.

[15] *Ibid,* Article 2.
[16] Opinion of *Riyāsat Al-Quḍāt* (collection of Regs., Vol. I, p. 38).
[17] Decision of Majlis al-Shūra No. 61 of A.H. 6/2/1350.

CHAPTER IX

ʿUqūbāt: Penal Law

NO OTHER parts of the sharīʿa are as inadequately worked out by Muslim jurists as the law of ʿuqūbāt. As a result, the caliphs and their viziers had more freedom in this field than in others to enforce their own executive decrees, based on custom and precedent.

The term ʿuqūbāt (singular, ʿuqūba) covers the two kinds of wrongs, namely, torts and crimes. But the line dividing the two is sometimes very narrow, since the rights of the public and of individuals are often combined. One of the tests is to determine to whom the law grants the remedy, to the public or to the individual. In the latter case, the wrong would be a tort, in the former a crime.

Islamic penal law combined the principles of the personality and territoriality of the law and, as a consequence, it applied, in the Islamic world, to all criminals, Muslims and non-Muslims alike, for the divine rules pertaining to wrongs applied in a general and comprehensive manner as will be discussed later.

Since Muslim law in principle applied to Muslims wherever they resided, be it inside or outside the Islamic world, Muslims who committed wrongs outside the Islamic world were punished when they returned to their country. Islamic law was thus close to the principles of territorial and personal criminal jurisdiction in modern law.

The existence of clear legal provisions defining offenses and their punishments and necessitating the strict infliction of penalties establishes an equivalent to the Western rule that all offenses must be defined and their punishment stipulated. The qāḍī may not punish an act which has not previously and explicitly been made punishable. He is likewise forbidden to impose a penalty other than that fixed by law; in conformity with the Qurʾānic stipulation: "And who so will not judge by what God has revealed, these be the evildoers" (Q. V, 51). The principle that a person may not be held criminally responsible for acts which at the time of their commission were not punishable by law was well known at the beginning of the Islamic era. The Prophet Muḥammad did not punish new proselytes for acts committed before their conversion, even though they were prohibited by Islam.

For purposes of simplification, this chapter is divided into three parts. The first discusses the general rules of penal law; the second deals with specific crimes and their punishments; and the third gives a brief synopsis of judicial procedure in criminal cases.

CATEGORIES OF PENALTIES

Penalties may be divided into four categories:

1. Physical penalties
   a. Punishment by death
   b. Cutting off of the hand
   c. Flogging
   d. Stoning
2. Restrictions of freedom, i.e., imprisonment or exile
3. Monetary fines
4. Admonition by the qāḍī

Islamic law has also known additional forms of punishment. The man who is convicted of false accusation of fornication, for example, is deprived of the right of testimony, a penalty which corresponds to some extent to the loss of civil status which accompanies some convictions today. The offenses which fall under each of these categories of punishment are well established in Islamic law.

CRIMINAL RESPONSIBILITY

The principle of the personal responsibility of the individual for crimes which he has committed is established by the following verse of the Qur'ān: "and no burdened one shall bear another's burden" (Q. VI, 164) and "pledged to God is every man for his actions and their desert" (Q. LII, 21). Islam put an end to the collective criminal responsibility which had been customary among the Arabs, but it continued to recognize the collective responsibility of the family for payments of damages resulting from a crime. Thus, it is stipulated that not only the criminal, but also his family (i.e., his relatives on his father's side) collectively are responsible for blood money and fines imposed for physical injury.

There is, perhaps, no clearer indication of the concern of Islamic law for confining criminal responsibility to the criminal alone than the will of Caliph 'Alī (A.D. 656-661) who, after suffering the fatal blow of Ibn Muljam, called his sons to his deathbed and told them, "Do not kill except him who killed me. Wait, if I die from his blow, revenge me a blow for a blow, and don't mutilate the man, for I heard the messenger of Allah say: 'Beware of mutilation even if it were an ailing dog.' "

This will, issuing from a man who had accompanied the message of Islam from its birth, supports not only the principle that criminal responsibility should be confined to the criminal alone, but also the rule of criminal investigation which demands proof that death is due to the act of the criminal and not to other causes. The jurists also studied the problem of criminal complicity and distinguished between the punishments of the criminal, the accessory, and the instigator.

RESPONSIBILITY OF THE MINOR AND IMBECILE

In conformity with the rule that a ḥadd (penalty) cannot apply to a person who has not reached his majority, Islamic law recognizes no criminal responsibility on the part of children. Judges reprimanded and admonished children who had committed criminal acts and even imposed reformatory punishments which were less severe than the legal penalties applicable to adults. Likewise, no responsibility attaches to insane or imbecile persons. To quote Abū Yūsuf in his study on al-iqrār: "the ḥadd cannot be imposed on the accused after his confession, unless it is made clear that he is not insane, or mentally troubled. If he is free from such deficiency, he should then be submitted to the legal punishment." It was imperative, therefore, that the qāḍī assure himself of the sanity of the criminal before pronouncing judgment.

CRIMINAL INTENT

Islamic law exonerates the criminal if it can be proved that he committed the act under duress or by mistake. This is in accordance with a ḥadīth which states "my community is excused for what it commits under duress, in error, or as a result of forgetfulness." This tradition clearly demands the presence of criminal intent as a basic condition for the infliction of punishment. Legitimate defense is also recognized as negating responsibility for a criminal act. An Egyptian fatwa declares: "The principle of self-defense is well established in Islamic law. If a person draws a sword on another, the person attacked may in self-defense kill the attacker without suffering punishment of any kind."[1]

[1] This *fatwa* is documented by legal arguments and is published in the *Journal of the Egyptian Bar Association*, Vol. 7, p. 146.

Abū Yūsuf says in his *Kitāb al-Kharāj,* "Whoever breaks into a house or a store and gathers his loot is not to be punished by cutting his hand if he were caught inside, before he escapes. He can only be flogged or imprisoned till he repents."[2] Thus, if a person is apprehended before he has consummated an act of theft, the regular penalty for stealing—cutting off of the hand—is commuted to flogging or imprisonment. Similarly, Ibn Taymiyya (d. A.D. 1328) states, "But if they draw the sword without killing a soul or taking any money, and then sheath it and retreat, they are to be exiled." Here, the penalties for killing and robbery are reduced from capital punishment to exile, in cases in which the offense does not exceed the stage of attempt.

Although Islamic law was primarily concerned with the moral aspects of crime, it did not fail to distinguish between criminal and civil responsibility, and provided for the payment of compensation in accidental transgressions as will be seen below in the discussion of homicide.

PENALTY AFTER DEATH

The pre-Islamic practice of judging the dead was discontinued under Islam. Islamic law stipulates that death terminates both the case and the punishment, and forbids the application of any measure after the death of the criminal except damage claims against his estate. The deceased carries with him his own crimes and sins to be judged before his God in the hereafter. In spite of the determination of the sharīʿa to maintain this rule, we find, however, one exception in the command of Allah to His Prophet concerning persons who ignored the call of the Apostle to the jihād (Holy War) and refused to join him. The Qur'ān states with regard to these offenders: "Never pray thou over any one of them who dieth, or stand at his grave, because they believed not in God and His Apostle, and died in their wickedness" (Q. IX, 85). This is, indeed, a form of punishment after death, an important exception to the rule stated above.

OFFENSES AND THEIR PUNISHMENT

Like modern students of penal law, Islamic jurists disagreed on the definition of crime. Al-Māwardī's definition is perhaps the closest to a modern one: "Crimes in Islamic law are legal prohibitions, imposed by God and punished with the penalty of ḥadd or

[2] Abū Yūsuf, *Kitāb al-Kharāj* (Cairo, A. H. 1352), p. 171.

with the penalty of ta'zīr."[3] According to this definition, crimes are of two kinds: (1) criminal acts whose penalty is specified by Qur'ānic stipulation; and (2) offenses punishable in the discretion of human authorities (ta'zīr). As to ḥadd (plural, ḥudūd), the qāḍī is not permitted to deviate from the penalty stipulated because God has bound the qāḍīs by His rule "And who so will not judge by what God hath sent down—such are the infidels (Q. V, 48)." Ta'zīr is the punishment of certain offenses, the extent of which is left to the discretion of the qāḍī. It may take many forms, but it may not exceed the legal ḥadd.

CRIMES PUNISHABLE BY ḤUDŪD

A study of the Qur'ānic provisions reveals that the crimes punished by specified ḥudūd can be divided into three categories: (1) crimes against life and limb, consisting of (a) homicide, and (b) physical injury; (2) crimes against the family and morality, consisting of (a) fornication, and (b) qadhf (false accusation of fornication); (3) crimes against property, consisting of (a) theft, and (b) highway robbery.

Crimes Against Life and Limb

Islam prohibits the killing of man by man in accordance with the Qur'ānic stipulation: "Neither slay any one whom God hath forbidden you to slay unless for a just cause" (Q. XVII, 35). The jurists have recognized three causes for the taking of life: a man's life may be taken in case of (1) apostasy; (2) intentional homicide; and (3) adultery. Apostasy, which is punishable by death, has become an obsolete rule.

According to the Qur'ān, there are three categories of homicide: (1) intentional, (2) accidental, and (3) homicide which is assimilated to accidental homicide.

Though the Qur'ān is clear on the subject of intentional homicide, the jurists have disagreed on its definition. The Qur'ān states:

> Retaliation for bloodshedding is prescribed to you; the free man for the free, and the slave for the slave, and the woman for the woman; but he to whom his brother shall make any remission, is to be dealt with equitably; and to him should he pay a fine with liberality. This is a relaxation from your Lord and a mercy. For him who after this shall transgress, a sore punishment (Q. II, 173-174).

[3] Māwardī, *Kitāb al-Aḥkām al-Sulṭāniyya,* ed. Enger (Bonn, 1853), p. 375.

And in the Sura of the Table it is stated: "And therein have we enacted for them, 'Life for life' " (Q. V, 49). It is to be inferred from these provisions that the punishment of the murderer is death plus the blood money which is paid to the family of the slain by the murderer and his family.

Accidental homicide arises, for example, if a man intends to kill an animal but unintentionally hits a man instead and causes his death. The rule applicable is stipulated in the Qur'ān as follows:

> A believer killeth not a believer but by mischance; and whoso killeth a believer by mischance shall be bound to free a believer from slavery; and the blood money shall be paid to the family of the slain, unless they convert it into alms. But if the slain believer be of a hostile people, then let him confer freedom on a slave who is a believer; and if he be of a people between whom and yourselves there is an alliance, then let the blood money be paid to his family and let him set free a slave who is a believer; and let him who hath not the means, fast two consecutive months. This is the penance enjoined by God (Q. IV, 94).

The jurists have agreed on imposing blood money and al-kifāra (the process of asking repentance from God through fasting and manumission of slaves) on the one who kills another by mischance; in addition, some jurists hold that the killer may not take under the victim's will or in intestate succession to the slain man's estate.

Homicide assimilated to accidental homicide may be divided into two types. The first is very close to the accidental killing discussed above. It is the direct result of an act which normally has no lethal consequences at all, and in which the intent to kill is absent; for example, a person rolls on another person in his sleep and causes his death. All rules which apply to accidental killing apply here also. The second type is described by jurists as similar to accidental homicide in some of its phases. It results directly from an act which is not in itself a cause of death, and which is not accompanied by the intention to kill; for example, a man digs a well in a public road or a mosque and another person falls in it and is killed. The person responsible in these cases is liable for blood money, but there is neither kifāra nor denial of inheritance rights.

Physical injury, like homicide, can be intentional or accidental. In the case of intentional injury, the same amount of pain is to be inflicted upon the offender as has been suffered by his victim. The former is also liable for civil compensation (al-irsh) which corresponds to blood money in homicide. If the physical injury is accidental, however, only the compensation has to be paid in conformity with the Qur'ān:

> And therein have we enacted for you, life for life and eye for eye and nose for nose and ear for ear and tooth for tooth and for wounds retaliation, who so shall compromise it as alms shall have therein the expiation of his sin (Q. V, 49).

Crimes Against the Family and Public Morality

The Qur'ān states: "The whore and the whoremonger—scourge each of them with a hundred stripes; and let not compassion keep you from carrying out the sentence of God, if ye believe in God and the last day; and let some of the faithful witness their chastisement" (Q. XXIV, 2). The punishment for fornication and adultery is, therefore, clearly fixed at a hundred stripes inflicted in public, but the jurists have gone further to distinguish between the punishment of the muḥaṣṣan (an offender who is or has been married) and that of the ghair muḥaṣṣan (an offender who is single). If the offender is single, the above-mentioned punishment applies, but if he is or was married, the jurists, relying exclusively on the authority of the sunna, have stipulated death by stoning as the legal punishment. Some jurists imposed the penalty of exile for one year in addition to the punishment of flogging, while others refused to recognize stoning to death because it is not provided for in the Qur'ān. They insisted on the need for complying with the Qur'ānic provisions, which do not distinguish between the punishment of married and single offenders.

If a person accuses another of fornication or adultery, he is required to support his accusation by procuring four reliable witnesses. If he is unable to do so he is guilty of al-qadhf (false accusation of fornication or adultery) and his punishment is eighty lashes. He is also deprived of the right to act as a witness in the future. This is in conformity with the Qur'ānic provision which states, "They who defame virtuous women and bring not four witnesses, scourge them with fourscore stripes and receive ye not their testimony for ever, for these are perverse persons" (Q. XXIV, 4). The jurists are agreed that a complaint in a case of this type may be filed only by the aggrieved, and that the case is dismissed if the aggrieved withdraws his complaint. These provisions are indications of the important position which morality and protection of the family occupied in Islamic law. As a counterweight to the severe punishment imposed on the adulterer or fornicator, the law stipulates definite requirements for the proof necessary to establish the crime. The jurists are not satisfied with the mere requirement of four reliable witnesses, but further stipulate that the witnesses must testify that they have witnessed the physical act of sexual intercourse.

Offenses Against Property

The jurists agree in defining theft (sariqa) as the clandestine taking of a thing not entrusted to the taker and belonging to someone else. Its punishment, according to the Qur'ān, is the cutting off of the hand. "As to the thief, whether man or woman, cut ye off their hands in recompense for their doings. This is a penalty by way of warning from God Himself; God is Mighty, Wise, but whoever shall turn him to God after this, his wickedness, and amend, God truly will be turned to him" (Q. V, 42-43).

There has been much argument among Muslim jurists as to the various forms of this crime and the conditions necessary for the application of the legal penalty. The disputes on this subject dealt with the object stolen, the place of theft, the condition under which the offense was committed, and the relationship of the thief to his victim. In the unanimous opinion of jurists, the penalty of cutting off the hand does not apply to petty larceny, that is, thefts in which the value of the stolen goods does not exceed ten dirhams.

The jurists also distinguished between thefts occurring in protected and unprotected places. Only in the first case was the hand cut off. As to theft among relatives, Abū Yūsuf writes in the *Kitāb al-Kharāj:* "No one shall suffer a cutting off of the hand for stealing from his father, mother, son, brother, sister, wife, or from anyone who, due to blood relationship, is forbidden to him in marriage; nor is a woman's hand to be cut off for stealing from her husband."[4]

In view of the severity of this punishment, the Prophet permitted its nonenforcement if it could be clearly determined that the criminal had repented and reformed himself in compliance with the Qur'ānic precept. Jurists disagreed, however, on the effects of repentance. A group of them, under the leadership of Abū Ḥanīfa, maintained that the repentance of the criminal could only dispense with punishment in the hereafter, but that it did not rule out the cutting off of the hand. The other school, the Shāfi'ī, maintained that repentance eliminated both punishment in this world and the next. In judicial practice, no definite stand

[4] Abū Yūsuf, *op. cit.*, p. 170.

was taken on either of these two interpretations, although many judges leaned toward Abū Ḥanīfa's thesis.

The Sharī'a imposes a heavy punishment on those committing highway robbery and endangering public safety with the purpose of ensuring public peace and security and safeguarding the community. The Qur'ān stipulates:

> Only, the recompense of those who war against God and His Apostle, and go about to commit disorders on the earth, shall be that they shall be slain or crucified, or have their alternate hands and feet cut off, or be banished from the land. This, their disgrace in this world, and in the next a great torment shall be theirs. Except those who, ere you have them in your power, shall repent (Q. V, 37).

What attracts attention in this provision is the variety of penalties. Jurists argued as to how these penalties should be applied, and the controversy was resolved by entrusting to the qāḍī the power to impose the punishment which, in his opinion, conformed to the criminal act. Another rule can be deduced from this Qur'ānic provision—the suspension of punishment for those who surrender before they are apprehended. This is similar to the modern practice of granting amnesty to participants in a conspiracy against the security of the state or in a revolt, if they voluntarily surrender with their weapons.

OFFENSES NOT PUNISHED BY ḤUDŪD

The offenses discussed so far belonged, for the most part, to the category of crimes whose penalty is stipulated by the Qur'ān. In addition, there are a number of offenses which, though difficult to define and not subjected to specific penalties, are, nevertheless, clearly prohibited by the Qur'ān. They differ from the preceding category in that they are less grave and do not injure individuals. The rule set by the jurists for defining these crimes stipulates that whoever commits a crime for which no ḥadd is provided, and through which no Muslim or non-Muslim is unlawfully hurt by word, deed, or inference, deserves ta'zīr. Offenses for which this discretionary punishment is provided can be divided into two categories: (1) offenses against religion, public order, and public morals, (2) offenses which interfere with rights of individuals.

Ta'zīr, as is evident from its basic meaning, comprises the various kinds of admonitions by which the qāḍī reprimands the offender. However, its meaning has been broadened to include the right of the judge to impose whatever penalty he deems appropriate, provided that it does not exceed the legal ḥadd. The severity of this punishment varies, in the unanimous opinion of the jurists, according to the age, sex, and social standing of the criminal, and the seriousness of the offense. Under the category of ta'zīr, the jurists have included various punishments, such as warning, imprisonment, and flogging; even fines were imposed under this heading.

The Qur'ān imposes religious obligations on Muslims under various penalties. Infringements of the rules on prayer, fasting, zakāt, and other religious duties are to be punished in the hereafter. However, since the dawn of Islam, general practice has recognized the imposition of punishments of the ta'zīr category on persons who neglect these obligations. Likewise, offenders in other matters not directly related to worship, such as fraud in weights and measures are subject to ta'zīr, for it is provided in the Qur'ān, "Be fair when you measure and weigh with the just scale," a rule which provides for no specific punishment. However, offenders have always been duly punished within the limits of ta'zīr.

The drinking of intoxicating beverages is also one of those acts prohibited by the Qur'ān without stipulation of specific punishment. The Qur'ān merely states: "Surely wine and games of chance, and statues, and the divining arrows, are an abomination of Satan's work! Avoid them, that ye may prosper" (Q. V, 92). A difference of opinion resulted when an attempt was made to determine a specific punishment for the consumer of liquor, and this disagreement was widened when the jurists failed to concur on the punishment imposed by the Prophet on those who committed this offense.

Offenses against individual rights include any infringement of the rights of one person caused by another, provided it is not an offense for which a ḥadd has been provided. The offender in this case is also punished by ta'zīr, in addition to possible curtailment of personal rights.

JUDICIAL PROCESS

The absence of clear and definite rules on this subject complicates the determination of the basic principles of organization of justice in Islam.[5] For, unlike the stipulations on offenses, the judges have sustained those which were in conformity with the law or established practice and set aside those which failed to meet

[5] For judicial organization, see Chap. X, below.

the tests. Trials are public and the principle, established by the classical jurists, that no qāḍī may hear a case *in camera* has been consistently respected. Decisions, likewise, are always delivered in public. Law courts in Islam are single judge courts. There are no benches of several judges and no jury system. Proceedings are simple, often the plaintiff bringing his opponent into court to seek a remedy; if he fails to bring him before the law, however, it is left to the judge to force his presence, resorting to the help of his aides or that of the police.

Islam has known something very similar to the modern system of public prosecution. Muslim jurists have studied public law-suits, that is, those concerning rights of God, and they have entrusted the authorities concerned to take the necessary measures in court. Cases such as theft, robbery, and the like, whose punishments are stipulated in the Qur'ān, fall under this category and, therefore, require no complaint by an individual plaintiff.

At first, the judges kept no record or registry of their decisions and it was only after the activities of the judiciary were extended that such registration was begun.

After full examination of all data, the judge began his decision with a summary of the plaintiff's case. He then gave a recital of the facts in the case, and referred to precedents, especially those of renowned judges. Finally, he pronounced his sentence on the basis of a Qur'ānic provision, a ḥadīth of the Prophet, or a consensus of the mujtahidīn. If none of these were available, he had to reach a decision by using his discretion and relying on analogy. It became customary for the judge to apply his seal and signature at the top of the decision which he began, "in the name of God, the Compassionate, the Merciful." The enforcement of a decision was rendered easy by the great prestige enjoyed by judges in the community. For this reason, the use of force was avoided, and the person sentenced as a rule willingly complied with the decision of the court.

On other occasions, the judges themselves have assumed the responsibility for enforcing their judgments. This is most common in civil matters, while the enforcement of ḥudūd has often been delegated to the rulers. Many judges, however, have had their powers defined at the time of their appointment. Some were authorized to hear ḥudūd cases and supervise the enforcement of the decisions, while others had no such power.

The principles governing the execution of penal rules correspond generally to the modern practice. We shall mention only two of them: Cumulation of punishments and the enforcement of sentences against pregnant women.

CUMULATION OF PUNISHMENTS

Abū Yūsuf writes in the *Kitāb al-Kharāj* as follows: "If a qādhif commits another qadhf (false accusation of fornication) before being punished for the first, he shall be punished only one ḥadd for the two crimes together."[6] If the qādhif were a slave, he received forty strokes, the ḥadd of the slave. If he were freed before being punished and then brought to justice, he still received only forty lashes because this was the punishment due to him at the time of al-qadhf; if he were not punished after gaining his freedom and then committed another qadhf, he was flogged eighty strokes only for the first and the second crime. This means that he is penalized for the two crimes by only one punishment, that of the repeated crime. Likewise, if he were punished by only a fraction of the ḥadd and then committed a qadhf, he would not be subjected to a new ḥadd of eighty strokes, but the flogging of the pending punishment of the former would be completed. No new ḥadd can be applied if even one lash is still pending from the old punishment. If he were punished eighty strokes, and then committed another qadhf, a new punishment of eighty would apply. In the same manner, if he stole more than once, the punishment of cutting the hand would be applied only once for all these thefts.

A person who is sentenced for a crime, and before the execution of that sentence commits another and is subsequently sentenced for the latter, shall suffer only the heavier of the two punishments. The principle of recognizing the right devolving from a prior status is equally established. A slave who is sentenced to be punished by the slave's ḥadd (i.e., forty strokes) for the crime of al-qadhf, would suffer the slave's punishment and not that of the free (i.e., eighty strokes), even if he attained freedom before the punishment was executed. The penalty he deserves is the one legally applicable at the time of al-qadhf.

THE ENFORCEMENT OF A SENTENCE AGAINST PREGNANT WOMEN

Physical punishment shall not be enforced on pregnant women except after delivery. Ibn 'Ābidīn states that:

[6] Abū Yūsuf, *op. cit.*, p. 169.

The ḥadd is enforced on the pregnant after delivery. If the ḥadd is stoning she should then be stoned after delivery. In case there is no other one to undertake the raising of the child, it shall be postponed until his livelihood can be assured. If the punishment is flogging, it shall also be postponed to after the post-natal period.[7]

In this respect, the classical jurists are more considerate to the pregnant woman and her child than modern legislation which merely delays the execution of a death sentence and the punishment of a pregnant woman until after delivery, without any regard to the fate of the child.

[7] Ibn 'Ābidīn, *Radd al-Muḥtār 'ala al-Durr al-Mukhtār* (Cairo, A.H. 1249), Vol III, pp. 204-205.

CHAPTER X

Judicial Organization

THE GENERAL CHARACTERISTICS OF THE JUDICIAL FUNCTION

ACCORDING to the classical concept of Muslim law, which developed under the influence of Byzantine and Persian thought, the state system is autocratic. The ruler himself holds all powers and, in particular, the power of jurisdiction. As the philosopher-historian Ibn Khaldūn said, the caliph is the temporal and religious head of the Islamic State and in his person are centered all the powers necessary for its rule. Regardless of the category to which they belong, all officials act only by virtue of a delegation of jurisdiction conferred upon them by the caliph, be that delegation direct, as in the case of officials whose investiture is received directly from the caliph, or be it indirect, as in the case of all the other officials, according to their position in the hierarchy. At the same time, this delegation is a representation. An official, whatever his status may be, is his superiors' representative as well as his delegate; and this is true to the very top of the hierarchy. One can say that the entire structure of the Islamic state is constituted by a series of delegations and representations. This idea of delegation-representation is extremely important and one of the principal concepts in the analysis of Muslim public law as a whole. This concept will be considered here only from the point of view of judicial administration.

THE LEGAL STATUS OF THE QĀḌĪ

The judge (qāḍī) is essentially a nā'ib (lieutenant), the delegate-representative of the governor. He does not have an independent or even autonomous position. Indeed, during this early period, the Muslim State, through the supreme and active power of a caliph, had not yet effectively asserted itself. The governor of a province, as leader of the conquering army, derived his judicial power from no one but himself, and this power he transmitted to subordinates by virtue of his position. With the development of caliphial authority, a superimposition of authority took place. Not every qāḍī is considered to be the direct and immediate delegate of the governor or of the caliph. Rather, the qāḍī is the delegate of whoever appointed him. Whenever the governor or caliph appointed a judge, the latter could subdelegate power to a third person who could, in turn, delegate his powers, and so on. Each one of these qāḍīs was considered to be the delegate of no one but the person by whom he had been appointed. This concept is apparent in the terminology which is used to designate the judges. The qāḍī of a district is the nā'ib of the qāḍī of the higher administrative division. When the chief qāḍī—the qāḍī al-quḍāt—appoints a person to a judicial position in the large provinces, he is merely appointing a lieutenant to carry on his work.

This principle of delegation enables those qāḍīs who have heavy judicial responsibilities to substitute others, not only in remote areas but also in the center itself. This practice of substitution became permanent even among the qāḍīs of important centers such as Cairo; they almost always had one or two deputies in the city itself and, at times, having obtained their appointment from Baghdad, they appointed their deputies even before they had reached their place of office. Numerous abuses resulted from this practice; one of the most prevalent among them was absenteeism. In order to remain close to their superior, maintain their position, and thwart possible intrigues against them, some qāḍīs developed the habit of remaining in the capital, and delegating a nā'ib to take charge of the district assigned to them. This abusive practice in the end received theoretical sanction and the permission was granted to the titular holder of a position to appoint a deputy before going to the post himself.

Was this delegation of power based on private law rules of agency? Did it depend equally upon the consent of both parties concerned? Clearly not. Just as the *mandatum* in Roman public law, the delegation discussed here constitutes, at the same time, an order. It is an act of investiture which becomes effective by the mere fact of its announcement and without the consent of the deputy being necessary; at the most, the deputy's concurrence is required.

This concept is derived primarily from the theoretical rule, mentioned in all the works and treatises, according to which the appointment to a judicial office must not be based upon a request but, rather, must come from the sole initiative of the authority. Investiture must appear to be acquired by the sole act of appointment. From this same concept stems the rule whereby the higher authority can force a person to accept a judicial function and can, to this end, use means of physical coercion such as fines and imprisonment. One must associate mainly with this rule all the anecdotes, authentic or legendary, that have been told about people who, having turned down a judicial position, were forced to accept it because of the punishments inflicted upon them. When a person wished to decline an appointment, he did not reject it, but rather offered excuses, pleading lack of experience, lack of competence. The correct doctrine concerning this point was set forth by al-Māwardī. After having mentioned the terminology which must be used in the acts of appointment and the conditions necessary to the accomplishment of the investiture, all emanating from the higher authority, al-Māwardī holds that "the consent" of the candidate only perfects the act of appointment.[1]

One of the most important consequences of this concept is that the appointment may be terminated by the sole desire of the appointing authority. That is why the authority can, at its own discretion, recall a qāḍī, except for the added condition that the interested party be notified. This also explains why the voluntary resignation of a qāḍī can only take effect if it is accepted by the appointing authority. Therefore all the texts, which mention cases of the relinquishment of duties through resignation, do not fail to add that the resignation was accepted.

The qāḍī thus merely administers delegated judicial functions and the principal retains the right to administer justice himself. This is why certain jurists, like Abū Yūsuf, mention only the imām or the governor, when they expound the rules of judicial procedure. It also explains the famous procedure known as that of the mazālim whose broad outlines will be set forth below. This concept likewise lies behind the singular theory of appeals from the qāḍī's decisions.

The principal's right to instruct his deputy concerning procedural rules is based on the same concept. Al-Kharashī reports that the qāḍī Ibn Bishr decided that in cases involving immovable property the court at the defendant's residence should have jurisdiction and accordingly sent instructions to his qāḍīs.[2] This concept of delegated justice is found at all levels. Just as the caliph or the governor retains the right to exercise justice himself, the qāḍī of an area does not lose his judicial rights over the entire area of his jurisdiction by the fact of having appointed deputies.

[1] Māwardī, *Kitāb al-Aḥkām al-Sulṭāniyya*, ed. Enger (Bonn, 1853), p. 107 ff.
[2] Kharashī, *Sharḥ Mukhtaṣar al-Khalīl* (Cairo, A. H. 1299), Vol. VII, p. 204.

On the other hand, the scope of the delegation can vary according to the wishes of the principal. The latter may deputize a private individual, one of his assistants or a formerly appointed qāḍī to deal with a specific case; he may likewise, when he appoints a new qāḍī, extend or restrict his jurisdiction as to venue, type of cases, type of litigants, etc. Thus, al-Māwardī relates that the governors of Baṣra were accustomed to appoint a qāḍī—a kind of justice of the peace—who heard cases in the principal mosque of the city, and who had jurisdiction in cases where the value involved did not exceed two hundred dirhams (drachmas) and twenty dinārs. The qāḍīs regularly sent certain cases for adjudication to private individuals whose legal knowledge was outstanding. Such individuals were given the title qāḍī by the public.

Because of its broad scope this concept of delegation was often applied in an exaggerated and distorted fashion. Even the designation of an expert, in the course of a lawsuit, took on the appearance of a delegation of jurisdiction.

Another consequence of the concept of delegation was the complete lack of separation between the judicial and executive powers. The drawbacks of this system were aggravated by the judge's subordination, not only to the central executive authority, but also to the various regional authorities as well as to the qāḍī whose deputy he was. As a reaction a system evolved later establishing a relatively autonomous relationship not only between qāḍīs but of the qāḍīs to the regional administrative authorities, and, although to a much lesser extent, to the central power itself. As of a comparatively late period, the former concept of the qāḍī-delegate's status was modified: the qāḍī at the lowest rung of the ladder, the nā'ib of the smallest district, was no longer considered, with respect to his judicial status, as officer-in-charge, personally responsible to his principal, but as the direct lieutenant of the caliph. Although appointed by a qāḍī, the nā'ib becomes the nā'ib of the sultan or of the imām. Two other concepts followed the same line of thinking. The qāḍī of a subordinate rank became the caliph or nā'ib of the Prophet or even of God. In a more positive manner, he was no longer considered to be the nā'ib of the caliph personally but of society in general. This new concept influenced the position of the qāḍī-delegate. He could no longer be dismissed by the qāḍī who appointed him and did not lose his position at the latter's death. Accordingly, the author of the work *Al-fatāwa al-hindiyya* (eleventh century A. H.), while continuing to report the traditional opinion that the nā'ib of a qāḍī can only be discharged by his principal or upon the latter's death, also states that a contradiction had grown up based on the concept that the nā'ib actually is the nā'ib of the sultan or of society. This is why, according to another author of the late period, the qāḍī cannot resign his office, because he is the nā'ib of the umma, the community, and his position is determined by the law of the community.

Another perversion of this same idea, set forth by jurists at the end of the fifth century A. H., consists in the qāḍī's being forbidden, whatever his rank, to delegate his powers of his own accord, in his inability and to appoint a nā'ib except with tacit or expressed authorization. This is why in the later period all the forms for acts of appointment of judges of the large districts contain a special clause conferring the power of delegation. However, this authorization to delegate can be tacit and can result from the nature of the judicial office. Thus, the appointment to the position of qāḍī al-quḍāt (chief qāḍī) entails, without its being expressly mentioned, the right to appoint nā'ibs; for the qāḍī al-quḍāt is the head of the judicial administration with the right to appoint and dismiss judges.

In its original form the concept of delegation implies the power of the principal to substitute himself at any time for his deputy, and any litigant could address himself directly to the principal. Later developments granted more independence to the position of the delegate. Although later legal treatises continue to emphasize that all litigants may have recourse directly to "the Sultan's Door" without going through the qāḍī, they also point out that an opposite practice has established itself and that litigants are not free to address themselves directly to the higher authority.

Another element which contributed to the establishment of a certain separation of powers as well as to the assurance of relative autonomy for the qāḍī appears to be the establishment, from the second century A. H. onward, of a general body of law. This body of law was superimposed upon the will of the principal as well as the deputy. The deputy had to apply a law which was distinct from the wishes of the delegating authority and which, in principle, imposed itself also upon the latter. The bonds of subordination were weakened accordingly; the qāḍī consequently acquired a position of much greater independence. The jurists of the later period created a rule that the command of the sultan, as the highest authority delegating judicial powers, must not be obeyed by the qāḍī if it does not conform to the rule of the sharī'a.

The uncertainty which was prevalent in legal matters before the definite establishment of a body of Islamic law and the "closing of the gate of ijtihād," as well as the lack of a legislative authority, influenced the status of the qāḍī and contributed to making him not only an instrument for applying the law but also an instrument for creating law. Thus, important legal institutions were created or refined through judicial practice. Among them are the shuhūd (office of the notary), the waqf, and administration of the property of minors and persons who are absent.

Another striking characteristic of the status of the qāḍī was that he was not exclusively a judge. Since the very beginning and especially during the first century of the hijra, almost all the qāḍīs were given, in addition to strictly judicial functions, duties which are either related, such as police, or which are completely different, such as the supervision of the public treasury. This expansion of duties was again due to the concept of delegation. Since the governor was the holder of all powers, he could entrust them to any of his appointees at his discretion. Later, the qāḍī specialized on his judicial attributes, but took on additional duties again in more recent centuries.

Contrary to other judicial systems where jurisdiction was at first given to a single judge, but later was entrusted to a bench of several judges, Islam adhered to the principle of a single judge. The origins of this principle are both logical and natural. Since the qāḍī was the delegate-representative of the governor, he had to be one, just as the governor was. In addition, judicial assemblies are derived from a democratic organization of the city-state, where the citizens participate in the exercise of governing power. Islam, by contrast, was built on the principle of personal autocratic power. The system of a single judge admits at most of the corrective influence of a *consilium,* consisting of a varying number of jurists who assist the judge by advising him, but who have no deliberative function.

THE QUESTION OF JURISDICTION

In Islamic law there is no distinction between various degrees of jurisdiction. The various delegations in a sense constitute gradations but these gradations emanate one from the other and constitute a whole. By contrast, appellate jurisdiction in modern law is clearly separate from original jurisdiction and has its own organization and procedural rules. Recourse from the qāḍī's decision to the authority responsible for his appointment or to the head of the State bears no resemblance to a modern appellate system. The office of the qāḍī al-quḍāt, which was created in the latter part of the second century A. H., and which corresponds to the qadā' al-jamā'a of Muslim Spain, does not constitute a degree of jurisdiction. The holder of this office is merely the highest judicial officer with important administrative functions.

Generally speaking, all categories of citizens in the Muslim world come under the qāḍī's jurisdiction. In the Muslim judicial system, there are no special jurisdictions for the burghers of a city, the nobles, or the commoners. There are many anecdotes telling how several caliphs, of their own free will, submitted to the qāḍī's jurisdiction. Autonomous municipal organizations and franchises were unknown to the Muslim world and the city burghers, therefore, did not consider establishing their own special jurisdictions. As for the nobles, great or small, they directed all their activity towards the acquisition of political independence from their suzerain: they did not attempt to claim for themselves the right to be judged by the suzerain or by their peers. There was no clergy in Islam. The jurists who devoted themselves to the study and teaching of the law constituted a truly distinct social class and did not enjoy any judicial privileges.

Justice, therefore, is everywhere that of the Chief of State. Doubtless, various governors attempted to interfere with judicial administration in their provinces and especially with the appointment of qāḍıs. Also, as independent Muslim states were set up, corresponding independent judicial organizations were formed. However, this is the political side of the question. Within the same state, there were no other forms of justice than that of the caliph or of the sultan. This is perhaps due to the absence, in Islam, of a feudal organization such as existed in the West during the Middle Ages.

Jurisdiction in Islam, however, is not unitary so far as the nature of the controversies is concerned. Contrary to what is usually assumed, the qāḍī is not the sole judicial authority to which any and all litigations are submitted. Thus, from the very beginning criminal jurisdiction was exercised by the governor even though he delegated his other judicial functions to the qāḍī; and later criminal jurisdiction was entrusted to a special order of officials, the shurṭa. Independent judicial institutions also appeared in the course of historical evolution and exercised judicial powers concurrent with, as well as superior to, that of the qāḍī. This was true, for example, of the institution of the ḥājib and of the mazālim. These jurisdictions dealt with matters according to custom and equity.

THE RELIGIOUS CHARACTER OF THE JUDICIAL FUNCTION

In the course of time the office of the qāḍī took on a decidedly religious character which steadily grew stronger and extended to all related institutions.

Ibn Khaldūn, in his enumeration of the religious functions of the caliph, mentions qaḍā' (justice) after the prayer and the futya (legal interpretation). According to Ibn Khaldūn's concept, which is representative of the classical doctrine, this characteristic of the judicial function stems from the religious character of the caliphate whose essential mission is to apply the sharī'a as it is laid down in the sacred texts. In the definition of the judicial office by the classical jurists, its religious character is even more pronounced. According to al-Sarakhsī, justice consists in "the application of the religious principle" and, therefore, "no temporal considerations must interfere with it."[3] Khushanī says: "The exercise of the qaḍā' is a vital principle of religion." Thus, the exercise of judicial functions no longer appears simply as fulfilment of a public duty of a religious nature but as a devotional act and the accomplishment of a religious obligation. To render justice, says al-Sarakhsī, "constitutes one of the most noble acts of devotion."[4] According to Kāsānī: "It is one of the best acts of devotion," and "one of the most important duties, after belief in God."[5] The qaḍā' is regarded as a farḍ al-kifāya, that is, one of those religious obligations which is imposed upon every believer when called upon and when he finds himself to be the only one to possess the necessary qualifications. Consequently, it was sinful to refuse a judicial position. The qāḍī became a religious magistrate and this religious character permeated all acts pertaining to his function.

Obviously, one of the requirements for the appointment of a qāḍī is that he be a Muslim. The dhimmī cannot be invested with a judicial function. The choice of a qāḍī should be inspired only by the desire to please God; he should be distinguished by his piety, his regular observance of religious duties, and by belief in God. He must act in such a way as to obtain heavenly rewards and to avoid the punishments of the after-life. No one must seek to

[3] Sarakhsī, *al-Mabsūṭ* (Cairo, A. H. 1324), Vol. XVI, p. 67.

[4] *Ibid.*, p. 60.

[5] Kāsānī, *Badā'i al-Ṣana'ī fī Tartīb al-Sharā'i* (Cairo, 1910), Vol. VII, p. 4.

obtain judicial office for its earthly reward, but one must allow oneself to be chosen solely on the basis of religious merits. A qāḍī also must know the Qur'ān and the sunna of the Prophet. Indeed, the qāḍī can only be chosen from among the 'ulamā. The qāḍī is considered as the heir of the Prophet himself. Just as he has inherited his knowledge from the Prophet, he has also inherited from Him his judicial power.

In order to bring out even more clearly this religious and disinterested character of the responsibility assumed by the qāḍī, the authorities emphasize its generally gratuitous character. Remuneration is a makeshift innovation. The virtue of certain qāḍīs who were said to have worked without compensation is celebrated by the historians.

The qāḍī's court was placed at the mosque. Shāfi'ī believed that the court should be placed elsewhere, but the Ḥanafīs retorted that the mosque was certainly the best place, since the rendering of justice was an act of devotion.

Because of the religious character of his office, the qāḍī must be especially qualified to carry out religious functions. He should supervise the safeguarding of the mosques, and administer waqf properties. Sometimes he also exercised the functions of a mu'adhdhin al-khaṭīb (preacher). He presided over the Friday prayer, and when, in years of drought, the people went to the country to implore Allah's mercy, the qāḍī led them and presided over the prayer of istisqā'; during funeral rites he delivered the ritual prayer. He announced the rising of the moon, thereby opening the fast of Ramaḍān. The abjuration of his faith by a non-Muslim and his conversion to Islam took place in the presence of the qāḍī.

The strengthening of the religious character of the qāḍī's office and the penetration of the religious element into nearly all of the institutions of public law further enlarged the scope of the qāḍī's functions by conferring upon him certain duties essentially political in nature. Thus, the qāḍī's concurrence was regarded necessary to lend religious legitimacy to the deposition or even to the execution of an heir presumptive to the throne, of a ruling prince, or of a pretender, and to justify the levying or the increase of a tax. According to al-Maqrīzī, under the Mamlūk dynasty nothing of a religious nature was outside the jurisdiction of the qāḍī al-quḍāt. Because of this concentration of the various religious functions in the hands of the qāḍīs, a group developed in Islam, despite its fundamental principles, which had the appearances of a clergy.

THE COMPOSITION OF THE COURT

The ordinary judicial tribunal in Islam is composed of a single judge, the qāḍī. The jurists rejected any possibility of a collegial formation. "The khalīf cannot," says Kharashī, "appoint two qāḍīs to pass judgment concurrently on the same matter; for, as Ibn Sha'bān put it, one judge cannot be half a judge."[6] The same rule is taught by the Shāfi'ī school. "It is possible to appoint two qāḍīs for the same town, each one having jurisdiction within a certain district; but they could not be appointed to pass judgment at the same time." Likewise, al-Māwardī, while describing the rules governing several qāḍīs in the same district or town, in no way considers the possibility of two or more qāḍīs sitting together. The only possibilities which he considers are: (1) qāḍīs who have each been appointed for a territorial district (jurisdiction *ratione loci);* (2) more than one qāḍī, each one having jurisdiction in certain types of cases (jurisdiction *ratione materiae);* and (3) qāḍīs having concurrent jurisdiction but sitting separately.[7]

Were there any exceptions to this principle that there should be only one judge? Certain works of jurists of the late period seemed to admit theoretically the possibility of exceptions. For example, the *Fatāwa al-Hindiyya* and the *Jāmi' al-Fuṣūlayn* discuss the case of a sultan who appoints simultaneously two qāḍīs to the court of a town. One of them renders judgments alone. The decisions of this judge would be null and void; for the same thing applies to these judges as applies to two agents (who cannot act separately without express permission). An even more explicit example is found in the *Fatāwa al-Khāniyya:* if the sultan endows two persons in a city with jurisdictional power, then neither of the two has the right to judge alone. Ibn al-Jawzī tells of a practical case representative of the collegial method: 'Ubaydallah al-Anbārī and 'Umar ibn 'Āmir were qāḍīs of Baṣra; they met and resolved jointly the lawsuits laid before them. But neither this historical precedent nor the speculations of jurists led, in practice, to the general development of courts with several judges. However, as in the Byzantine judicial system where the magistrate sought the advice of a *consilium* of jurists, the qāḍī did not pass judgment alone; he was generally aided by assessors who advised him concerning legal difficulties arising from the case.

The *consilium* system is one of the most neglected aspects in

6 Kharashī, *op. cit.,* Vol. VII, p. 169.

7 Māwardī, *op. cit.,* p. 123.

the study of the Islamic judicial system. Modern writers having exclusively concentrated upon the principle of the singleness of the qāḍī—mainly because, starting at a late period, this rule was rigorously applied owing to decadence or transformation of the *consilium* system—they were not aware of this particular feature of qāḍīvial justice. Al-mashūra (taking counsel from somebody else) is one of the principles most emphasized by the Muslim authors who dealt with the general rules of government. In their treatises, a special chapter is devoted to a discussion of the need of every public official to have recourse to the advice of informed persons, thereby emphasizing the advantages of the mashūra.

The application of these principles in the administration of justice is characteristic. Those who assisted the qāḍī like those who assisted the Roman and Byzantine judge, were not assessors in the proper sense of the word. Rather, they formed a *consilium* which was called upon to furnish advice to the judge. This advice was not binding and the decision always remained in the hands of the qāḍī and the qāḍī only.

According to some jurists the qāḍī must consult legal experts. Others appeared to regard such consultation as optional for the judge. In general, however, the qāḍī had to consult the experts (fuqahā') only if he encountered legal complications. In that case consultation was recommended not only for the ignorant judge but even for the 'ālim, the qāḍī who was also a legal expert.

Should this consultation apply both to questions of law and of fact? This question is not raised in any legal writing. The general scheme of the system appears to indicate that consultation applied exclusively to points of law. Were it otherwise, one could not understand why the judge could consult only a person considered to be an expert. As Kāsānī puts it, the qāḍī consults the fuqahā' if he is unable to find the legal solution of cases submitted to him.

Did the obligation to seek the advice of experts entail their obligation to be present during the hearing of the case? On this point the views of the various schools differed. According to the Ḥanafīs and Shāfi'īs the qāḍī could decide whether or not the consilium should be present while the case was argued. If the presence of advisers at the public hearing of the case inconvenienced him in any way, he could ask their advice outside the hearing. However, the presence of the advisers at the hearing is recommended, and some jurists of these schools state categorically that the qāḍī must not hold a hearing alone since such action would give rise to suspicion.

To the Mālikī jurists, the presence of advisers at the hearing is imperative, at least when important matters are involved. In minor cases a simple consultation is sufficient, according to Dasūqī, but Ibn Farḥūn believes the qāḍī[8] can hold a hearing only with the assistance of legal experts.

This divergence of opinions between the Ḥanafī and Shāfi'ī schools, on the one hand, and the Mālikī school on the other, is simply the theoretical consecration of the independent evolution of the institution of the *consilium* in oriental and occidental countries.

The adviser does not have any official status, according to the jurists. He gives his advice to the qāḍī exclusively as a private citizen. The qāḍī is entirely free as to the number of people whom he wishes to consult, or whose presence at the court sessions he desires. He can require the advice of one, two, or more counsellors. The jurists generally took it for granted that there would be several advisers.

There are elements in the traditions which prove that the qāḍī was assisted by a *consilium* from the earliest period. While these traditions cannot be deemed completely authentic, they at least confirm the manner in which justice was carried out at the time when they were first circulated.

In the fourth century A. H., Ibn Ḥajar pointed out (in the chronicle concerning the Egyptian qāḍī, Ibn al-Ḥaddād) that the latter always held hearings with four people in attendance, two of them on his right, and two on his left. The Caliph al-Muṭī', when he appointed in 363 (973) the qāḍī al-quḍāt Abū Ḥasan al-Hāshimī, instructed him to have people attend his hearings who could enlighten him with their knowledge and advice. When the Faṭimīd caliph appointed Ibn al-'Awwām to the Cairo seat in 405 (1014), he intimated in the writ of investiture that "he [Ibn al-'Awwām] should not hold hearings without the assistance of four fuqahā' of the court, in order to avoid the rendering of judgments contrary to the doctrine adopted by the khalīfa."[9]

During the period of decadence, the official texts continued to point to the persistence of this institution. Thus, when speaking of the court clerks, the treatise *Nihayat al-'Arab* says that these clerks must have adequate legal knowledge; and states the following reason for this condition: "He [the clerk] is always close to

[8] Dasūqī, *Ḥāshiyat al-Dasūqī* (Cairo, A. H. 1295), Vol. IV, p. 157; Ibn Farḥūn, *Tabṣirat al-Ḥukkām*, Vol. I, p. 29.

[9] Kindī *Kitāb al-Wulāt wa al-Quḍāt*, p. 610.

the qāḍī who, during his hearing, is often surrounded by legal experts who discuss points of law and give advice."[10] The clerk had to be able to follow these discussions intelligently.

THE FUTYA (LEGAL OPINION)

The futya or iftā' is an institution closely related to the Islamic judicial system, and represents the practical expression of the principle of mashūra. It consists of answering legal or religious questions and corresponds to the Roman institution of the *ius respondendi.* There are many analogies between the two institutions.

In Islam, where legislative power does not exist in principle, the jurists' contribution to the elaboration of the law was extremely important. The legal opinions of the muftīs were not reasoned and therefore the muftī enjoyed a great deal of freedom. It was through these opinions that the theoretically unchangeable doctrine was, through the centuries, adapted to practice and that judicial evolution was imperceptibly accomplished. Thus, in controversial cases—in all cases where ancient doctrines clashed with new realities of social life—the solution adopted was that which conformed to practical necessities, and its adoption was made possible by a fatwa. The rule, according to which the futya can only be applied to cases arising from practice but not to theoretical examples, emphasized even better the role and influence of the Muslim *ius respondendi.* This work of elaborating the law gained such importance that it became necessary to collect into great volumes the fatwas of famous jurists.

It was mainly because of the great influence exercised by the jurists upon legal interpretation and development that the state invaded the legal profession and finally gained control over it. At a very early stage the need was felt in Islam for persons with legal education and training. The expansion of the new religion, the increasing number of converts with only a vague understanding of their new faith, the tendency of this faith to rule over both the temporal and spiritual aspects of daily life, and, finally, the surviving laws and customs of conquered countries which had to be reconciled with the new precepts and rendered understandable and acceptable to the new rulers—all of these factors necessitated having constant recourse to the advice of legal experts. This need was first felt by private citizens who wished to conform to the rules

[10] Nuwayrī, *Nihāyat al-Arab fī Funūn al-Adab,* Vol. IX, p. 4.

of the new religion and who wanted guarantees for the validity of legal acts arising in daily life.

Towards the end of the first century A. H., the supreme authority itself appointed jurists to the responsibility of the futya which, at that time, corresponded essentially to the Roman *ius publice respondendi*. The oldest document, to our knowledge, which deals with this function is a text by al-Maqrīzī according to which the Umayyad caliph, 'Umar ibn 'Abd al-'Azīz (96/714-101/719) appointed three persons whom he put in charge of the futya in Egypt. Two of them were natives, mawla, and the third was of Arab origin. When it became apparent that this choice of two mawlas angered the Arabs who were settled in the country, the caliph bluntly replied: "How can I help it if the mawlas are better than you?"[11]

Futya did not, however, become an exclusive concern of the state. Aside from those jurists who were appointed by the central government to give certain concrete advice, everyone was free to set himself up as a muftī, if public opinion held that his knowledge of law was adequate. It does not even appear that the opinions delivered by the official muftīs were any more binding than those given by independent jurists. Appointment of certain jurists by the government was merely made to serve the needs of the population and to ensure a sound choice by the interested parties.

It seems that, at first, the institution of the futya was placed exclusively at the disposal of private individuals—and this was done as much for their own instruction as to help them when they were defending a case in court. In view of their special aptitudes, the muftīs were generally assigned to give opinions to the judge and to take part in his *consilium*. The two duties then began to overlap. The lawyer, the faqīh, whom the qāḍī was wont to consult, became, by the same token, a muftī exercising *ius respondendi*. This confusion is especially noticeable in texts dealing with the nature of justice in Muslim Spain. The *mushāwar* (adviser) of the qāḍī was the one who delivered the fatwas to the qāḍī; it was from such an individual, a member of the *consilium*, that the judge "sought fatwas."

THE INTERVENTION OF THE AUTHORITIES IN THE FUTYA

From the very beginning, the central government made itself felt within the function of the futya. But its role had been limited

[11] Maqrīzī, *Kitāb al-Khiṭaṭ*, Vol. IV, p. 143.

to the appointment of one or more jurists who were particularly competent. During the later development of the institution, the interference of the central government became more pronounced and manifested itself in two ways. On the one hand, the government set up official positions of the futya, to which it appointed men responsible to itself, thereby making the institution a public concern and part of the judicial organization. On the other hand, it claimed the right to control and discipline the independent jurists.

In enumerating public functions of a religious nature in Islamic countries, Ibn Khaldūn puts futya after prayer but before the judging of lawsuits. However, Ibn Khaldūn does not regard the futya as an exclusive public function. He distinguished between those jurists who could be consulted in the principal mosques of the cities and those who could be found in mosques of lesser importance; one must include among the latter those muftīs who received people in their homes or in other places. The management of the principal mosques is directly subordinate to the central government; all matters and all functions of religious legal life which take place there come under the authority of the caliph or his agents. Just as no imām may lead the prayer and no qāḍī may dispense justice in one of these mosques without having been appointed by the central government, the muftīs who functioned there had to be government appointed. All these muftīs received salaries as state employees.

During the Mamlūk period, the official nature of the institution became more pronounced because of the creation of positions of muftīs, personally attached to the sultan or to the governor of the larger provinces. At that time the position of muftī and qāḍī became closely related. This new function was called iftā' dār al-'adl. In Cairo, four persons were appointed to this position, each belonging to one of the four orthodox rites. Their duties consisted in being present, with the qāḍī al-quḍāt and other high functionaries, at the audiences held by the sultan, during which they acted as his advisers. Similar posts were established in Damascus, Aleppo, Tripoli, Hama, and Ṣafad.

The government supervised and controlled the independent muftīs and those muftīs which it had appointed. Individuals must not be led astray or deceived through the ignorance or malice of those from whom they might be seeking advice. The ruler was to keep a constant watch over the behavior of the muftīs and, if necessary, could debar from the exercise of their profession those muftīs who were inefficient or immoral. Qāḍīs likewise had disciplinary power over the muftīs which may have been of greater importance in practice than that of the administrative officials. The qāḍī could go so far as to disbar an "irresponsible muftī." Ibn Khaldūn says that when he was appointed to be the qāḍī al-quḍāt in Cairo (ninth century A. H.), his attention was immediately drawn to the deplorable character of the muftīs under him; therefore, he debarred most of them from exercising their profession.

THE QĀḌĪ'S CONSILIUM IN ANDALUSIA

The institution of the *consilium* of the qāḍī became one of the essential elements of the judicial system in Muslim Spain. The doctrine set forth by Maghribian and Spanish authors, following the Mālikī school, as well as practice itself, turned the right of a judge to call upon the *consilium* in the exercise of his functions into a definite obligation.

The *consilium* in Spain has been given a time-honored name: it is the shūra, and the lawyer who exercises shūra is called a mushāwar. These terms can be translated literally as: council and councillor.

Ḥusāmī relates that the amīr advised newly appointed qāḍīs to seek the counsel of men versed in the law with respect to the judgment of cases. He tells the story of Yaḥya ibn Ma'mar who had been appointed qāḍī in Cordova during the time of Amīr 'Abd al-Raḥmān II (206/822-238/852). This qāḍī refused the assistance of the mushāwars Yaḥya ibn Yaḥya and Sa'īd ibn Ḥasan, with the result that all judicial activity was stopped until the return of the amīr made possible the appointment of a new councillor. In the practical treatise of ibn 'Abdūn, which was written at the end of the eleventh century A.D., it was stated categorically that the qāḍī could hold a hearing only if aided by two jurists whose advice he must seek in judging the cases.

It is obvious, from these texts, that the jurisdiction of the qāḍī was valid only if he were aided by a *consilium* of jurists. Ḥusāmī does report that one of the qāḍīs in office at the time of Amīr 'Abd al-Raḥmān, Muḥammad al-Ma'afirī, held hearings alone. But this is an exceptional case which differs from all the others related in contemporary as well as later documents. During the second and third centuries A. H., no set rules appear to have existed concerning the number of jurists who had to assist the qāḍī.

After the third century A. H., the texts no longer mention the case of a mushāwar being sole adviser to a judge. There could be three or four counsellors, but the number was usually limited to two. The aforementioned text of Ibn 'Abdūn, which is confirmed by the weight of other historical documents, clearly proves that a regulation was finally made providing that there be two mushāwars for each qāḍī. This number applied only to those counsellors who collaborated with the qāḍī in the judgment of litigations; within the same jurisdiction, there could be a greater number of jurists available to assist the magistrate in his function. Nevertheless, in Ibn 'Abdūn's time, there could not be more than four of them.

What was the legal nature of the function of the mushāwar? Was it a free profession whose members were occasionally called upon to give advice to the career judge, or did it rather constitute a public office? One cannot categorically say that it was either one or the other. It is certain that the shūra was not really a free profession, and in numerous texts it has many of the characteristics of a public function. On the other hand, one cannot classify it completely as a public function. From the very origins of the institution, all the documents which we have been able to consult indicate that not every jurist could be freely called to give advice to the qāḍīs. He had to be appointed by the government through investiture by the ruler or by the amīr.

Although appointment to the function of the shūra emanated in principle from the sovereign, it was made in many cases at the request of the qāḍī who wanted the services of a particular candidate. As a consequence, the authority of the qāḍī steadily increased in scope, a process which was accelerated by the decadence of the central government. During this period qāḍīs even became independent governors of provinces and veritable petty kings. The qāḍīs always seem to have enjoyed a great deal of freedom in choosing their counsellors since they could call upon any of the various mushāwar attached to their court or could dispense with the collaboration of mushāwar already exercising their functions. Numerous texts mention cases of newly appointed qāḍīs refusing to seek the advice of their predecessors' mushāwar. The qāḍī also has disciplinary rights over his mushāwar. As Ibn 'Abdūn puts it, the qāḍī supervises the behavior of the people of the shūra, holds them to a strict observance of their obligations, and, if need be, dismisses them.

Shūra was closely linked to futya. The mushāwar, attached to a court by official appointment, retained the prerogative to exercise the free profession of the futya. In many texts the terms are used interchangeably one for the other and the biographies of many mushāwar stress that they were equally distinguished in free futya.

WITNESSES

The shahāda (testimony; [shāhid, witness; plural, shuhūd]) is one of the most important institutions, not only within the system of evidence but also within the judicial organization of Islamic law. In Islamic law, testimony by witnesses is the best proof. Al-bayyina (the proof) means, in current juridical language, with no added explanation, the testimony of witnesses. Written testimony has always been looked upon with disfavor by judicial practice and doctrine. It never could by itself make proof. Even when written material was widely used in legal matters, even when regular clerks, with all their documents and archives, were appointed to tribunals, the contents of public and private documents was proven not so much by the text itself as by the witnesses who attested to the documents. That is why all legal documents, whether private or notarized, also had to be witnessed by at least two persons. Judgments, too, had to be witnessed. In practice this reliance on witnesses led to many inconveniences: the witnesses could always be suspected, and the transaction itself remained threatened. This is why the institution of the shahāda (*stricto sensu*) was developed.

This institution consisted of a procedure according to which the judge, after having ascertained the reliability of an individual, recognized him as a truthful witness whose testimony could not, in principle, be doubted. Such persons became accredited witnesses and were called shuhūd ʻudūl (singular, shāhid ʻadl, reliable witness), or, for the sake of abbreviation, shuhūd or ʻudūl. The judge's designation of a shāhid ʻadl was called al-rasm bi al-shahāda. Of course, the designation of shuhūd ʻudūl did not make it impossible for the interested parties to call upon other people as witnesses; but the testimony of these witnesses ran the risk of being discarded as worthless. This new institution was inaugurated in 174 (790) by the qāḍī of Egypt, al-Mufaḍḍal ibn Fuḍalā', who, according to al-Kindī, designated ten people as shuhūd. It gave rise to much discontent among the masses and drew much criticism to Ibn al-Mufaḍḍal. People failed to understand why a limited number of persons should alone be recognized as witnesses worthy to be trusted. An uprising even occurred in 177 (793) when the Qāḍī Ibn Masrūq designated the shuhūd. The number of shuhūd appointed by the qāḍīs within their respective jurisdictions, at first limited, was soon increased considerably. At the beginning of the fifth century A. H., there were 1,500 shuhūd in Cairo.

While the system of shahāda was developed originally to protect the validity of legal acts, the shuhūd later became necessary assistants of the qāḍī. Their primary function then was to serve as witnesses to the hearings and the judgment in a suit. The principle of shuhūd assistance to the judge is particularly stressed in the writings of the Mālikī school. This assistance appears to be more clearly compulsory than that given by the *consilium*. All the authors agree that the judge "cannot hold a hearing unless the shuhūd are present." That the institution of the shuhūd is just as firmly established in the Ḥanafī and Shāfi'ī schools is proved in historical texts dealing with the judicial organization in countries under the influence of these schools. The assistance of the shuhūd as witnesses to the litigation and to the judgment was so vital that it was not restricted to common law procedure, but was generally applied to all legal procedure, even of an exceptional nature such as that of the mazālim.

As to the number of shuhūd a magistrate could have, no precise regulations are stipulated in the texts. It seemed to depend upon the consideration of practical expediency, and the opinion of the judge was most influential in this matter. It appears that practice eventually brought about the definite adoption of four shuhūd. In any case, the minimum requirement was two shuhūd, following the general rule that one witness is no witness (*testis unus, testis nullus*).

Since the purpose of the institution of the shuhūd was to furnish incontrovertible proof of procedural acts and of judgments, it might be concluded that there were no court clerks recording the proceedings and the judgment. However, both institutions existed and functioned at the same time. The clerk had always been an indispensible assistant to the qāḍīs even though they had to receive the aid of the shuhūd. Certainly the institution of court clerks antedates that of shahāda. According to historical texts court clerks existed in the beginning of the second century A. H., whereas the shahāda of the qāḍīs is found only toward the end of the same century. The reason for the coexistence of these two institutions is the general failure to recognize written documents as conclusive proof.

THE COURT ASSISTANTS

The system of court assistants was fully developed by the third century A. H. Aside from the shuhūd, court clerks, and the interpreters, there were assistants entrusted with the maintenance of order while the court was in session and with calling upon the parties, as well as those assistants to whom the judge assigned the exercise of a few supplementary judicial functions. These various officials were called a'wān which literally means auxiliaries, even though this term had a more restricted meaning when applied to a special category of legal assistants.

THE COURT CLERK, KĀTIB

The kātib's duties consisted in making a full written record of the statements of the parties in the lawsuit, the claims of the plaintiff, the defense of the defendant, rebuttals, the deposition of witnesses, etc. At the trial he read into the record all documents submitted in evidence by both parties. Just as the qāḍī also exercised the functions of a notary, so the clerk was called upon to draw up all the legal documents to which the interested parties wished to lend authentic value. The clerk was in charge of keeping all the registers, files, and archives of the tribunal.

However, the kātib's functions were not limited to recording trials. He also took part in the discussions between the qāḍī and his *consilium*. In addition, the qāḍī might call upon the clerk or the shuhūd to take over certain judicial functions occasionally or permanently. According to the jurists, the clerk legally had the position of a deputy, or nā'ib.

THE MUZZAKĪ

This term designated two different officials: one of them, also called ṣāḥib al-masā'il, was entrusted with investigating the character of shuhūd; the other investigated the character of ordinary witnesses.

THE INTERPRETER (MUTARJIM)

The judge was required to have an interpreter. This official was not called upon merely for a particular suit, but held a permanent position. He acted as a legal aid in charge of translating for the judge statements made by litigants who did not know Arabic. Certain authors, treating translations as testimony, insisted that the qāḍī have two mutarjims at his disposal at the same time, but this was always an isolated opinion and according to the time-honored practice established by prevailing opinion, a single interpreter sufficed.

THE BAWWĀB, THE JILWĀZ, AND THE 'AWN

The bawwāb (literally, the doorkeeper) is comparable to the usher in modern courts. He was stationed at the door of the court room and maintained order among the litigants and the public. He established the order in which litigants were to appear before the judge according to the time of their admission to the court room and assigned to each litigant the place where he should stand before the qāḍī. The bawwāb was sometimes assisted by another official named the ḥājib, who was closer to the person of the qāḍī. His duties were to allow only the interested parties to have access to the judge and to act as a bodyguard to the qāḍī.

Another official entrusted with the internal order of the hearing was the jilwāz, who is still called, in the Orient, ṣāḥib al-majlis. He was charged with the maintenance of order at the hearing, and held himself near the qāḍī. He carried a whip which he used against any person whose behavior was not proper or who was creating a disturbance. He also saw to it that the litigants appeared before the judge to present their case only at their proper turn.

The a'wān (singular, 'awn) were bailiffs who made known to the parties the judge's orders and who used force, if necessary, to make them appear before him. (The 'awn is also called mushkhis or rasūl). He attended the hearings.

THE QASAM OR QĀSIM

This official was put in charge of supervising the division and apportioning of goods, and was appointed by the qāḍī because of his technical knowledge. The qāḍī only approved the decisions of the qasam, for this legal assistant actually rendered the decisions in cases involving the division of goods.

AMĪN AL-ḤUKM

In the third century A. H., the qāḍīs adopted the habit of entrusting to the shuhūd, for safekeeping, the assets of legally incompetent persons, orphans, absentees, etc. Later an official called amīn al-ḥukm was especially appointed to safeguard and administer the property of orphans. Since he was under the direct control of the qāḍī, the amīn al-ḥukm had only administrative powers. He could dispose of property in his trust only through a special procedure before the qāḍī. In the tenth century A. H., according to Ibn Nujaym, this office had become obsolete and the properties of minors and orphans were entrusted to their guardians.

KHĀZIN DIWĀN AL-ḤUKM

This official, who is mentioned in several texts, was entrusted with the safekeeping of the court's archives. Until the fifth century A. H., in Egypt at least, these documents were deposited at the home of the judge or of his clerk. Ibn al-'Awwām, qāḍī of Cairo during the years 405/1014-418/1027, transferred these archives to the mosques which served as courts and there were deposited in a specific place. From the middle of the fourth century A. H., conclusive evidence is found of the existence of the khāzin diwān al-ḥukm.

The qāḍī is, finally, advised to appoint a trustworthy person whose duties are to keep him informed about the people's opinion of his behavior, his judgments and the shuhūd who assist him in carrying out his duties.

THE WAKĪLS

In Muslim law there is no bar as an institution *sui generis,* as in Western countries. There are no attorneys in Islamic law, in the special sense of the word. In theory, defending a party's interests before a court is, both in Muslim theory and practice, purely an application of the contract of agency. The person to whom the legal interests of another party are entrusted is treated as an ordinary agent. Neither in legal nor in colloquial Arabic is there any term corresponding to "attorney." He is an agent, a wakīl; and the contract which binds him to his client is a wakāla (contract of agency). In accordance with the accepted and traditional doctrine, Muslim authors relate the institution of the agent in court to origins reaching back to the Prophet and to Arab practice from early Islam. From this it can be concluded that this type of agency has always been practiced.

To represent someone in court became a profession open to people qualified by their legal knowledge and especially to those skilled in court practice. Their profession did not require any particular conditions for admission, and its members did not constitute an order or an association; nevertheless, they form a distinct group of legal men. They are the wukalā' (agents) or the khuṣamā' or khuṣūm, in the restrictive sense of the words.

The contract between the attorney and his client is usually drawn up according to the ordinary rules of agency. There are only a few restrictions on the choice of the wakīl. According to an opinion attributed to Abū Ḥanīfa and taught by his school and by certain Mālikī authors, such as Saḥnūn, a litigant may be represented in court by counsel only if he obtains the consent of his adversary. It was argued that the appointment of counsel to defend the interests of a litigant would harm the interests of his adversary since, as a general rule, the interested party himself should appear before the judge and uphold his claims, and since the defense of these claims by an attorney is usually more effective than defense by the interested party himself. But this opinion did not prevail and practice generally recognized the freedom of each litigant to find an agent to plead his case without obtaining the consent of his adversary. This practice was in accordance with the Mālikī doctrine, and was acknowledged by Article 1516 of the Majalla (which is drawn from the Ḥanafī school of law).

The judge may refuse to permit representation of a litigant by counsel if he believes that the statements which the litigant might personally make would be more likely to reveal the truth. Counsels also are not allowed to plead cases which are manifestly unjust. On the other hand, the judge may also forbid a litigant to appear in court in person, and force him to be represented by an agent. Thus, a woman "of outstanding voice and beauty" may not defend her own case before the judge.

The role of the agent in court is not limited to arguing a case before the judge, but is concerned with every act occurring during the litigation. The agents are, at the same time, barristers and solicitors.

The causes for the termination of this type of agency are, as a general rule, the same as those that apply to an ordinary contract of agency. The death of the party who appointed an agent, however, does not terminate the contract if the agent has almost accomplished his task. The agent will, in this case, carry through his responsibility to the end as the agent of the deceased party's heirs who may not discharge him.

The client is also restricted in his right to discharge an agent. If the agent has already pleaded a case for his client during three successive sessions, his client no longer has the right to discharge him, even in the case of a gratuitous mandate, unless the wakīl has been charged with grave professional misdemeanors, such as collusion with his adversary or other fraudulent action. It is even more understandable that the wakīl cannot be dismissed if the arguments are almost closed. Moreover, the rules for the cancellation of an agency contract differ when they apply to a gratuitous or a remunerated contract. In the first case, cancellation follows the rules already indicated. But in the case of the remunerated contract—in which are included all the cases of an interested third party or of the agent who is not actually paid but is remunerated in some other way—the rules of a contract of lease are applied by analogy and the client can cancel the contract if he has sound reasons for withdrawing his trust from his representative.

The judge's right to refuse a dishonest litigant the assistance of a wakīl implies his right to dismiss a wakīl who manifests dishonesty during a suit. The qāḍī enjoys the same disciplinary and regulatory power over a wakīl as he does over all his legal assistants and over all persons who are engaged in any judicial activity whatsoever. The qāḍī may officially appoint wukalā' for worthy parties who do not themselves have the means to engage the services of an agent.

An administrative official, the muḥtasib, exercised, from the seventh century on, the same disciplinary control over the attorneys as the qāḍī. The muḥtasib must see to it that lawyers do not let themselves be corrupted by their clients' adversaries, that they do not encourage their clients to deny what they have previously admitted, etc. If need be, the whip, or even disbarment, may be used as a sanction.

THE FUNCTIONS OF THE QĀḌĪ

In the Muslim judicial system, the qāḍī basically represented ordinary justice, in contrast to the other magistrates and to officials of other categories, who exercised extraordinary justice. It is true that these or similar terms, originating in Roman law, are not to be found in legal texts and in judicial terminology. But it is certain that there existed, side by side, in Muslim law, a court practice which operated in accordance with rigid rules and followed a procedure and methods of proof which were definitely set and imposed upon the interpreter of the law, and, on the other hand, a court practice that was freed from these rules, worked out in a manner left to the judge's discretion, and generally based upon equity. The first type of court was the qaḍā', the second corresponded mainly to the institution called al-maẓālim. The functions of the qāḍī, his jurisdiction *ratione materiae,* can only be those which have been set by the law, that is to say, by the works of the jurists, such as the compilations of the fiqh or the writings of the authors on public law, like al-Māwardī. The same law determines the rules to which court procedure must conform.

There are certain important exceptions to these principles. In the Mālikī school of law, aside from his ordinary judicial powers, the qāḍī enjoys a power of extraordinary justice, called al-siyāsa al-shar'iyya, which allows the judge freedom in finding an equitable solution to litigations. In Morocco and in the West, where the Mālikī rite was most widespread, this resulted in the institution of the mazālim being considerably restricted in its application. Even in Islamic countries which adhered to other schools, the effect of the mazālim's decadence increased the importance of the function of the qāḍī. There were frequent cases of the qāḍī combining, by express permission of the government, extraordinary jurisdiction, mazālim, shurṭa, etc., in addition to his ordinary jurisdiction.

In the exercise of ordinary justice, the qāḍī had much coercive power—with *iurisdictio,* he possessed *imperium.* To assist in finding out the truth or to assure the carrying out of procedural and investigative acts, the law grants the judge a certain coercive power which is extensive in the Mālikī school and much more restricted in the other schools. The Ḥanafī school holds that if the defendant in a lawsuit is obliged to admit or deny the allegation of the plaintiff, the qāḍī has not only the right but the duty to jail a defendant who refuses to do so. Similarly, the defendant who refuses to produce in court the chattel with which the litigation is concerned, in accordance with the procedural rules of Islamic law, can be forced to do so under penalty of imprisonment. This imprisonment can last until the judge's injunction has been obeyed or until there is conclusive proof of the loss of the chattel. The Mālikī school states that the defendant who appears before the court but who refuses to defend the suit may be lashed as well as imprisoned. A similar coercive power is granted the judge over the litigants with regard to certain acts of investigation.

In its general appearance, the jurisdiction of the qāḍī becomes progressively more extensive. It creates and appropriates new attributes and arrogates functions which were previously in existence but were not part of the jurisdiction of the qāḍī. In several cases, this extension of jurisdiction was not brought about by a spontaneous concession by the administrative authority but by initiative on the part of the judicial organism itself. In the other cases, the government, finding itself unable to guarantee the functioning of certain services, handed them over to the judicial organization, whose activity constantly increased.

Indeed, during the course of the development of the institution, the qāḍī became increasingly conscious of the scope of his mission, which consisted in the arbitration of suits between individuals and the safeguarding of the interests of those who require protection of the state. Thus the qāḍī became the guardian of the interests of orphans and of absentees whose property had been left without provision for its administration. He was a notary, the guardian of ownerless property, and the administrator of waqfs. The qāḍī also exercised functions which were actually foreign to the nature of his office, but which required an identical type of knowledge. It was normal for the qāḍīs to teach law, to write legal treatises, and to issue fatwas.

Because of the religious characteristics which soon made themselves felt in all the institutions of public law in Islam, and especially in the caliphate, the qāḍīs were naturally called upon to consecrate the investiture of each new caliph, during which they occupied places of honor. The qāḍīs were also called upon to legitimize, through legal advice, the deposition of a ruler through a palace revolution or the change of sovereigns. No doubt other free consultants were asked to corroborate the advice of the qāḍīs. Advice alone did not suffice and the pronouncement of a judgment was required for the confirmation of a deposition. The qāḍī was the only person competent to render this judgment. The qāḍī was also called upon for acts of much lesser importance which were entirely alien to the judicial function. Thus historical chronicles relate that when the government wished to establish or modify a customs regulation, it would ask the chief qāḍī to legitimize this administrative act through his advice.

The judge's functions also were extended to certain essentially administrative matters. The qāḍī took over the function of the ḥisba, a type of administrative police; he became controller of weights and measures and of the mint; he took over the construction of harbors, the supervision of fisheries, etc.

The judicial functions indicated by al-Māwardī—other authors mention a few variants—are the following: (1) the settlement of litigations between individuals; (2) the enforcement of rights established in court; (3) the protection of the weak; (4) the administration of waqf property; (5) the execution of wills; (6) providing for unmarried women who have no guardians; (7) the application of the ḥudūd, i.e., the penalties laid down by the Qur'ān; (8) the policing of buildings and of public highways; (9) controlling the shuhūd and judicial assistants as well as the choice and appointment of the qāḍī's deputies.[12]

One notes that no rational classification directs this enumeration of the various judicial functions. In particular, there is no distinction between the qāḍī's acts as a judge in litigation and his judicial acts outside litigation. But most of the jurists have noted this distinction and discussed it in connection with the definition of the term "judgment." They make a distinction between "judgment" properly speaking (al-ḥukm, al-ḥukm al-qawlī, al-qaḍā') on the one hand, and the "command" or "action" of the judge (al-ḥukm al-fi'lī) on the other. The authors state that the judgment consists of the decision rendered by the judge following litigation before him; it necessarily presupposes two conflicting claims. No proceedings in which a conflict is not involved can terminate with a judgment. The action which the qāḍī takes in administering property of which he is guardian or in carrying out his functions as the protector of the weak, even the action whose purpose is to settle certain rights but which does not imply a conflict, is fi'l. Into this category would come the marriage of a minor who has no guardian, the purchase of a property for the benefit of a legally incapable person who is under the guardianship of the qāḍī, the division of real estate, etc.

In theory, the judge functions only at the request of the interested party. This is strictly laid down by Ibn Farḥūn: *al-qāḍī la yaḥkum illa fīma rufi'a ilayhi.* This rule is perfectly natural insofar as it applies to cases of private conflicts, which constituted the original main area of competence of magistrates. But this rule was expanded to apply to proceedings where public interests were involved. In criminal law, i.e., in all matters concerning wrongs to a private individual, for instance a case of theft, it is only on the initiative of the victim that the case can be brought before the judge; on the other hand, in the case of offenses punishable by legal penalties or ḥudūd and constituting a specific menace only to the public interest, the judge may act on his own initiative. In an opinion attributed to Abū Ḥanīfa, even in the latter situation the

[12] Māwardī, *op. cit.*, pp. 117-119.

judge cannot act on his own initiative, but must await the action of an individual before taking up the case, thus upholding a kind of *actio popularis.* In the exercise of jurisdiction concerning what will be called, for the sake of convenience, municipal regulations (e.g., buildings jutting out onto a public thoroughfare), some jurists following Abū Ḥanīfa maintained that the qāḍī could not act on his own initiative, and that express action had to be undertaken by the interested party. The Mālikī school conforms to this theory.

THE MAZĀLIM

Aside from the ordinary justice carried out by the judicial magistrates for the settlement of private conflicts and other related situations whose main categories we have already mentioned, and aside from the justice exercised by certain exceptional jurisdictions, there existed a superior justice whose field of action was not limited by any fixed and precise rule and which is designated by the term mazālim.

This type of justice stems from the absolute authority of the sovereign and from his fundamental competence to deal with all litigations and to right all wrongs. It was developed after the establishment of a strict body of law which placed the judge within a legal system and eliminated the free consideration of equity. It also developed through the inability of the ordinary judiciary to guarantee equal justice to all people.

There are no texts, nor written or customary rules, which define and limit the categories of litigations which come under the jurisdiction of the mazālim. It extends to all conflicts which are justiciable by the qāḍīs or by extraordinary courts. In addition, through an exaggerated extension of the concept of justice, the mazālim procedure was applied to all sorts of torts, caused not only by an individual, a group or an administrative body to another individual, but by many other diverse means, when the victim is an individual. In other words, this procedure can apply to all prejudicial situations. By this one must understand not only any violation of the subjective right of an individual, but instances of erroneous or faulty application of the objective rules of law, either in specific cases or in a general way, such as the bad administration of a foundation or negligence in the observance of municipal police regulations. One can mention the following principal cases:

(1) Any injustice committed in the carrying out of public services or by the personal action of government agents, irregularities

in the collection of taxes, delay or failure in the payment of salaries and wages to those entitled to receive them.

(2) Usurpation of property or violation of rights committed by agents of the government or by powerful people.

(3) Recourse against the decisions and actions of judicial magistrates. This is not an appeal along the lines of modern appellate procedure. As we shall see in the examples of practical application which follow, recourse before the judge of the mazālim is different in nature from that of the appeal and its field of application is infinitely greater. On the one hand, it is not merely a matter of an appeal from formal decisions, but also from all the acts which the ordinary judge performs in the exercise of any of his functions. On the other hand, the purpose of complaint may be the judge's actions completely outside the exercise of his official functions, that is, his personal and private behavior which might indicate his incompetence or his unworthiness. This control over the decisions and acts of the magistrate seems to be a manifestation of the supervisory right which the sovereign or his delegates have over the administration of justice, and the jurisdiction of the judge of the mazālim derives from the general power of control over the public services.

(4) In the enforcement of judicial decisions, the judge of the mazālim has only subsidiary jurisdiction. In theory, the enforcement of a decision is the responsibility of the judge who made it; the holder of the mazālim jurisdiction may only be asked to enforce such a decision if the judge is incapable of doing so himself. It is not necessary, however, that the ordinary judge have previously been the object of controversy, or that he have been urged in vain to carry out said decision.

Certain considerations determine which authority is competent in questions of mazālim jurisdiction. If, as we have just said, the ordinary judge is powerless to guarantee the sanction or punishment of an act coming within his jurisdiction, it is necessary to have recourse to a more powerful authority whose power and influence cannot be broken by the author of this act. Al-Māwardī says: "The one who is competent in matters pertaining to mazālim jurisdiction must have, for the exercise of his duties, and in order to guarantee the enforcement of law, a coercive authority and power which the qāḍīs [as ordinary judges] do not possess . . . he may use threat and coercion when seeking out the truth."[13]

[13] Māwardī, *op. cit.*, pp. 128-29.

The procedure of mazālim is an arbitrary one so far as the power of decision and the means of establishing proof are concerned; it is not subject to the limitations and the strict regulations of ordinary procedure. Mazālim jurisdiction can therefore only be carried out by those people to whom such restrictions do not apply in the exercise of their powers. Since the possessor of mazālim jurisdiction is naturally called upon to make decisions whose theoretical contents are not to be found in positive law or which even contradict the text of this law, he must find within himself the justification for these decisions.

As already indicated, the various acts which are amenable to mazālim procedure encroach upon the domain of ordinary justice. The injustice which may have been caused is not only injustice *stricto sensu.* Therefore, the person in charge of mazālim, through his personal position, must have authority, both in fact and in law, over everybody and all things; he must normally be the supreme corrective force whose competence cannot be challenged in any field or by virtue of any doctrine. Only the head of the State, the absolute ruler, combines the necessary qualifications corresponding to these considerations.

The exercise of mazālim jurisdiction in Islam is one of the most characteristic and startling functions of the sovereign. It is closely parallel to the rise and decline of the royal authority. The ruler—caliph, sultān, amīr—jealous of his authority and conscious of his duties and prestige, maintained this procedure. During the history of the Islamic dynasties, one of the first actions of a leader who had shaken off the central authority and set himself up as an independent ruler was to hold mazālim meetings which, in the eyes of the public, consecrated and emphasized the new rule. The decline of a dynasty or of a certain regime was characterized by a progressive and often complete relinquishment of the practice of mazālim. Royal audiences, if and when held, took place only as a matter of form and for show. The powerful minister or another person exercising mazālim power in fact took the ruler's place. The exercise of mazālim jurisdiction by the sovereign does not appear to be distinct from the exercise of ordinary jurisdiction. These two procedures are, to him, but the manifestation of the same theory of power appearing under different forms. The exercise of mazālim jurisdiction by provincial governors or by ministers is an application of the essential attribute of the ruler in this matter. They exercise this jurisdiction only insofar as they are, in theory or in fact, the representatives of the ruler. In general, the mazālim jurisdiction cannot be delegated permanently to an autonomous and distinct body of judges.

THE POWER OF DECISION

The nature and extent of the power of decision in questions of mazālim are closely related to the character of the authority entrusted with the exercise of this form of justice. Since this authority is essentially vested in the sovereign, the power of decision will be sovereign and absolute. Mazālim justice appears to be a rebellion against the strictures of positive law, of the sharī'a: it freed itself from the fetters and the rigid rules of this law. Doctrine brings out very clearly this characteristic of mazālim justice. In his comparison between mazālim and ordinary justice, al-Māwardī says: "The qāḍīs can act only in accordance with the rules imposed by the sharī'a whereas the mazālim judges are not bound by such rules; their freedom is limited only by those legal regulations which establish express prohibitions."[14]

The extent of the power of decision in questions pertaining to mazālim has these apparent aspects: the mazālim judge is free in his choice of sanction and has discretionary power; he may apply penal sanctions in a civil case; the sanction can also be dual, both penal and civil. In the doctrinal concept of the mazālim, this power is considerably restricted. The jurists state that in ordinary litigation, that is, litigation which cannot legally be kept from being submitted to an ordinary judge, the mazālim judge cannot pronounce a sanction which the ordinary judge is not empowered to pronounce.

The mazālim judge can freely defer the rendering of judgment. After having examined the case himself, he can delegate the power of rendering a decision to a third party. This delegation may be limited and may only be effected according to the manner and extent authorized by law. The sources divulge that the mazālim judge was often assisted by ordinary judges and that at times he delegated to them the task of judging cases which came under their normal competence; naturally, the magistrate who was thus put in charge of the case could decide only in terms of the common law. But in other cases, the delegation was much broader. The mazālim judge could make the litigants appear before a body of arbitrators, for an amicable settlement, whereas the qāḍī could do this only with the consent of the litigants themselves.

14 Māwardī, *op. cit.*, pp. 140-41.

PROCEDURE

The mazālim judge is not bound by any rules of procedure. He can take action by virtue of his office even though a purely civil question is involved. The complaint of the litigant does not even appear as the juridical fact which results in the judge being seized of the case. Its only effect is to make the authority aware of the wrong which has been committed.

The mazālim judge was not required to hold a hearing for the parties himself, but could entrust the examination of the claim to special officials appointed for this purpose. Those to whom the sovereign, the ministers, or the governors delegated mazālim jurisdiction, even the ṣāḥib al-mazālim, often found that their powers were limited to receiving complaints and collecting the evidence and the facts upon which a decision might be based.

In investigating the facts, the mazālim judge could use threatening and coercive measures and allow the establishment of proof by means of hints and presumption; he could listen to evidence not legally admissible before qāḍīs, swear in the witnesses, demand the testimony of as many witnesses as he deemed necessary to form an opinion, and (even before hearing both sides) start the procedure by listening to the witnesses. No system of legal evidence is imposed upon the mazālim judge.

The organization of the mazālim court was not subject to strict regulations. The judge or his delegate was present, even though the latter's functions might be more or less extensive and might or might not include the power of decision. Moreover, the mazālim judge, or his delegate, enacted decrees, either independently or with the aid of assessors. The role of these assessors was not always the same; sometimes they attended the hearing as passive spectators to enhance the authority of the judge; sometimes the latter delegated to them a part of his powers.

One must be cautious in the use of certain terms: jurisdiction, judge, and tribunal. The mazālim judge was not exclusively concerned with stating which of two litigants was right or with guaranteeing protection of the rights of one of the litigants, nor did he have to wait to be called upon by a litigant to start proceedings. In the terminology of the authors who write concerning public law and in that of historians and chroniclers, the mazālim institution is not termed qaḍā' which is the word used to designate true jurisdiction. The office which was established under the authority of the ruler, the minister, or the governor to exercise mazālim jurisdiction, was called wilāyat, wazīfat, or nazar al-mazālim; the official entrusted with this task was not called a qāḍī, but ṣāḥib al-mazālim, walī al-mazālim, or nāzir al-mazālim.

Mazālim procedure was not integrated in the system of fiqh, in Muslim positive law, for it was *extra-ordinem*. With the exception of the Mālikī school, one would search in vain for mention of the mazālim institution in the works on fiqh and in the collections of fatwas. The fuqahā' refused to consider this institution as an institution of the sharī'a. Only the authors on public law (such as al-Māwardī and Abū Yūsuf) and historians and encyclopedists (such as al-Maqrīzī, al-Qalqashandī, and al-Nuwayrī) recognized the existence of the mazālim and gave details concerning its organization and procedures.

Because mazālim was the supreme controlling organization of the public services and of the department of justice and because, no matter how high the standing of a certain office within the administrative hierarchy, it was theoretically subordinate to that of the mazālim (which is thus one of the most striking manifestations of the sovereign power), it was natural that the principal organ for carrying out mazālim jurisdiction was the ruler who possessed this supreme and overall power in a State. Every person who, by virtue of the ruler's delegation, assumed the general direction of State affairs (the minister [wazīr], any other official of the government, and, with the exception of a territorial limitation of competence, the provincial governor), also possessed the right to exercize mazālim jurisdiction. Such jurisdiction was not originally exercised as a special function but as an application and manifestation of a supreme power. The mazālim later freed themselves from this power and acquired the appearance and accoutrements of an autonomous institution. Although there developed a special and autonomous position whose functions were conferred on officials who did not possess supreme power, this phenomenon did not result in a threat to the power of the sovereign, the minister, or the governor.

The exercise of mazālim jurisdiction by the caliphs and sultans was a means of demonstrating their sovereign power in a striking way, characteristically by holding hearings. During the solemn public occasions (mawākib) presided over by the ruler, a special moment was reserved for a hearing at which any victim of an injustice could voice his complaint (mazlama). To render this function more impressive, the rulers built palaces which were specially adapted to the exercise of mazālim jurisdiction. When the royal custom of direct and effective exercise of mazālim jurisdiction became outdated, the sovereign still maintained the tradition, at least in appearance. According to al-Maqrīzī, the Sultan Barqūq of the Mamlūk dynasty held bi-weekly mazālim hearings in his palace as his predecessors had done, but the hearing was held very early in the morning and was very short. A few requests were read to the sultan during the meeting, but the historian quickly adds that this was purely a formality whose sole purpose was to maintain the royal traditions.

Next to the sovereigns, the people best qualified, by virtue of their positions, and empowered to exercise mazālim jurisdiction, were the ministers and the provincial governors. Al-Māwardī, and after him other authors, declared competence in this matter to be a natural function of those state officials who had general executive and administrative power. Conversely, the mazālim institution required its administrator to be endowed with effective superior power and presupposed the capacity to enforce his decisions against any opposition. Ministers and governors naturally had this power. This also explains why, in theory, only the ministers with an effective power of decision (wuzarā' al-tafwīḍ) are qualified to exercise mazālim jurisdiction. Those ministers who, because of the authoritarian character of the sovereign, have not received a general delegation of power and are only executive agents (wuzarā' al-tanfīdh) are not qualified.

SUNDRY SPECIAL JURISDICTIONS

Besides the ordinary jurisdiction of the qāḍīs and the mazālim, there existed certain limited jurisdictions which were determined either by the persons amenable to a certain jurisdiction or by the nature of the disputes.

THE QAḌĀ' AL-ASKAR

The formation of this jurisdiction is closely connected to that of the qāḍī himself. Just as with the latter, the starting point was the principle of the personal consideration of the laws of the judiciary organization. During the first period of the invasions, the new Arab-Muslim communities which were set up in the conquered territories and which existed side by side with the former inhabitants of the country who had been permitted to maintain their customs and their courts, required a competent authority for the settlement of disputes arising among their members. The military formations, the Arab-Muslim armies which set out to conquer new territories or settled down in conquered territories, were not different, in this respect, from other communities adhering to the new religion. Here, as mentioned earlier, disputes would arise which necessitated a competent authority for their settlement. Originally, this need could only have been felt among those armies which were in the field and far from their base and were, therefore, deprived of an ordinary judge appointed for the civil community of new converts. The awareness of the need for a judiciary authority among the armies was heightened by the fact that the purpose of the military expeditions was not only the conquest of territories and the establishment of the new Arab-Muslim rule, but also the seizure and acquisition of rich booty of various types which was mostly distributed among the conquerors by themselves.

The qāḍa' al-'askar (the institution, as distinguished from qāḍī al-'askar, the man) did not appear during the first stages of the conquest and at the same time as that of the ordinary qāḍī. The reason for this is obvious: at that time, the Arab-Muslim communities were nothing more than the body of the conquering forces, and the ordinary qāḍī appointed for these communities was precisely the same magistrate who was appointed by the conquerors. The qāḍa' al-'askar took on the aspect of an autonomous institution only when a distinction was actually made between the civil communities established in the conquered territories and the armies which carried on the task of war and conquest.

The first consistent evidence which we have been able to discover of the qāḍī al-'askar in Islam dates back to the first half of the second century A. H. At the end of the Umayyad period in Spain, the qaḍā' al-'askar takes on the appearance of a normal function which must necessarily exist within any army. During the first stages of the 'Abbāsid period, numerous works mention appointments of qāḍīs al-'askar.

The judicial status of the qāḍī al-'askar does not differ from that of the qāḍī, the ordinary magistrate; and there does not exist a judiciary body of qāḍīs al-'askar which differs in nature from the ordinary magistracy. The only basic difference resides in the field of competence. This identical status appears more distinctly at the origin of the institution than later on.

The function carried out by the qāḍī al-'askar is the qaḍā', that is, the ordinary jurisdiction exactly as it is exercised by the qāḍī. The qāḍīs al-'askar were included in the common qāḍīvial hierarchy. This characteristic was brought out in certain ways. Until the Fāṭimid period, the qaḍā' al-'askar does not appear, in the enumeration of public functions, as an autonomous function, distinct from that of common magistracy. The law which the qāḍī al-'askar must apply is identical to that which the ordinary magistrate applies, differing thereby from the mazālim judge or the ḥājib, who adjudicates both according to strict law and to equity.

The nature of the qāḍī al-'askar is that of a religious magistrate, just as with the ordinary qāḍī. One of the evidences of this religious characteristic is revealed by the fact that whenever the qāḍi al-'askar is not campaigning with the army, he holds hearings in the mosque, just as the common magistrate does. Under the Mamlūks, in the general classification of public functions, the qaḍā' al-'askar appears immediately after common magistracy within the category of religious functions.

An important transformation, dating from the Ayyūbid period, took place in the organization of the qāḍā' al-'askar. Actually, there was no fundamental change in the nature and in the competence of this magistracy. But it seems to have reached full maturity and a high degree of development. It appears to have acquired its own existence and a vitality conducive to allowing it to free itself from the general system of the common judiciary organization and to constitute an autonomous body of magistracy. During the Mamlūk period, this institution broadened considerably in scope. Having sprung from the common judiciary hierarchy, it attempted to conform to this hierarchy in its new organization.

THE ḤĀJIB

Since it is basically political and administrative in nature, the institution of the ḥājib received judiciary competence only as the result of a purely arbitrary extension of power which took place only at a late period in historical evolution and only within certain parts of the Muslim world.

The office of ḥijāba usually indicates the function of chamberlain, of the "master of the door" of the sovereign. It would seem from the detailed works of Ibn Khaldūn and al-Maqrīzī that the transformation undergone by the ḥijāba did not take place before the Mamlūk period. During this new period of Islamic history, the ḥājib no longer has anything in common with the ḥājib of the defunct dynasties: he is no longer the "chamberlain" of the Umayyad and 'Abbāsid periods. Neither is he any longer the chamberlain promoted to the position of prime minister as in the

Western dynasties. In the Mamlūk empire, it is certain that the ḥājib possessed judicial competence.

The texts which deal with this competence lack clarity. Nevertheless, one can gather the following evolution from the various texts. In a first phase, the personality of the ḥājib does not yet stand out from his administrative character and, naturally, his competence is still restricted to the surroundings to which he belongs. The ḥājib is still the minister entrusted with the settlement of suits filed against the amīrs and the soldiers, and likewise litigations between soldiers, and especially disputes arising over the endowments and the fiefs which are granted to members of the army. There seems to be, in this respect, a competence concurrent with that of the qāḍī al-'askar. But this competence is more specialized and is restricted to important conflicts in which higher ranking military figures are involved and which is concerned with the rich endowments from which those military figures benefitted.

This competence grew as a result of another function which later was entrusted to him and which consisted in the ḥājib becoming a sort of assistant or deputy of the prime minister of the realm, the nā'ib al-salṭana. Engrossed as he was in his duties as general director of public affairs, it was natural for him to entrust to his chief assistant the task of carrying out mazālim jurisdiction. This is how this jurisdiction came to be the principal function of the ḥājib.

During the Mamlūk period, a confusion arose between common jurisdiction and the extraordinary jurisdiction of the mazālim. The mazālim jurisdiction extended also to ordinary civil litigations, with the only difference, however, that the magistrate enjoyed the power of evaluation in equity as to the fundamentals of the problem, and a complete freedom of procedure, in form, such as had never been enjoyed by the ordinary qāḍīs.

This mingling of mazālim jurisprudence and ordinary jurisprudence is again obvious in a text of Ibn Khaldūn. In order to justify the ḥājib's competence in judicial matters, this author describes his jurisdiction as proceeding from that of the nā'ib al-salṭana who possesses "a power of jurisdiction over both State officials and the common people," which is therefore similar to the power of the mazālim.

The transformation which took place within the nature of the ḥājib's jurisdiction becomes apparent the day when this official claims, as belonging to his own jurisdiction, common litigations which come under the competence of the qāḍī and whose characteristics in no way justify the application of mazālim procedure. According to al-Maqrīzī, the ḥājibs, at the time when they lacked all competence to deal with certain disputes involving military figures, "often forced people subject to ordinary justice to appear at their own courts."

Actually, the competence of the ḥājib had become broader and more comprehensive. According to other texts of al-Maqrīzī himself, the ḥājibs had become competent to deal with "all sharī'a matters [this must be understood as meaning all litigations falling under the ordinary competence of the qādīs], such as marital suits, and also matters of debt and obligations."[15] And, from the point of view of those to come under his justice, the author adds: "The ḥājib finally exercised his jurisdictional power over everybody, be he humble or powerful, and whether ordinary or mazālim jurisdiction was involved." Thus was the jurisdiction of the ḥājib definitely established as an ordinary jurisdiction, with this characteristic that it was carried out not according to strict law, as in qāḍī jurisdiction, but according to the siyāsa, to equity. The ḥājib thus appears to be exercising a jurisdiction in competition to that of the qāḍī. But the institution of the ḥijāba did not extend beyond the Mamlūk empire and shortly thereafter became obsolete.

OTHER SPECIALIZED JURISDICTIONS

In the exposé of the general theory of judicial competence, doctrine admits that some of the functions of the ordinary judge, or qāḍī, can be removed from his competence and given over instead to a judge who is specially appointed for this purpose. Thus, al-Māwardī states that a special qāḍī can be designated to settle litigations dealing with conflicts between debtors and creditors, or marital conflicts, or litigations whose value does not exceed a certain sum. Kharashī, of the Mālikī school, declares that the ruler can appoint two or more magistrates, each one competent in a special category of litigations, such as the qāḍī of marital matters, the qāḍī of the shurṭa, the qāḍī of waterways, etc. Ibn Farḥūn states that magistrates can be specially appointed to deal with marital affairs, or with the administration of the property of minors who have no natural guardian, etc., and also specifies that the competence of these magistrates be restrictively interpreted, doubtless because of its specialized character.

[15] Maqrīzī, *op. cit.*, Vol. III, p. 356.

PUNITIVE JURISDICTION—THE SHURṬA

THE COMPETENCE OF THE SHURṬA

If one were to refer to the theory of penal law only as it is written up in the works of the jurists, one would get a very erroneous impression of the punitive system in Islamic countries, not only from the point of view of fundamental and procedural rules but also from the point of view of the organizations charged with their execution. There again one finds the same contrast, previously observed in other matters, between the various schools' juridical doctrine and practice.

In a general way, punitive justice escaped coming under the ordinary jurisdiction of the qāḍī. It was carried out by a special organization, that of the shurṭa. The shurṭa is both a police organization which is charged with the maintenance of public order, and an organization of punitive jurisdiction and of execution of penalties. The carrying out of public punitive jurisdiction is the main function of the shurṭa, to the extent that it is the only function mentioned by certain ancient authors in their definition of this institution. Thus, Ibn Khaldūn defines the ṣāḥib al-shurṭa as being the official whose duty it is to deal with infractions of the law and to inflict punishment. Another author even calls the head of the shurṭa the wāli al-jarā'im, or the official to whom are entrusted cases involving breach of law. The most important powers of the shurṭa, which al-Maqqarī mentions in order to describe this function, consist in the application of the death penalty and the punishment to persons guilty of legal offenses, of fornication, of drinking, etc. This same fundamental competence is also pointed out by al-Māwardī in his statement of the Muslim doctrine of penal law. In order to determine accurately the competence of the head of the shurṭa, certain authors add to his title the phrase "entrusted with the enforcement of penalties."

In official acts, and especially in the writs of investiture, the main function of the shurṭa is indicated as being the investigation of breaches of the law and the punishment thereof. The acts which terminate with the inflicting of punishment and which modern judicial organization subdivides into indictment, examination of the facts, judgment, and execution, are all treated as one in Muslim law, and they all come under the competence of the shurṭa. Acting by virtue of his office, the duty of the ṣāḥib al-shurṭa is, all at once, to seek out the criminals, to hear the accusation drawn up against them, to judge them and, if necessary, to execute the sentence. In Muslim penal law, there is neither a public prosecutor nor an examining magistrate. Nor did Muslim law conceive of distinguishing between the various procedural steps which lead either to the sentencing of the guilty party or to his acquittal.

The offenses which come under the jurisdiction of the shurṭa can be classified into three categories. In the first place, all the misdemeanors are included which are mentioned in religious law and which are punishable by set penalties or ḥudūd. One must beware of a possible misunderstanding with regard to this matter: one might assume that, given the religious and legal character of fixed punishments, it is the qāḍī who is charged with the application of religious law, who would possess exclusive competence in this case. But this is not true. All the texts concerning the shurṭa mention, in the first place, his competence to deal with legal misdemeanors. In the very definition of the institution, Ibn Khaldūn says that its purpose is to ensure the application of the ḥudūd, using this term in the generally accepted sense which includes both fixed and arbitrary punishments.

The second type of punitive function of the shurṭa consists in applying the penalty of retaliation or qiṣāṣ. This sanction, essentially and originally purely private in nature, since it involves the exercise of the right of revenge within the limits set for it by Qur'ānic legislation, should therefore be personally carried out by the injured party. But this sanction, in practice as well as in theory, is no longer carried out by any one except the representative of public authority. This is one of the aspects of the transformation of qiṣāṣ into a public sanction. Although the jurists continue to assert that it is the injured party or his heirs who exercise qiṣāṣ, what they really mean is that the victim has the right to demand that the authority itself apply this sanction. They use synonymously the expressions "to exercise" qiṣāṣ and to "request" the application of qiṣāṣ. According to certain jurists, the right of the individual simply becomes his right "to authorize" the State to exercise qiṣāṣ. One finally arrives at a very clear statement: "In questions pertaining to bodily injuries or to murder, the theory is that the individual cannot render justice unto himself since the very duty of the judge is precisely to judge between two litigants." Ibn Khaldūn expressly mentions qiṣāṣ among the sanctions whose application comes under the competence of the shurṭa. The official acts also make allusions to it.

Finally, the shurṭa can condemn as constituting an infraction of law any act which it deems reprehensible according to the principles of the siyāsa, which corresponds to the principle of arbitrary judgment of offenses and arbitrary penalties.

This power of the shurṭa stems from the power of the supreme ruler of the community, the caliph or the sultan—whose shurṭa, in theory, is no more than an executive instrument—who, outside of the limits of strict law, or sharī'a, constitutes an absolute autocratic power. It is a fact that the sultan has always, in practice if not in theory, exercised discretionary punitive power over his subjects. This accounts for the innumerable occasions in history when one finds Muslim rulers, or their representatives, inflicting various punishments and even the death penalty for often trifling reasons. This arbitrary power of incrimination is used to such an extent that even in matters foreseen and formally regulated by common law or by the text of the Qur'ān, one finds completely opposite solutions being enforced.

There are also two other very characteristic aspects to this power of arbitrary justice. In the first place, a mere doubt concerning the guilt of an individual sufficies to allow the ṣāḥib al-shurṭa to enforce punitive measures. One might compare these types of sanctions to the voluntary or extraordinary penalties of ancient French law.

In the second place, it is allowed that the public interest, and the need for intimidation can, in certain exceptional circumstances, justify the infliction of a punishment upon an accused person who is recognized as being pardonable.

This third type of function is by far the most important, not only because of the numerous matters which it draws under the jurisdiction of the shurṭa, but also and especially because of the nature itself of the powers which are recognized as belonging to this jurisdiction, the shurṭa becoming an organization not only for the execution but also for the creation of law. This fact enables it to guarantee the adequate exercise of punitive justice in society.

PROCEDURE BEFORE THE SHURṬA

Special rules of procedure are followed in the exercise of the punitive jurisdiction of the shurṭa. They are freed from the shackles of ordinary procedure. Contrary to the ordinary judge, the agent of the shurṭa, by virtue of his office, initiates penal proceedings. This power of immediate action is also strengthened in the shurṭa by the fact that it includes the functions of the police which enable it to prevent infractions and to deal with them after they have taken place. In this prosecution of the offenders, the subordinate agents of the shurṭa make them appear before their superior's court. Ibn Khaldūn brings out this seizing procedure which is common to the shurṭa, when he defines the function of this system as being both the indictment of those who are presumably guilty of breaches of the law, and also the application of penalties. Moreover, in all the historical examples, the shurṭa appears to prosecute by virtue of its own position.

This same action can be initiated by a private individual who is the victim of the infraction. But, before this jurisdiction, the individual is not really a plaintiff since he is not the principal figure in the suit. Actually, the suit could take place without him. Even when the case would lead to the application of an established sanction, in accordance to legal principles exclusively in the interest of individuals, such as the talion penalty, or even in the case of calumny or theft, the victim of such an offense does not actually play the role of the plaintiff before the judge of the shurṭa, since the proceedings can even be undertaken and carried on in his absence and, in any case, the action is not taken in his name.

There is no separate organization for the examination of a criminal case. This procedure is also entrusted to the shurṭa. Here again, the ṣāḥib al-shurṭa enjoys discretionary powers. Doctrine itself recognizes that the ṣāḥib al-shurṭa has the right to use a variety of means in ascertaining the truth. Action is taken on behalf of the public interest and this is sufficient justification for the means employed. In particular, the use of coercive methods to provoke an admission of guilt is clearly recognized and approved by doctrine. This coercion can consist of imprisonment, torture, and especially flogging. Tricks are obviously authorized.

One must not think that, in criminal procedure, the first phase of preparatory examination is followed by the judgment of the case. The examination of the case is closely tied to the judgment. But a particular question arises concerning the judgment which takes place. Does the procedure before the shurṭa take place, according to the judicial pattern, with a debate between the judge and the accused, during which the accusation is stated and the defense is made, and is the decision rendered in judicial form? Or is the procedure purely administrative? Here again, the shurṭa is not bound by any rules. The principle of discretionary power, of siyāsa, always holds good, thus enabling the ṣāḥib al-shurṭa to guarantee the carrying out of punitive measures according to the procedure which he deems most appropriate. Nevertheless, the general tendency has been to adopt forms of a judicial nature. This tendency is evidenced in many ways. The possessor of shurṭa functions is often called by the same name as that used to designate a magistrate: the ḥākim.

The examination of a criminal case is often described as taking place before "the praetorium of the shurṭa." The evidence which is given during this examination, the confession which one tries to obtain, the testimony which is heard, the opinions which are formed and interpreted, all these things presume a judicial procedure. Moreover, the criminal case which is debated before the shurṭa is often known by the same term applied to all cases which are debated according to strictly judicial form: it is a da'wa litigation. The judgment rendered by the ṣāḥib al-shurṭa is called a jurisdictional decision, ḥukm, a term which is especially used in official acts.

Thus, the shurṭa organism becomes a judicial organism, with the characteristic that it applies extraordinary procedure with the use of discretionary powers. Not only is the judge of the shurṭa free to choose, from among the various customary punishments used in a certain place and at a given time, the punitive measure which seems to him to be the most appropriate, but he may also invent new penalties.

CHAPTER XI

Development of the Sharī'a Under the Ottoman Empire

BEFORE THE proclamation of the Imperial Decree of Reform of 1839 (Hatti-Sherif of Gülhane), there were three different aspects to the legal system of Turkey.

First, there were principles of private law, or rules of civil law which in turn were taken from fiqh. The necessity of abiding by these principles was stressed in a special decree sent by the Seldjuk ruler Alaeddin to the founder of the Ottoman state, Osman I, which conferred upon him due authority and power and acknowledged his independence. According to this letter-patent, the administration of law was to remain in the hands of the existing judges, thus insuring that the sharī'a would remain the law of the new principality. Sultan Osman's answer—"When the decree, whose nature was final and decisive and which demanded the obedience of all, was read in the presence of the people, they all exclaimed: 'We have heard, and shall obey!' "—made it clear that this principle had been accepted and established in the country by general consent. Thus, in matters concerning personal status, family relations, inheritance, contracts, and the acquisition of real estate, the principles of fiqh were observed and enforced. Only in cases concerned with agricultural land did the Turks, inspired by their national customs, apply their own rules.

In penal law, the rules of fiqh pertaining to al-'uqūbāt (torts, crimes, and misdemeanors) were applied in most cases. This is mentioned in the letter-patent and recommended with the following statement: "One should act with the utmost caution and treat with due consideration the political criminals who are to be executed." Only in the case of murder, where the heirs of the murdered person prefer indemnity to retaliation, are the judges warned not to deviate from the passage of the Qur'ān which says: "There is life for you in the law of retaliation." Since ululemr (the ruler) was the person who determined the degree of deceit or corruption in accordance with the principles of fiqh, these different degrees were determined at all times by the laws of the country.

The rules and regulations of public law were inspired by everyday matters and were called law (kanūn.) Orders and commands issued from time to time, beginning with the reign of the founder of the Ottoman Empire, Osman I, were called laws, although their legal validity did not go further than the tacit acceptance of the commands of the ruler as regulations. Most of these were given the name of the vizier who had received the approval of the ruler for the command. Orders concerning land, taxes, and revenues were in this category. The decree of Osman I, pertaining to the distribution of official posts, was called a law. The tariff containing the fees of legal tribunals and revenues to be collected by the judges of a province was communicated to them under the title of law, during the reign of Bayazid I. Likewise, the order pertaining to the distribution of copies of title deeds to the owners of timār (fief) on State Lands (miri topraklar) which was issued on the return of Mehmet II, the Conqueror, from the Danube campaign in the year A.H. 881 (A.D. 1476) was named law. It is not possible to find a compilation of all these orders. Because classification is still going on in the archives, it is difficult to build up even a brief general picture from known examples of these laws by inductive reasoning. In many works whose contents have been based mainly on foreign sources there appears a compilation of laws attributed to Mehmet II, but its authenticity is doubtful. This compilation and the imperial handwriting (*manu proprio*) which appears at the beginning of it are preserved in the National Library at Vienna, and have been justly the subject of a great deal of serious and enlightened criticism. Although the handwritten introduction attributed to Mehmet II states "This law was my father's and my grand-father's; it is also mine. I want my sons, generation after generation, to abide by it," no mention has been made of this compilation by Ottoman historians. Had it been authentic, it would have been important, but when we observe that the Western historians have cited this compilation through Greek historians, we can scarcely wonder that the shadow of doubt falls upon it—a shadow caused by century-long hostility and enmity. Reliable jurists of our century, after long research and investigation, have come to the conclusion that this compilation is not authentic.

Katip Celebi (Kiatip Tchelebbi), in his well-known work, *Kesfelzunun,* has mentioned three compilations of the Ottoman state in detail, but has not said a word about this compilation. Ali Himmet Berki, the famous jurist, has recently published a book examining the legislative achievements of Mehmet II (on the occasion of the 500th anniversary of the Conquest of Istanbul). This is a summary of his criticisms of the compilation: The date on this compilation is A.H. 1029 (A.D. 1620), that is, 143 years after the death of Mehmet II. Although this is the date of the copyist of the compilation, one undoubtedly has the right to ask the question: Who was the copyist, and from what did he copy? Why can the original, which undoubtedly should have been preserved in the Imperial Treasury, not be found? How could one imagine Turkish historians overlooking such an important law?[1]

In the introduction, it is stated that these laws were codified by order of Mehmet II and that they were compiled by Lis Zade Muhammed ibn Muṣtafa, the officer in the Imperial Chancery at the time, who had been entrusted with the task of writing the sultan's orders and putting his cipher on the documents. However, during the reign of Mehmet II, there was no officer of that name in the Imperial Chancery. The name of Lis Zade Celebi, a well-known personality during the reigns of Mehmet II and Bayazid II, was not Muhammed but Nureddin Hamza, and his father's name was not Muṣtafa but 'Alī.

The contents of the handwritten introduction attributed to Mehmet II are also suspect, because this compilation does not comprise the laws of the ancestors of Mehmet II. It does not even contain one-tenth of their material, and most of the principles appearing in it are in contradiction to the laws of Mehmet's ancestors.

In view of the accepted importance of the subject, it is strange that the code is neither well-written nor well-organized. Since it is necessary to acknowledge the erudition and eminence of him who occupied the highest office of the Imperial Chancery during the reign of the Conqueror, it is impossible to imagine that he would compile a work full of spelling mistakes, and vague and ambiguous in phraseology. Nor could such a compilation have pleased Mehmet II, who had acquired a unique position in the field of science and literature. It would be an injustice to Ali Himmet Berki not to accept his point of view on this matter, since it is a well-known historical fact that Mehmet II was exceptionally meticulous, oversensitive, and difficult to please on matters concerning expression and style. Consequently, he had his letters announcing the conquest of Istanbul written by the most distinguished men-of-letters of his time.

[1] Ali Himmet Berki, *Büyük Türk Hükümdarı, Istanbul Fatihi Sultan Mehmed Han ve Adalet Hayatı* (Istanbul, 1953), pp. 141-47.

Had this collection of laws been a real code of law, as is claimed by foreign sources, and not a book pieced together at random, it would have passed from one generation to another, it would have been quoted on various occasions and used as evidence by historians. Thus, it would have been handed down to us.

The principle of fratricide is further evidence to prove the code suspect. Von Hammer-Purgstall quotes it thus: "The majority of jurists have declared it permissible that whosoever among my illustrious children and grand-children may come to the throne, should, in order to secure the peace of the world, order his brothers to be put to death. Let them hereafter act accordingly." It is absolutely certain that in a country whose basic law is the law of Islam, which forbids the unlawful killing of a human being, this legalization of fratricide would not have been tolerated. Von Hammer had to add a clause to the article indicating that it was accepted by the majority of jurists, since he was aware that it was at variance with Islamic law. This additional clause has no basis whatsoever, for it would be impossible to find even a minority of jurists who thought fratricide permissible. One must conclude that this spurious codification cannot be utilized as a source of Ottoman law.

Before the proclamation of the imperial decree of 1839, there existed two different forms of codification in the Ottoman Empire, collections of fatwas and of laws. In each case compilations were made by different authors from time to time and distributed throughout Turkey. The fatwas were classified according to their contents on the basis of the sharī'a and pasted in notebooks under different chapters and headings. They were then collected in four large volumes and preserved in the Fetva-hâne, the special bureau which assisted the muftī in preparing decisions until the abolition of the office of the Shaykh al-Islam.

According to Ottoman historians, the system of codification started with the reign of Sulayman II (1520-1566), known as the kanuni, or the legislator. Here credit must be given to the fourteenth Shaykh al-Islam of the Ottoman Empire, Imadi Mehmet Ebussuud Efendi, an eminent jurist. He was appointed to this high office in A.H. 952 (A.D. 1545), and held it for twenty-two years during the reign of Sulayman and for six more years during the reign of Selim II. It was he who collected the best known kanun-name (collection of laws) of Sulayman, and who by applying the Ottoman kanuns to the sharī'a wrote 1400 fatwas per day.

Shaykh al-Islam Ebussuud Efendi's aim was to maintain the

good order of the state and of its religion, and to establish harmony in public affairs. In order to act in accordance with the ideas of the interpreters of Islamic law, he obtained the consent of the sultan to collect and codify these under the title of *Ma'ruzati Ebussuud Efendi*. The laws written by Ebussuud on the occasion of the conquest of Budin, as well as his proposed law for the improvement of legal procedure drafted to record the title deeds in the provinces of Uskup and Selanik (where he had discovered some faults in the legal procedure), are still known as *Sultan Sulayman's Kanun-name*. Although the sources of some of the principles laid down with the assistance and under the direction of Ebussuud are taken from the sharī'a, others are based upon local and Turkish customs. In particular, the principles concerning state lands are based upon custom rather than on the sharī'a. Even in the period when the sharī'a was the main source of law, there had been decisions contrary to its principles in the courts or divans judging crimes and misdemeanors in the Ottoman Empire.[2]

It is possible to reduce all rules and regulations pertaining to written or unwritten law and enforced in the Ottoman Empire to four types according to their sources:

(1) the sharī'a; (2) regulations and principles contrary to the principles of sharī'a, those created in the fields which are not covered by sharī'a, or those deliberately left to local custom; (3) official interpretations made according to the necessities or requirements of the social environment at the time the law was to be applied, without regard for the intention of the legislator; (4) principles adopted from various codes of the Western European countries.

The Ottoman Turks, the ruling element in the Ottoman Empire, could make use of their own opinions and of their urfs (custom) only in fields where the sharī'a had been silent. For instance, the first penal laws in the Ottoman Empire were introduced simply because there were no definite penalties for some crimes in the sharī'a. The right to determine such penalties was granted to the sultan. Similarly, through legal evasions the sharī'a rules for agricultural land were replaced by the introduction of arazi kanunu (land law), inspired by and in conformity with the urf of the country. These rules and regulations were enforced regularly in cases dealing with agricultural land before and after the Tanzīmāt

[2] See *Hukuku Islamiye Kamusu* of Ömer Nasuhi Bilmen, the present Muftī of Istanbul, for the duties and functions of the administrative court called "Divani Mezalim."

(reforms) until the new civil law, adapted from Swiss law, was put into effect.

Codification in its modern meaning started with the proclamation of the Hatti Sherif of Gülhane, 1839, which marks the beginning of the Tanzīmāt in the Ottoman Empire. This decree of reform, published by the government, indicates that a new order had replaced the old in the country. The factors which played a role in this fundamental change included elements of natural law, the need for introducing new principles governing social and economic relations, the strengthening of the central government, and the trend towards bringing the law in accord with national feeling.

The principle of natural law spread to the Ottoman Empire as a result of its closer relations with the West. This is evidenced by the incorporation of the principles of the French Revolution in the Hatti Sherif of Gülhane. Social and economic relations in the eighteenth and nineteenth centuries took an altogether different form from those previously known, and it was necessary to adapt to these new conditions. This is shown in the following excerpt from the Hatti Sherif concerning the reform to be made in financial matters:

> . . . . and it is our belief that banks should be opened in order to raise the prestige of the finances of the Empire by adjusting and protecting the value of money, that capital funds should be created to augment the sources of material wealth, that roads and canals should be opened for the transportation of products, that all obstructions preventing the growth and development of agriculture and commerce should be removed and the necessary facilities provided, and that for the accomplishment of these aims, means shall be sought to profit by European culture, science, and capital.[3]

Internal policy was to increase the central power of the state through codification of the laws. External policy, on the other hand, was to counteract the pressure exerted on public opinion abroad through the propaganda of foreign nations with ambitious and aggressive designs against the Ottoman Empire. Policy was particularly directed against claims that Muslim and non-Muslim subjects were not treated equally and that Muslims enjoyed privileges denied to non-Muslims, for, in conformity with the rules of the fiqh, equality between Muslim and non-Muslim subjects prevailed generally.

No one intended to evolve a national law in the country, for

[3] For the full text of the decree, see Edward Hertslet, *Map of Europe by Treaty* (London, 1875), Vol. II, pp. 1002-1005.

during that period the concept of remodelling the law according to national feeling was unknown in the Ottoman Empire. It was only in fields such as land law and penal law, where the sharī'a was silent, that Grand Vizier Mustafa Rashid Pasha, the author of the Ottoman reform decree of 1839, chose and supported the application of laws inspired by the customs of the Turks.

During the preparation and codification of the new laws beginning in A.H. 1262 (A.D. 1846), the Grand Vizier requested from the office of the Shaykh al-Islam the designation of a scholar particularly well versed in the principles of sharī'a, yet able to understand the needs of modern times. Ahmet Cevdet Pasha was introduced to the Grand Vizier by the then Shaykh al-Islam as the most suitable person for the purpose.

Cevdet Pasha accomplished as much as Ebussuud Efendi had during the reign of Sulayman the Magnificent. As the chairman of the Committee of Justice, Ahmet Cevdet Pasha sought to codify the various laws that had never been brought together in a systematic collection. The Penal Code of 28 Zilhicce A. H. 1274 (A.D. 1858), and the Land Law of A. H. 1274 were both the work of his committee. But his masterpiece crowning all the others was the famous Majalla. It is true that no new law was created by the codification of the Ottoman Land Law which has outlived even the Majalla in present-day Turkey, but the principles and regulations appearing in the old codes were improved.

In sum, the nationalization of law should be interpreted as an indication of the development of the reform movement, for the educated class was convinced that only in this way could the security of the country be guaranteed.

The supporters of modernization even consented to the adoption, with modifications, of foreign codes in the hope of achieving this goal. They acclaimed the Hatti Sherif of Gülhane of 1839 because they believed this the only way to establish a modern state and to remove the evil effects arising from disorder and violation of law. In any case, this clause which appeared at the opening of the decree clearly indicated this point of view:

> For a hundred and fifty years, because of ever increasing troubles and anxieties of various origins, our once powerful and prosperous State has become weak and disintegrated, for the sole reason that we have not obeyed and complied with either the religious law or the kanuns....

The decree then stated that all these disorders would be prevented by the enforcement of newly enacted laws and regulations, and that the first law to be issued should be a penal code prepared in conformity with the Hatti Sherif of Gülhane. The decree also set forth the method for the drafting of these new laws:

> Although in other instances, it has been necessary to take decisions by unanimity of votes, the membership of the Committee of Justice has been increased, and our noted jurists and statesmen will meet on appointed days to discuss with the members of the Committee the contents of the laws; they will express and defend their views in all possible liberty. . . . Thus, the necessary laws will be prepared . . . after the preparation of each it shall be submitted for our approval and then enforced for as long a period as God wills.

The new laws put into force as a consequence of the promises made in the Hatti Sherif of Gülhane can be classified under two separate headings: local laws codified according to modern principles and laws adapted from foreign sources.

Some of the most important statutes based on local principles were the penal codes of A. H. 1256 and 1267 (A.D. 1840 and 1851). Although the Committee consulted European laws on the subject, the resultant laws were in no way adaptations of foreign codes. The Penal Code of A. H. 1256 comprised an introduction, a conclusion, and thirteen chapters. The sultan approved this code and put it into effect a year after the proclamation of the Hatti Sherif of Gülhane, with the following significant words:

> We have seen it. Since this law has been set forth in detail and—to tell the truth—with utmost skill, our approval and acceptance goes with it. As it is an absolute necessity and a moral obligation to all to abide by it, and as the maintenance thereof and its application fall on our Imperial Selves, it is required that all should act as carefully and as meticulously as possible in this respect.

In the year 1267 (1851) a new code, composed of three chapters, was substituted. Most of its articles were almost identical with those of the code of 1256. The new code was in turn superseded by the Penal Code of A.H. 1274 (A.D. 1857).

Regulations concerning land were enacted by the first ruler of the Ottomans, Osman I. They were expanded and improved in the reign of Orkhan, the second Ottoman ruler. In the reign of Sulayman the Magnificent a cadastral office was established to record property rights and issue title deeds. Regulations and principles governing land were collected and codified, particularly the laws concerning the hereditary tenancy of land (tapu), fallow fields and uncultivated lands, joint ownership, etc.

The Land Law of A. H. 1274 was adequate for the needs of the people, and only minor changes and additions were made until the proclamation of the constitutional regime in the Empire for the second time. One amendment was made by the law of the 17th Muharrem A. H. 1284 (May 1867), which contained new regulations governing inheritance, especially the inheritance of state lands. After the proclamation of the constitutional regime, on the 16th and 21st of February A.H. 1328 (A.D. 1910), temporary laws were enacted to regulate the ownership of real estate by corporate entities and the inheritance of real estate.

These two laws contain important radical changes in land law jurisdiction. Previously, the right to own real estate had been granted to such legal entities as governmental or municipal bureaus, waqfs and monasteries, but with the enforcement of the new law, Turkish corporate entities were also granted the right to own real estate.

The rules concerning inheritance were adopted with slight alterations from the German Civil Code, but, as the result of negligence, the regulations which the German code enforced only for the real property in towns and not for cultivated land and forests were applied to cultivated lands and forests in the Ottoman Empire. Because of these regulations, the land was divided into small plots and the actual owners, who had been the masters of these lands for centuries, had to relinquish them. Thus, the seeds of deep discontent and great disorder were sown in the country.

Further amendments to the Land Law were contained in the law of February 25, A.H. 1328 (A.D. 1910), which was adopted from the French law and regulated such matters as mortgages; the law of March 30, A. H. 1329 concerning the right of ownership of real estate; the law dated December 1, A. H. 1329 concerning the division of a real estate under joint ownership; and the law of February 16, A. H. 1328 concerning the abolition of feudal tenures.

The Land Law was divided into the following sections: the introduction defines the various kinds of lands. The first section deals with state lands (arazii emiriyye), their ownership, transfer, inheritance and reversion to the State. The second section deals with public lands (arazii metruke), their definition and the principles to be applied to uncultivated and ownerless lands. The third section contains miscellaneous principles and is followed by a conclusion.

The various kinds of land are:

(1) arazii memluke: land held in unqualified ownership by private individuals. (2) arazii emiriyye: state lands were lands whose title remained with the State and which were rented to indi-

viduals. The lessee benefited from it in accordance with the conditions laid down by the Land Law. The Government received some money when renting the land, which was called tapu muaccele (advance payment for a lease). It also received annually a share of the produce (one-tenth or one-fifth) or collected a fixed sum under the names of zemin icaresi (rent of the plot), usur bedeli (an amount of tithe), or mukataa (a public revenue), which are called müeccele (postponed payment for a lease).

Arazii emiriyye were of two kinds:

(a) Arazii emiriyyei sirfa (pure state land) was land whose profits were assigned to the State Treasury.

(b) Arazii emiriyyei mevkufa (endowed state land) was land whose profits, and sometimes whose right of use, were devoted by the government to religious endowments (waqf).

(3) Arazii mevkufai shaiha (real waqf land) was land which had been held in unqualified ownership by individuals, but which was later devoted to religious endowments.

(4) Arazii metruke (public land) was land which could not be privately utilized, but was reserved for the use and enjoyment of the public. Just as in the case of state land, title to public land was vested in the Treasury, but public land could not be leased. In this category was communal land, such as pastures, forests, etc., reserved for the use of the inhabitants of specific towns or villages and land devoted to the use of the general public, such as public roads.

(5) Arazii mevat: Uncultivated and unowned land.

Majallat-i Ahkami Adliye (the Majalla), or Ottoman Civil Code,[4] like the land and penal codes, was based on local tradition.

A great majority of the laws borrowed from the West after the proclamation of the Hatti Sherif of Gülhane were adapted from French law. Some provisions were omitted intentionally to conform to internal policy, others were abridged or distorted through the negligence of translators and heedlessness or contempt in using legal terms.

First and most important of the laws adopted from the West is the Commercial Code, dated 18 Ramazan, A.H. 1266 (A.D. 1850). The reasons for its adoption are explained in the introduction of the code, which states its guiding principles:

> As is well known, commerce, public order, welfare, development, and prosperity are the foundations of a country's social conditions and the life of the mechanism of State. The expansion and increase of this

[4] See below, Chap. XII.

commerce from day to day is a very important matter, and it, in turn, is dependent on the strength and praiseworthiness of regulations governing commercial transactions. . . . Although commercial lawsuits have been dealt with according to current commercial regulations, these regulations were not recorded and organized; consequently, they do not meet the commercial needs of present conditions.

Upon the Imperial order for the speedy preparation of a new law to meet commercial needs and to create the necessary principles for the development of commerce, with every detail taken into consideration, this project, inspired by the existing commercial laws with special attention given to the establishment of confidence in trade, was submitted to the Agricultural Assembly, where all concerned, traders, businessmen, merchants, etc., were present for a final revision of the draft.

The project was divided into four parts. The first part included rules for general commercial transactions and principles for contracting partnerships, forming companies and corporations, as well as principles for using checks and drafts. Maritime trade and maritime insurance were the subject of the second part. Rules for bankruptcy proceedings formed the third part, while the fourth concerned the organization of commercial courts.

After discussion, it was decided to delete the fourth part on the organization of commercial courts since it was in contradiction to current procedure in the country. The codification of the second part, which dealt with maritime trade, was postponed since it was not as pressing as the other parts. Parts one and three of the project were considered fundamental to the development of commerce, and after a thorough discussion, they were rewritten to correspond with current procedure in the country.

The Maritime Code of France, with those of Sardinia and Sicily, inspired the Ottoman Maritime Code, dated 6 Rebiulevvel, A.H. 1280 (A.D. 1863). Certain articles suggest that the maritime laws of Belgium, Spain, and Prussia were consulted.

French law served as the basis for the Code of Commercial Procedure (dated 10 Rebiulahir, A.H. 1278 [A.D. 1861]). It was enforced in all commercial and civil courts until the new code of commercial procedure replaced it in A.H. 1297 (A.D. 1880).

The Penal Code of A.H. 1274 (A.D. 1857) is discussed in Ahmet Cevdet Pasha's *Memoirs,* for he spent a great deal of time and energy in its preparation. Because its fundamental provisions were adopted from the French Penal Code, it differed greatly from the earlier Ottoman Penal Codes.

The Code of Civil Procedure (dated 2 Recep, A. H. 1297) was prepared by the Council of State on the basis of the French Law of 1807.

Except for the omission of the jury system, the Code of Criminal Procedure (dated 5 Recep, A.H. 1296 [A.D. 1879]) is almost identical with the French Code.

These codes, with certain amendments, remained in force until superseded by the new codes enacted by the Turkish Republic in the 1920's.

The history of the laws of the Ottoman Empire can be divided into two periods. The first period runs from the foundation of the Ottoman Empire until the Tanzīmāt (1839). Texts of the laws put into force during the first period are recorded in the Divani Humayun (the records of the Imperial Chancery). But with the publication of the *Takvimi Vakayi* (an official paper giving in full all laws and decrees in A.H. 1247 [A.D. 1831]), these texts were printed and announced therein. There is no official printed source for the laws of the first period, except the *Takvimi Vakayi.* There followed the period from the Tanzīmāt to A.H. 1324 (A.D. 1906) when the constitutional system of government was reinstituted. It is also possible to classify the laws promulgated after the reinstitution of constitutional government to the end of the First World War as a third period.

It is to be noted that laws were published on various subjects with the aim of transforming the country into a modern state by turning from East to West with the reforms started with the proclamation of the Hatti Sherif of Gülhane in 1839. These laws were published by the Government under the title of "dustur" (codex) and were translated into foreign languages. Such was the *Corps de Droit Ottoman* of George Young, who translated the statutes of the Ottoman Empire in seven volumes.

These codes include the laws, interpretations and decrees enacted by the legislative power, as well as the regulations, contracts and the like which were prepared by authorized offices in conformity with the provisions imposed by laws, interpretations and decrees.

The dustur was codified in three series. The first series contained the texts previous to A.H. 1324 (A.D. 1906). It comprised eight volumes, four of which were appendices. It contains the laws and decrees up to A. H. 1302 though it is incomplete. Laws from 1302 to 1324 were not compiled and printed in the form of a dustur. The compilation entitled *Mutemmim* (Addenda) contains only a part of these.

The second series of dustur contains all judicial texts from 1324 to 1336 (1918). Of this series, seven volumes were published at the time, containing texts up to the year 1331 (1912), but the part which went up to 1338 (1919) was printed later in five volumes, making a total of twelve. Only the twelfth volume, being put into force after the formation of the National Government, was considered null and void; thus, it contains laws which were not accepted by the Turkish Republic.

The third series of dustur contains in full all laws promulgated by the Grand National Assembly and all governmental decrees of the Turkish Republic in thirty-three volumes.

Laws codified before the Constitution of A.H. 1293 (A.D. 1876) were submitted by the Government to his Imperial Majesty for approval and were enforced by His Majesty's decree. Laws after this date were enacted by the Parliament in accordance with the provisions of the Constitution.

CHAPTER XII

The Majalla

THE REFORM movement which started in 1839 with the Gülhane charter brought about numerous changes in the Ottoman Empire. Many administrative and judicial institutions were reorganized along Western lines, and European law was introduced in various fields. The Majalla was one of the important means of preserving Islamic institutions while the Ottoman Empire was changing from an Islamic to a Western society.

Although the Majalla was a product of the Ottoman reform movement, it was based upon the Ḥanafī school of law. It did not introduce new principles of law, but codified the Islamic principles which had served as the civil law of the Ottoman Empire. Its very name indicates this fact, for the word Majalla means a digest of legal rules and principles. The full name of the code is *Majallat-i Ahkami Adliye,* the Book of Rules of Justice.

To understand the nature of this code it is necessary to know why and how it was compiled as an official code of law, and to see its importance within the Ottoman legal system.

PREPARATION OF THE MAJALLA AND ITS LEGAL NATURE

The Majalla is a product of the Tanzīmāt. The outstanding characteristic of this period is the presence of two separate legal systems derived from different sources. Before 1839 there was only one system of law within the Ottoman Empire—the sharī'a. The prerogatives of the sultan, based on the ancient rights of ta'zīr, enabled him (as the supreme ruler of the country) to make rules for the regulation of public affairs. These rules, however, could not interfere with the rights of the people, which were protected by the sharī'a, nor could they contravene the general principles of Islam. Before 1839 the law of the country was primarily Islamic; after 1839 new laws were adapted from Western codes. From then on a dual system of law developed within the Empire, one having its origin in Islamic religious law and the other based on continental European, especially French, codes.

The immediate causes for the development of this dual system may be found in the problems which arose during the reign of Sultan Selim III in 1789. At a time when Europe was making great progress, Ottoman power declined because the Empire failed to take advantage of Western progress in science and technology. When the sultans began to understand the Empire's weakness vis-a-vis the West, they sought to save themselves from disaster by adopting European institutions and techniques. At the same time, Turkey needed new institutions and procedures to facilitate its increasingly active relations with European states.

Reforms were begun in the army in the late eighteenth century, but met strong resistance that led to the assassination of Sultan Selim III in 1807. In 1826, during the reign of Maḥmūd II, reforms were resumed (this time extending beyond the military field), and in the year of 1839 when Abdul Majid was on the throne, reached their climax with the charter of Gülhane which opened the era of the Tanzīmāt. Because Islamic law failed to deal with such problems as foreign exchange, corporations, and commercial transactions, it was difficult to settle controversies arising out of business relations between Ottoman subjects and foreigners, and in 1850 the French Commercial Code was adopted to facilitate trade with European countries. In other fields where Islamic law was clearly antiquated, such as admiralty, criminal law, and the enforcement of court decisions, European codes were likewise introduced.

It was obvious that these new laws could not be applied through the old sharī'a courts, and that a new judicial system was needed. In 1837, prior to the proclamation of the Gülhane charter, a committee had been established to prepare administrative and judicial reforms, to draft new laws and regulations, and to supervise their application. In 1868, this committee was divided into two sections: Shura-i Devlet, the Council of State, which continued to have the duty of preparing laws and supervising their enforcement; and Divani Ahkami Adliye, the Judicial Committee, which decided cases to which the new Westernized law was applicable. After 1840 a special commercial court dealt with disputes arising between European and local merchants. A new system of secular courts was created by special decree in 1871 and expanded in 1880.

The application of the new laws and regulations produced a certain amount of confusion. Compilations such as the Commercial Code were Western, but Ottoman civil law continued to be based on the sharī'a. Thus, there existed a basic irreconcilable difference between the traditional law of the Empire and the new statutes derived from foreign sources.

This difficulty was thus stated by the committee which prepared the Majalla:

> During this century trade relations have expanded to so wide an area and have acquired so complex a character that Turkish law cannot settle problems concerning matters such as bills of exchange or bankruptcy, and there is need for a new and special Code of Commerce to apply to these cases. But for matters outside the scope of this Code, recourse must be had to the civil law of the country. For instance, in the Commercial Court where a suit is conducted according to the provisions of the Commercial Code, recourse must be had to the civil law on matters such as pledge, guarantee, and agency.

The initial difficulty faced by the committee was that no single Muslim code existed. Rules were scattered throughout the works of various jurists, and most of their works were written in classical Arabic, of which the lawyers practicing in the new secular courts had little or no knowledge. Muslim jurists, in turn, were not only unacquainted with the principles of Western law, but often found it difficult to deduce principles from the divergent and scattered sources of the sharī'a.

In discussing this situation the committee declared:

> . . . . If the provisions of mu'āmalāt (transactions) were sufficient for the needs of the people they [i.e., the judges] would apply these; but the people think that, as the judges of civil courts are not experts of the religious law, they will not solve these disputes as they should according to law, but decide according to their own discretion. In the courts of commerce where commercial law is applied, great difficulties have arisen on points outside the scope of commercial law. It is impossible to have recourse to the laws of Europe because they are not the laws of Turkey, and no judgment can be based on a provision which is not the law of the land. It is equally impossible to refer these purely commercial matters to religious courts, because for the sake of a minor point they would apply religious law to the whole of the matter. Moreover, the procedure of the two courts is entirely different. The judges of the courts of commerce do not make reference to religious law books because they have no knowledge of them.

The committee felt that it would be impossible to assign persons with a sound knowledge of religious law to the civil courts, since there were so few of them and even they had great difficulty ascertaining the proper legal provisions because of the large number and diversity of sources.

To resolve these difficulties, a new civil code was needed. Some

Turkish statesmen, led by 'Alī Pasha (d. 1871), took account of the fact that the commercial courts were applying laws adopted mainly from France and argued that the French *Code Civil* should be accepted as the civil code of the Ottoman Empire. Others of a more conservative and religious school held that the civil code should be a compilation of Islamic principles, taken primarily from the Ḥanafī school. This group was led by the eminent scholar and statesman, Cevdet Pasha.

The viewpoint advocated by Cevdet Pasha prevailed and an official committee was formed in 1869 to prepare a civil code based on the principles of the Ḥanafī school. The committee sat until 1888 but was dissolved before it had completed its work. During the committee's existence there were many changes in its membership. Even Cevdet Pasha, who acted as its chairman, relinquished this office from time to time because of the pressure of other duties, but he always retained a keen interest in the work of the committe and played the most prominent part in the preparation of the Majalla.

The object of the Majalla and the procedures used in compiling it were set forth by Cevdet Pasha in the committee's report as follows:

> The work of compiling religious principles to make a code containing provisions to satisfy the needs of our society was vested in us by a decree of the Sultan. We met in the office of the High Court and collected the opinions and ideas of the most eminent Ḥanafī jurists on the subject of mu'āmalāt to suit the present conditions. The result of our work is classified according to various subjects of law and the code is called *Majallat-i Ahkami Adliye.*

The various parts of the Majalla were published and put into effect over a period of several years. The first part (containing an introductory section and a book on sale) was published in 1870, the sixteenth and last in 1877. The Majalla was submitted to the Sultan and after receiving his approval acquired an obligatory character. This is stated in the report of the committee as follows:

> According to Muslim doctrines, in a controversial matter the opinion held by the Sultan is the one to be obeyed; therefore, if the opinions expressed in this book are found acceptable it should be submitted to the Sultan for approval.

Although the committee later codified the law of procedure, it was dissolved by the suspicious Sultan 'Abdul Hamid II in 1888, before it began to work on other branches of the civil law.

The Majalla had the force of law and was applied as the civil code of the Ottoman Empire. It has only gradually been replaced in the successor states. However, it was not a code in the strict European sense, because it was not a complete and exclusive statement of the law as it existed at the time of codification, but rather a nonexclusive digest of existing rules of Islamic law.

ORGANIZATION AND BASIC PRINCIPLES OF THE MAJALLA

Although the Majalla was the civil code of the Ottoman Empire, it did not contain all the provisions of a civil law. It consisted of an introductory section and sixteen books, each treating a different subject: sale, hire, guarantee, transfer of debt, pledges, trust and trusteeship, gifts, wrongful appropriation and destruction, interdiction, constraint and pre-emption, joint ownership, agency, settlement and release, admissions, actions, evidence, and administration of oath and administration of justice by the Court. The total number of articles is 1,851.

The introductory section of the Majalla contains general principles which were intended to serve as a guide for judges in applying its provisions to specific cases. For example, Article 2 states that ". . . . the effect to be given to any particular transaction must conform to the object of such transaction," and Article 3, "in contracts effect is given to intention and meaning and not to words and phrases." These two rules embody important principles for the interpretation of contracts, which are identical with the principle of intention accepted by modern civil codes. Article 5 states that ". . . . a thing shall remain as it was originally," and Article 6, "Things which have been in existence from time immemorial shall be left as they were," i.e., the existence of a situation must be accepted unless it can be proved that it has been changed by a legal act.

Some of these general principles are applicable to damages and compensation cases. Thus, Article 7 states that "injury cannot be removed by a similar injury"; Article 27, "severe injury is removed by lesser injury"; and Article 31, "injury is removed as far as possible." It follows that a harmful situation cannot be considered legal even if it existed for a long time, since injury cannot create a right. Harmful situations constitute an exception to the principle laid down in Articles 5 and 6, and must be remedied. A harmful situation cannot be eliminated by creating another harmful situation; it can be eliminated only by an act causing less damage.

Articles 36 and 45 recognize custom as a source of law, and establish the principle that it should be applied when necessary. Article 40 states that custom may change the meaning of a law, and a law may change with the passing of time (Article 39). According to Article 43, a matter which is in accordance with custom is accepted as a contractual obligation even if it is not made part of the text of the agreement. Likewise, a rule established by custom has the same force as a rule established by law (Article 45).

Among other important general principles are Article 55, which states: "A thing which is not permissible at the outset may become permissible at some later period," and Article 56: "Continuance is easier than commencement." The Majalla gives the following example to illustrate the principle of Article 55. It is not acceptable to give a share of undivided joint property as a gift, because according to Article 57, a gift becomes absolute only when delivery thereof is completed, and it is impossible to deliver joint property. However, if someone later claims title to a share as co-owner and the property is divided, the recipient of the gift is entitled to a share. The object of the law is to interfere with the rights of the individual only when it is absolutely necessary and to respect the desires of the contracting parties.

As a general rule, moral principles are placed above economic needs. Article 30 states: "Repelling an evil is preferable to securing a benefit," for, even though there may be an economic benefit in the perpetuation of a wrong, it should be remedied for the sake of justice. If a house is built illegally on the land of another person, the building shall be demolished if the owner of the land so desires, regardless of the financial loss.

The theory of objective responsibility or risk is set forth in several of the preliminary articles. "Disadvantage is an obligation accompanying enjoyment" (Article 87), and "the burden is in proportion to the benefit, and the benefit to the burden" (Article 88). It follows that if a situation creates a benefit for a person, that person should also be responsible for the risk involved, i.e., a businessman or factory owner should be responsible for the harm he causes to other persons even if he himself is not at fault. In continental European law, responsibility is based largely on the principle of negligence. If damage is not due to a person's negligence, he is not liable for compensation; objective responsibility is applied only in certain exceptional cases. In the Majalla, by contrast, objective responsibility is an essential principle.

The first book of the Majalla deals with sale which is regarded as the basic contract. It is divided into an introductory part and seven chapters, each divided into a number of sections. The introductory part (Articles 101-166) contains explanations and definitions of many of the legal terms and phrases used in the book. For example, the terms "sale" and "property" are defined and their various forms illustrated. The second book deals with hire and is divided into an introductory part and eight chapters. In the introduction to that book, the terms used are explained and the various forms of hire classified.

Each book of the Majalla contains definitions and a classification of the subject treated. But the classifications are neither complete nor well organized. The Majalla suffers from lack of uniformity and some of its subjects are dealt with in various places. For example, the book on trusts contains certain provisions concerning both deposit and loan, and in the book on joint ownership there are some provisions quite alien to the subject.

The last four books of the Majalla deal with civil procedure and court organization rather than with substantive civil law. In the book on admissions there are rules on the various forms of admitting a claim; the book on actions contains provisions on bringing and defending a suit and on estoppel; and the book on evidence deals with various aspects of evidence, such as witnesses, documents, and oaths. It is to be noted that there are no rules concerning marriage, divorce, inheritance, or waqf. The committee was anxious to add special sections on these subjects but it did not have the time to do so before its dissolution.

Privately-owned real estate was considered within the scope of the Majalla but was governed by noncodified provisions of the sharīʿa. The land law, promulgated before the Majalla, applied to arazii emiriyye and arazii memluke. In the case of State land, the State was the owner of the land and individuals acquired some rights on the land by permission of the State. Relations between the State and the individual were considered contractual and were governed by statutory rules.

The Majalla is based exclusively on the Ḥanafī school of law, and in order to satisfy the conservatives, only the opinions of the most eminent jurists of that school were considered. Thus the sources of the Majalla were very restricted; each chapter may be said to be a summary of a certain book of fiqh. The treatment of the subjects and the terms used in each chapter gave the Majalla the character of a textbook rather than that of a civil code.

BASIC PROVISIONS OF THE MAJALLA

The provisions of the Majalla fall within the following general categories: contracts, property, torts, wrongful appropriation, and procedure.

CONTRACTS

The Majalla embodies principles of contract quite different from those generally accepted by continental European and Anglo-American law. The fact that the rules of the Majalla are founded mainly on moral principles rather than on economic necessities is clearly shown in the rules on contracts. The Majalla does not accept the Western principle of freedom of contract, but instead sets narrow limits in an effort to protect the individual in the exercise of rights he acquired by contract. In the West, freedom of contract is limited by public order and general rules of behavior, but individuals are free to make any contract within these limits. The Majalla, by contrast, defines the types of contracts which may be concluded and the conditions which may be attached thereto. The pertinent provisions are found in the chapter on sale.

In the report of the drafting committee, the problem of conditions attached to contracts was discussed as follows:

> Commercial transactions are generally carried on subject to certain conditions . . . the Ḥanafī school [holds] that the majority of the conditions stipulated upon the conclusion of a contract of sale subject to a condition render the sale invalid.

After citing the opinions of eminent jurists of the various schools, the report continued:

> . . . . a middle course has been adopted in the Ḥanafī school and conditions have been divided into three categories: a valid condition, a voidable condition, and a condition which is null and void. Thus, any condition stipulated in favor of one of the contracting parties and which is not of the very essence of the contract, or which does not serve to assure one of the essential elements thereof, is voidable and renders the sale voidable. A condition which brings no advantage to either of the parties is regarded as null and void, the sale being valid, since the object of buying and selling is to confer and obtain ownership of the thing sold and for the vendor to obtain ownership of the price without any let or hindrance. But if a condition existed in favor of one of the contracting parties alone, who insisted on the execution of such condition, and the other party sought to escape therefrom, such conduct would give rise to disputes, and it could not be claimed in such cir-

cumstances that the sale was complete. Sale subject to a condition of this nature, however, is permissible when it is allowed by custom, because in such a case the dispute itself would be finally settled by custom. . . . We have contented ourselves with mentioning in Section 4 of Chapter I the conditions which do not make a sale voidable according to the Ḥanafī school, a procedure adopted in the other sections.

Chapter 1, Section 4, of the book on sale deals with sale subject to condition. According to Article 186, "if a contract of sale is concluded with an essential condition attached, both sale and condition are valid." The Majalla permits the seller to retain the thing sold until the price is paid and Article 187 declares a sale valid if it is subject to a condition which "is to assure the due performance of the contract." Article 188 stipulates that sales and conditions are valid where the condition is sanctioned by local custom. Finally, Article 189 states that "in the case of sale subject to a condition which is not to the benefit of either party, the sale is valid, but the condition is voidable." The example given is the sale of an animal on the condition that it shall not be sold to a third party. In such a case the sale is valid but the condition is null and void. In other chapters, the Majalla does not repeat these provisions about conditions but emphasizes conditions which are not acceptable. For example, in the chapter on lease and hire, Article 428 states that a condition prohibiting subletting is void.

In the treatment of contracts, there is a tendency to establish within the limits of the Majalla a consistent concept of justice and to prevent the acquisition of unlawful benefits. There is also an endeavor to regulate every detail and to leave nothing to individual interpretation. There are few counterparts in continental European codes to these provisions which must be observed by the parties. For example, in the contract of lease, according to Article 449, "the subject matter . . . must be specified." Thus, if one of two shops is leased and the shop in question is not specified or the lessee is not given an option as to which one he will take, the contract is invalid. Since the contract is void, no judicial interpretation or inquiry into the intent of the parties is possible. If the services of skilled workmen are hired, the nature of the work to be performed and the method of performance must be stated in full detail (Article 455). Even though the provisions of an illegal lease are fulfilled by the lessor, the payment of rent by the tenant is not necessary since the contract is considered void. However, an equivalent sum of money may be awarded by the court to the lessor. Although this sum is considered as a compensation and not as payment in fulfillment of the contract, it must not exceed the amount fixed by the contract.

Freedom of contract is also restricted by the Majalla's detailed rules on its object. The most extreme examples may be found in the contract of sale. Article 105 states: "sale consists of exchanging property for property." According to Article 126, "property consists of something desired by human nature and which can be put aside against time of necessity." Things whose use is forbidden by Islam may not be sold. In this category are wine, pork, dead animals, and rubbish. Things which have no material existence likewise may not be the subject of sale. Article 210 stipulates in general that "the sale of a thing which is not generally recognized as property . . . is void."

By defining economic concepts from a noneconomic viewpoint, the Majalla excluded many things from the scope of the contract of sale, limited the objects of sale, and left itself far behind the economic requirements of its time. The fact that things which do not have any material existence, such as electricity, could not be objects of a contract of sale, impeded many transactions, including credit sales, and led to much criticism of the code.

REAL PROPERTY

The concept of real property in the Majalla is the same as that in Western European codes. Article 1192 states that any person may deal with his property owned in absolute ownership as he wishes, provided the rights of others are safeguarded. According to Article 1194, absolute ownership extends to the airspace above and the soil beneath the property without restriction. The Majalla attached great importance to relations between neighbors and regulated them in detail in Chapter 3 of the book on joint property.

In Chapter 4 of the book on joint property, the Majalla deals with property reserved for public use such as water, grass, and fire. Thus, Articles 1235, 1236, and 1237 state that the water which runs under the surface of the earth, natural wells, the sea, and large lakes belong to no one, and are available for public use. Rivers are divided into two categories: those which are subject to private property rights and those which are not. Rivers whose beds do not pass solely through property absolutely owned by a person or a group of persons are not subject to the rights of private property.

Rivers which can be subject to acquisition by private persons are divided into two categories: rivers which are not exhausted in private property but continue their course through vacant land which is free to the public, and rivers that flow entirely in private property. To the latter category applies the right of pre-emption, i.e., if a river flows through the property of several owners and one owner sells his lot, the other riparian owners have an option to buy his land under the same condition as the prospective third buyer.

The right of pre-emption (shuf'a)—a legal option to buy another person's real property—is very important in Islamic law in general and is dealt with in detail in the Majalla. According to Article 1008, there are three situations in which pre-emption is possible. One is joint ownership of the property involved: if one of the co-owners sells his share, the other co-owners have the right to buy the share for the same price as the third party involved. Holders of joint easements, such as joint road and water rights, also enjoy the privilege of pre-emption. The case of joint beneficiaries of a private river belongs to this category. Thirdly, the Majalla extends the right of pre-emption to immediate neighbors. Articles 1009 and 1010 define priority of persons having the right of pre-emption, and Articles 1011 and 1012 define situations of doubtful claims to pre-emption.

The Majalla attaches considerable importance to the relations among joint owners (Chapter 5 of the book on joint property). According to Article 1308, joint owners are responsible for the upkeep of the property in proportion to their shares. If one of the co-owners repairs the whole of the property with the consent of the other owners, the latter must reimburse him. In the case of absence of the co-owner, the latter's consent can be replaced by permission given by the court for the repairs in question (Article 1310). If one of the proprietors repairs the property without obtaining permission from the other co-owners or the court, or against the wishes of the co-owners, he forfeits the right to ask for reimbursement or to apply to the court for approval of the repairs. The court may, however, order partition of the property (Articles 1311 and 1312). The denial of the right to ask for court permission for such repairs is based on the general principle of Article 25 that an injury cannot be removed by the commission of a similar injury. Joint property may be divided except in a few cases. If in these exceptional cases one of the proprietors wishes to repair the property and the others do not consent, the repair work may be performed with the permission of the court and the rest of the proprietors are then liable to pay their appropriate shares of the costs.

Section 2 of the same chapter contains provisions concerning the dredging of river beds and water courses. Article 1321 provides for the dredging of rivers which are not private property but are within the public domain. The dredging of these rivers is the duty of the State, but if the financial situation of the State makes it impossible for it to dredge the river, then the dredging becomes the duty of the public.

WRONGFUL APPROPRIATION AND DESTRUCTION

Regulations concerning wrongful appropriation and destruction are to be found in Book VIII. Article 881 defines wrongful appropriation as the taking and keeping of property of another person without his consent. Destruction can be either direct (Article 887) or indirect (Article 888), depending on whether the person himself destroys the thing or merely is the cause of the destruction.

Wrongfully appropriated property has to be returned to the owner at the place from which it was taken (Article 890). If such property is destroyed, the person who has appropriated it is liable for the loss whether or not it was his fault (Article 891). If the thing taken has changed (for example, if fruit has become dry) the owner has the option of taking the property back or demanding equivalent payment (Article 897). If the person who took the property has added something to it, the owner is free either to claim payment for the original property or to accept the improved property after paying the value of the increase (Article 898). If the value of a thing decreases after its wrongful appropriation, the owner may not refuse to accept it. However, if the value has decreased because of the use made of the thing, the person who appropriated it must compensate the owner to the extent of the decrease in value (Article 900).

If real property is wrongfully appropriated, it must be restored without alteration (Article 905). If a house is built or a tree is planted on land which has been wrongfully appropriated, they must be removed before the land is returned. If the removal of buildings or trees would cause injury to the land, the landowner may acquire them by paying the cost of removal (Article 906). The Majalla thus endeavors to protect the landowner rather than the person who improves the property, ignoring the loss which the latter must suffer. An exception is made only if the value of the buildings or trees is greater than that of the land and if the person who built or planted believed he had a legal right to do so. In that case, the owner of the buildings or trees may acquire the land by paying its price.

Where destruction of property is concerned, the Majalla makes the destroyer responsible for the damage (Article 912). Consequently, a child who destroys property or a person who destroys another's property by accident is held liable to pay compensation (Articles 913, 916). Intent or negligence are not considered and liability is based exclusively upon the result of the action. If the actions of both parties involved caused the damage, liability is shared (Article 15). If a person pulls another man's coat and tears it, he alone is liable for damage. But if he holds the coat and the other person pulls and tears it, or if he sits on the tail of another person's coat and that person tears his own coat in getting up, the compensation is only half the price of the coat.

In contrast to the above, if destruction is indirect, the destroyer is liable only if his act was of a wrongful nature (Article 924). Consequently, if a person performs an act (in itself legal) which may in its turn cause the destruction of a thing and, meanwhile, some other act supervenes, the author of the second act is held liable (Articles 90, 925). For example, A digs a well and B drives C's animal into it. Only B is responsible in this case. Similarly, the owner of an animal is not liable for damage caused by it unless he is negligent or has been warned that the animal is destructive (Article 920).

Book XIII deals with admissions, Book XIV with actions, Book XV with evidence, and Book XVI with the administration of justice, but the Majalla does not codify these topics systematically. Admission is defined as "a statement by one person admitting the claim of some other person against him." To make a valid admission a person must be of age and of sound mind, act of his own free will, and be free of deficiencies which would put him in the care of a guardian. In addition, his admission must not be contrary to obvious facts (Articles 1572-1578).

The effects of an admission are dealt with in Chapter 3 of Book XIII. According to Article 1587, a person is bound by his admission unless it is proved false by a judgment of the court. If the right of another is admitted, the admission may not be retracted (Article 1588). If a person claims that his admission has not been truthful, the person who has benefitted from his admission has the right to swear that it was correct. For example, A acknowledges in writing that he borrowed a sum of money from B and later denies that he borrowed the sum by claiming that he never received the money. In this case, B may testify under oath that the acknowledgement was correct (Article 1589).

Section 3 of the book on admissions deals with admissions made during mortal illness, that is, an illness which usually results in death and where death actually occurs within a year. In such instances, admissions are either held invalid or are regarded as bequests. Article 1608, in Section 4, which regulates written admissions, states that entries in the books of businessmen should be considered as written admissions.

Book XIV (Actions) contains rules on conditions for an action and its validity, defense of an action, the parties to an action, estoppel, and limitation. Action is defined as "a claim made by one person against another in court" (Article 1613). Both parties must be of sound mind and of age, although lunatics and minors may sue or be sued through their tutors or guardians (Article 1616). The defendant must be known; no action can be brought against persons unknown (Article 1617).

In principle, both parties have to be present or represented when the action is tried. If the defendant fails to appear or appoint a representative, the court must issue a summons to him on three separate occasions to appear. If he still fails to appear, the court will appoint a representative for him and proceed with the case (Articles 1618 and 1834). Even after judgment has been given, the defendant may appear in court and show that he had a defense against the action. In this case, the defense shall be heard and judgment may be reversed (Article 1836).

Although the Majalla does not deal with corporations or persons entitled to act for a corporation, there are two articles connected with this subject. In a village whose inhabitants exceed one hundred, one person or more among them may bring or defend an action on behalf of the community in matters concerning the whole village, such as water or grazing rights. In villages having a population of less than one hundred, the action must be brought by the entire population (Articles 1645-1646). Actions regarding public places, such as highways, may be brought by any citizen (Article 1644).

Chapter 2 of the Book on Actions deals with the statute of limitations. In general, actions may be brought for fifteen years, but thirty-six years are allowed for bringing action relating to the fundamental constitution of a pious foundation (waqf) [Articles 1660 and 1661]. Actions relating to government land, private roads or water rights may be heard for ten years only. (The period begins from the time the action could first be brought.) According to Article 1674, a right is not lost merely by the passing of time. If a defendant explicitly admits the right of another party in court after the statute of limitations has expired, he may not plead this defense later.

Although the period of limitation should pass without intervals and interruptions, there are some causes which interrupt the period: the minority of the plaintiff, insanity, a journey to a distant place (the distance is defined by the Majalla), or fear on the part of the plaintiff of the powerful position of the defendant (Article 1663). If an action is brought, the period is interrupted, but claims made out of court do not constitute an interruption. No period of limitation applies to actions concerning public highways, rivers, and pastures (Article 1675).

Chapter 15 treats of evidence by witnesses, documentary and presumptive evidence, and administration of the oath. The basic type of evidence is that given by witnesses. However, numerous formal conditions must be fulfilled to make testimony valid. There must be either two male witnesses or a male and two female witnesses. Should the witnessing of males be impossible in view of the circumstances involved, the witnessing of women is acceptable. Evidence supported by an insufficient number of witnesses, as well as the evidence of the dumb and the blind, is not admissible (Articles 1685 and 1686).

As a rule, hearsay evidence is not generally admissible. In cases concerning the establishment of a pious foundation or presumption of the death of a person, hearsay evidence is admissible if characterized as such by the witness. In matters of state administration, paternity, and death, hearsay evidence may be accepted even if the witness does not specify that he is repeating hearsay (Article 1688). After evidence has been given by a witness, the judge shall inquire into his credibility. If it is established that the witness is an honest and reliable person, his evidence is accepted. Detailed rules concerning this inquiry are found in Section 6 of Chapter 1.

Section 1 of Chapter 2 of the Book on Evidence contains rules on documentary evidence. Writing or seal may become a valid ground for action if it is free from any taint of fraud or forgery (Article 1736). Presumptive evidence may be accepted by the court according to Section 2 of this chapter. Presumption is defined in Article 1741 as "an inference which amounts to positive knowledge." For example, A is found escaping from a place where a man has been murdered, holding a blood-stained knife. He is held to be the murderer and other possibilities, such as that of suicide, are not considered.

The last book of the Majalla (Book XVI) deals with the administration of justice. The judge is the person appointed by the sovereign to settle disputes according to the rules of law (Article 1785). He should be intelligent, upright, reliable, and firm (Article 1792); he should have a sound knowledge of fiqh and legal procedure (Article 1793); and he should be capable of settling disputes and of distinguishing right from wrong (Article 1793). The judge is the representative of the sovereign in conducting the proceedings and in rendering judgment (Article 1800). He must hold the trial in public but never indicate his opinion before the trial is completed (Article 1815). Arbitration is accepted by the Majalla and Chapter of Book XVI contains regulations for it. It is to be noted that the rules concerning procedure are very detailed and do not leave a wide discretionary power to the judge.

REVISION AND ABOLITION OF THE MAJALLA

There is no doubt that the Majalla contains many sound principles which satisfactorily served the needs of the Ottoman Empire; however, its tendency to deal with details rather than broad principles often restricted the power of the judge and the freedom of action of the parties. The style and scope of the Majalla gave it an important place among other legal systems and it was favorably received by Western scholars. The real weakness of the Majalla lay in its rigidity; since its provisions were based on unchangeable principles of the Islamic religion it could not be adapted to the needs of a rapidly changing society. Although its compilers tried to codify principles that would fit the needs of the people, their sources were limited. They restricted themselves to the principles and opinions of the Ḥanafī jurists and could not make use of the opinions of jurists of other schools.

After the establishment of constitutional government in Turkey in 1908, criticism was leveled at the Majalla, but amendment was difficult, and the revision of its principles was considered dangerous. The code on civil procedure, which was enacted in 1880 and amended in 1914, was based on French law. Many of its provisions ran counter to the Majalla but were in keeping with the needs of trade and commerce. It accepted the principle of freedom of contract and increased the discretionary power of the judge.

In 1920-21, a committee of experts began to prepare amendments to the Majalla. Although the committee was limited to Islamic law, it was not obliged to depend upon jurists of the Ḥanafī school for all of the principles embodied in its revisions. The committee altered many provisions, especially those concerning the contracts of sale and lease, but its proposals never came into force. In 1923, another committee was formed with wider powers to prepare a new civil code based not only on Islamic principles but on the modern civil law of Western countries. It had not finished its work when the Government of Ankara decided in 1926 to adopt the Swiss civil code and code of obligations. These codes replaced the Majalla, as well as other laws contrary to the new codes.

CHAPTER XIII

The Development of Western Judicial Privileges

BACKGROUND

THE JUDICIAL and other privileges accorded by Muslim rulers to subjects of foreign powers have their roots not only in Islamic law but also in institutions which were common in the Mediterranean area at the time these privileges developed in the Muslim World. In general, the exemption of foreigners from local judicial jurisdiction and the recognition of their right to live according to their own laws can be fitted easily into a legal system which is dominated by the principle of the personality of the law. This principle means that the law applicable is not determined territorially but on the basis of the origin, nationality, or tribal or religious affiliation of the individual involved. In antiquity this principle of the personality of the law was controlling.[1] Only during the period when the Roman Empire held sway around the coasts of the Mediterranean and created in that region a universal empire did the principle of territoriality of the law make strong inroads upon the existing system, primarily through the decrees of the Roman Emperors which were applicable to all subjects to whom they related or to whom they could be applied.[2]

With the disintegration of the Roman Empire in the West and the development of the Germanic states, the principle of the personality of the law again assumed major importance. Of particular interest from the point of view of the status of foreign merchants is the provision in the laws of the Visigoths, compiled in the sev-

1 Raphael Taubenschlag, *The Law of Greco-Roman Egypt in the Light of the Papyri, 332 B.C. to 640 A.D.*, Vol. 1 (New York, 1944), pp. 2-41; Vol. 2, (Warsaw, 1948), pp. 11-16 and 35-36; L. Mitteis and Ulrich Wilcken, *Grundzuege und Chrestomathie der Papyruskunde* (Leipzig, 1912), Vol. I, p. 12; Leopold Wenger, "Nationales, Griechisches und Roemisches Recht in Aegypten," *Atti del IV Congresso Internazionale di Papirologia, Firenze, 28 Aprile—2 Maggio 1935* (Milano, 1936), pp. 158-181.

2 Leopold Wenger, "Rechtstheoretische Fragen in der juristischen Papyrusforschung," *Actes du Vᵉ Congres International de Papyrologie* (Brussels, 1938), p. 528, and the further literature cited there.

enth century, that foreign merchants should be judged according to their laws by the so-called *telonarii* (persons levying duty).[3] This stipulation of the Visigothic law provides a pertinent early medieval example of the exemption of foreign merchants from the ordinary jurisdiction of the country in which they were doing business. It also shows that it is a logical step, on the basis of the personality of the law, to recognize that the foreigner as well as the local subject should live according to his own laws. This idea of the personality of the law penetrated, slowly but surely, into the Byzantine orbit, even though the concept of the universal Roman Empire was essentially territorial.[4]

Outside the Christian area, in the Islamic countries, the principle of the personality of the law also was recognized. There was, however, one modification of this principle which did not change its essential features but influenced its range. Islamic law was religious law and Muḥammad had replaced the old concept of the tribal group by a new concept, that of the community of believers.[5] Islamic law therefore could be applied to all those who believed but by the same token was not applicable, at least in principle, to nonbelievers. As the Muslim Empire expanded and enveloped communities which did not embrace Islam, certain accommodations became necessary and the right of these communities to live according to their own laws was recognized within certain limits.[6] However, aside from these non-Muslim subjects of the Muslim state, another group had to be taken into account increasingly—the non-Muslim foreigners who came to the dār al-Islam (territory of Islam) but without the intention of staying there permanently. As in other laws of antiquity and the early Middle Ages, the foreigner was basically without rights in Islamic law. Nevertheless, he could receive protection through the means of amān (safe-conduct) which could be given individually or arranged through treaty for the subjects of a given state; in the latter case such pro-

[3] It is not certain whether these *telonarii* were foreigners elected by the merchants to collect dues and exercise jurisdiction or whether they were Visigothic customs officials entrusted with jurisdiction over foreign merchants. See Eugen Wohlhaupter, *Gesetze der Westgoten* (Weimar, 1936), p. 295; and Theophil Melicher, *Der Kampf zwischen Gesetzes-und Gewohnheitsrecht im Westgotenreiche* (Weimar, 1930).

[4] See M. de Taube, "L'apport de Byzance au developpement du droit international occidental," in Academie de droit international de La Haye, *Recueil des Cours* 1939 (Paris, n.d.), I, 291-92.

[5] David Santillana, *Istituzioni di diritto Musulmano Malichita* (Rome, 1938), Vol. I, p. 1.

[6] For further details, see below Chap. XIV, p. 335 ff.

tection was likely to be based on the principle of reciprocity.[7]

Thus, the underlying legal principles and the practice of the states in the Mediterranean orbit, both Christian and Muslim, provided a ready basis for the development of special privileges for foreign merchant settlements. This development received a decisive impetus through the commercial activities of the Italian city states, such as Venice, Pisa, and Genoa, activities which were aided and extended by the Crusades. Judicial and other privileges of these settlements therefore did not develop as an isolated institution or one peculiar to Islamic countries, but as an institution common in the eleventh and twelth centuries around the coast of the Mediterranean. Thus, the Crusaders granted the Venetians part of the city of Acre in 1110 for the aid given in its capture, and a third of Tyre in 1123, together with the right of jurisdiction over their citizens residing in these cities. Similar privileges were granted to the Pisans by the King of Jerusalem in 1157. The right to establish consulates with judicial jurisdiction over Pisans in Antioch and Tripoli was granted in 1170. In Tyre and Acre the citizens of Marseille were permitted during the same period to establish a quarter with their own judicial jurisdiction and the Genoese had an official (consul) with the right of jurisdiction in Antioch.

These settlements enjoyed a genuine extraterritorial status. They were headed by officials who were appointed by the home authorities and who were vested with judicial as well as administrative powers. Their usual title was that of consul, except for the Venetian official who was called *bailo*. Judicial jurisdiction extended both to criminal and civil matters, the only exceptions being suits involving real estate and, in general, crimes punishable by death; with regard to those categories the ordinary tribunals of the state retained jurisdiction.[8]

During approximately the same period the privileges of the foreign settlements in Constantinople were gradually extended. The first treaty in which the judicial jurisdiction of the head of a foreign merchant settlement was set forth in detail was the *chrysobulum verbum* of November 1198 between Emperor Alexis III and Venice. According to this treaty the Venetian emissaries had charged that Byzantine subjects had filed complaints

[7] This problem is dealt with in considerable detail in Julius Hatschek, *Der Must'amin* (Berlin, 1920); see below, Chap. XV.

[8] For further details, including references to other Christian states such as Armenia, see Karl Lippmann, *Die Konsularjurisdiction im Orient* (Leipzig, 1898), pp. 1-20.

against Venetians in other courts even though the suit had been heard before the Venetian representative in Constantinople and the Venetian defendant had been acquitted. This had resulted in the renewed imprisonment of Venetians, a state of affairs which Venice emphatically sought to remedy. From this complaint it would appear that the Venetian representative exercised judicial jurisdiction before the treaty of 1198. In view of the Venetian complaints this treaty endeavored to define more closely the extent of this jurisdiction, especially in disputes between Venetians and Byzantine subjects. Briefly, suits by Byzantines against Venetians had to be brought before the Venetian representative, and suits by Venetians against Byzantines before a high Byzantine official concerned with affairs of foreigners, the *logothetes tou dromou* or his representative. Rules were somewhat different in cases of assault and battery between Byzantines and Venetians; basically, jurisdiction lay with the above-mentioned Byzantine official, though jurisdiction, possibly concurrent, was granted to the Venetian representative if the Byzantine subject involved was not of senatorial rank or belonged to the imperial court.[9]

The Venetian position in Constantinople increased in importance under the Latin Kingdom. However, after the restoration of the Greek empire the Genoese, old rivals of the Venetians, were granted extensive privileges in a treaty of March 13, 1261, which among other things exempted Genoese merchants from the jurisdiction of the courts of the empire, and submitted them to the jurisdiction of the Genoese *podestat*.[10] In the same year the rights of the Pisans and of the Venetians to maintain consuls in Constantinople with jurisdiction over their citizens was confirmed by the Emperor.[11] The merchants of other cities and regions in Europe, such as the Florentines and the Catalans, enjoyed similar privileges which continued until the end of the Byzantine Empire.

CAPITULATIONS IN MUSLIM COUNTRIES PRIOR TO THE OTTOMAN EMPIRE

In spite of the basic hostility between Muslim and Christian states, commercial needs led the Muslim countries around the Mediterranean to grant privileges to European merchants similar

[9] Summary in Franz Dolger, *Regesten der Kaiserurkunden des Ostromischen Reiches von 565-1453,* Part II (Munich, 1925), pp. 104-05.

[10] Summary in *ibid.,* Part III (Munich, 1932), pp. 36-37; see also Lippmann, *op. cit.,* pp. 16-18.

[11] W. Heyd, *Histoire du commerce du Levant au Moyen-Age* (2nd. ed., Leipzig, 1936), Vol. I, pp. 430-31.

to those which the latter enjoyed in the Christian states of the area. Apparently the first of the capitulations, so called from their subdivision into chapters *(capitula),* were concluded between Pisa and Morocco and between Pisa and the Muslim ruler of Valencia in 1133 and 1149 respectively. A short time later, in 1154, the first capitulation between Pisa and Egypt was concluded which accorded to the Pisans the right of commerce in Alexandria, liberty of person and inviolability of property, and authority to maintain consuls and to exercise judicial jurisdiction. The capitulation was renewed in 1155 and 1173. A further capitulation of 1215 granted Pisans the right of appeal to the Amīr of Alexandria and, if he did not give satisfaction, even to the sultan, in cases where Pisans had been injured by Egyptian subjects. Egypt granted capitulations to Venice soon thereafter, in 1238, 1254, and 1302. They guaranteed personal liberty and inviolability of property to Venetians, and required that all suits of Christians and Muslims against Venetians be filed in the court of the Venetian consul. The jurisdiction of the amīr was restricted to serious crimes. Suits of Venetians against Muslims had to be filed in the court of the amīr but with the consent of the Venetian consul such causes could be brought before the sultan. Civil and criminal suits concerning Venetians exclusively were orginally under the consul's sole jurisdiction but later capitulations stipulated that crimes punishable by death should come under the jurisdiction of the amīr even if only Venetians were involved. The consul also had the right to take into custody the estates of Venetians who died in Egypt and goods from Venetian vessels stranded in Egypt.

Other Italian cities concluded similar treaties with Egypt, such as Genoa in 1290. Florence, having conquered Pisa and achieved access to the sea, was granted in 1422 the same privileges which the Pisans had enjoyed. The Florentine privileges were reaffirmed in later capitulations. Other European nations which likewise had privileges in Egypt were the Catalans and Aragonians, chiefly Barcelona, and the French.[12] During the negotiations with Egypt in 1447, France was assured by the sultan that the French consul would be treated on a most-favored-nation basis.[13] It has also been stated that the French consul had the title "Consul of the Francs and the foreigners" and as such had jurisdiction not only over French subjects but also over other Christians whose governments did not have consular representatives in Egypt.[14]

[12] Lippmann, *op. cit.,* pp. 37-46; see in general, Heyd, *op. cit.,* Vol. I, pp. 378-426.
[13] A. de Miltitz, *Manuel des Consuls* (London, 1838), Vol. II, Part 1, p. 206.
[14] Lippmann, *op. cit.,* p. 45.

The lively trade between Christian countries and Egypt gave rise to misgivings on both sides. Thus, in 1182 Sultan Saladin sent a letter to the caliph in which he pointed out that the Venetians, Genoese, and Pisans imported into Egypt choice occidental goods, especially arms and war materials, thus creating an advantage for Islam and a disadvantage for Christianity.[15] On the part of the Christians, efforts were made to stop the export of war materials and arms. The trade in these goods nevertheless flourished and a situation was created in which privileges were accorded to European merchants by Muslim rulers at the same time that the latter were fighting the Crusaders—in many cases probably with war materials supplied by Christian merchants.[16]

The conquest of the Crusader kingdoms in Syria and Palestine by the Muslims interrupted the trade between Europe and the Levant for a time, but fairly soon the Italian cities and others were able to re-establish their consulates. Venice asked the Egyptian Sultan for permission in 1415 to establish a consulate in Jerusalem with jurisdiction over pilgrims, most of whom traveled on Venetian ships. The sultan granted the request as being "based on the old customs of the Venetians."[17] Trade between North Africa and the Italian cities likewise was brisk and treaties embodying capitulatory rights were concluded between the Muslim rulers there and Italian city-states beginning in the twelfth century.[18]

The practice of Muslim sovereigns with regard to granting extraterritorial rights to foreign merchant colonies thus did not differ appreciably from that followed by Christian rulers in the Mediterranean orbit. Finding their legal basis in the principle of the personality of the law, the capitulations reflected the economic need of encouraging commerce between the Arab-dominated areas and the states in Italy and the Western Mediterranean. Essentially, therefore, these agreements were commercial treaties which conceded special custom rates and regulated other commercial matters at the same time as they gave the right to establish merchant colonies with separate jurisdiction. Difficulties doubtlessly existed on both sides in justifying the conclusion of such agreements between Muslims and Christians, but the requirements of

[15] Heyd, *op. cit.*, Vol. I, p. 386, note 2.

[16] *Ibid.*, pp. 386-87.

[17] Lippmann, *op. cit.*, p. 47.

[18] These treaties are collected in M. L. de Mas Latrie, *Traités de paix et de commerce et documents divers concernant les rélations des Chrétiens avec les Arabes de l'Afrique Septentrionale au Moyen Age* (Paris, 1866).

commerce and the desire on the part of the Christian merchants to utilize and exploit the old established commercial routes and markets apparently overcame whatever hesitancy existed with regard to commercial treaty relationships.

DEVELOPMENT OF CAPITULATORY RIGHTS AFTER THE ESTABLISHMENT OF THE OTTOMAN EMPIRE

When the Ottoman Turks conquered Constantinople in 1453, capitulatory rights thus were already a well-established feature in the eastern Mediterranean. However, it was in the Ottoman Empire that extraterritorial jurisdiction based on capitulations found its full development and systematization. That the Ottoman Sultans would continue the grant of capitulatory rights became apparent soon after the fall of Constantinople. In fact, one day after the conquest of the city, Mehmed II granted the Genoese who had surrendered unconditionally, personal liberty and security of property and also gave them the right to choose from their midst an elder for the administration of their settlement and the adjudication of disputes.[19] In 1454 a treaty was concluded between the sultan and Venice through which "peace and friendship" were established between the two parties. The treaty contained stipulations regarding Venetian commerce in Ottoman territory and in Article 16 the Venetian *Signoria* was granted the right to send a consul *(bailo)* to Constantinople with the right of civil but not criminal jurisdiction over the Venetians.[20] The right of the *bailo* to receive the estate of Venetians who had died intestate within Ottoman territory was maintained. However, in spite of this treaty relationship, the Ottoman Empire and Venice were frequently at war as a result of the rivalry between the two states in Greek waters. By contrast the relationship between Florence and the Ottoman Sultans was relatively peaceful and judicial privileges, possibly broader than those accorded to Venice, were granted to Florence though not all the details can be ascertained because of the loss of the original documents.[21]

While the position of the Italian cities as the principal commercial links between the Muslim countries and Europe gradually declined, the importance of France in European relations with the Ottoman Empire increased, primarily due to political cir-

19 Julius von Hammer-Purgstall, *Geschichte des Osmanischen Reiches* (Pest, 1827-35), Vol. I, p. 576.

20 Domenico Gatteschi, *Manuale di diritto publico e privato Ottomano* (Alexandria, 1865), pp. 16-20.

21 Heyd, *op. cit.,* Vol. II, pp. 336-45.

cumstances such as the common enmity of the two states toward the Hapsburgs in Spain and Austria. In 1528 the capitulatory rights of the "French and Catalans" in Egypt were reaffirmed by Sulaymān II. This grant applied to Egypt only and extended to the "Catalans and Francs and the other nations which are under their consulate in Alexandria." It granted the consul judicial jurisdiction in all disputes among French and Catalans except for cases punishable by death.[22] Nothing was said about mixed cases and the principle of *actor sequitur forum rei* (i.e., of the trial of suits in the court of the defendant) which had been embodied in earlier capitulations, was apparently abandoned. The inviolability of the consul was guaranteed and all complaints against him had to be brought before the Sublime Porte. The provisions with regard to the protection of estates of Catalans and Francs who had died in Egypt were more or less the same as in older capitulations.

Soon after this reaffirmation of French rights in Egypt a treaty was concluded between France and the Ottoman Empire in 1535 which became the prototype of the capitulatory agreements later negotiated by European countries with the Ottoman Empire and other non-Christian nations.[23] The object of this treaty was first to establish "a valid and sure peace" between the two countries during the lifetime of their respective rulers. Secondly, it was to ensure commercial relations between France and the Ottoman Empire, stipulating that non-prohibited merchandise should move freely between the two countries and that Turks in France and Frenchmen in Turkey should pay only such customs dues as the respective country charged its own subjects. Thirdly, the treaty was to regulate the French establishments in all parts of the Ottoman Empire. The French King was granted the right to send a consul to Constantinople, Pera, or any other place in the Empire. These consuls had exclusive jurisdiction in all civil and criminal causes arising among French subjects, including crimes punishable by death. Disputes between Frenchmen and Ottoman subjects were still to be submitted to the Ottoman courts but certain safe-

[22] "S'il survenoit quelque différant entre les Cathelans ou Francoys, le consul aye à le juger, exceptant toutesfoys s'il y intervenoit sang; que en ce cas noz presidens l'auront à juger. . . ." See the text in E. Charrière, *Négociations de la France dans le Levant* (Paris, 1848), Vol. I, pp. 121-29.

[23] The text of this treaty has been published in various places. The French text and the Italian text are given by *ibid.*, pp. 283-94. An English translation can be found in G. Bie Ravndal, *The Origin of the Capitulations and of the Consular Institution*, Senate Document, 67th Congress, 1st Session, Document no. 34 (Washington, 1921), Appendix II-Bis, pp. 94-99, and in Nasim Sousa, *The Capitulatory Regime of Turkey* (Baltimore, 1933), Appendix I, pp. 314-20.

guards were erected for the protection of the French, such as the compulsory presence of a dragoman in any hearing or trial before a Turkish qāḍī or other official. Criminal cases against French subjects could not be heard by qāḍīs or other Ottoman officials but had to be referred to the Sublime Porte, or in the absence of the Porte, to the principal lieutenant of the sultan. If a French merchant departed from the Ottoman dominions leaving debts, neither the consul nor the relatives of the debtor nor other persons could be held responsible, but the king promised that full justice would be done to the plaintiff should the debtor or his goods be found within French territory. Freedom to dispose by will was likewise guaranteed, as in earlier capitulations, and if a Frenchman died intestate his estate was to be distributed to the heirs by the consul. If a consul was not present the qāḍī could take over the effects of the deceased but had to hand them over to the consul or his representative upon demand. The rest of the treaty dealt with the mutual freeing of slaves and prisoners of war; maritime matters; exemption of French subjects who had resided in the Ottoman Empire less than ten years from the head tax, forced labor, and other dues; and reciprocal rights of Ottoman subjects in France. Finally, at the proposal of the King of France, a provision was inserted which permitted the Pope, the King of England, and the King of Scotland to adhere to the treaty within eight months from the date of its conclusion.

This capitulation was reaffirmed by the successor of Sulayman I, Selim II, in 1569. In form the new capitulation differed from the older one. Whereas the capitulation of 1535 was embodied in a treaty of amity and commerce, the new grant was one-sided, having the form of an "order" of the sultan.[24] Substantively there were several interesting new features. The grant was extended for the first time to those non-Frenchmen, "such as Genoese, Sicilians, Aconese, and others" to whom the King of France had given the privilege of sailing to Ottoman ports under the French flag. Also, it was expressly stated that all privileges granted to the Venetians by the sultan's capitulations should equally apply to France, thus formulating in essence a most-favored-nation clause.[25] The jurisdictional rights granted were basically the same as in the treaty of 1535; all suits between French subjects and

24 Text in I. de Testa, *Recueil des traités de la Porte Ottomane avec les puissances étrangères* (Paris, 1864), Vol. I, pp. 91-96.

25 The Italian text of the renewal of the Venetian capitulation, which took place in 1567, is published in J. du Mont, *Corps universel diplomatique du droit des gens* (Amsterdam, 1778), Vol. V, Part 1, p. 140.

Ottoman subjects remained under Ottoman jurisdiction and the prohibition against suits involving Frenchmen without the presence of a dragoman was again stressed. Suits among Frenchmen remained under the jurisdiction of the French "Ambassadors and consuls." The tax exemption which the treaty of 1535 had restricted to a ten-year period of residence was now granted without limitation.

The important French privilege of protecting non-French Christian merchants in Ottoman territory was further expanded in the capitulation granted by Selim's successor, Murād III, in 1581. This capitulation reaffirmed the rights granted in the earlier documents and stipulated that those nations which until that time had traveled under the French flag should continue to do so; Genoese, English, Portuguese, Spanish, Catalan, Anconese, and Sicilian merchants were mentioned specifically. The Venetians were exempted since they lived and traded under capitulations of their own. The stipulation of the earlier grant that all privileges accorded to the Venetians should also be applicable to the French was repeated.

The Venetian capitulation had again been renewed early in Sultan Murād III's reign, in August 1575.[26] This document is of considerable interest as to form. Throughout, it is the sultan who speaks, but many of the stipulations, which are political as well as commercial in nature, are mutual: the sultan thus formulates his own obligations as well as those undertaken by Venice. While unilateral in form the document, therefore, is bilateral in content. As far as Venetian jurisdiction was concerned, the old privileges were upheld.

France's endeavors to maintain a position of preponderance, if not monopoly, as protector of foreign Christians in the Ottoman Empire were not successful, in spite of the stipulations of the capitulation of 1581. The right to establish consulates in the Ottoman dominions and to trade with the Empire under the English flag was granted by the sultan to Queen Elizabeth in 1580 in spite of French efforts to prevent such an agreement.[27] The first English ambassador was appointed in 1582. In 1593 England was granted the same privileges accorded to France.[28] Under Murād III's successor, Mehmed III, the existing capitulations with Venice, France,

[26] Text in *ibid.*, pp. 244-47.

[27] Charrière, *op. cit.*, Vol. III, pp. 884, 913, 924.

[28] Gabriel Noradounghian, *Recueil d'actes internationaux de l'Empire Ottoman* (Paris, 1897), Vol. I, p. 37.

and England were renewed, as was customary upon the accession of a new sultan; and one new country was expressly granted extraterritorial privileges. At the request of the French ambassador the right was given to the merchants of the Netherlands to trade in the Ottoman Empire under the name and flag of the King of France and the protection of the French consuls.[29]

During the following reign of Sultan Ahmad I, the struggle between France and England over the right to protect other Christian nations under their respective flags became more intense. The very detailed capitulation granted to France in 1604 provided that all Christian states trading with the Ottoman Empire, with the exception of Venice and England, had to do so under the flag and protection of France.[30] In addition it granted France the protection of the pilgrim traffic to the holy places in Jerusalem and promised security and freedom of movement for the Christian clerics in Jerusalem, Bethlehem, and other places of the Holy Land. The judicial privileges remained basically unchanged but the right of the French ambassadors and consuls to jurisdiction "according to French laws and customs" in the case of murder or other crimes among French subjects was specifically recognized. Again, it was expressly stipulated that all privileges accorded to the Venetians should also apply to the French. The capitulation was in the form of a unilateral declaration which concluded, however, with a solemn oath containing the following stipulation:

> [We promise and swear] not to run counter to or contravene what is established by this treaty of peace and capitulation, provided the Emperor of France is constant and firm in the preservation of Our friendship. We accept as of now his [friendship] with the will of holding it dear, and this is Our intention and Imperial promise.

Thus, substantively the capitulation was based upon the mutual obligation of continued peace and friendship between the two powers.

However, despite the unequivocal language of this document, the French monopoly of protection of the subjects of other Christian states in the Ottoman Empire was disturbed by England which, in the renewal of its capitulatory rights in 1606, managed to secure the privilege of extending to other nations the protection of its flag and consequently, of its consuls. This had been accomplished during a time when there was no French ambassador in Constantinople and the next year, after an envoy had arrived,

[29] Du Mont, *op. cit.*, Vol. V, Part 1, pp. 558-59.
[30] Text in Noradounghian, *op. cit.*, Vol. I, pp. 93-102.

the French were able to obtain from the sultan a reaffirmation of the French monopoly and a revocation of the rights granted to England.[31] In 1612, however, the Netherlands succeeded in establishing direct relations with the Ottoman Government and were granted an exemption from French protection.[32] In a very detailed capitulation, again unilateral in form, the sultan expressly granted to the Dutch Estates General all the rights and privileges previously accorded to France and England (Articles 3 and 41). The Dutch ambassadors and consuls were to have judicial jurisdiction in all matters involving Dutch subjects, including cases of murder. An interesting provision is contained in Article 54 which stipulates that no one should prevent Dutch subjects from visiting the holy places in and around Jerusalem on the grounds that they were Lutherans. Though the Dutch capitulation follows the earlier capitulations in all of its main provisions, a steady tendency toward more and more detailed stipulations is noticeable. For example, the French capitulation of 1535 can be subdivided into 16 articles (they are actually unnumbered), the French capitulation of 1604 is divided into 50 articles, and the Dutch capitulation of 1612 consists of 65 articles.

Somewhat different from these capitulations were the rights granted to Austria following the treaty of peace of Sitvatorok between Rudolph II of Austria and Sultan Aḥmad I, signed on November 11, 1606. The treaty was renewed with some modifications between Sultan Aḥmad and Emperor Matthias in 1615 and further modified in 1616. In 1617 a firmān (imperial decree) confirmed the rights of Austrian merchants in the Ottoman dominions.[33] As laid down in these documents, the principal rights were: to trade freely in the Ottoman Empire under the imperial flag, to enjoy certain customs privileges, and to have the goods of deceased merchants delivered to the consuls of the emperor. The consuls, however, did not have judicial jurisdiction. All suits, whether among Austrian merchants or between them and other persons were to be adjudicated by Ottoman authorities. If the value exceeded 4000 *kreutzer* the suit had to be brought before the qāḍī al-'askar (military judge) in Constantinople. The merchants, however, could not be questioned in a qāḍī's court without a dragoman being present. While the subjects of the emperor

[31] *Ibid.*, pp. 108-10.

[32] Du Mont, *op. cit.*, Vol. V, Part 2, pp. 205-14 (text in Dutch and French).

[33] The text of the treaties of 1615 and 1616 can be found in *ibid.*, pp. 264-66 and 280-82. A French translation of the German text of the firman of 1617 is given in Miltitz, *op. cit.*, Vol. II, Part 2, pp. 1413-21.

were thus granted commercial privileges comparable to those of the French, Venetians, Dutch, and English, the important right of judicial jurisdiction was not given to the imperial representatives. This is probably explained by the reluctance of the sultan to grant to the subjects of a power which had for so long been hostile to the Ottoman Empire the same position as subjects of other Christian states which had had friendly relations with the Ottoman Government for a considerable period.[34] The rights of the Austrian merchants as granted in 1615 were confirmed in a treaty between Emperor Matthias and Sultan Osman II in 1618.[35]

Under the succeeding sultans the various capitulations were periodically renewed with little change in their substance. During the reign of Mehmed IV the dispute between France and Great Britain over the right of foreign nationals to sail under their flags again achieved prominence. In 1673 the French capitulation was renewed along basically the same lines as the earlier capitulations, but the right of France to extend to nations not represented at the Porte by ambassadors the protection of the French flag was confirmed in a long article which reviewed some of the history of that privilege.[36] In 1675 the sultan renewed the English capitulation and mentioned therein difficulties that had developed between the English and French ambassadors concerning the protection of nationals of states not represented in Constantinople. The sultan now leaned toward England's point of view and conceded to the latter country the right to permit foreign vessels to fly the English flag in Ottoman waters, at the same time enjoining the French ambassador not to interfere in any way.[37] The English capitulation has several other interesting features: suits between Englishmen and Turks involving a sum of more than 4,000 aspers (Turkish monetary unit) were to be heard by the Sublime Porte. Cases of murder or other crimes were to be tried by the local governors in the presence of the ambassador or consul, and decided by the Ottoman and English officials "together without their [i.e., the governors] presuming to give them [i.e., the English] the least molestation by hearing it alone, contrary to the holy law and these

[34] The ambassadors of the emperor usually were subjected to a much more humiliating treatment by the sultans than the ambassadors of other Christian rulers.

[35] Du Mont, *op. cit.*, Vol. V, Part 2, pp. 309-10.

[36] French text in Noradounghian, *op. cit.*, Vol. I, pp. 136-45.

[37] The various French and English texts of this capitulation differ from each other. A French translation is given in *ibid.*, 146-69, with other translations noted on pp. 52-53. An English translation, which was followed above in the quotations, is contained in Hertslet's, *Commercial Treaties,* Vol. II, pp. 346-69.

capitulations" (Article 42). The French capitulation of 1673, like its predecessors, granted the French representatives the right to sole jurisdiction in cases of crimes among French subjects. The English capitulations stipulated in Article 16 that in "any suit, or other difference or dispute, amongst the English themselves, the decision thereof shall be left to their own ambassador or consul, according to their custom, without the judge or other governors our slaves intermeddling therein." From these provisions it would appear doubtful that the sole jurisdiction of the English consuls in criminal matters was recognized at the time that this capitulation was granted.

It might be noted that the capitulation for the Netherlands granted in 1680 stated in Article 5 that "all suits and differences, even suits concerning murder in which the Netherlands subjects are involved, shall be judged and decided, according to their laws and customs, by their ambassadors or consuls without any of our qāḍīs or other officers having the right to interfere."[38] On the whole the Dutch capitulation of 1680 follows closely that of 1612. All the capitulations here discussed which were granted by Mehmed IV contain most-favored nation clauses.

After this period the contents of the capitulations appear to have been stabilized and formalized. The form, however, changed during the eighteenth century. In connection with the peace of Passarowitz of 1718, a treaty of commerce and navigation was concluded between the Ottoman Empire and Austria which was definitely bilateral in form and content. Austrian subjects now received the same rights in the Ottoman Empire as the subjects of other nations, the Austrian consuls had the right to judicial jurisdiction in suits among Austrians and, similar to the English capitulation of 1675, any suits between Austrians and others whose value exceeded 3000 aspers had to be brought before the Sublime Porte. However, the treaty had a number of reciprocal features. Thus, customs privileges were stipulated for subjects of both powers and Article 9 provided for most-favored-nation treatment of Ottoman merchants sailing on Austrian merchant vessels. Article 6 of the treaty provided for the appointment of Ottoman consuls (shahbender) in the Austrian states and for the delivery to them of the assets of Ottoman subjects who died in Austrian territory. The Ottoman consuls did not have any judicial jurisdiction, however, since at that time the judicial systems of the European countries

[38] French text in Noradounghian, *op. cit.*, Vol. I, pp. 169-81.

had come to be organized on the basis of the doctrine of territoriality of the law, with the law of the land in principle being applicable to foreigners and subjects alike.[39]

A treaty of commerce and navigation concluded between Sweden and the Ottoman Empire in 1737 granted the former the same privileges as other European nations on a most-favored-nation basis.[40] The judicial privileges of Swedes in the Ottoman dominions were the same as those of the nationals of other Western countries, with one exception. Article 8 stipulated that no dispute between a Swedish and an Ottoman subject should be judged except in the presence of the Swedish consul or dragoman. The Swedish diplomatic and consular representatives were enjoined to see that no Swedish subject committed an offense, but if one were nevertheless committed, the offender was to be punished by the ambassador or consul. Thus, the principle that in mixed cases the Ottoman authorities should have jurisdiction was breached. Another Scandinavian state, Denmark, concluded a commercial treaty along very similar lines with the Ottoman Empire in 1746 but it contained no provision parallel to the one discussed above. The reciprocity of the privileges accorded in the treaty to Danish merchants and goods was expressly stipulated in the final article (Article 17).[41] A similar provision was contained in the commercial treaty with Prussia concluded in 1761.[42]

More detailed with regard to reciprocity of treatment is the treaty of friendship, commerce, and navigation concluded between the Ottoman Empire and the Kingdom of the Two Sicilies in 1740. Of particular interest is Article 5 which states:

> S'il naissait des controverses entre les marchands et sujets du Roi des Deux-Siciles, ils sera examiné et terminé par nos consuls et interpretés suivant les propres lois, et usages et constitutions et, la necessité l'exigeant, il sera procedé de la même manière pour les sujets et marchands de l'Empire Ottoman qui se trouvent dans les domaines du Roi des Deux-Siciles.

Article 7 gave the Sublime Porte the right to establish in Messina a consul "et les dits sujets de la Sublime Porte seront respectés comme le sont ceux du serenissime roi dans l'Empire Ottoman."[43]

39 French text in *ibid.*, pp. 220-27.

40 Latin and Swedish text in F. A. W. Wenck, *Codex iuris gentium recentissimi* (Leipzig, 1781), Vol. I, pp. 471-503.

41 French translation in Noradounghian, *op. cit.*, Vol. I, pp. 308-14.

42 *Ibid.*, pp. 315-19.

43 *Ibid.*, pp. 270-77.

Similar provisions as to reciprocity were embodied in Article 5 and 7 of the commercial treaty with Spain of 1782,[44] and in Article 8 of the Anglo-Turkish treaty of 1809.[45] However, this does not mean that Ottoman consuls were granted judicial jurisdiction over Ottoman subjects in these European countries. The reciprocity was limited in the sense that the Ottoman representatives enjoyed only such rights as were at the time accorded to the representatives of other foreign powers which, of course, did not then include extraterritorial jurisdiction. This was expressed in one of the commercial treaties of the time, that with Russia of 1783, which stipulated most-favored-nation treatment for Ottoman subjects and promised the rendering of "justice complète aux sujets Ottomans dans les tribunaux."[46] The same idea was even more clearly stated in the Russo-Turkish treaty of 1846 which provided in Article 17:

> Les droits et les dispositions stipulés par la présente Convention à l'égard des sujets et negociants Russes ne pouvant pas, d'aprés les lois commerciales observées en Russie, être entiérement appliquées dans les États Russes envers les sujets et négociants de l'Empire Ottoman, c'est-a-dire une pleine reciprocité à cet égard ne pouvant pas avoir lieu, les sujets et les negociants de la Sublime Porte et ces navires de commerce qui fréquentent les États Russes et qui y exercent le commerce, ainsi que les produits des États Ottomans, seront traités dans les États Russes conformement aux dispositions qui sont adoptées envers les sujets et les négociants, les navires et les produits des Puissances étrangères les plus favorisées.[47]

In this developing pattern of clearly bilateral treaties embodying capitulatory rights there is one important exception, the capitulation granted to France in 1740. In this document the traditional form was fully preserved and the old rights of France reaffirmed in great detail in 85 articles.[48] The rights of France to allow the vessels of nations lacking direct relations with the Porte to sail under its flag, and to protect subjects of "enemy nations" on the pilgrimage to Jerusalem were reaffirmed (Articles 32 and 38). However, in view of the vastly expanded relations between the Ottoman Empire and Europe, these privileges had less meaning than they had had in earlier times. Of particular interest is the provision of Article 52 which stipulates that cases between Frenchmen and subjects of other foreign powers may be heard, at the option of the parties, by

[44] *Ibid.*, pp. 344-49.

[45] *Ibid.*, Vol. II (Paris, 1900), pp. 81-84; the statement is not as explicit as those in the treaties with Denmark and Spain.

[46] *Ibid.*, Vol. I, pp. 351-73.

[47] *Ibid.*, Vol. II, pp. 371-49.

[48] *Ibid.*, Vol. I, pp. 270-306.

the French ambassador, or by the local Ottoman judges. Thus, the principle of exempting mixed foreign cases from the Ottoman jurisdiction was established and was later incorporated in other commercial agreements. Another important provision was that of Article 47 exempting Ottoman subjects in the service of the ambassador up to a maximum number of fifteen from all taxes and dues. Search of a Frenchman's premises could only take place in the presence of the ambassador, a consul, or their agents (Article 70).

By the end of the eighteenth century, therefore, a number of Western countries had achieved judicial privileges for their nationals in the Ottoman Empire and still more were to secure them during the nineteenth century. Among the countries which concluded commercial agreements with the Porte during the first half of the nineteenth century was the United States. In a treaty of commerce and navigation of 1830, the two countries granted each other the same customs privileges as those given to the most-favored nation and the right to establish consulates.[49] The right of judicial jurisdiction in cases involving only American citizens was not expressly granted to the American consuls but was assumed to exist. In mixed cases between American citizens and Turkish subjects hearings were not to be held or judgment pronounced unless the American dragoman was present. Difficulties arose as to the interpretation of part of the Article dealing with jurisdiction (Article 4), which read:

Citizens of the United States of America, quietly pursuing their commerce, and not being charged or convicted of any crime or offence, shall not be molested, and even when they may have committed some offence, they shall not be arrested and put in prison by the Local Authorities, but they shall be tried by their Minister or Consul, and punished according to their offence; following in this respect, the usage observed towards other Franks.

An identical provision appears in Article 8 of the Ottoman-Belgian commercial treaty of 1838 and in Article 8 of the Ottoman-Portuguese treaty of 1843. However, in its relations with the United States at least, the Porte tried to maintain that the American representatives did not have criminal jurisdiction in cases involving American citizens and Turkish subjects. The Ottoman Government argued that the provision was based upon a mistranslation

[49] English text in *British and Foreign State Papers, 1830-31*, Vol. 18, pp. 1361-63. On the history of this treaty and the difficulties concerning Article 4 see Moore, *Digest of International Law*, Vol. II, pp. 668-714.

from the Turkish and was not found at all in the original. The controversy continued during most of the nineteenth century with the U. S. Government asserting in theory and practice the right to try in consular courts American citizens guilty of crimes or misdemeanors against Ottoman subjects in Ottoman territory.

In its fully developed form, extraterritorial jurisdiction in the Ottoman Empire in the nineteenth century thus included complete jurisdiction of consular officers over their citizens in civil and criminal cases. In mixed cases between the citizens of two or more Western powers, mixed commissions had jurisdiction according to a verbal agreement of 1820 among the ministers of Austria, France, Great Britain, and Russia which was later adhered to by the representatives of the other powers. These commissions replaced earlier mixed tribunals and were composed of three members, one appointed by the plaintiff's legation and two by the defendant's legation. The jurisdiction of the Ottoman courts in these cases was thereby eliminated.[50] The sentences of these commissions had to be approved by the consuls. According to a report of Mr. F. Dainese, one time American consul at Constantinople, written to Secretary of State Webster in February 1852, this system was the worst ever devised. The commissions, in his opinion, were often biased and "under such a system a fair and equitable adjustment of litigated cases cannot be hoped for."[51] Later in the nineteenth century this system was abolished and the principle of *actor sequitur forum rei* was strictly applied.[52]

LEGAL NATURE OF THE CAPITULATIONS

By the nineteenth century the capitulatory rights of the various powers had thus grown into a well-systematized framework of law and procedure.[53] Much has been written about the legal nature of the capitulations and scholars have differed over whether they should be regarded as unilateral privileges granted by the sultan

[50] A detailed description of the jurisdiction of the consular courts can be found in Stamatios Antonopoulos, "Ueber die Exterritorialitaet der Auslaender in der Tuerkei mit Ruecksicht auf die Gerichtsbarkeit in Civil-und Strafprocessen," *Jahrbuch der internationalen Vereinigung fuer Vergleichende Rechtswissenschaft und Volkswirtschaftslehre* (1895), Vol. 1, pp. 95-190.

[51] Moore, *op. cit.*, Vol. II, p. 674.

[52] Antonopoulos, *op. cit.*, p. 124.

[53] A detailed discussion of the system of extraterritorial jurisdiction in the Ottoman Empire in the nineteenth and early twentieth centuries may be found in André Mandelstam, *La Justice Ottomane dans ses rapports avec les puissances étrangères* (2nd ed., Paris, 1911), and in Pelissié du Rausas, *Le régime des capitulations dans l'Empire Ottoman* (2nd ed., 2 vols., Paris, 1910).

or as treaties. This discussion was not without political overtones. If the capitulations could be construed as unilateral favors granted by the sultan, the right of the Ottoman Government to abrogate these privileges at will could be justified much more easily than if the capitulations were regarded as treaties.[54] In the light of the historical development of the capitulations, however, it appears that these grants, although in earlier times frequently in the form of privileges granted by the sultan, embodied rights and duties of both parties and thus could be regarded as bilateral agreements.

An important feature of the earlier capitulations—the French capitulation of 1740 is the first exception—was that they were valid only during the lifetime of the sultan who had granted them. Capitulatory rights were renewed whenever a new sultan came to power. The reason for this limitation has likewise been discussed in considerable detail. One possible explanation is the rule of Islamic law which disapproves of perpetual treaties with unbelievers. However, Pelissié du Rausas suggests as another possible reason for this limitation that the idea of perpetual treaties transcending the lifetime of the ruler is relatively recent and presupposes a concept of the state and its rights and duties which the Ottoman Turks of the sixteenth and seventeenth centuries could not know.[55] It is likely that both of these considerations may have played a role. Pelissié du Rausas' theory would explain why these grants were limited to the sultan's lifetime and not to a given number of years.

OTTOMAN JUDICIAL REFORMS AND THE ABOLITION OF THE CAPITULATIONS

With the development of the modern concepts of territorial sovereignty, including the exclusive rights of the organs of the territorial state to judicial jurisdiction for the capitulations began to be regarded in the Ottoman Empire as undue restrictions upon sovereignty. They were no longer an institution logically developed on the basis of the principle of the personality of the law, but were considered by the Ottoman Government as privileges claimed by the powerful states of Europe and impositions upon the weakening Ottoman Empire. This feeling was reinforced by the fact that the European powers claimed protection not only of their own subjects but also for certain subjects of the Ottoman Empire. Al-

[54] Mahmoud Essad, *Du régime des capitulations Ottomanes, leur caractère juridique d'après l'histoire et les textes* (Istanbul, 1928).

[55] Pelissie du Rausas, *op. cit.*, Vol. I, pp. 23-24.

though originally restricted to dragomans and other Ottoman subjects in the employ of foreign consular and diplomatic officers, this system of so-called protégés was extended to others, especially members of the Christian minorities in the Empire, and led to considerable abuses which were finally curbed by an Ottoman law of 1863. The history of the capitulations, therefore, especially in the nineteenth century, is one of continuous attempts by the Porte to limit the jurisdiction of the foreign tribunals and to avoid at least any further extension of capitulatory rights.

A new element was injected into the picture by the endeavors of the Porte to introduce judicial reforms which were aimed at the establishment of state courts and of equality before the bar of justice for all subjects of the Empire regardless of their religion. The impetus for these reforms came in part from the European powers, and in part from the desire of the sultans to reorganize the administrative and judicial system of the declining Empire on the pattern successfully employed in contemporary Europe. The first step was taken in 1839 when Sultan Abd al-Majīd solemnly proclaimed the hatti-sharif of Gülhane which stipulated the basic equality of all subjects of the Empire regardless of race or religion. The European concept of a territorial state with equal status for all its citizens was thus basically established by the Porte and the principle of the personality of the law on the basis of religion was, though not abandoned, relegated, at least in theory, to a minor role. The first judicial reform affecting foreigners was the creation in 1840 of commercial tribunals which were reorganized in 1848, and again in 1860 after the enactment of a Commercial Code. The commercial tribunals as finally constituted were composed generally of three judges and four assessors, the former appointed by the Ottoman Government, the latter by the merchant community. In mixed cases involving Ottoman subjects and foreigners the latter's consuls selected two of the assessors from among prominent members of their respective national communities. The courts had jurisdiction in mixed civil cases not concerning real estate if the value exceeded 1000 piasters. In commercial cases their jurisdiction was unlimited.[56]

In spite of the establishment of the commercial tribunals, the judicial and administrative reforms promised by the Hatti-sharif of 1839 were implemented only slowly. Under the pressure of the European powers the sultan therefore issued, on the eve of the

[56] For further details see Mandelstam, *op. cit.*, pp. 1-6 and Antonopoulos, *op. cit.*, p. 131.

Congress of Paris of 1856 which ended the Crimean War, another and more detailed reform decree, the Hatti-Humayūn.[57] Designed primarily to weaken Russian claims at the peace conference to the right of protection of all Greek Orthodox in the Ottoman Empire, the decree promised complete equality and religious liberty to the Christian subjects of the Porte. Mixed tribunals for commercial, correctional, and criminal suits were to be established to hear cases between Muslims and non-Muslim subjects of the Empire and between non-Muslims of different sects. Codes of substantive law and procedure for the use of these tribunals were to be enacted as quickly as possible. A number of codes were adopted, mostly on the French model, with the law of contracts and evidence being codified in the Majalla on the basis of Islamic law of the Ḥanafī school. The personal status law of the various communities remained untouched.[58]

Of particular importance from the standpoint of the rights of foreigners was the enactment on June 10, 1867 of a law permitting them to own real estate in the Ottoman Empire. The Porte had attempted, and failed, to obtain the abolition of the capitulations at the Congress of Paris but had remained insistent that rights of ownership of real estate could not be given to foreigners unless they were submitted to the laws of the Empire. After prolonged negotiations the European powers had to admit this principle and the law of 1867 thus permitted foreigners to own real estate in the Ottoman Empire, except in the then province of the Hijāz, provided that with regard to such real estate they would be submitted to the same laws and court procedures as Ottoman subjects.[59] Although the law guaranteed the maintenance of the established privileges of foreigners with regard to their persons and personal property, a protocol issued in its implementation and accepted by the European powers, after some hesitation, especially on the part of the Russians, extended Ottoman jurisdiction over foreigners to some degree. The extension applied primarily to persons residing more than nine hours' march from the seat of the nearest consul and, briefly, dispensed with consular intervention in petty civil and criminal cases as far as these persons were concerned.

The establishment of Western-type civil and criminal tribunals in the Ottoman Empire and the desire of the Porte to limit foreign

[57] English translation in Hertslet, *Map of Europe by Treaty*, Vol. II, pp. 1243-50.

[58] For further details see Chapters XI and XII.

[59] This law, referred to frequently with its Turkish date as the law of Sefer 7, 1284, is discussed in detail by Mandelstam, *op. cit.*, pp. 6-18.

privileges as far as possible led to constant friction and difficulties which cannot be discussed in detail. The need for reform of the system became obvious to the European powers as well as the Porte, and after the Young Turk revolution of 1908 the endeavors to abolish the capitulatory regime gained a new and stronger impetus. No agreement with the European powers was reached, however, and after its entry into World War I on the side of the Central Powers the Ottoman Government on October 1, 1914, unilaterally declared the capitulations abrogated.[60] This unilateral abrogation was not recognized by the Allied powers and led to specific difficulties with the United States which, though not a belligerent at the time, was also affected by the abolition of the extraterritorial privileges. The United States refused to abide by this unilateral act and American consular tribunals continued to function in the Empire until the severance of diplomatic relations with the Porte in 1917. The re-establishment of the capitulatory regime in Turkey was envisaged in the Armistice of Mudros of October 30, 1918, and the abortive Treaty of Sèvres reserved to the powers the right to permit the introduction of a system of judicial reforms at a date to be set by them. However, the successful establishment of the Turkish Republic by Kemal Atatürk brought about the complete abolition of the capitulations by Article 28 of the Treaty of Lausanne of July 24, 1923. Although the United States was not a signatory of the Treaty of Lausanne it acquiesced in the abolition of the capitulations.

THE MODIFICATION AND ABOLITION OF CAPITULATORY RIGHTS IN EGYPT

The developments in Egypt leading to the establishment of Mixed Courts and, ultimately, to the abolition of the capitulations, differed from those in the rest of the Ottoman Empire. Muḥammad 'Alī (died 1849) and his successors led Egypt along a course which was independent in all but name from the government in Istanbul. Muḥammad 'Alī's desire to attract European cooperation in the execution of his many projects led to an extension of foreign judicial privileges which resulted in jurisdictional chaos because of the coexistence of a number of unrelated consular courts. A radical reform of the judicial system was therefore carried through by Nubār Pasha, the first minister of Khedive Ismaīl (1863-1880). In 1874-75 the system of the Egyptian Mixed Courts was created which, though inspired to a degree by the Ottoman mixed com-

[60] Charles C. Hyde, *International Law* (2nd ed., Boston, 1945), Vol. II, pp. 863-68.

mercial tribunals, went much further in the establishment of a workable judicial structure. The Mixed Courts, which were staffed by foreign and Egyptian judges, assumed jurisdiction in all civil and commercial cases between Egyptians and foreigners and between foreigners of different nationalities. The Mixed Courts also had jurisdiction in all cases involving land arising between foreigners even if they were of the same nationality. An important extension of the jurisdiction of the Mixed Courts took place with regard to corporations. They assumed jurisdiction even in cases where an Egyptian corporation was involved against Egyptian litigants if there was foreign capital invested in the corporation, as was usually the case. This so-called theory of "mixed interest" thus enabled the Mixed Courts to adjudicate practically all cases concerning corporate interests with the exception, after World War I, of the Bank Miṣr and its subsidiary institutions where ownership of stock was limited to Egyptians.

In the field of criminal law the jurisdiction of the Mixed Courts originally remained seriously restricted because of objections on the part of the foreign powers. The consular courts therefore retained criminal jurisdiction over their nationals with the exception of police offenses and offenses directly touching the administration of justice by the Mixed Courts themselves. The Mixed Courts were organized in three District Courts, at Cairo, Alexandria, and Mansura, and a Court of Appeals at Alexandria. The law which they applied was laid down in a series of codes based primarily on French models. In 1883 native or National Courts were organized in Egypt which followed more or less the pattern of the Mixed Courts and which had jurisdiction in matters involving Egyptians only. Personal status matters continued outside the jurisdiction of both the Mixed Courts and the National Courts. They were handled by the religious tribunals for Egyptians and by the various consular courts for foreigners.[61]

Even though the system of the Mixed Courts functioned rather well, it was increasingly felt as a burden by Egypt and in 1937 a convention was concluded at Montreux which set the stage for the abolition of the system in 1949. During the transitional period all vacancies up to two-thirds of the total membership of the district courts were to be filled by Egyptian judges who were also permitted for the first time to become presidents of these courts.

[61] The history of the Mixed Courts until 1930 can be found in the basic book by Jasper Y. Brinton, *The Mixed Courts of Egypt* (New Haven: Yale University Press, 1930).

In the Court of Appeal the membership ratio of one-third Egyptian to two-thirds foreign was maintained, however. At the same time criminal jurisdiction and such civil jurisdiction as was still exercised by the consular tribunals in matters concerning their nationals only (other than in personal status cases) was transferred to the Mixed Courts. Personal status cases still remained outside the jurisdiction of the Mixed Courts. The codes to be applied by the courts remained the same, except that a unified Criminal Code to be applied by Mixed and National Courts alike was introduced. On October 15, 1949, the Mixed Courts and the consular courts were closed, jurisdiction was transferred to the National Courts, and the law codes were revised and unified. Thus, the era of consular jurisdiction and its outgrowth in the Mixed Courts had ended in Egypt, not without establishing, however, through the Mixed Courts an important judicial tradition in the country.[62]

IMPORTANCE OF THE CAPITULATIONS IN THE LEGAL DEVELOPMENT OF THE NEAR EAST

Although the capitulations were a natural extension of the idea of the personality of the law and a practical solution for the problem of jurisdiction over nonbelieving foreigners in a Muslim state, they became an anachronism and were regarded as an intrusion upon sovereign rights with the ascendency of nationalism and the idea of the territoriality of the law. The secularization and Westernization of large areas of the law in most Islamic countries further militated for the abolition of this institution. Historically, however, the capitulations have been an important factor in the legal development of the region once included in the Ottoman Empire. They were one avenue through which Western legal thought and legal procedure were introduced. Also, since the capitulatory rights came to be felt in the nineteenth century as an infringement of sovereignty, they served as a stimulant for judicial reform, since modernization and reform of the judicial system were one way to prove that the capitulations were no longer needed to protect the European merchant from possible abuses of local courts. The capitulations can thus be regarded as one of the factors which induced the Ottoman Empire and Egypt to adopt continental European codes and procedures and to endeavor to follow European standards in the administration of justice. In

[62] For further details on the end of the Mixed Courts, see Jasper Y. Brinton, "The Closing of the Mixed Courts of Egypt," *American Journal of International Law*, Vol. 44 (1950), p. 303.

Egypt particularly the Mixed Courts with their international personnel served to introduce into Egypt the legal thought not only of continental Europe but also, although to a lesser degree, of the Anglo-American system.

Today broad extraterritorial privileges are maintained in the Near and Middle East in a few cases only. The United States still has extraterritorial rights in Morocco, and though not at present exercised, in Muscat.[63] Great Britain has extraterritorial jurisdiction over its own nationals and foreigners in the Persian Gulf principalities under its protection. In these cases, however, British judicial jurisdiction appears based upon custom, usage, and informal agreements rather than upon a formal grant of capitulatory rights. In Muscat, Great Britain has jurisdiction over its nationals.[64] The interesting and often stormy history of the capitulations has thus practically come to an end.

[63] See in general Richard Young, "Recent American Policy concerning the Capitulations in the States of the Middle East," *American Journal of International Law,* Vol. 42 (1948), pp. 418-23. On the extent of U. S. jurisdiction in Morocco see "Case Concerning Rights of Nationals of the United States of America in Morocco (France v. United States)" International Court of Justice, *Reports,* 1952, p. 176, digested in *American Journal of International Law,* Vol. 47 (1953), p. 136.

[64] Further details in Richard Young, "The United Kingdom-Muscat Treaty of 1951," *American Journal of International Law,* Vol. 46 (1952), pp. 704-08; and Herbert J. Liebesny, "International Relations of Arabia: The Dependent Areas," *Middle East Journal,* Vol. II, pp. 148-68.

CHAPTER XIV

Conflict of Law

AN EXHAUSTIVE study of conflict of law in Islam cannot be presented in a limited number of pages. This is particularly true of private international law during the first centuries because it has not yet been thoroughly examined.[1] It will be useful, however, to state some facts from the works of ancient Muslim jurists and try to systematize the empirical solutions recommended in various schools of law in order to compare them with the law of conflicts in modern systems. The first section will discuss the situation of the non-Muslim inhabitants of Islamic territory and examine their legal and legislative status. The second section will present the conflicts born of the multiplicity of laws and customs in Muslim countries where the law of the believers differed from the law of other religious communities. This survey will be limited to the Islamic period (from the reign of the first caliph to the Conquest of Constantinople by Muḥammad II).

During the following period the emphasis falls on the nature of the conflict between Muslim and non-Muslim personal status law in the various oriental countries. In passing it is necessary to note the origin of the religious laws which still govern the inhabitants of countries detached from the Ottoman Empire. This study will require a discussion of the legal status of these communities prior to the break-up of the Empire.

The discussion will be limited to an examination of the sources and evolution of problems of private international law as they relate to doctrine and custom in countries which are still making a distinction between religious and secular legislation. Turkey has adopted the Swiss Civil Code in an amended form to replace much of her law, including personal status law. Because matters of personal status are no longer based on religion, the solutions of conflicts have lost a unique quality derived from the particularism of a diversity of religious groups and community laws. Even thus limited, the survey will not include all the countries in which com-

[1] See, however, Chucri Cardahi, "The Concept and Practice of Private International Law in Islam" in *Recueil des Cours de l'Academie de Droit International de la Haye*, 1937, Vol. II, pp. 511-646.

munity personal status law has survived but only the ones considered as the lands most typical of such conflicts of law: Egypt, Lebanon, and Syria. In these states detached from the Turkish Empire, religious laws continue to bring up the most difficult judicial problems. Legislative reform inspired by European codes left this legacy of the past almost intact in these countries.

LEGAL STATUS OF THE "SCRIPTURARIES" (AHL AL-KITĀB, OR AHL AL-DHIMMA)

The name dhimmī or "scripturary" was given to the Christians and the Jews as followers of religions which Islam considered revealed. To these were joined in time the Zoroastrians and the Sābians. If they submitted to the caliph and agreed to pay a poll tax, the jizya, they were to enjoy the protection of Islam and of the Muslim authorities. According to the jurists, the dhimma was a contract between the dhimmī and the Muslim community. Such a contract gave the dhimmī the right to stay in Islamic territory, security for his person and his belongings, freedom to practice his religion, and defense against an enemy. On his part, the dhimmī pledged loyalty to the Muslim authority and promised to pay to the Muslim treasury a poll tax: the jizya. The Ḥanbalīs stipulated in addition that the dhimmī should promise not to speak ill of the Prophet's religion and also that he should abstain from any act detrimental to believers.[2] They declared further that the dhimmī should be subject to the laws of Islam in all cases concerning damages, weregeld, or rape.

It would lead too far to discuss here in detail the legal position of the dhimmī. A very brief outline of their condition with regard to civil and criminal law is needed, however, as a background for a discussion of the conflicts of law and their solution.[3]

CIVIL LAW

Marriage between dhimmīs and Muslims was not permitted in all cases. A dhimmī could not marry a Muslim girl; however, a Muslim could marry a Christian or Jewish girl, but not a Zoroastrian. Although such marriages were legal, they were not recommended and the Mālikīs regarded them as objectionable (makrūh).

Because of the difference of religion, a dhimmī could not in-

[2] 'Abd al-Qadir al-Shaybānī, *Kitāb Nayl al Ma'ārib bi Sharḥ dalīl al Ṭālib,* Vol. I, p. 97.

[3] For a discussion of the status of the dhimmīs in Muslim public law, see below, Chap. XV.

herit from a Muslim nor a Muslim from a dhimmī.[4] It was permissible for one dhimmī to inherit from another of the same creed provided that they both lived in Islamic territory. Succession was then governed by their own law, which will be discussed later. When a dhimmī died heirless, the following distinction had to be made: if he belonged to a community subjected by pacific means, the vacant estate reverted to his community, but if he belonged to a group subjected by force of arms, then the property went to the Muslim treasury (bayt al-māl).

The question now arises: if dhimmīs belonged to different religions, could one inherit from the other? For instance, could a Jew inherit from a Christian? On this matter, there are several opinions: Mālik thought that difference of creed barred inheritance. His views were based on a tradition of the Prophet which states: "Adherents of different religions are not called to succeed to each other." On the other hand, according to Shāfi'ī and Abū Ḥanīfa, there was no objection to a dhimmī inheriting from a dhimmī of a different faith. These jurists base their opinion on another ḥadīth of the Prophet: "The Muslim does not inherit from the nonbeliever and the nonbeliever does not inherit from the Muslim." This, in turn, was taken to mean that a Muslim could inherit from a Muslim and a nonbeliever from a nonbeliever.

Whatever his sex, a dhimmī could establish a waqf for his heirs, provided that at the extinction of his family, it would revert to the poor of his religion.[5] The dhimmī was also free to make a will. The conflicts which arose from their right to make a will and the manner in which these problems were solved will be discussed below. The dhimmī could own all kinds of properties, even those the use of which was prohibited to believers, but he could not buy a Muslim slave or a copy of the Qur'ān.[6]

PENAL LAW

In the realm of penal law, the pre-Islamic law of retaliation (talion), which had been sanctioned in part by the Qur'ān, was the only law applied to the dhimmīs. The Qur'ān had established it, and its decisions confirm the status of inferiority of the dhimmī, whose murder, as in the Germanic laws of the West *(leges Barbarorum),* was more easily expiated than that of a Muslim. Ac-

[4] Suyūṭī, *Sharḥ Muwaṭṭa' Mālik,* Vol. II, p. 59.

[5] See Qadrī Pasha, *Qanūn al 'Adl wa'l-Inṣāf,* Art. 88.

[6] Santillana, *Istituzioni di diritto musulmano malichita,* (Rome, 1938), Vol. I, p. 81.

cording to the Mālikīs, the blood money (diyya) for the unintentional killing of a dhimmī by a Muslim was much lower than for a like offense committed against a Muslim.[7]

JURISDICTION OVER DHIMMĪS

In principle, dhimmīs were under the jurisdiction of their religious leaders. The Muslim qāḍī had jurisdiction in suits arising between two dhimmīs belonging to the same community only if they had agreed to bring their suit before him. He also had jurisdiction in cases concerning scripturaries of different communities. The question arose whether the Muslim judge had to try the case if two dhimmīs brought it before him. On this point, opinions vary: the Ḥanafīs held that the qāḍī had to try the case, whereas the Mālikīs and the Shāfi'īs decided that the qāḍī had a choice. The latter based their opinion on the rule of the Qur'ān which reads: "If, therefore, they [the dhimmīs] have recourse to thee, then judge between them, or withdraw from them," (Q. V, 46). Another opinion (which did not prevail) would have imposed on the dhimmīs the jurisdiction of the qāḍī and would have denied them the right to be judged by their own courts.[8]

CONFLICTS BETWEEN MUSLIM LAW AND THE LAW OF NON-MUSLIM COMMUNITIES IN ISLAMIC TERRITORY

In a civil suit between a Muslim and a non-Muslim, the Muslim judge was required to apply his own law, for Islam must dominate and not be dominated (Q. V, 54-55; IV, 140).[9] The same principle applied in criminal cases. When an offense was committed by a dhimmī against a Muslim, Muslim law was applied. Thus, if a dhimmī killed or wounded a Muslim, the law of retaliation was applied to him. According to the Mālikī school, a Muslim committing the same crime toward a dhimmī was liable only to a fine and a prison term, that is, he had to pay the diyya. If the crime was unintentional, he had to pay only half the compensation required in the case of a Muslim. According to the Ḥanafī school a Muslim who murdered a musta'min (i.e., the non-Muslim beneficiary of a safe-conduct) was not punished by talion but instead

[7] Sidī al-Khalīl, *al-Mukhtaṣar,* trad. Perron, p. 511. Among the Shāfi'īs, according to Shirazi, the diyya of a Christian, a Jew, or a Zoroastrian was one-third of the Muslim diyya (*Kitāb al-Tanbīh,* p. 129).

[8] See, for all these questions, Ibn Rushd (al-Hafid) *Bidayat al-Miytahid* (Istanbul, A. H. 1333) p. 113, and Shāfi'ī, *Kitāb al-Umm,* Vol. VI, p. 146.

[9] Santillana, *op. cit.,* pp. 84 ff.

paid the diyya. Likewise, when a Muslim intentionally gouged out the eye of a musta'min or cut off his leg or his hand, the penalties were not applicable but the Muslim was liable to pay damages. An exception to this rule was made when the Muslim committed adultery with a musta'min girl; in that case he was subject to the legal punishment.[10] When in Islamic territory under a safe-conduct, a musta'min was not generally subject to Muslim jurisdiction. If he committed an offense against a Muslim, however, punishments (ḥudūd) were applied.[11]

One question, however, arises. If dhimmīs brought a lawsuit before a Muslim qāḍī, which law was the latter to apply? As has been stated above, the Shāfi'is held that the Muslim judge was not bound to entertain their suit. Because he was established to administer justice to believers, he could refuse jurisdiction over nonbelievers if he wished.[12] In principle, they were strangers to him. A similar problem arises in modern law as to whether national courts may assume jurisdiction in civil suits involving only foreigners. According to Baydāwī and Abū Ḥanīfa by the contract of the dhimma, Islam undertook to dispense justice to the dhimmīs, and the Muslim judge had to retain jurisdiction.[13]

When a Muslim judge agreed to hear a suit, he did so as an arbitrator trying to reconcile the parties. But what law did he apply? The Mālikīs stated that he should apply the national law of the litigants unless it directly contradicted Muslim law in which case it was to be rejected for reasons of public order. (The concept of public order among a people who relate everything to God and have established their law on the depth of their faith is essentially a religious one.)

This principle can be clarified by examples of its application. A Muslim judge had to enforce a contract concluded among dhimmīs unless its provisions infringed upon the precepts of Muslim law. For example, in case of a wine sale, which was considered illegal by Muslims, the judge had either to decline jurisdiction or to apply Islamic law.[14] Questions concerning intestate succession or the validity of a will were settled according to the inheritance law of the decedent's creed. A dhimmī's bequests, however, were limited. If the will he probated violated the Islamic rule that a

[10] Ṭabarī, *Kitāb al-Jihād,* p. 54, no. 46.

[11] Santillana, *op. cit.,* p. 85.

[12] Q. V, 46, 50, 51.

[13] See Bayḍāwī, *Tafsir al-Qur'ān,* p. 125.

[14] Saḥnūn, *al-Mudawwana al-Kubra,* Vol. XI, p. 42; Vol. XIII, p. 56; Vol. XIV, pp. 32, 74.

man might bequeath only a third of his estate to persons who would not inherit if he died intestate, the Muslim judge would reduce bequests to the established quota.

Other aspects of inheritance law merit further study. For example, Islamic law provides that a legal heir may not receive a bequest. This rule was apparently applied to dhimmīs and the Muslim jurists unanimously approved it as necessary to the maintenance of public order.[15] In contrast, the limitation of bequests to those who were not legal heirs had a sacred character. Ibn Rushd stated that the jurists unanimously forbade all bequests exceeding one-third of the estate by a testator with heirs, because of the tradition established by the Prophet after he saw Sa'd Ibn Waqqāṣ.[16] On this point, therefore, Muslim law was applied to the ahl al-kitāb but with certain important restrictions. The Ḥanafī jurists held, in various cases, that the law of the community, even if opposed to Muslim doctrine, determined the validity of the will. Even in this matter, many controversies arose among the jurists concerning the applicability of the laws of the community.[17]

Various types of cases concerning the validity of wills were distinguished:

(1) If the object of the will was illegal according to the law of the community as well as according to Muslim law, it was null and void.

(2) A will submitted to the Muslim judge might have had an object which was legal in the religion of the testator, but illegal in Islamic law. This would be the case of a decedent dhimmī making a bequest for the construction of a church or a slaughter house to distribute pork to his coreligionists. Abū Ḥanīfa considered such a will to be valid, since the validity of the bequest should be determined according to the law of the testator's community whether or not the beneficiaries of the bequest were explicitly named. His disciples, Abū Yūsuf and Shaybānī, did not admit the validity of such a will unless the legatees were specifically designated.

(3) If the contested will had an object legal under Islamic law but illegal under the testator's religious law, all jurists held it invalid.

(4) Contracts: The Muslim judge had to recognize a contract between dhimmīs unless the provisions violated the principles of

15 Q. IV, 37. See also Ibn Rushd, *op. cit.*, Vol. II, p. 280.
16 *Ibid.*, p. 281; Da'ud Effendi, *Majma' al-Anhur*, Vol. II, p. 718.
17 *Ibid.*, Vol. II, pp. 716-17.

Muslim law. In a case concerning the sale of wine, the judge, according to the Mālikīs, had either to decline judging the case or to apply Islamic law.[18]

(5) Pre-emption frequently gave rise to conflicts of law. For instance, when a dhimmī bought a house from another dhimmī and paid for it not in money but in wine or pork (both goods prohibited by Islam), pre-emption was valid. If the pre-emptor was a dhimmī, nothing prevented him from substituting himself for the buyer, and from paying the latter the quantity of pork or wine he had given for his purchase of the building. If, however, the pre-emptor was a Muslim, Islamic law applied, and the buyer could not be given wine or pork but had to be paid in money.[19]

CONFLICTS OF LAW BETWEEN DHIMMĪS OF DIFFERENT RELIGIONS

Such conflicts could arise in a lawsuit between a Christian and a Jew. Since a dhimmī could sue only his coreligionists in his own religious court, the Muslim judge had jurisdiction and Islamic law applied. The same rule was followed in penal matters. If a Christian committed an offense against a Jew, the Muslim judge, having sole jurisdiction, applied Islamic law.[20]

In case of a civil or criminal action between dhimmīs of the same faith, such as two Christians or two Jews, the judge of their religious court had jurisdiction. So extensive was his judicial power that he could impose a death sentence if his religion provided that penalty.[21] According to Mālik, if a non-Muslim committed fornication with a Muslim woman, the Muslim woman was to be judged by the Muslim qāḍī and the non-Muslim man would be referred to his religious judge.

This solution was generally accepted, except in cases where considerations of public order were involved. Thus, in cases of murder, theft, or highway robbery committed by an unbeliever against another unbeliever in the territory of Islam, the penalties applied were those stipulated by Islamic law. Because these acts constituted serious violations in the world of Islam, Islamic law

[18] Saḥnūn, *op. cit.*, Vol. XI, p. 42; Vol. XIII, p. 56; Vol. XIV, pp. 32, 74.

[19] *Fatāwa al Hindiyya*, Vol. V, pp. 382 ff.

[20] Zurqānī, *Sharḥ Mukhtaṣar Khalīl*, Vol. VIII, p. 130; Saḥnūn, *op. cit.*, Vol. XVI, p. 53.

[21] Saḥnūn, *op. cit.*, Vol. VIII, p. 97 in fine, 98; Zurqānī, *op. cit.*, Vol. III, p. 226; Van den Berg, *Principes du droit Musulman d'après les rites de Abou Hanifa et de Chafei* (Algiers, 1896), p. 207; Santillana, *op. cit.*, p. 82.

had to provide the punishments. This is the principle of the territoriality of penal law.

Abū Ḥanīfa did not accept this rule in the case of an offense committed by a ḥarbī musta'min (a protected foreigner) against a dhimmī. The guilty foreigner should pay damages only, and no penalty based on Islamic law (ḥadd) should be imposed upon him. This presupposes, of course, commission of the offense in Islamic territory. Had the offense been committed in the dār al-ḥarb, the Muslim qāḍī could not take jurisdiction.[22]

A dhimmī guilty of fornication with another dhimmī was penalized as prescribed by his own law since the provisions of Islamic law regarding this offense applied to Muslims only. However, if the offense caused a scandal or otherwise attracted public attention, the qāḍī intervened and applied Islamic law.[23]

CONFLICTS OF LAW AMONG SCHOOLS OF LAW WITHIN ISLAM

A conflict could arise between two schools of law. Here, more than anywhere else, it could be said that the conflict was not one of private international law, for both laws were Islamic. The problem arising from a conflict between rules established by two of the four orthodox schools has not been directly examined by the Muslim jurists, but principles can be deduced from their works.

These principles, briefly, are the following:

If the parties belonged to different schools of law, the defendant had the right to choose the system of law according to which the case was to be judged. The defendant was not necessarily the one summoned to appear before the judge, but the one "whose declaration was supported by presumptions resulting from the usual state of facts." This principle was followed by the Ḥanafī school of law, at least in Tunisia. In the words of the Shaykh al-Islam of Tunis: "If the plaintiff has sued in the court of the judge of one school, and if the defendant, before any statement has been made before the judge, asks for the transfer of the case to a judge of a different school, such a request cannot be refused."[24]

The Majalla seems to follow the same line. Article 1803 stipu-

[22] Ṭabarī, *op. cit.*, p. 54.

[23] This principle was established by Ibn Sarrāj, Supreme Judge in Cordova, who died in A. H. 456 (1664). Wancharisi, "La pierre de touche des fetwas" *Moroccan Archives*, Vol. XII, p. 213; Santillana, *op. cit.*, p. 76.

[24] See Morand, "Le droit musulman et le conflit des lois," *Acta academiae universalis jurisprudentiae comparativae*, Vol. I, pp. 321 ff.

lated that in case of a suit between parties belonging to different schools of law, the defendant could demand the transfer of the case to a judge of his own school.

This right of the defendant in a suit to choose the qāḍī was not an obligation. He could, if he wished, submit to the qāḍī of the plaintiff,[25] for the submission of a Muslim to an orthodox school other than his own is permissible. Therefore, the sovereign could decree that justice be dispensed according to the school of his choosing. In Egypt, for example, where there are no Shāfi'ī qāḍīs, the Shāfi'īs have always accepted without protest the jurisdiction of the Ḥanafī qāḍīs.[26]

CONFLICTS OF LAW RESULTING FROM A CHANGE OF RELIGION

Religion being equivalent to the present-day idea of nationality, such a change was considered as we would consider a change of nationality. The main conflicts created by such a change in the citizen's civil status were the following:

CIVIL LAW

If two dhimmīs were married according to their law without witnesses and then accepted Islam, their marriage remained valid although Islamic law required two witnesses.[27]

If the dhimmī husband only was converted to Islam and his wife remained a Christian or a Jewess, their marriage remained valid since no rule of Islamic law prevented a Muslim from marrying a Christian or a Jewess. The marriage would not have remained valid had the wife been a Zoroastrian, for a Muslim was forbidden to marry a Zoroastrian. In that case, the wife had a month in which to decide whether she wanted to adopt Islam or not. If she remained a Zoroastrian, the matrimonial bond was severed. If a polygamous pagan (idolater) was converted to Islam and had more than four wives, his marriages with the first four wives remained legal while those with the remaining wives were annulled.[28]

When the wife alone was converted to Islam, a distinction was made as to whether the marriage had or had not been consum-

[25] A Girault, *Principes de legislation coloniale,* Vol. IV, p. 357, and Morand, *op. cit.,* p. 335.

[26] *Fatāwa al-Hindiyya,* Vol. II, p. 359.

[27] This is admitted in Ḥanafī law as well as in Mālikī or Shāfi'ī law. For the Ḥanafī doctrine, see *ibid.,* Vol. I, p. 360.

[28] *Ibid.,* Vol. I, p. 365.

mated. According to the Mālikīs, a marriage which had not been consummated was considered dissolved automatically since a Muslim woman could not be married to a nonbeliever. A marriage which had been consummated was dissolved if the husband refused to adopt Islam, but in contrast to the first case, he retained the mahr.[29] In Ḥanafī doctrine, a dhimmī whose wife had become a Muslim was given three months (three menstruation periods) to become a Muslim. If he refused to do so, their marriage was dissolved.[30]

A dhimmī was not permitted to marry a Muslim woman and such a marriage was dissolved even if the dhimmī later became a convert to Islam. The law of contracts being applicable to marriage, the contract of marriage was considered null and void and a later event could not validate it. If a Muslim husband and his Christian wife both wanted to be converted to Judaism, their marriage was dissolved. According to Ḥanafī authors, this did not happen if the wife alone has converted, since a Muslim was permitted to marry a Jewess.[31]

A nonbeliever could not inherit from a Muslim because of the Qur'ānic rule: "God will by no means make a way for the unbelievers over the believers."[32] The Qur'ānic stipulation was reinforced by a ḥadīth of the Prophet, saying: "The Muslim will not inherit from the unbeliever nor the unbeliever from the Muslim."

An unbeliever who adopted Islam after the succession was opened could not inherit from the believer, for his capacity to inherit had to exist at the time of the decedent's death. This is why Ibn 'Āṣim ruled that the unbeliever and the slave could not inherit even if their condition changed after the decedent's death (i.e., if the unbeliever became a Muslim or the slave was given his freedom).

What was the effect of the conversion to Islam of a non-Muslim heir after the death of the testator, but before the partition of the property? The majority opinion holds that the moment of death is decisive in such a case. If on the day of the Muslim's death the potential heir was not a Muslim, he would not inherit from his father who died a Muslim. No importance was attached to a conversion which occurred after the death of the decedent. Another group of jurists believed that the time of the division of

[29] Mālik, *al-Muwaṭṭa'*, Vol. III, p. 69.
[30] *Fatāwa al-Hindiyya*, Vol. I, p. 360.
[31] *Ibid.*, Vol. I, p. 362.
[32] Q. IV, 140.

the estate should govern. If, at that time, the potential heir had become a Muslim, he could inherit his father's estate. This solution, though not a very judicial one, is attributed to Caliph 'Umar Ibn al-Khaṭṭāb.[33]

Unless the obligations assumed are contrary to Islamic law, contracts entered into before conversion to Islam are valid because in principle dhimmīs have the legal capacity to enter into contracts. Since interest is forbidden by Islamic law, a stipulation of interest becomes invalid if the creditor adopts Islam. Thereafter, he is entitled to the principal only. A contract of loan with interest concluded between two unbelievers, although valid under their own law, becomes void if they are converted to Islam.

The Ḥanafī jurists' interpretation of the effects of a conversion to Islam upon a contract of sale vary according to the circumstances. It is well known that any transaction involving wine is forbidden by Islamic law. When, for example, a house is sold by a dhimmī to another dhimmī (a Christian to another Christian) against the delivery of a certain quantity of wine, the agreement is legal. If one of the contracting parties is converted to Islam, one must distinguish between two situations. Conversion after the delivery of the wine and before the delivery of the house does not affect the transaction. On the contrary, conversion after the delivery of the house, but before the stipulated delivery of the wine, renders the sale void. This difference in treatment is probably due to the fact that in the first case the delivery of wine took place before conversion to Islam, while in the second case a Muslim could not be bound to participate in a transaction which his religion forbade.[34]

PENAL LAW

In contrast to the application of certain principles in matters of civil law, the law applicable to an offense is the one which governed the offender at the time the offense was committed. A subsequent event, such as his conversion, cannot impose on him the law of his new creed.[35] Sidī al-Khalīl stated that even though a Christian declared that he became a Muslim before any sentence determined by his former law (in case of murder, theft, slander, or assault) had been pronounced, the sentence had to be pronounced.[36] This solution seems to have been inspired by an ad-

[33] Ibn Rushd, *op. cit.*, Vol. II, p. 302.
[34] *Fatāwa al-Hindiyya,* Vol. V, p. 217.
[35] Sahnūn, *op. cit.*, Vol. XVI, p. 170.
[36] Khalīl, *op. cit.*, Vol. VI, p. 24.

vanced legal technique which uses the principle of nonretroactivity of law. It appears to have been due to general legal considerations rather than the more restricted aim of preventing persons from changing their religion to mitigate their punishment. Otherwise, one cannot understand why the jurists found it necessary to apply the Muslim law to a believer guilty of an offense against another believer who later denied his faith. Islamic law applied Qur'ānic punishments in case of offenses against believers only, giving lighter punishments to those guilty of offenses against unbelievers.

This line of argument prevailed only if the offense (committed by an unbeliever prior to his conversion) was by its nature detrimental to others, such as murder, theft, slander, and assault. Sidī al-Khalīl said that there is a human right involved calling for compensation which is incumbent even upon a Muslim.

In case of an offense of a religious character, such as fornication or illegal cohabitation, which implied some compensation to God, the penalty could be commuted or set aside.[37] The offender was held responsible according to his own creed; when he lost his former belief and became a Muslim, the punishment provided by his own creed was set aside or softened.

CONFLICTS RESULTING FROM A MUSTA'MIN'S RETURN TO AN ENEMY COUNTRY

If a musta'min, that is, a foreigner granted a safe-conduct, returns to the land of war (dār al-ḥarb), his legal status changes. Instead of being a musta'min with full exercise of the rights inherent in this condition, he becomes again a ḥarbī, i.e., an enemy. What effects does this change of status have on acts he performed in dār al-Islam? If he died in dār al-ḥarb, what happens to his estate and what law is applied to the succession?

When a musta'min, who was the creditor of a Muslim or a dhimmī, or had left a deposit with one of them, returned to the dār al-ḥarb, he lost the status of musta'min, his claim was extinguished and, according to Shaybānī and Abū Ḥanīfa, the deposit was considered as war booty to be divided among the warriors as provided in the Qur'ān. Abū Yūsuf, however, held that the deposit became of the depositary property because he had it in his possession, and therefore must be given preference over the warriors. According to some Ḥanafīs, if a musta'min secured a loan by his property in Islamic territory and later entered enemy territory,

[37] *Ibid.*, p. 29.

the property given as security passed into the creditor's ownership. Abū Yūsuf and Shaybānī, however, whose opinion was generally accepted, believed that the Muslim or dhimmī creditor had to sell the property given as security by the musta'min. From the proceeds he would first satisfy his own claim and the remainder, if any, would be given to the Muslims as booty.[38] The benefit arising from the safe-conduct is thus retroactively lost, and transactions entered into by the musta'min before the change of this legal status are thus affected by that change.

However, if the musta'min died (or, if the Muslims did not attack their enemies), the musta'min's heirs can benefit from his property; they can institute actions to recover debts owed to the musta'min or property given by him as security. Because the treatment imposed on the musta'min—the loss of his rights—is the punishment for his desertion from dār al-Islam, it is personal and does not apply to his heirs.

According to the Ḥanafī law as codified by Qadrī Pasha in Article 97 of his book,[39] the musta'min's return to his native country had no influence on the waqf he had established in Islamic territory. The property of a musta'min who dies in the territory of Islam reverts to the Muslim Treasury only if the deceased was a permanent resident and had no heir.[40]

CONFLICTS RESULTING FROM PARTIAL ADOPTION OF WESTERN CODES

The privileges given to the dhimmīs by the caliphs were maintained by Muḥammad II after the conquest of Constantinople in 1453. On the basis of this precedent, and realizing the advantages of a policy of appeasement, he respected the customs and habits of the population which was Orthodox Christian with a few Jews. The treatment of unbelievers, whether mild or cruel, was always humiliating; but the Ottoman Empire signed the treaty of Küchük-Kainarji (1774), in which the Ottoman Government promised to protect the Christian religion and its churches. Then came the Tanzīmāt period, the reform era, which opened in 1839 with the Imperial Decree of Gülhane. In this decree, Sultan Abd al-Majīd made a number of promises for reform which were only partially carried out, but were to be renewed and carried through by the Hatti-Humayun of 1856. This decree started with some

[38] Da'ud Effendi, *op. cit.*, p. 666.
[39] Qadrī Pasha, *op. cit.*, Art. 97.
[40] This principle was stated by Ibn Sarrāj; Wansharīsī, *op. cit.*, Vol. XII, p. 213.

very wise provisions, which guaranteed the non-Muslim communities the right to enjoy their traditional privileges, free exercise of their religion and the administration of their properties.

JURISDICTION

In the field of procedure, it was stipulated that commercial and criminal cases between Muslims and Christians, or between Christians of different communities, be judged by joint tribunals composed of Muslims and non-Muslims. Among the Christian Patriarchates, the most favored was the ecumenical one of Constantinople, to which special privileges were granted first.[41] These privileges were extended to other communities by means of a berat, i.e., the decree of investiture issued by the Sublime Porte to confirm the election of the religious leaders of a community.

Several imperial decrees, having the force of law, were issued in 1891 to define the extent of the judicial power of non-Muslim communities. The first of these (February 3, 1891) stated that matrimonial cases (including suits involving dowry, separation from bed and board, and divorce) were under the exclusive and compulsory jurisdiction of the patriarchates. No provisions were made for matters such as parent-children relationship, legal capacity, etc. It may be inferred, however, that this silence meant that the exclusive and compulsory jurisdiction of the patriarchates in these cases was to continue. So far as inheritance was concerned, the patriarchates did not have exclusive jurisdiction in cases involving wills unless the parties belonged to the same religious community, and their jurisdiction was optional in cases concerning intestate succession.[42] This system of communal jurisdiction was further developed in the successor states of the Ottoman Empire.

INHERITANCE

Under Ottoman rule, only personal property of a resident alien might be inherited by his relatives (in accordance with the law of his country). After 1867 an alien could own land, but could not inherit it from an Ottoman subject. He was disqualified because his usual residence was outside Islamic territory. This principle prevailed in Syria and Lebanon until the Lebanese law of June 18, 1929 and the Property Code promulgated by the High Commis-

[41] Van den Steen de Jehay, *La situation legale des sujets ottomans non-musulmans,* pp. 90 ff.

[42] S. Messina, *Traité de droit civil égyptien,* Vol. 3, pp. 135 ff.

sioner of Syria and Lebanon in 1930. Article 231 of the Code gave an alien the right to inherit immovable property (through testamentary or intestate succession), but only if the alien's country extended reciprocal rights to the Syrians and Lebanese.

Ikhtilāf al-dīn (difference of religion) continues to be a barrier because inheritance law has not been secularized. Consequently, it is important to determine which law of inheritance should be applied to the estate of a member of a non-Muslim community. The simple solution would be to decide an inheritance case in accordance with the law of the decedent's community, but in Syria—as in Egypt—the Christians have long followed the Islamic law of inheritance.

CHAPTER XV

International Law

IT HAS been observed throughout the various civilizations so far known to us that the population of each civilization, in the absence of a vital external threat, tended to develop within itself a community of political entities, that is, a "family of nations," rather than a single nation. This is indicated by the fact that there existed, or coexisted, several families of nations in such areas as the ancient Near East, Greece and Rome, China, Islam and Western Christendom where at least one distinct civilization had developed in each one of them. Within each civilization a body of rules and practices developed for the purpose of regulating the conduct of states in peace and war. "The mere fact of neighborly cohabitation," says Baron Korff, "creates moral and legal obligations, which in the course of time crystalize into a system of international law."[1] Even among primitive people such rules seem to have existed as part of the mores before they developed into a rational system among civilized groups.

Such systems of international rules and practices, however, were not truly *international,* in the modern sense of the term, since each system was primarily concerned with the relations within a limited area and within one (though often more than one) civilization and thus failed to be world-wide. Further, each system of international law was entirely exclusive since it did not recognize the principle of legal equality among nations which is inherent in the modern system of international law. It was for this very reason that there was no possibility of integrating one system with another. Though each freely borrowed from the others without acknowledgment, each system claimed an exclusive superiority over others. Consequently, each system of international law disappeared with the disappearance of the civilization (or civilizations) under which it flourished.

The rise of Islam, with its universal appeal to all people, inevitably raised for the Islamic State the problem as to how it would conduct its relations with the non-Islamic states and with the tol-

[1] Baron S. A. Korff, "An Introduction to the History of International Law," *American Journal of International Law,* Vol. XVIII (1924), p. 248.

erated religious communities within its territory. The jurist-theologians developed a special branch of the sharī'a, known as the siyar (based on the same sources as the sharī'a) which was the Law of Nations for the Muslims. In theory the siyar was designed to be only a temporary institution, until the Islamic State would correspond to the then known world, but failure to achieve this end inevitably rendered the siyar an elaborate and permanent part of Islamic law.

THEORIES

The modern law of nations presupposes the existence of a Family of Nations composed of a community of states enjoying full sovereign rights and equality of status. Islamic law recognizes no other nation than its own since the aim of Islam was the subordination of the whole world to one system of law and religion, to be enforced by the supreme authority of the caliph. Similar to Medieval Christian international law, the Islamic law of nations was based on the theory of a universal state. Both Christendom and Islam assumed mankind to constitute one community, bound by one law and governed by one ruler. The character of such a state is entirely exclusive; it does not recognize, by definition, the existence of a second world state. The aim of both these states was the proselytization of the whole of mankind. Their rules of foreign relations, accordingly, were the rules of an imperial state which would not grant an equal status to the other party (or parties) with whom it happened to fight or negotiate. It follows that the binding force of such a law of nations was not based on mutual consent or interest; it was merely a self-imposed system of law binding on its adherents, even though the rules often ran against their interests, because the sanction of the law was moral or religious.

In theory the Muslim world had to deal only temporarily with non-Islamic state communities, but the failure of Islam to convert the whole world made such dealings a permanent problem. The world accordingly was sharply divided, under Muslim law, into the dār al-Islam (abode of Islam) and the dār al-ḥarb (abode of war). The first corresponded to the areas under Islamic rule. Its inhabitants were Muslims, by birth or conversion, and all the people of the "tolerated" religions who preferred to remain Christians, Jews, Sabians, and Magians (Zoroastrians) at the sacrifice of paying a poll tax. The Muslims enjoyed full rights of "citizenship"; the members of the tolerated religions enjoyed only partial rights, and submitted to Muslim control in accordance with special rules regulating their relations with the Muslims.[2] The dār al-ḥarb consisted of all states and communities outside the World of Islam. Its inhabitants were often called infidels, or, more accurately, unbelievers.

On the assumption that the aim of Islam was the world, the dār al-Islam was always, in theory, at war with the dār al-ḥarb. The Muslims were required to preach Islam by persuasion, and the caliph, or his commanders in the field, to offer Islam as an alternative to paying the poll tax or fighting; but the Islamic state was under legal obligation to recognize no other authority than its own and to enforce Islamic law and supersede any other authority even though non-Islamic communities had willingly accepted the faith of Islam without fighting. Failure to accept Islam or the poll tax (jizya) by non-Muslims made it incumbent on the Islamic state to declare a jihād (holy war) upon the recalcitrant individuals and communities. Thus the jihād, as an alternative to paying the jizya, was the State's instrument of transforming the dār al-ḥarb into the dār al-Islam. But the jihād was not the only legal means of dealing with the unbelievers since peaceful methods (negotiation, arbitration, and treaty making) were applied in regulating the relations of the believers with unbelievers when actual fighting ceased. The Islamic law of nations was, accordingly, the product of the contact of an ever expanding state with its neighbors which led to the development of a body of rules and practices followed by the Muslims in war and peace. The mores followed by the Arabs before Islam in their intertribal warfare were regarded by Islam as too ungodly and brutal; thus Islam abolished all war except the jihād, and the jurist-theologians consciously formulated rules to subordinate all other considerations to *raison d'état* based on religous sanction.

NATURE AND SOURCES OF LAW

The Islamic law of nations, as part of the sharī'a, may be regarded as an effort to rationalize the relations of a society with the outside world in which chaos and conflict predominated. The aspiration was order. In the same way that natural law was regarded as the ideal legal order consisting of the general maxims of right and justice, so was Islamic law looked upon as the ideal system designed by God, the author of nature, for the Muslims. Man cannot make law, for the sharī'a, as a divine law, tolerates no other

[2] See section on the *dhimmīs,* below.

law than its own. Just as natural law exists in nature, to be discovered by reason, so the sharī'a, as an Islamic natural law, was revealed to, or "discovered" by, the Prophet Muḥammad. On the basis of Muḥammad's revelations and Traditions the law was later developed by the jurist-theologians who made use of analogy and consensus for the interpretation and elaboration, if not for the "discovery," of derivative laws. In theory the sole source of law is Allah, the head of the Islamic State, who alone is the fountain of right and justice. Man can only obey, and in his attempt to consummate his obedience to law he realizes his religious ideal. Divine law is infallible. It includes dogma as well as social and political rules, for in the Islamic State the religious and the political are not separate aspects of life. Law has the character of a religious obligation; at the same time it constitutes a political sanction of religion.

The divine law, it is held, existed in a complete heavenly book which was revealed piecemeal to the Prophet Muḥammad.[3] But this flow of divine legislation was not possible after Muḥammad's death, since the caliphs were not entitled to communicate with the Divine Legislator. The need for further legislation, however, was pressing as the Islamic State was rapidly expanding and new situations necessarily arose. New sources of law had to be used, if the state was to continue its relations with the outside world. The Muslim jurist-theologians undertook the matter and developed the so-called fiqh, or Muslim jurisprudence. The doctors of fiqh did not, in theory, make new law; they only developed a system which enabled them to deduce derivative laws from the Qur'ān, the sunna, and such other sources as analogy and consensus which were accepted by the various schools of law.[4] In the early conduct of the Islamic State opinions of the caliphs as well as their practices were often followed as rules of international law; but such rules were regarded valid as law only after they were sanctioned by tradition, analogy, or consensus.

Analyzed in terms of the modern law of nations, the sources of the Islamic law of nations conform to the categories defined by modern jurists and the statute of the International Court of Justice, namely, agreement, custom, reason, and authority. The Qur'ān represent the authoritative source of law; the sunna is equivalent to custom; rules expressed in treaties with non-Muslims fall in the category of agreement; and the opinions of the caliphs and jurists, based on legal deduction and analogy, may be

[3] Q. XVII, 107; LXXVI, 23; XLIII, 4.

[4] See Chap. IV, above.

regarded as reason. Such opinions, fatwas, or decisions had great influence in the development of the law.[5]

THE DOCTRINE OF THE JIHĀD

The popular idea in the West was that Islam attained its great success by violent means. The identification of Islam with violence was, perhaps, the result of comparing Islam with Christianity. This approach, needless to say, is quite erroneous, since Islam, in contrast to Christianity, combined both the religious and civil authority in the hands of the head of the state. It was natural therefore that violent as well as peaceful means were employed for the expansion of the Islamic State and for the spread of Islam.

War, however, was not introduced into Arabia by Islam. It was already in existence among the Arabs. But it was a tribal war. Its nature was peculiar to the existing social order. There were no organized political entities; the tribe (in certain instances, the clan) was the political unit. Wars, as such, were raids; mainly for robbery or vendetta. This state of affairs had, as observed by Ibn Khaldūn, developed among the Arabs a spirit of self-reliance, courage, and cooperation among the members of the single tribe. But these very traits intensified the character of warfare and hatred among the tribes and created a state of instability and unrest.

The importance of Islam lay in shifting the focus of attention of the tribes from their intertribal warfare to the outside world; Islam abolished all "wars" execpt the jihād, that is, the holy war in the "path of Allah"—war that would spread the belief in Allah and make His word supreme over the world.[6] Thus no war was legally permitted in Islam unless it was a war for a definite religious purpose. The jihād was a sanction against all those who failed to believe in Allah, and the Muslims were under legal obligations to punish them. In this sense, it represents in Muslim law what is known among Western jurists as *bellum justum.*

Nor was this all. The jihād, like the *jus fetiale,* had to be conducted according to certain specific rules in order to be just. The violation of these rules deprived the jihād of its religious sanction and entailed punishment by Allah or the imām whether in this world or the next.

In the first place, the jihād was a required duty of the whole Muslim community, binding the Muslims en masse rather than individually. If the jihād were accomplished, regardless of who

[5] See M. Ḥamīdullah, *Muslim Conduct of State* (Lahore, 1945), pp. 15 ff.

[6] Q. VI, 108; XXII, 77.

undertook the task of its accomplishment (but obviously only by those who were fit to fight), the duty was considered as fulfilled and those who performed it were rewarded; but if no Muslim would consecrate himself to it, then the whole Muslim community was in delict and liable for punishment.

Secondly, the jihād may be regarded as a doctrine of *permanent war*. If the objective of Islam was to achieve the universalism of a state and of a religion (at least as the Islamic creed was developed by the Muslim publicists), then the jihād naturally meant continuous "exertion of power" until the whole world was converted to Islam and constituted the Islamic State.[7] All the early jurist-theologians agreed, in principle, that the jihād was the normal condition in the conduct of the Islamic State, and that conditions of peace were only short intervals of recess. The Shāfi'ī school of law limited the interval of peace, if established by a treaty, to a maximum period of ten years.[8] The Ḥanafī school argued that suspension of the jihād was only possible when there was an urgent necessity, due to internal conflict or the overwhelming power of the enemy.

Thirdly, the jihād, though a doctrine of permanent war, did not necessarily mean continuous fighting. The objective of the jihād was not fighting per se, but the conversion of unbelievers to Islam. If means other than fighting were used (such as propaganda or persuasion) then the jihād duty was fulfilled. The essence of the doctrine was that the Muslims could not relax their effort to convert the unbelievers. The jihād, in this sense, meant a state of war rather than actual fighting. Later, publicists began to argue that the mere preparation for fighting would fulfill the jihād obligation.

The validity of the jihād (like that of the *jus fetiale*) depended on the observance of certain rules. The imām had to declare the jihād, to invite the unbelievers to adopt Islam before fighting began, and to agree to negotiations if they were requested by the enemy before actual fighting had taken place.[9]

[7] This is implied, for instance, in the following Qur'ānic verses: "fight [always] those infidels who are near to you and let them find in you hardness" (Q. IX, 123); and "slay the idolaters wherever you find them" (Q. IX, 5). There is also a ḥadīth to the same effect. The Prophet Muḥammad had declared, "I am ordered to fight idolaters until they say: 'there is no god but Allah.' "

[8] This rule is based on the precedent of the Hudaybiya peace treaty concluded by Muḥammad with the Meccans. See section on treaties, below.

[9] For details of these rules, see M. Khadduri, *Law of War and Peace in Islam* (London, 1941), Chap. VII,

THE LAW OF LAND WARFARE

The objective of the jihād, it will be recalled, was not fighting per se, but the prosyletization of unbelievers. Hence the general principle that unnecessary damage in life and property were to be avoided was stressed. In his address to the first expedition sent to the Syrian borders, Abū Bakr (d. 634), the aged first caliph said:

> Stop, O People, that I may give you ten rules to keep by heart. Do not commit treachery, nor depart from the right path. You must not mutilate, neither kill a child or aged man or woman. Do not destroy a palm tree, nor burn it with fire and do not cut any fruitful tree. You must not slay any of the flock or the herds or the camels, save for your subsistence. You are likely to pass by people who have devoted their lives to monastic services; leave them to that to which they devoted their lives. You are likely, likewise, to find people who will present to you meals of many kinds. You may eat; but do not forget to mention the name of Allah.[10]

The commander of the jihādists was permitted, once actual fighting began, to kill or capture enemy combatants, to besiege enemy cities, and to use all kinds of weapons such as mangonels (siege artillery) and incendiary materials which might bring a speedy capitulation of the enemy. Surprise attack, as well as night fighting, were permitted. Even such extreme measures as poisoning or cutting off water supplies were permitted by certain jurists.[11] Noncombatants might be killed in self-defense or accidentally during fighting, provided that they should not be killed treacherously and with mutilation. As a general rule, noncombatants, including women, children, and slaves, were excluded from molestation unless they took part in actual fighting. Non-Muslim spies were usually killed, but Muslim spies were subject to severe punishment and imprisonment until they were forgiven.

Prisoners of war were considered as part of the "spoils of war," and consequently were liable for molestation. The detailed treatment differed with the different schools of law. The Shāfi'ī school contended that the imām, if the prisoners did not adopt Islam, should follow one of four courses. He might order their immediate execution, he might condemn them to slavery, he might ask them to pay ransom (fidā'), or he might set them free without ransom. If the prisoners adopted Islam, they were safe from immediate execution and the imām might apply one of the other three

10 Ṭabarī, *Ta'rīkh,* ed. de Goeje (Leiden, 1890), Series I, Vol. IV, p. 1850.

11 Shaybānī, *al-Siyar al-Kabīr,* with Sarakhsī's commentary, (Hyderabad, A. H. 1335), Vol. III, p. 212.

rules. The Mālikī school restricts the treatment of prisoners to execution, slavery or ransom in persons or property. The Ḥanafī school reduces it to execution or slavery.

Finally, the imām might condemn the population of a conquered country to be slaves and be divided among the Muslim warriors as spoils of war if they did not accept Islam and the imām did not let them work and pay tribute. The Muslims had the liberty of employing the slaves any way they liked. If the slave were a woman, the Muslim might treat her as his concubine. Married slaves were usually not separated. The Muslim system of slavery, however, carried with it the possibility of emancipation. The master might give liberty to his slave either as an act of favor or by ransom.[12] Thus the slaves were not condemned to live permanently in slavery; they had a chance of obtaining liberty in their life-time at a time when the rules of slavery were far more rigid outside the Islamic world.[13]

THE SPOILS OF WAR

The expansion of Islam did not only enlarge the Muslim community by conversion, but also brought immense riches and wealth from the occupied dominions of Persia and Byzantium. To avoid quarrels among the warriors, the division of this property had to be regulated and rules were provided based in the main on the Qur'ānic revelations and the precedents established by the Prophet Muḥammad. The spoils of war, including movable and immovable property, were either acquired by force as ghanīma or acquired without fighting as fa'y.

PROPERTY

The rule for the division of property acquired by force was established after the battle of Badr when a Qur'ānic verse was revealed to this effect:[14] ". . . When you have taken any booty, one-fifth belongs to Allah and to the Apostle, and to the near kin, and to orphans, and to the poor, and to the wayfarer. . . ."[15] The other four-fifths were to be divided among the jihādists.

The one-fifth share may be regarded as the share of the State.

[12] Q. XLVII, 4; LC, 13.

[13] See M. Ḥamīdullah, *op. cit.*, pp. 195 ff.

[14] Before Islam the custom among the Arabs was to assign one-fourth of the booty to the chief. Muḥammad tried at first to have free choice to divide the spoil among the believers, but this led to quarrels which led to the above Qur'ānic revelation.

[15] Q. VIII, 41.

But its expenditure led to serious differences of opinion. The Shāfi'ī school maintained that the one-fifth share should be divided into five parts in accordance with the Qur'ānic verse, *i.e.*, one part for Allah and the Apostle, the second for the near kin, the third for orphans, the fourth for the poor, and the fifth for the wayfarer.[16] There was difference of opinion also as to the treatment of the share of "Allah and the Apostle" after the death of Muḥammad. One point of view was to redistribute this share among the other recipients; others argued that it should be given to the imām (caliph);[17] still others held that it should be spent on preparation for the jihād. The Ḥanbalī school maintained that the one-fifth share should be divided into four parts. The clause concerning Allah is only a "prelude" to the other parts and as such should not be counted. The rest of the parts are the Apostle and his kin, the poor, the orphans, and the wayfarer. The Ḥanafī school held that the one-fifth share should be divided into three parts only, for the death of Muḥammad had rendered the clauses concerning his share and that of the kin obsolete. The division should be therefore among the orphans, poor, and the wayfarer. The Mālikī school argued that the one-fifth share should be divided evenly among the poor and the rich of the Muslim community.

The four-fifths share is divided among the warriors who were in the field in such a way as to assign two parts to the horseman and one to the foot soldier, according to Abū Ḥanīfa; or three parts to the horseman and one to the foot soldier, according to Shāfi'ī and Abū Yūsuf.

The imām had the authority of increasing the share of a warrior by the so-called power of tanfīl (supererogation), that is, promising larger share before the battle; but this was only a temporary measure which the imām might follow or omit at his own discretion.[18]

Finally, restored property of Muslims which had been appropriated by non-Muslims was treated according to one of the following rules. First, according to Shāfi'ī, such property was to be given to its original owner. Secondly, according to a view ascribed to 'Alī, the fourth caliph, it was to be treated as part of the spoils of war. Thirdly, if the restored property was claimed after its di-

[16] Shāfi'ī, *Kitāb al-Umm* (Cairo, A. H. 1321), Vol. IV, p. 64.

[17] This view was based on the ḥadīth that "whenever Allah has rewarded His Apostle, it would be to his successors after his death."

[18] While the jurists never questioned this power of the imām, they differed as to the source and the quantity to be given. See Shāfi'ī, *op. cit.*, Vol. IV, p. 68; Shaybānī, *op. cit.*, Vol. IV, p. 20.

vision as part of the spoils, the owner lost his right; if he claimed it before the division, he could regain it. Fourthly, if the restored property had been seized by the non-Muslims by force, the original owner could only regain it before the division of the spoils; if the restored property had been taken by the non-Muslims without force, the original owner could regain it before or after the division of the spoils.

LAND

Immovable property acquired by force was treated differently according to the different schools of law. The Shāfi'ī school regarded land as part of the *ghanīma,* and as such to be divided among the jihādists unless they declined to take it and allowed it to become state land. The Ḥanafī school held that the imām had free choice to divide the land among the jihādists, to regard it as state land, or to let its inhabitants retain ownership, provided they paid the kharāj (land tax). The Mālikī school insisted that conquered land should be public property owned by the state, and its products part of the state revenue.

TERMINATION OF FIGHTING

The Muslim jurists are silent regarding the termination of the jihād on the assumption that this was a doctrine of permanent war; but they are also silent about an unsuccessful war with the enemy. The caliph is advised by al-Māwardī to have constant patience for the continuation of fighting until he wins a victory however long it may take him to reach that end.[19] If the caliph were forced to make peace with the enemy, such peace had to be regarded—by its very nature—a truce until he felt strong enough to resume fighting. The truce should not last longer than the Hudaybiya treaty, but if the caliph felt that he was unable to resume fighting, the truce might be renewed for a similar period.[20]

To sum up, the following may be regarded as the chief methods by which fighting was terminated:

First, by complete surrender of the enemy forces without conditions ('anwatan).

Secondly, by a treaty of peace. The Muslim commanders, on behalf of the caliph, concluded peace treaties by virtue of which the people of the conquered territories were guaranteed their lives, property, and religion, if they accepted the status of dhimmīs and

19 Māwardī, *Kitāb al-Aḥkām al-Sultāniyya,* ed. Enger (Bonn, 1853), p. 81.
20 Ṭabarī, *Kitāb al-Jihād,* ed. J. Schacht (Leiden, 1933), p. 15.

paid the jizya, or by concluding treaties of peace for the suspension of fighting which could not exceed, in theory, a period of ten years. In the latter case the caliph might even agree to pay tribute to the non-Muslim rulers in order to avoid their attack, as was the case of Mu'āwiya and 'Abd al-Malik. Under Harūn al-Rashīd war was terminated with the Byzantines by concluding treaties of peace which stipulated that the Byzantine emperor should pay annual tribute; but when the 'Abbāsid caliphs became weak the situation was reversed and the caliphs were required to pay the tribute.

Thirdly, by arbitration, which was used for avoiding war as well as for terminating fighting. This method will be discussed later under the law of peace.

THE LAW OF PEACE

The doctrine of the jihād presupposed the condition of war as normal between the Islamic State and the outside world. But this war condition, in theory, was only temporary until the whole world be transformed into the Islamic state. We may argue therefore that war was not considered a permanent condition in the Islamic society, but merely a means to achieve ultimate peace under Islam. If that end was ever achieved, the *raison d'être* of the jihād would come to an end.

The impossibility of universalizing Islam and the failure to set up a world state divided the world into the *world of Islam* and the *world of war*. It is true that this division, in Muslim theory, was only transitory; yet in practice it persisted throughout the life of the Islamic State. The relations between these two worlds were normally unpeaceful; each world was legally at war with the other. But this state of war should not be construed as a state of actual hostilities, for the Muslims concluded treaties of peace with the enemies on more than one occasion. This state of war was rather in practice equivalent to what is termed "nonrecognition," that is, the incapacity of the world of war to possess a legal status under Muslim law so long as it lacked the essential elements of the true faith. This nonrecognition did not imply, as in modern international law, the impossibility of concluding treaties or initiating official relations, for such actions were not considered to imply equality between the two contracting parties,[21] and were only temporary.

This state of affairs induced a few jurists, especially the Shāfi'īs, to devise a third "temporary" division of the world called dār al-

[21] See section on treaties, below.

ṣulḥ (world of peace) or dār al-'ahd (world of covenant).[22] Its relations with the world of Islam were defined by treaties of peace which were never, in theory, to last long. Other jurists, however, especially the Ḥanafīs, never recognized the existence of a third division of the world. Abū Ḥanīfa argued that if the inhabitants of a territory concluded a treaty of peace (and agreed to pay the *jizya*) they were considered as dhimmīs and their territory as part of the world of Islam since otherwise it would be a part of the world of war. Peace accordingly was not a definite term to mean entirely normal relations under Muslim law. Certain Qur'ānic rules, it is true, emphasize the tendency towards peace, but the jurists' interpretations do not stress this tendency and they even hold that the imām should not resort to peace unless he were under necessity.

JURISDICTION

The jurisdiction of the Islamic State is derived from the binding force of the sacred law upon individual Muslims as well as things acquired by Muslims. Since the concept of territorial sovereignty had not yet developed under Muslim law and since the Muslims were bound by the law regardless of the country or the territory they resided in, it follows, at least in Muslim legal theory, that the jurisdiction of the Islamic State would extend to Muslims, regardless of their place of residence. Conversely, a non-Muslim was not bound by the sacred law except in his relations with the Islamic community (for example, paying the jizya, respecting things Islamic, and doing no harm to Islamic interests). The jurisdiction of the Islamic State, accordingly, was limited, even within the territory of the Islamic State, since the character of the sacred law was and still is personal rather than territorial, and the non-Muslims, either as aliens who happened to reside temporarily in the dār al-Islam or permanently as dhimmīs, were not bound by all the provisions of the law. In their own personal behavior or their intergroup relations, they were bound only by their own religious laws as individuals or groups; in their relations with Muslims or in matters connected with the State, they were governed by Muslim law. The sharī'a, accordingly, provided rules for non-Muslims residing in the Islamic State only insofar as it governed their relations with Islam, but it did not require them to conform to the Muslim way of life while they resided among the Muslims. The law regulating prayer, marriage, divorce, and inheritance (not even

[22] Shāfi'ī, *op. cit.*, Vol. IV, pp. 103-104.

all the taxes paid to the State) were not binding upon non-Muslims, unless they chose to conform to them, since Islam provided special rules for their relations with non-Muslims if they resided in the Islamic State.

NON-MUSLIMS IN THE ISLAMIC STATE: THE MUSTA'MIN

Non-Muslims may be permitted to stay in the dominions of Islam in the capacity of dhimmīs, by virtue of a treaty, or as *musta'mins* by obtaining amān, that is, a pledge of security or safe-conduct.

The amān may be secured in one of two ways, either from the imām or from one of his representatives or from individual Muslims. The first, which may be called an official amān, is done by concluding a treaty of peace or a truce by the terms of which the non-Muslims agreed to pay a sum of money or commodities in lieu of getting safe-conduct to live in the world of Islam unmolested for a period not to exceed a year.[23] If this time limit was exceeded, the must'amins were considered dhimmīs and had to pay the jizya. If the amān proved to be harmful to the interests of Islam, the imām might repudiate it. This was done either because the must'amins abused the privileges given to them or because the imām discovered that the grant of the amān was inconsistent with the interests of Islam.

The unofficial amān could be given by any adult Muslim, free or slave, a man or a woman, to a non-Muslim. Children and insane persons were not permitted to grant amāns; and the dhimmīs, who were not, strictly speaking, full "citizens" of the Islamic State, were also denied right.[24]

The procedure of granting the amān was very simple; it was enough, for instance, when a non-Muslim was told that he was safe, this being equivalent to the grant of amān. Even a sign or a hint was enough to confer such a privilege. The musta'min, however, must not be a spy and must not enter the world of Islam with the intention of helping his people or government; if his intentions were known to be such, he was liable to be killed.[25] On the other hand, if the musta'min killed a Muslim, acted as a marauder, or

[23] Mālik reports a case where a commander in the army had given an amān to a non-Muslim and then killed him. Caliph 'Umar disliked the action and called the attention of the commander to live up to his pledge of amān. See Mālik, *al-Muwaṭṭa'* (Cairo, 1339), Vol. I, pp. 249-50.

[24] Shāfi'ī, *op. cit.*, p. 196; and Saḥnūn, *al-Mudawwana al-Kubra,* Vol. I, p. 401.

[25] Abū Yūsuf, *Kitāb al-Kharāj,* p. 117.

entered into sexual intercourse with a Muslim woman (which is not permitted by the sacred law) or a dhimmī woman, he was not considered to have violated the amān, though he was liable for punishment for violating the law.[26] Because the Islamic State, in a permanent state of war, would not permit the exportation of military supplies to the enemy,[27] the musta'min was not permitted to carry back to his country implements of war or goods or slaves valuable for war purposes. If he had paid for them, he was to be given back his money. He was permitted to conduct business transactions and to buy or sell commodities, but never those which were prohibited by Islam, such as liquor or pork. Usury contracts were also prohibited.

If the non-Muslim entered the world of Islam without an amān, or was unable to secure one, he was killed unless he adopted Islam. The Shāfi'ī school permitted him a period of four months to leave the Islamic State, pay the jizya as a dhimmī, or adopt Islam.[28] If the musta'min died in the Islamic State leaving his property there, the amān granted was valid for his property too, and his heirs could take it from the Islamic State. But if the musta'min went back to his country and died, leaving his property in the Islamic State, the property could not be taken from the Islamic State by his heirs since the amān expired with the departure of the musta'min.[29] The imām might repudiate any amān given to a non-Muslim and might even punish the Muslim who gave it, if he discovered that it was inconsistent with the interests of Islam.

NON-MUSLIMS IN THE ISLAMIC STATE: THE DHIMMĪS

The Jews, Christians, Zoroastrians, and Sabians, who failed to adopt Islam after the Muslim conquest and preferred to maintain their religious beliefs by accepting certain disabilities imposed upon them, were not considered unbelievers because they shared the Muslims' belief in Allah. But they were not regarded as true believers because they failed to believe in the Qur'ān and the Prophet Muḥammad. Consequently, in the words of Hughes, they were "not guilty of an absolute denial, but only of a partial perversion of the truth; [therefore] only part of the punishment for disbelief is due."[30] These scripturaries, or ahl al-kitāb (People of

26 *Ibid.*, p. 117.
27 Abū Yūsuf, *op. cit.*, pp. 116-117.
28 Shāfi'ī, *op. cit.*, p. 201.
29 *Ibid.*, p. 191.
30 T. P. Hughes, *A Dictionary of Islam* (New York, 1885), p. 710.

the Book), were allowed to live in the Islamic State unmolested on the condition that they paid the poll tax and accepted the status defined by treaties or charters issued to them by the Muslim authorities. The rules governing the relations between the Muslims and the dhimmīs were partly derived from the Qur'ān and ḥadīth and partly from local traditions and practices which the Muslim jurists later expounded as part of the sacred law. The following may be regarded as the fundamental terms defining the status of the dhimmīs:

(1) The Muslims guarantee the security of lives, property, churches, and religious rites of the dhimmīs.

(2) Every male, adult, free and sane dhimmī was required to pay the jizya (poll tax), the amount of which was to be fixed by agreement.[31] The jizya, an Aramaic word, was partly paid as "a punishment for their infidelity," but mainly for the protection they received from the Muslims.[32] The refusal to pay the jizya was not construed, from a strictly legal point of view, as a breach of the obligation. The significance of the jizya is not the payment of the tax per se, but the acceptance of the status of the dhimmī, which, in turn, leads to the requirement of paying the tax. The jizya was lifted when the dhimmī accepted Islam.

(3) The dhimmī was required, likewise, to pay the kharāj for the land. If the land were taken by the state the dhimmī might remain to till the land and pay the kharāj.[33]

(4) The dhimmī was required not to show disrespect to the Prophet, discredit the Qur'ān, or attack the religion of Islam.

(5) A dhimmī was not permitted to marry a Muslim woman, nor enter into sexual connection with her. A Muslim, however, could marry a dhimmī woman.

(6) The dhimmī was not allowed to help non-Muslims against Muslims nor give refuge to them.

(7) The dhimmīs were not allowed to build new churches nor pray or ring their church bells loudly. Likewise, they were not supposed to show their crosses, drink wine, or eat pork in public.

[31] Q. IX, 29. Women, children, slaves and the poor were exempted. See Māwardī, *op. cit.*, p. 137; C. H. Becker, "Djizyah," *Encyclopedia of Islam*, Vol. I, pp. 1051-1052; and D. C. Dennett, *Conversion and the Poll Tax in Early Islam* (Cambridge, Mass., 1950).

[32] Saḥnūn, Vol. I, pp. 394-395; and Ibn Rushd, *Al-Muqaddimāt al-Mumahhidāt* (Cairo, A. H. 1325), Vol. I, p. 279. The dhimmīs were exempt from military service if they paid the poll tax, but (as in the case of certain Christian tribes) if they fought as allies with the Muslims, they were exempted. See T. W. Arnold, *The Preaching of Islam* (London, 3rd ed., 1938), pp. 60-62.

[33] Balādhurī, *Kitāb Futūḥ al-Buldān*, ed. de Goeje (Leiden, 1866), pp. 447-448.

(8) Dhimmī houses should be built no higher than those of the Muslims, if not lower.

(9) The dhimmī was required to distinguish himself from a Muslim in dress by wearing a zinnār (belt) and a colored turban, and could not ride on horseback nor carry weapons. He was allowed to ride on donkeys or mules, distinguishing them by hanging a wooden ball on the saddle.

(10 The dhimmīs, on certain occasions, were required to serve as hosts to Muslim officials or travelers who passed through their community for a limited time.[34]

The foregoing conditions, though they hardly left any respectable position for the dhimmīs, were often ignored or violated by both sides. The Umayyad caliphs were probably more lenient towards their Christian subjects, while some of the 'Abbāsid caliphs, like al-Manṣūr and al-Mutawakkil, restricted their activities.[35] But the dhimmī communities were, on the whole, tolerably treated in a time when religious differences were taken more seriously by other peoples. The dhimmīs were granted a sort of self-rule, each community was left to be governed by its religious head who was responsible to the Muslim ruler. Thus the dhimmīs were not full citizens of the Islamic State, since they were not bound by all the Islamic (municipal) law but were subject to their own canon laws.

TREATIES

The treaty-making power in Islam rested in the hands of the head of the State who, as the person charged with the duties of prosecuting the jihād, was *ipso facto* the ultimate authority who would decide when the jihād was to be relaxed and a peace treaty signed. This power was often delegated to the commanders in the field. During the early Muslim conquests, they were empowered to negotiate treaties with the inhabitants of the occupied territories regarding their paying the jizya as an alternative to acceptance of Islam.

While the Muslim jurists did not stress the tendency towards establishing peaceful relations with their enemies, the caliphs in practice were often forced to come to terms with them, justifying their action by the force of "necessity" and by the precedent established by the Prophet Muḥammad in coming to terms with the non-Muslims of Mecca.

[34] The Christians of Najrān were required to accept a maximum period of a month, while the Christians of Damascus were required only three days. *Ibid.*, p. 64 (Hitti's translation, pp. 98-99).

[35] See A. S. Tritton, *The Caliphs and Their Non-Muslim Subjects* (Oxford, 1930).

The model treaty which later the caliphs and the jurists often cited from the Prophet's tradition is the so-called Hudaybiya treaty which, in its form, procedure of negotiation, and duration, supplied a precedent (if not indeed a source for the law of treaty-making) which was followed by the Muslims.

After a bitter struggle between the Prophet in Medina and the stubborn pagan Arabs of Mecca (e.g., Quraysh) who resisted his mission, the two parties were ready for peace. For Muḥammad such a peace was necessary, even though by no means permanent, to accomplish the pilgrimage to Mecca. He sent 'Uthmān, the future third caliph, to carry the peace message of Muḥammad to the people of Mecca. The Meccans accepted and sent Suhayl, their representative, to negotiate a peace treaty. 'Alī, the future fourth caliph, acted as a secretary, while a number of persons from both sides were brought who swore to observe the terms of the treaty. The text of the treaty follows:[36]

> In your name, O Allah;
>
> This is what Muḥammad ibn 'Abdullah has agreed upon peacefully with Suhayl ibn 'Amr;
>
> They agreed peacefully to postpone war for a period of ten years. People shall be secured and guaranteed [from attack] by each other;
>
> If anyone from the Quraysh wishes to join Muḥammad without authorization of his walī [protector] he should be sent back; if any one of Muḥammad's followers wishes to join Quraysh, he will not be refused;
>
> Unbecoming acts between each of us are prohibited; and that there should not be between us defection, nor treason;
>
> Those [people] who want to join Muḥammad's alliance and his pact may do so; those who want to join Quraysh's alliance and its pact may do so.

This treaty, which stipulated that the duration of peace was to last for ten years, supplied a precedent for the jurists that no peace treaty with the enemies should last longer than that. But its violation within less than two years renewed hostilities and offered the Muslims justification for taking Mecca by force. The reason for the violation was the attack of Quraysh on Muḥammad's adherents. Negotiations were conducted to resume peaceful relations but to no avail since the Muslims disliked the violation of the treaty. The Meccans, it seems, were very weak at this time and Muḥammad captured the city without difficulty.[37]

[36] Ibn Hishām, *Sirat Sayyiduna Muḥammad,* ed. by Wüstenfeld (Göttingen, 1858-1860), Vol. II, pp. 747-748. For an English translation of the text, see M. Khadduri, *op. cit.,* p. 89.

[37] This explains why the Shāfi'ī school considered the taking of Mecca by peace, and the Ḥanafī school by force.

The treaties which the Prophet Muḥammad concluded with the non-Muslims were models which the caliphs followed after his death. With the exception of those treaties which the caliphs (or their representatives) had concluded with the peoples of the occupied territories, all Muslim treaties were concluded for a limited period to fulfill certain specific functions. The Umayyad caliphs often concluded peace treaties with the Byzantines in order to avoid war with them, and some of these treaties, like those which Mu'āwiya I and 'Abd al-Malik had concluded, were unfavorable treaties which required the Muslims to pay tribute during the time when there was civil war within the Islamic State. The 'Abbāsid caliphs concluded similar treaties in which either the Byzantine Emperors paid tribute to the caliphs or vice-versa.[38] Further, the 'Abbāsids and Byzantines often concluded fidā' (ransom) treaties for the purpose of releasing prisoners of war by paying a certain amount of revenue for the state treasury. It also made it possible to save the lives of thousands of warriors who would otherwise have been killed.[39]

Once a treaty had been signed by the Muslims, though the Muslims were reluctant to come to terms with the non-Muslims, the terms of the treaty were strictly observed. This is urged not only by the Qur'ānic injunctions, but also by the ḥadīths and supported by practice. The Qur'ān urges the Muslims "not to break oaths after making them,"[40] and if the non-Muslims did not break them, then "fulfill their agreement to the end of their term."[41]

The following may be regarded as general characteristics of the treaties which the Muslims concluded with the non-Muslims:

(1) The texts of the treaties were, on the whole, brief and general. The phraseology was simple and even, at times, vague due to the brevity of the text. The content of the treaties dealt with certain specific issues rather than principles of law.

(2) The form of the treaties was simple; it included the preamble, the content of the treaty, and ended by stating the names of the witnesses who swore to observe its terms. The preamble consisted of the so-called basmala (i.e., the name of Allah, etc.) and the names of the representatives of the two parties.

(3) The terms of the Muslim treaties we possess, as reported by the Muslim publicists, show in most of the cases that they were

[38] See further details in Khadduri, *op. cit.*, pp. 95-96.

[39] For an interesting example of a *fidā'* treaty signed in 811 during the reign of Harūn al-Rashīd, see Ṭabarī, *op. cit.*, Series III, Vol. II, pp. 706-07.

[40] Q. XVI, 91.

[41] Q. IX, 4; III, 75-76.

pledges by one party to the other rather than contracts between equals. This is particularly true of the Muslim treaties with the people of occupied territories who agreed to live in the Muslim state. This is evidenced by the terms which demanded security of lives, property, and religion in lieu of submission of the people (the dhimmīs), and their payment of the jizya. Further, the treaties bore the names of the Muslim witnesses but not the names of the dhimmīs. This special type of treaty had the character of constitutional guarantees to the people of the annexed countries rather than an agreement between "independent" countries.

(4) The duration of a treaty was specified by Muslim jurists. The Shāfi'ī school held that a peace treaty with the enemy should not exceed the term of ten years, that is, the term of the Hudaybiya treaty which the Prophet Muḥammad concluded with the Meccans. The Ḥanafī and Mālikī schools maintained that the Hudaybiya peace did not last ten years and argued that no peace treaty should last for more than three or four years. (The treaties with the dhimmīs, which were in the nature of "charters" to guarantee their rights so long as they resided in the Islamic State, were indefinite.)

(5) Finally, the system of taking human rahā'in (hostages) to insure the sanctity of treaties was followed by the Muslims. If the treaty were violated, however, the Muslims did not kill the hostages. If the Muslims started the war, the hostages were sent back home, but if war was started by the other party, then the hostages were kept.[42]

ARBITRATIONS

Arbitration was practiced among the Arabs before Islam. The Prophet Muḥammad respected this tradition and himself acted as an arbitrator. The Qur'ān refers to arbitrations in the following verse:[43]

> O you who believe! Obey Allah, and the Apostle and those in authority among you; if you differ, bring it before Allah and the Apostle, if you believe in Allah and in the last day.

Probably the most notable case of arbitration to be found in Muslim annals is the arbitration between 'Alī (A.D. 565-661) the fourth caliph, and Mu'āwiya, the governor of Syria, to end civil war. Though this case was used by Mu'āwiya as a political device to escape military defeat, yet the way the case was handled reflects

[42] Māwardī, *op. cit.*, pp. 84-85.
[43] Q. IV, 59.

the nature and procedure of arbitration as then conceived by the Muslims.

The appeal to arbitration was demanded by Mu'āwiya, on behalf of the Syrians, who were fighting the caliph's forces in 'Iraq. The astute 'Amr ibn al-'Āṣṣ, commander of the Syrian army, demanded appeal to the rules of the Qur'ān as the basis of the arbitration between the two contending parties. 'Alī, the caliph, who was anxious to end the civil war by attaining military victory, was aware of the trick, but could not turn down an appeal to the Qur'ān as an arbiter between him and his opponent.

The two parties agreed to appoint arbitrators who met at Adhruḥ in A.D. 658 and were given full powers to discuss and give a decision on the basis of the Qur'ān and sunna within a period not to exceed one year.[44] Mu'āwiya appointed 'Amr, and 'Alī appointed Abū Mūsa al-Ash'arī. The two arbitrators met and drew up a draft treaty for a truce which was to last one year and which stated that the Qur'ān and the sunna were to be the legal bases of arbitration. The text of the treaty follows:

> In the name of Allah, the Compassionate, the Merciful;
>
> This is what is agreed upon for arbitration, between 'Alī ibn Abī-Ṭālib and Mu'āwiya ibn Abī Sufyān. 'Alī represented the people of Kūfa and their followers of the believers and Muslims; and Mu'āwiya represented Ash-Shām (Syria) and their followers of the believers and Muslims;
>
> We appeal to the arbitration of Allah and His Book; and that there is no other basis than this . . . and that the two arbitrators Abū Mūsa al-Ash'arī and 'Amr ibn al-'Āṣṣ will act on the basis of Allah's Book . . . and if nothing were to be found in Allah's Book, then the justiciable sunna would be the basis. . . .

The text of the treaty is obviously very brief and vague. It is entirely silent about the object of arbitration and the specific issues to be discussed. The only point mentioned is that the Qur'ān and sunna were to be the basis of arbitration. This brevity and vagueness gave 'Amr an excellent opportunity to ignore the original issue, and he shifted the discussion by addressing the following question to Abū Mūsa:

"Abū Mūsa, don't you agree [with me] that 'Uthmān [the late caliph] was assassinated unjustly?" Abū Mūsa replied in the affirmative.

'Amr then added: "Don't you agree that Mu'āwiya and his relatives are ['Uthmān's] heirs?" Abū Mūsa agreed to this.

'Amr then said that Allah has declared: ". . . whosoever shall

[44] For the full story of this case, see Ṭabarī, *op. cit.*, Series I, Vol. VI, pp. 332 ff.

be slain unjustly, to his heirs we have given authority; he shall not exceed the limits in slaying, and surely he is assisted" (Q. XVII, 32). "Why therefore," said 'Amr, "is not Mu'āwiya the heir of 'Uthmān?". "But," 'Amr continued, "if you fear that the people will complain that Mu'āwiya will rule without qualifications, then you may reply that Mu'āwiya is the heir of 'Uthmān [who was assassinated] unjustly . . . and that he is artful in politics and administration, and that he is the brother of Umm Ḥabība, the wife of the Prophet, and he was a companion of the Prophet. . . ." Abū Mūsa replied: "O 'Amr, be fearful of Allah . . . 'Alī ibn Abī-Ṭālib is more distinguished in Quraysh. . . ."

Discussion continued in this way. It dealt very little with ways and means to end the civil war, and was confined to determining who was the best fitted for a caliph. Abū Mūsa was inclined to nominate for the caliphate 'Abdullah ibn 'Umar (the son of the second caliph) and 'Amr supported Mu'āwiya. Finally, 'Amr addressed the following question to Abū Mūsa: "What is your opinion?" Abū Mūsa replied: "My opinion is to depose these two men and to leave the matter for popular election to the Muslims who will choose for themselves whom they like." 'Amr said: "My opinion is as yours."

The two arbitrators, having apparently reached an agreement, proceeded to announce officially their decision to the public. 'Amr politely asked Abū Mūsa, on the basis of seniority, to give the decision first. Abū Mūsa praised Allah and announced:

> O people! We have examined the matter of this nation and could not find a better solution . . . than to depose [both] 'Alī and Mu'āwiya, so that this nation will take the matter and entrust for rulership whom it would like. I have [decided] to depose [both] 'Alī and Mu'āwiya . . . and you may choose whom you consider is qualified. . . .

'Amr succeeded Abū Mūsa and declared, after he praised Allah, the following:

> You have listened to this man [Abū Mūsa] who had [decided] to depose his companion. I have [also decided] to depose his companion as he deposed him, [but] I confirm my companion Mu'āwiya, as he is the heir of 'Uthmān . . . and the best qualified for this position. . . .

This disagreement in the announcement of the decision naturally induced the 'Iraqi side to declare that the decision was not binding. 'Alī condemned the arbitrators on the grounds that they had

> left the rules of the Qur'ān behind them . . . and that each one had followed his own opinion without [taking into consideration] a standard.

Their decision [therefore] has no ground of evidence or precedent; and [moreover] they have disagreed on their decision. . . .

The nature of this arbitration was obviously not entirely legal. 'Amr tried to shift the discussion from a legalistic into a political issue. In this he was entirely successful because of Abū Mūsa's unawareness of the misleading procedure which they were following. Thus the political aspect of the arbitration decided the victory of the Syrians by causing dissension and confusion among the 'Iraqi army.

DIPLOMACY

Diplomacy existed in the Middle East before the rise of Islam, and the Prophet Muḥammad made use of it for the propagation of his religion in Arabia and elsewhere. Muslim chroniclers record the account of emissaries sent to Byzantium, Persia, Egypt, and Ethiopia. These emissaries, according to traditions, were provided with official letters and were instructed to address them to the heads of the states concerned. The identical phraseology of these letters raises the question as to the authenticity of these documents as well as the actual sending of these missions. Nonetheless the recording of the traditions about these emissaries, regardless of the historicity of the action, suggests the implicit acceptance of diplomacy as a principle of Muslim law of nations. The story goes that the Emperor of Ethiopia and the Governor of Egypt accepted Muḥammad's invitation to adopt Islam; the Byzantine Emperor replied that his nation was not of the opinion of accepting Islam; and the King of Persia tore up the letter and dismissed the emissaries. On learning the news about the Persian King, Muḥammad remarked, "His kingdom will be torn."[45]

In early Islam, especially during the life of Muḥammad, diplomatic relations were chiefly religious in character, but they became primarily political during the Umayyad and 'Abbāsid periods. The Muslim commanders conducted negotiations on behalf of their caliph during the wars of expansion for the purpose of extending invitation to Islam before fighting took place and for the conclusion of peace treaties. The Umayyad and 'Abbāsid caliphs entered into almost continuous diplomatic correspondence with the Byzantines for the negotiation of peace treaties, the payment of annual tributes, exchange of prisoners of war and payment of ransom as well as for the exchange of gifts. While commercial relations were

[45] See Ya'qūbī, *Tar'īkh*, ed. by M. Th. Houtsma (Leiden, 1883), Vol. II, p. 83; and Shāfi'ī, *op. cit.*, Vol. IV, p. 94.

privately conducted by Muslim individuals with the dār al-ḥarb, such contacts were not always encouraged by the caliphs or the jurists. Thus Mālik insisted that the Muslims should avoid as much as possible trade with the dār al-ḥarb, whether by land or sea.[46] Abū Yūsuf advised the caliph to permit the non-Muslims to trade with the Muslims, but not with forbidden goods or war materials.[47] Mālik shares opinion with Abū Yūsuf, but does not approve of Muslims going to the dār al-ḥarb for this purpose.[48]

The Muslims carefully respected the immunity of envoys and diplomatic missions. Non-Muslims were permitted to enter the dār al-Islam unmolested as official messengers,[49] even without securing amān, provided they declared that they were carrying diplomatic messages.[50] The rule of diplomatic immunity goes back to the time of the Prophet Muḥammad when two envoys were received from Musaylima, the so-called "liar Prophet," who, in spite of their unfavorable declarations to Muḥammad, were secured in their lives. This tradition was usually, though not always, observed by Muslim rulers.

CONCLUSION

The political ascendancy of Islam was followed by a period of stagnation and decline which was paralleled in the West by far-reaching development. Thus the Islamic international law was abandoned by the Islamic States when the European Powers, in their contact with the Islamic countries, gradually began to recognize these states and to conduct their foreign relations on the basis of Islamic law. This naturally meant that the European system of international law, which originally had developed as a European and Christian law, had to undergo certain changes in its character in order to include non-European and non-Christian countries. At the opening of the nineteenth century the European system had already changed in scope and nature to meet the new circumstances of the world. The emergence of the United States and the South American republics changed its scope from a regional to a world-wide system; the participation of the Ottoman Empire in the Concert of Europe and the emergence of Japan as a Great Power rendered it no longer Christian in character.

The development of the European system of international law

46 Ibn Rushd, *op. cit.*, Vol. II, p. 285.
47 Abū Yūsuf, *op. cit.*, p. 116.
48 Ibn Rushd, *op. cit.*, Vol. II, p. 287.
49 There is a ḥadīth to the effect that "messengers should never be killed."
50 Abū Yūsuf, *op. cit.*, p. 116.

from a continental into a world-wide system might have helped to integrate the various systems of the law of nations of Islam, India, and the Far East. But the disintegration of these Eastern societies had already gone too far to enable them to deal on a par with the European Powers. In the circumstances, the contact of Europe with the East, the domination of the latter by the former, helped to set in motion the slow but disruptive process of the Westernization movement—a movement which almost caused the destruction of the older legal systems of the East, including their traditional systems for the conduct of foreign relations.

The modern system of international law, however, is far from being complete or satisfactory to meet the needs of a rapidly changing World Community. Not only the last two World Wars, which have rendered the Law of War almost completely obsolete, but also the urgent need for an effective World Government require the further development of a truly worldwide international law. Further, the participation of Eastern and Islamic peoples in the new World Order has given these people an opportunity to make their influence felt in the development of modern international law. The Statute of the International Court of Justice permits the adoption of new maxims of law from the legal systems of "civilized nations." This possibility of using non-European sources of law opens the way for the Eastern and Islamic nations to make their contributions to the development of modern international law.

Glossary of Legal Terms

'abd: slave
'āda: custom
ahl al-bayt: family of the Prophet Muḥammad
ahl al-kitāb: see *dhimmīs*
ahliyya (kafā'a): legal capacity
'amal: practice, precedent
amān: pledge of security, safe-conduct
'aqd (pl. *'uqūd):* contract
'aql: intellect, reason
arāḍī amīriyya (mīrī): state land
arāḍī matrūka: public land
arazii emiriyye: See *araḍi amiriyya.*
'aṣaba: clan, agnate

bāṭil: void
bay': sale
bay' al-wafa: a mortgage by conditional sale
bay'a: in theory the election of a caliph; in practice fealty or homage paid to him.
bayt al-māl: public treasury
al-bayyina: evidence
bid'a: innovation

caliph (khalīfa): chief of state

dār al-'ahd: territory in covenant with Islam
dār al-ḥarb: territory of war (enemy territory)
dār al-Islam: territory of Islam
dār al-sulḥ: territory at peace with Islam
ḍarar: damage
ḍarūra: necessity
da'wa: claim
dhawū al-arḥam: uterine heirs
ḍhawū al-furūḍ: shares
dhimmīs (ahl al-kitāb): People of the Book, scripturaries (Christians, Jews, Sabians, Zoroastrians)
diyya: compensation

faqīh (pl. *fuqahā'):* jurist
farḍ: obligatory
farḍ 'ayn: individual obligation
farḍ al-kifāya: collective obligation

fāsid: irregular, invalid
faskh: revocation, annulment
fatwa (pl. *fatāwa*): legal opinion
fay': booty
fidā': ransom
fi'l (pl. *af'āl*): act, practice
fiqh: jurisprudence
firmān: imperial decree
furū': branches of the law
futya (iftā'): the institution of giving *fatwas* or legal opinion. See *fatwa.*

ghanīma: spoils of war
ghayba: absence of the *imām,* a Shī'ī doctrine

ḥadd (pl. *ḥudūd*): penalty
ḥadīth: tradition
hadiyya: gift
ḥājib: door-keeper, usher
ḥajj: pilgrimage
ḥakam: arbitrator
ḥaqq (pl. *ḥuqūq*): right
ḥarām: prohibited
ḥarbī: foreigner (one who belongs to the *dār al-ḥarb*)
ḥawāla: novation
hiba: gift
ḥiḍāna: custody
hijra: migration of the Prophet Muḥammad to Medina in A.D. 622; the beginning of the Muḥammadan era.
ḥiyal: casuistry, legal devices
ḥukm (pl. *aḥkām*): command, law
ḥusn: beauty, good

'ibādāt: devotional duties
'ibāḥa: permission
'idda: the period specified for termination of the legal effects of marriage
iḥrāz: original acquisition
ijāb: offer, proposal
ijāra: hiring, letting
i'jāz: miracle (of the Qur'ānic revelation)
ijmā': consensus, agreement
ijtihād: independent reasoning
ikhtilāf: legal controversy, differences among jurists on matters of law
ikrāh: duress
'ilm: knowledge
imām: (1) leader of people, *caliph;* (2) head of state.
iqrār: confession, acknowledgment
irsh: compensation
'iṣma: infallibility, impeccability
isnād: claim of authorities in a *ḥadīth* (traditions)
istiḥsān: equity, juristic preference

istiṣlāḥ: opinion based on public interest

jā'iz: permitted. See *mubāḥ.*
jamā'a: community
jihād: holy war
jizya: poll tax

kafā'a: suitability, competence
kafāla: suretyship
kāfir: unbeliever
kāhin: soothsayer
kalām: theology
khalīfa: see *caliph* and *imām*
kharāj: land tax
khaṣm: opponent
khuṭba: Friday sermon
kifāra: blood money

li'ān: accusation

madhhab: school of law
mahdī: messiah
mahr: bride-price, dowry given to the wife by the husband
makrūh: objectionable
māl: property
mandūb: commended act
mansūkh: abrogated. See *naskh.*
maslaha: public interest
mawāt: literally, dead-land; uncultivated or waste land
mazālim: complaints
milk: ownership
mirāth: inheritance.
mu'āmalāt: transactions
mubah: permitted
muftī: counsellor
muḥtasib: administrative superviser, disciplinary control
mujtahid: one who exercises *ijtihād,* or independent reasoning
mukallaf: subject of the law
mulk: sovereignty, authority
mushāwar: adviser
mustaḥab: See *mandūb.*
musta'min: one who is granted safe-conduct. See *amān.*
mut'a: temporary marriage
mūwrith: testator

nabī: prophet
nafaqa: support (for a wife)
nā'ib: lieutenant of a caliph or his subordinates
nasab: lineage, blood kinship
nāsikh: abrogating. See *naskh.*
naskh: abrogation. See *mansūkh* and *nasikh.*

naṣṣ: text of scripture or the *sharī'a*
nikāḥ: marriage
niyya: intention
nubūwwa: prophethood. See *nabī.*

pādishah: monarch

qabūl: acceptance
qaḍā': judgment
qadhf: charging the wife with adultery
qāḍī: judge
qasam: oath
qāḍī al-'askar: military judge
qāḍī al-quḍāt: chief judge
qānūn: regulation, ordinance, statute
qanūn-nâme: statute-book
qarāba: blood relations
qibla: direction toward Mecca in prayer
qiṣāṣ: talion, punishment
qiyās: analogy
qubḥ: ugliness, bad
Quraysh: a tribe to which the Prophet Muḥammad belonged

rahn: pledge
rajm: stoning to death
ra'y: legal opinion
riba: usury
riḍā'a: suckling

ṣadāq: bride-price
ṣaḥīḥ: authentic
salam: a form of sale where the price is paid in advance
ṣalāt: worship, prayer
sariqa: theft
ṣawm: fasting
shahāda: testimony
shāhid (pl. *shuhūd*)*:* witness
sharī'a: sacred law
sharika: association, partnership
shī'a: partisan of 'Alī, the fourth caliph. The leading heterodox sect
shuf'a: preemption
shūra: consultation
shurṭa: police
ṣidāq: see ṣadāq
siyar: branch of the sharī'a dealing with the conduct of state
ṣulḥ: transaction, compromise
sulṭān: temporal ruler
sunna: custom, tradition
sunnī: Orthodox Muslim
sūra: chapter of the Qur'ān

tafsīr: commentary on the Qur'ān
tafwīḍ: delegation of authority
taḥkīm: arbitration
ṭalāq: divorce
tanfīl: supererogation
tanzīmāt: Ottoman reform movement
ṭāpū: land registry
taqlīd: imitation, conformism: following the opinion of an acknowledged jurist
ta'wīl: esoteric knowledge of the *imām*
tawrīth: to bequeath
ta'zīr: corrective punishment (less than a *ḥadd*)
tha'r: vendetta, vengence
timār: fief

'udūl: (1) withdrawal; (2) upright
umma: community
'uqūba (pl. *'uqūbāt*)*:* penalty
'urf: usage, practice
'ushr: tithe
usra: family
uṣūl: roots or sources of the law

wājib: obligatory
wakīl: guardian
walāya: devotion (to 'Alī)
waqf: pious endowment
waṣī: executor
waṣiyya (pl. *waṣāya*)*:* will
wilāya: delegation of authority

zakāt: alms
zinā': fornication

Select Bibliography

It would be quite impossible to compile and set forth a complete list of the published works on Islamic law, let alone the unpublished original sources, whether in Arabic, Turkish and Persian, or in Western languages. There are a few bibliographical works which may well serve the purpose of scholars without the need of going into the task of reproducing such bibliographies without sifting them. Mention may be made of the extensive bibliography of Aghnides in his *Mohammedan Theories of Finance* (London and New York, 1916), Part I, pp. 157-96, which is in turn based on Hajjī Khalīfa's *Kashf al-Zanūn* and Ibn al-Nadīm's *Fihrist*. The suggested readings which follow are works in Western languages (including translations from original sources) intended to provide the reader with materials for further study of Islamic law.

Chapter I

For background material on the subject of constitutional organization, D. B. Macdonald's *Development of Muslim Theology, Jurisprudence and Constitutional Theory* (New York, 1903), Part I, gives a general historical survey. From an institutional viewpoint, Demombyne's *Muslim Institutions* (London, 1950) treats in a general way the whole field of Muslim public institutions.

Perhaps the best general survey of the rise and development of the institution of the caliphate is still that of Sir Thomas Arnold, *The Caliphate* (Oxford, 1924), which should be supplemented by more recent researches on the subject. H. A. R. Gibb's "Some Considerations on the Sunnī Theory of the Caliphate," in *Archives d'histoire du droit Oriental,* Vol. III (1948), pp. 401-410, and his "Al-Māwardī's Theory of the Khilāfah," in *Islamic Culture,* Vol. XI (1937), pp. 291-302, are particularly useful for a critical study of the views of Muslim writers on the subject. For a comprehensive treatment of the subject by modernists, Laoust's translation of Rashīd Riḍa's *Le Califat* (Beyrouth, 1938) and Sanhoury, *Le Califat* (Paris, 1926) are probably the best representatives. Emile Tyan's *Institutions du droit public Musulman* will cover the whole subject of constitutional organization, the first volume of which deals with *Le Califat* (Paris, 1954).

Chapters II and III

The best treatment of the historical origin and development of the schools of law is J. Schacht's *Origins of Muhammadan Jurisprudence* (2nd ed., Oxford, 1953), and *Esquisse d'une histoire du droit Musulman* (Paris, 1953). D. B. Macdonald, *op. cit.,* part II, is still useful.

Studies which emphasize certain aspects of the sharī'a, or a particular school, are: I. Goldziher, *Die Zahiriten* (Leipzig, 1884); C. Snouck Hurgronje, *Verspreide Geschriften* (Bonn, Leipzig, or Leiden, 1923 ff.), Vols. II and IV; J. Berque, *Essai sur la methode juridique maghribine* (Rabat, 1944); and H. Laoust, *Contribution à une étude de la methodologie canonique d'Ibn Taimiya* (Cairo, 1939).

Chapter IV

A comprehensive treatment of the subject of jurisprudence is to be found in Aghnides, *Mohammedan Theories of Finance* (New York, 1910), Part 1; D. S. Margoliouth, *Early Development of Mohammedanism* (London, 1914), Chap. 3; and I. Goldziher, *Le dogme et les lois de l'Islam* (Paris, 1920), Chap. 2.

For a detailed study of the sources of law, especially the *Qur'ān* and Traditions, the reader may be referred to R. Blachère, *Introduction au Coran* (Paris, 1947); R. Roberts, *The Social Laws of the Koran* (London, 1925); I. Goldziher, *Muhammedanische Studien* (Halle, 1890), Vol. II; and A. Guillaume, *The Traditions of Islam* (Oxford, 1924). For the development of analogy and consensus, Schacht's *Origins of Muhammadan Jurisprudence* (Oxford, 1953) is the most penetrating. For a treatment of the subject of foreign influence on Muslim law, see J. Schacht, "Foreign Elements in Ancient Islamic Law," *Journal of Comparative Legislation and International Law,* 3rd Series, Vol. XXXII (1950), pp. 9-17; and S. V. Fitzgerald, "The Alleged Debt of Islamic to Roman Law," *Law Quarterly Review,* Vol. 67 (1951), pp. 81-102.

Chapter V

Few are the works on Shī'ī law in Western languages, but reference may be made to D. M. Donaldson, *The Shī'ite Religion* (London, 1933); Fyzee, *A Shi'ite Creed* (London, 1942); B. Lewis, *The Origins of Isma'ilism* (Cambridge, 1940); and W. Ivanow, *Brief Survey of the Evolution of Ismailism* (Leiden—Bombay, 1952) which deal with Shī'ī theory and practice. A translation of Shī'ī law is to be found in A. Querry, *Recueil de lois concernant les Musulmans Schyites* (Paris, 1881).

Chapters VI to IX

There are several works dealing with the detailed branches of the sharī'a in accordance with the recognized schools of law. Abdur Rahim's *Muhammadan Jurisprudence* (Madras, 1911) gives a fairly detailed treatment of the whole subject, based in the main on Ḥanafī writings; David Santillana, *Istituzioni di diritto Musulmano Malichita* (Rome, 1926-1938), 2 vols., gives an excellent survey of the law according to the Mālikī and Shāfi'ī schools. S. Vesey-Fitzgerald's *Muhammadan Law* (London, 1931); and Ameer Ali's *Personal Law of the Mohammedans* (London, 1880) provide the contents of the sharī'a relating to the law of personal status. Louis Milliot's *Introduction à l'étude du droit Musulman* (Paris, 1953); and A. A. A. Fyzee, *Outlines of Muhammadan Law* (2nd ed., Oxford, 1953) are the best recent surveys of the whole subject of Islamic law. Mention must also be made of a monograph on waqf by Muhammed Ahmed Simsar, *The Waqfiyah of Ahmed Pasa* (Philadelphia, 1940).

Chapter X

The best work on judicial organization in Islam is E. Tyan's *Histoire de l'organisation judiciaire en pays d'Islam* (Paris, 1934-1943), 2 vols. Reference may also be made to the chapters on this subject in the French translation of Mawardi's *Al-Aḥkām al-Sulṭāniyya,* by E. Fagnan (Algeria, 1915); and Demombynes, *op. cit.,* Chap. 9.

Chapters XI and XII

Works on the development of the sharī'a during the Ottoman period in Western languages are not too numerous. For the study of the Ottoman Reform Movement, see J. H. Kramers' article on the "Tanẓīmāt" in the *Encyclopedia of Islam,* Vol. IV, pp. 656-660; and E. Engelhardt, *La Turquie et le tanzimat* (Paris, 1882), 2 vols. For a general treatment of the development of law during the Ottoman period, see J. N. D. Anderson, "Recent Development in Sharī'a Law," *The Muslim World,* Vol. 40 (1950), pp. 244-56 and subsequent issues; "Ottoman Law and the Shari'a," *Journal of Comparative Legislation and International Law,* 3rd series, Vol. XXII (1940), pp. 95-98; and H. J. Liebesny, "Religious Law and Westernization in the Moslem Near East," *American Journal of Comparative Law,* Vol. II (1953), pp. 492-504.

For texts of Ottoman legislation, reference must be made to the monumental work of George Young, *Corps de droit Ottoman* (Oxford, 1905-1906); and the translation of the *Majalla* in Charles A. Hooper, *Civil Law of Palestine and Transjordan* (Jerusalem, 1933), Vol. I.

Chapter XIII

Few subjects have been treated so extensively in Western languages as the subject of Western privileges in the Ottoman Empire, and it would be a hopeless task to enumerate all that has been written by Western writers. The best general surveys in English are G. Bie Ravndal, *The Origin of the Capitulations and of the Consular Institution* (Washington, 1921); Philip Marshall Brown, *Foreigners in Turkey* (Princeton, 1914); and Nasim Sousa, *The Capitulatory Regime of Turkey* (Baltimore, 1933). On the Egyptian Mixed Courts, J. Brinton's *The Mixed Courts of Egypt* (New Haven, 1930) is the standard work.

Chapters XIV and XV

Public and private international law in Islam have aroused great interest among Western writers. Several studies have been published which treat this subject with considerable detail. Most important of these works are the following: Julius Hatschek, *Der Musta'min* (Berlin, 1920); Wilhelm Heffening, *Das islamische Freundenrecht* (Hannover, 1925); Najib Armanazi, *Les principes islamiques et les rapports internationaux en temps de paix et de guerre* (Paris, 1929); Majid Khadduri, *Law of War and Peace in Islam* (London, 1941); M. Hamidullah, *Muslim Conduct of State* (new ed., Lahore, 1954); and Hans Kruse, *Islamische Völkerrechtslehre* (Göttingen, 1953). Shorter studies in the same field include: Ch. Cardahi, "La conception et la pratique du droit international privé dans l'Islam" in *Recueil de cours de l'Academie du droit international de la Haye,* 1937, Vol. II, pp. 509-650; and Ahmed Rechid, "L'Islam et le droit des gens," *ibid.,* pp. 373-506.

Index

'Abbāsids: administrative and judicial policy of, 57-62, 71; diplomacy of, 370; status of Islamic law under, 72-73; treaty relations with Byzantine empire, 359, 366
'Abd al-Qāhir al-Baghdādī, on the caliphate, quoted, 7-11
Abū Bakr: on land warfare, quoted, 355; on share of grandfather in estate, 171
Abū Ḥanīfa: 52-53; on acts of *negotiorum gestor,* 187; on bride-price, 142, 143; on divorce, 148, 149; on freedom of woman to choose husband, 138; on inheritance by dhimmī, 336; on interdiction of the debtor, 197; on interdiction of the prodigal, 197; on jurisdiction over dhimmī, 338; on liability for damage, 186; on liability for loss of profit, 189; on musta'min's return to enemy country, 345; on offense of protected foreigner against dhimmī, 341; on powers of the qāḍī, 262-63; on punishment for the repentent thief, 230-31; on representation by counsel, 258; on revocability of waqf, 206; on share of grandfather in estate, 171; on suitability in marriage, 138, 140; on support of relatives, 159; on validity of will of dhimmī, 339. *See also* Hanafī school of law
Abū Isḥāq al-Shāṭibī. *See* Ibrāhīm Mūsa al-Lakhmī
Abū Yūsuf: 92; on attempted crime, 226; on caliphate, quoted, 5, 15; on criminal responsibility of the insane, 225; on cumulation of punishments, 234; doctrines of, 52-53; first Chief Qāḍī, 58; on homicide and bequests, 176; on liability for damage, 186; on musta'min's return to enemy country, 345-46; on non-Islamic customs, 35-36; on perpetuity of waqf, 207; on punishment for theft from relatives, 230; on revocability of waqf, 206-7; on share of grandfather in estate, 171; on trade with non-believers, 371; on validity of will of dhimmī, 339; treatise of, 57
acceptance: 191-92; in marriage contract, 133
accessio, 183
action in court in Majalla, 304-6
actor sequitur forum rei, principle of, in capitulations, 316, 326
administration of justice in Majalla, 307. *See also* judge, judicial organization, qāḍī
admissions, 304-5
adultery: and attribution of paternity, 152; with musta'min girl, 338. *See also* fornication
agency, defined, 200
agent, unauthorized. *See negotiorum gestor*
Agha Khan, 97, 116
Agha Khan case, 118
agnate relatives. *See* relatives, agnate
ahl al-ḥadīth, 92
ahl al-kitāb. *See* dhimmī
ahl al-ra'y, 92
ahl-i-ḥaqq, 120
Ahmet Cevdet Pasha, 285, 289, 295
'Alamgir, Mogul emperor, 81
'Alawī, 119
'Alī, Caliph: 45, 114, 119; status in relation to the Prophet, in Shī'ī doctrine, 116, 117; will of, and criminal responsibility, 224-25
Ali Himmet Berki, 280-81
'Alī ibn Abī Tālib: 119; on share of grandfather in inheritance, 171
'Alī-Ilāhī, 119
'Alī Pasha, 295
Allah. *See* God
Almoravid, 81
amān, form of, 361-62; granting of, 361
amīn al-ḥukm, 256-57
Amīr al-Mu'minīn. *See* caliphate
amīriyya. *See* land, state owned
analogy: early use of, 49-50; as source of Islamic international law, 352. *See also* qiyās
Andalusia, qāḍī's *consilium,* 251-53
Anglo-Muḥammadan law, 81-82
Apostle. *See* Muḥammad

'aql, in Shī'ī doctrine, 97
arazii emiriyye. *See* land, state owned
arazii memluke. *See* ownership, absolute, of lands
arazii metruke. *See* public land
arbitration: defined, 201; in Islamic international law, 359, 367-70; in pre-Islam, 29, 31, 33; regulations in the Majalla, 307
ascendants, entitled to assured shares of inheritance, 168-72; support of, 160
aṣḥāb al-furūḍ, 167-72
al-Ash'arī, 15
assault, against musta'min by Muslim, 338
attempted crime, 226
attorney, substitute for, 257-59
Austria: capitulations with Ottoman empire, 320-22; mixed commissions in Ottoman empire, 326
aval. See debts, transfer of
'awn, 256
awqāf. *See* waqf
Awzā'ī, 51
al-bā'in baynūnatan kubra, 149

bar, substitute for, 257
Baṣra, school of law, 41, 45
bawwāb, 256
bay'a, 11-12
bay' bil-wafā', 102-3, 108
Bayḍāwī, on jurisdiction over dhimmīs, 338
Bedouin, customary law of, 28-29
Belgium, capitulations with Ottoman empire, 325
bequests: acceptance of, 175; conditions attached to, 175-76; exceeding third of estate, 177; to heirs, 175; mandatory, 177-78; not to exceed third of estate, 175; obstacles to execution of, 176; passing of title, 175; revocability of, 175; validity of, 175-76
betrothal: defined, 132; effects of withdrawal from, 133
bidā' divorce, 104
blood money, 224, 228. *See also* diyya
blood relationship, impediment to marriage, 134
Bohora, 97
bride-price: 141-44; deferred, 142
Byzantine empire: diplomacy with Islamic state, 370; granting of extraterritorial privileges by, 310-12; influence of judicial organization, 38; treaties with the Islamic state, 359, 366

caliph: responsibility for declaring and prosecuting jihād, 354, 364; responsibility for treatment of prisoners, 355-56; role in judicial organization, 60; treaty-making power, 364. *See also* caliphate
caliphate: 4-27 *passim;* absolute power of, 17-20; circumscription of legislative powers, 61-62; compared with sultanate, 20-27; conditions of leadership, 7-11; delegation of powers, 236; derivation of authority, 5; establishment of, 4-5; legislation during, 33; maẓālim jurisdiction, 265, 268; relation to imāmate in Shī'ī doctrine, 121-22; relation to the community, 14-17; religious character of, 243; Sunni doctrine of, 6-14. *See also* caliph, imāmate
capacity, to contract, 196
capitulations: 312-33 *passim;* abrogation of in Ottoman empire, 330; as commercial treaties, 314; with Egypt, 312-14; form of treaties, 316-17, 322; legal importance of, 332-33; legal nature of, 326-27; modifications of, 329; most-favored-nation clauses in, 313, 317, 322, 323-24; with Ottoman empire, 315-26; pre-Ottoman, 312-15; reciprocity in, 323-24; renewal of, 317-22 *passim,* 326-27; unilateral grant v. bilateral treaty, 326-27
Cevdet Pasha. *See* Ahmet Cevdet Pasha
children: care of, 154-56; guardianship of, 154-57; period of dependence, 154-55; rights of, defined, 151; spiritual guardianship of, 156; support of, 157-58
children's property, guardianship of, 157
Christians: legal position of, *see* dhimmī; as receivers of revelation, 88-89
civil code, Ottoman. *See* Majalla
civil procedure: in Majalla, 295, 298, 307; Ottoman code of, 290
claim, transfer of, 202
codification: lack of in earlier Ottoman empire, 294; in Ottoman empire, 282-91 *passim. See also* dustur, Hatti Sherif of Gülhane, Majalla, tanẓīmāt
coercion, impeding consent, 193
cognate relatives. *See* relatives, cognate
collateral relatives, entitled to assured shares of inheritance, 170-71

commercial cases, jurisdiction of Mixed Courts in Egypt, 331
commercial code, Ottoman, 288-89, 293-94
commercial procedure, Ottoman code of, 289
Community of Muslims. *See* umma
Companions of the Prophet: 44-46, 92-93; on divorce, 147, 148; on share in inheritance of grandfather, 171
complaints, courts of, 59
conditions, of contract, in Majalla, 300; in marriage contract, 140-41
conflict of law: 337-48 *passim;* as affected by conversion, 342-45; among dhimmīs, 340-41; concerning foreigners, *see* musta'min; between Muslims of different schools of law, 341-42; between Muslims and non-Muslims, 337-40, 342-45; in Ottoman empire, 346-48
consensus, as source of Islamic international law, 352. *See also* ijmā'
consent: of contracting parties, 192; impediments to, 193
consideration. *See* contract, consideration in
consilium: 245-47; in Andalusia, 251-53
constitutional theory, formality of law as check on despotism, 106
consular jurisdiction, 311-32 *passim*
consultation: principle of, 245-47; in Andalusia, 251-53
contract: 191-202; cancellation of, 201; conditions for validity, 192; consideration in, 195; defined, 191; among dhimmīs, 339-40; between dhimmīs and Muslim community, 335; form of, 192, 198; freedom of, 194; general causes for termination, 202; illicit, 195; legal capacity to enter into, 196; in Majalla, 299-301; object of, 194; purpose of, 195; special, 198-201; termination of, 201
conversion: and contracts, 344; legal effect of, 342-45; and marriage, 342-43; as objective of jihād, 354; and penal law, 344-45
corporation, in Majalla, 305
court assistants, 254-57
court composition, 244-48
crime: in dār al-ḥarb, 341; defined, 226-27; against peace and security, 231; punishable by ḥadd, 227
criminal cases, jurisdiction of Mixed Courts in Egypt, 331
criminal procedure, Ottoman code of, 290
custom: in marriage suitability, 140; as source of law governing dhimmī, 363; as source of law in Majalla, 297; as source of reform, 109-10
customary law: as applied to contracts and obligations, 77-78; of Bedouin, 28-29; of Ottoman Turks, 283; in pre-Islam, 28-33 *passim;* reliance on written documents, 79-80
cy pres doctrine, analogy in law of waqf, 207-8

damages, for deception in betrothal, 133
dār al-'ahd, 359-60
dār al-ḥarb: 350-51, 359, 371; crime in, 341; return of musta'min to, 345-46
dār al-Islām, 350-51, 359
dār al-ṣulḥ, 359-60
Daudi Bohora, powers of the dā'ī, 97
Dawud ibn Khalaf, 67, 74
death, simultaneous and succession, 166
death sickness: as cause for partial interdiction, 197; defined, 162; disposition of property during, 162-63; gifts during, 175; as start of compulsory succession, 164
debts: as cause for interdiction, 197; contracted during death sickness, 163-64; deferred, payment after death, 163-64; transfer of, 202
decedent, 160-78 *passim*
defendant: 305; right to choose school of law, 341-42
Denmark, capitulations with Ottoman empire, 323
deposit: defined, 200; termination of, 201
descendants, entitled to assured shares of inheritance, 168-69
destruction of property, 303-4
device, to circumvent inalienability of waqf, 209-10. *See also* ḥiyal
dhimma. *See* contract, between dhimmīs and Muslim community
dhimmī: duties of and guarantees to, 363-64; jurisdiction over, 337-38, 340-41; legal effects of conversion of, 342-45; legal position of, 335-44, 346-48; in the Ottoman empire, 346-48; relation between different dhimmī communities, 336, 340-41; relation to Muslim community, 335-40; status under Is-

lam, 350, 362-64. *See also* jizya and kharāj
difference of religion, as bar to marriage, 136
diplomatic immunity, 371
disposable third. *See* succession, optional
divorce: 146-49; clear, 149; effect on bride-price, 143; and guardianship, 156; manifest, 149; revocable, 149; role of 'idda in, 148, 150-51; triple, as bar to marriage, 136; triple, effects of, 148, 149; wife wanting, 147-48; wife wanting, character of, 149
diyya, in case of dhimmī, 337; for murder of musta'min, 337-38
dominium. *See* ownership, absolute
dowry. *See* bride-price
drunkenness, validity of contracts concluded during, 198
Druze; belief in divinity of imām, 116; doctrine, 119, 120
duress, 193
ḍurūra, 102-3
dustūr, 290-91

easement, 182
East India Company, policy toward law in India, 81-82
Ebussuud. *See* Mehmet Ebussuudd Efendi
Egypt: capitulations with, 311-14, 316; legislation on waqf, 218-19; Mixed Courts in, 329-30; termination of Mixed Courts, 331-32
enforcement, of decision in criminal cases, 233
equity. *See* istiḥsān
error, impeding consent, 193
estate: claims against, 161-64; debts of, 160-64; distribution of, 160-78; increment of property, disposal of, 164; recipients of assured shares of, 167-72; sale of future, 194; under debt, treatment of, 164. *See also* inheritance
estoppel, 184
evidence, rules on, in Majalla, 306-7
executor of estate: appointed by qāḍī, 165; appointed by testator, 164
extra-territorial jurisdiction: 311-32 *passim;* of Great Britain in Persian Gulf, 333; in Ottoman empire, 315-26 *passim. See also* capitulations, personality of law

family, defined, 158
family law, Muslim, defined, 132
farḍ, 98-99
fasting, infringement of rules on, punished, 232
father, as guardian, 154-58
Fāṭimid, 117, 120, 122, 124
fatwa: 75, 76; collection of, 282; as precedent, 105. *See also* futya
fa'y. *See* spoils of war
felony. *See* crime
financial status, consideration in marriage suitability, 139
fiqh, defined, 86
five values, of human acts, 98-100
Florence. *See* Italian city states, extraterritorial privileges
fornication: and conversion, 345; false accusation of, 229-30, 234; involving dhimmīs, 340, 341; proof of, 229-30; punishment of, 229
France: capitulations with Egypt, 313, 315; capitulations with Ottoman empire, 316-26; influence on Egyptian law, 331; influence on Ottoman law, 329; mixed commissions in Ottoman empire, 326; predominance of, in Ottoman empire, 315-20
fratricide, 282
fraud, impeding consent, 193
free status, consideration in marriage suitability, 139
fuḍūlī. *See negotiorum gestor*
Fulānī, 81
fuqahā', 91-92, 246, 247, 268
futya, 248-51, 253

Genoa. *See* Italian city states, extra-territorial privileges
ghanīma. *See* spoils of war
al-Ghazzālī: on caliphate, quoted, 19-20; on istiṣlāḥ, 101-2
gift: acceptance of by minor, 196; consideration in contract of, 195; defined, 199; made during death sickness, 162-63; return of, if betrothal terminated, 133
God: as Head of Muslim community, 3-5; on ibāḥa, 99; imposing legal prohibitions, 226; judging the deceased, 226; as owner of all things, 181; as owner of waqf, 208; rights demanded from man, 100; as sharing in war booty, 356-57; in Shī'ī doctrine, 115-16, 117, 121; as source of law, 85-90 *passim,* 104-5, 351
governor, jurisdiction of, 242-43
Great Britain: capitulations with the Ottoman empire, 318-26; extra-terri-

torial jurisdiction in Persian Gulf, 333; and mixed commissions in Ottoman empire, 322; struggle with France for predominance in Ottoman empire, 319-21
Greeks: influence on Muslim philosophy, 25; political thought contrasted with Muslim, 12-13
guarantee, defined, 200
guardian: approval of contract by, 196; permission to ward to engage in business, 196; of woman, assisting in marriage contract, 137
guardianship: of children, 154-57; of children, defined, 154; of children, spiritual, 156; of children's property, 156; and divorce, 156; of property, and maturity, 157

ḥadd: applied to musta'min, 338; crimes punishable by, 227; cumulation of, 234; defined, 227
ḥadīth: 61, 65, 67; aḥādīth qudsiyya, 92; fabrication of, 93-94; as a root of the sharī'a, 92-94; in Shī'ī doctrine, 120. *See also* Traditionists
ḥājib, jurisdiction of, 271-73
ḥakam. *See* arbitration
al-Ḥākim, Caliph, 119
Ḥammād ibn Abī Sulaymān, 43
Hammer-Purgstall, von, quoted, 282
Ḥanafī school of law: 92; basis of family legislation of Egypt, 132; basis of Majalla, 292, 295, 298, 307-8; on compensation for pain, 190; on conditions in waqf, 211; on consultation of *consilium* by the qāḍī, 246; on contract of gift, 199; on contracts concluded during drunkenness, 198; on criminal cases involving musta'min, 337-38; on definition of waqf, 203; on definition of wrongful appropriation, 189; on diplomacy, 371; on division of world, 360; doctrine of, 64, 65; on doctrine of jihād, 354; on duration of treaties, 367; on estates under debt, 164; formalism in, 107; geographic distribution of, 68-69; on influence of time on law, 110; on inheritance of dhimmī, 336, 339; on jurisdiction over dhimmī, 337, 338; on *laesio enormis,* 193; on legal effects of conversion, 343-44; on limitation, 184; on musta'min's return to enemy country, 345-46; on non-support of wife, 145; on paternity, 151; on perpetuity of waqf, 206-7; on powers of qāḍī, 260; on recognition of custom, 109-10; on sale of futures, 194; on services as property, 180; on suitability in marriage, 139, 140; on transfer of claim or debt, 202; on value of wrongfully appropriated property, 189; on wāqif as first beneficiary, 203; on witnesses, 254; on written documents, 79. *See also* Abū Ḥanīfa
Ḥanbalī school of law: on applicability of Islamic law to dhimmī, 335; on claims against the estate, 162; on conditions in marriage contract, 141; on conditions in waqf, 211; on estates under debt, 164; geographic distribution of 69-70, 132; on illicit contracts, 195; on *laesio enormis,* 193; on payment of deferred debts after death, 163-64; on spoils of war, 357; on value of wrongfully appropriated property, 189: *See also* Ibn Ḥanbal
ḥarām, 98-99
Hārūn, Caliph, 57, 58
Ḥasan-i 'Āmilī, 124
Hatti-Humayun, 329, 346-47
Hatti Sherif of Gülhane, 279, 284-86, 328, 346
ḥawāla. *See* debts, transfer of
head of state. *See* caliph, caliphate, imāmate
heir, 160-78 *passim*
highway robbery: 231; by unbeliever from unbeliever, 340
al-Ḥillī, on status of imāmate in relation to the Prophet, 117
hire: defined, 198-99; in Majalla, 300; types of, 199. *See also* lease
ḥiyal, 77-80, 107-8
holy war. *See* jihād
homicide: 227-29; accidental, 228; assimilated to accidental, 228; as impediment to inheritance, 165-66; intentional, 227-28; as invalidating a bequest, 176. *See also* murder
hostages, 367
Hudaybiya treaty, 358, 365, 367
ḥudūd. *See* ḥadd
Ḥusāmī, on consultation of experts by by qāḍī, 251
husband, share of estate of wife, 167

Ibāḍī, 122
ibāḥa, 99-100
Ibn 'Abbās, 44
Ibn 'Ābdūn, on consultation of experts by the qāḍī, 251, 252

Ibn 'Ābidīn, on physical punishment during pregnancy, 234-35
Ibn Abī Layla, 51-52
Ibn Farḥūn, on functions of the qāḍī, 262, 273
Ibn Ḥajar, on consultation of *consilium* by the qāḍī, 247
Ibn Ḥanbal: 67; on divorce, 149; on homicide as impediment to inheritance, 165-66; on paternity, 151; on services as property, 180; on share of grandfather in estate, 171; on suitability in marriage, 140; on support of relatives, 159; on transfer of claim, 202. *See also* Ḥanbalī school of law
Ibn Ḥazm, on bequests to infirm relatives, 177-78
Ibn Jamā'a, on the caliphate, quoted, 23
Ibn al-Jawzī, on the qāḍī, 245
Ibn Khaldūn: on the caliphate, 236, 243; on futya, 250; on maẓālim and ḥājib jurisdiction, 272; on need for Divine law, quoted, 13-14; on penal procedure, 275; on shurta, 274, 277
Ibn Mas'ūd, 44-45
Ibn al-Mufaḍḍal, policy on witnesses, 253
Ibn Muqaffa', on state control of law, 61-62
Ibn Nujaym, as source of legal maxims, 103
Ibn Qayyim al-Jawziyya: 69-70, 74; on acts of *negotiorum gestor,* 187-88; on freedom of contract, 194
Ibn Rajab al-Ḥanbalī, on ownership, 181-82
Ibn Taymiyya: on attempted crime, 226; on caliphate, 23-24; on paternity, 151; teachings of, 67-69 *passim,* 74
Ibn 'Umar, 45
Ibrāhīm Ḥalabī, 105
Ibrāhīm Mūsa al-Lakhmī, on liability for damage, 187
Ibrāhīm Nakha'ī, 40, 43, 44
'idda: 148, 150-51; repudiation of child born during, 152; as temporary bar to marriage, 136, 137
iftā'. *See* futya
ijāratayn. *See* waqf property, exchange, lease, sale of
ijmā': early development of, 42-47; ijmā' al-'ā'imma, *see* ijmā' of the scholars; ijmā' al-umma, 95; as a root of the sharī'a 95-96; of the scholars, 42-43, 51, 64, 65, 74, 95; in Shī'ī doctrine, 97, 127
ijtihād: 73, 104-6; closing of the gate of, 73-75, 105-6; in Shī'ī doctrine, 122-23
imāmate: relation to Nestorian Christ in Shī'ī doctrine, 119-20; in Shī'ī doctrine, 97, 113, 114-21; in Shī'ī doctrine contrasted with caliphate, 121-22. *See also* caliphate
imbecile, criminal responsibility of, 225
imbecility, as cause for interdiction, 196-97
impediments to inheritance, 165-66
imprisonment, for non-support of wife, 145
infallibility. *See* 'iṣma
inheritance: 160-78; of agnate relatives, 172-73; of ascendants, 169-73; assured shares, reduction of, 172; of cognate relatives, 173-74; conditions of, 165-66; and conflict of law in Ottoman empire, 347-48; of descendants, 168-69, 172-73; impediments to, 165-66; involving dhimmīs, 335-36, 338-39; law of, 111, 160-78; of musta'min, 346; among non-Muslims, 166; sale of, not yet due, 194; in Shī'ī law, 130-31; between spouses, 166-67. *See also* estate, succession
inheritor, 160-78 *passim.*
injurious act, 190
insane, criminal responsibility of, 225
intent: criminal, 225-26; in injurious exercise of rights, 186-87; in Majalla, 304
interdiction, causes of, 196
interest, on loan of commodities, 199-200
international law (Islamic): 349-71 *passim;* arbitration in, 359, 367-70; compared to Western, 352; decline of, 371-72; on jihād, 353-59; on prisoners, 355-56; sources of, 351-52; on spoils of war, 356-58; on status of non-Muslims, *see* musta'min, dhimmī; on treaties, 358, 364-67
interpretation. *See* ijtihād
intoxicating beverages, prohibition of, 232
'Irāq, law of waqf, 222
irsh, correspondence to blood money, 228-29
Islamic law: and decree legislation, 109; influence of Roman and Rabbinical law, 89; influence of Qur'ān, 87-90; influence of sunna, 90-95; instruments of reform, 107-10; parallels from Roman, Talmudic and Christian canon law, 110-11; subjection to practice, 80-81
Islamic state: allegiance to the caliphate,

11-15 *passim;* cleavage between umarā' and fuqahā', 91; constitutional organization, 1-27; delegation of power, 237-40; influence of Persian thought, 15, 21, 26; position of the individual, 14-16 *passim;* structure, 236; universality of, as basis for Islamic international law, 350
'iṣma, 121
Ismā'īlī, doctrine on the imāmate, 114, 115
Ismā'īlī Khoja, dogma regarding the Agha Khan, 116-19
istiḥsān, 101, 110
istiṣḥāb, 102
istiṣlāḥ, 101-2
Italian city states, extra-territorial privileges: in Byzantine empire, 311-12; in Egypt, 313-14; in Ottoman empire, 315-21
Ithna 'Asharī, 97; doctrine on bidā' divorce, 104; doctrine on ijmā', 127; doctrine on imāmate, 114, 115, 120, 122; doctrine on mut'a, wills, and inheritance, 128-31; doctrine on qiyās, 123, 124; geographic distribution of, 132; relative status of imāmate to the Prophet, 116
ius respondendi, 248-49

Jalāl ud-Dīn Dawwānī, on the caliphate and organization of the state, 26-27
Jews: legal position of in Islam, *see* dhimmī; as receivers of revelation, 88-89
jihād: 98; defined, 353; doctrine of, 353-54; refusal to join, punishment for, 226; as a religious duty, 353, 354, 358; as a religious sanction, 351; rules of, 355-59; termination of, 358
jilwāz, 256
jizya, 335, 351, 360, 363-64
John of Damascus, 35
joint ownership, in Majalla, 301-2. *See also* joint tenancy
joint tenancy, of heirs, 165
Jordan, law on waqf, 222
judge: permission to minor to engage in business, 196; qualification of, 307; as representative of the sovereign, 307. *See also* qāḍī
judicial organization: 236-78; courts of complaints, 59; muḥtasib, 59-60. *See also* administration of justice, judge, qāḍī
judicial procedure, in criminal cases, discussed, 232-33. *See also* judicial organization
judicial reform: in Egypt, 330-31; in Ottoman empire, 328-30
jurisdiction: and community law in Ottoman empire, 347; over dhimmī, 337-38, 340-41; of the Islamic state over Muslims, 360; of the Islamic state over non-Muslims, 360-64; of Mixed Courts in Egypt, 331-32; over a musta'min, 337-38; of qāḍī in cases between Muslims belonging to two different schools of law, 341-42. *See also* extra-territorial jurisdiction
jurisprudence: development in the Umayyad period, 36-42; early development of, 28-56; incorporation of ḥadīth into, 46-56; influence of foreign legal systems, 35-36; Islamic, as science of classification, 100; Islamization of, under the Umayyads, 38-56; use of witnesses, 35. *See also* Islamic law

kanūn, in Ottoman empire, 280
Kāsānī, on consultation by the qāḍī, 246; on religious character of qāḍī, 243
kātib, 255
Katip Celebi, 280
khalīfa. *See* caliph, caliphate
kharāj, 358, 363
Khārijī: 34; on the caliphate, 6
khaṣṣāf, 79
khāzin diwān al-ḥukm, 257
khilāfa ijbāriyya, compulsory succession, 160-61
khilāfa ikhtiyāriyya, optional succession, 160
Khoja Shahādi, quoted, 118
Khushanī, on religious character of qāḍī, 243
Khurashī, on the qāḍī, 245, 273
kifā'a. *See* marriage, suitability in
kifāra, 228
al-Kindī, on witnesses, 253
kinship by marriage, impediment to marriage, 134, 135
Kitāb al-kharāj. See Abū Yūsuf
Kūfa, school of law, 41, 43-56 *passim*

laesio enormis, 193
land: common, defined, 181; dead, defined, 181; state owned, defined, 181
land law, Ottoman: 286-88, 298; based on custom, 283
larceny. *See* theft
last illness. *See* death sickness

law, Western concept contrasted to Islamic, 85
lawful acts, defined, 191
laws, collections of, in Ottoman Empire, 280-83, 291-92
lease, in Majalla, 300-301. *See also* hire
Lebanon, legislation on waqf, 219-20
legal devices. *See* ḥiyal
legal dispositions: 185-88; categories of, 185
legal fictions. *See* ḥiyal
lex talionis: in case of murder of musta'min, 337; concerning dhimmī, 336-37; in Qur'ān, 229
liability: of borrower, 199; for damage, as result of exercise of rights, 186; of depositary, 200; for destruction, theory of, 190-91; for loss of use, 189-90
limitation: as estoppel, 184; period of, 184; terminating contract, 202. *See also* statute of limitations
lineage, consideration in marriage suitability, 138-39
loan, for use, defined, 199; of commodities, 199
lunacy, as cause for interdiction, 196-97

Magians. *See* Zoroastrians
al-Mahdī bi'l-lah, 125
mahr. *See* bride-price
Majalla: 285, 288, 292-308; on administration of justice, 307; amendment and abolition of, 308; cited, 179-202 *passim;* compilation of, 294-96; content of, 299-307; on contracts, 299-301; on evidence, 306-7; general principles of, 296-98; on joint ownership, 302; on liability for damage, 186; on procedure, 304-7; on real property, 301-4; reasons for enactment of, 294-95; on representation by counsel, 258; rigidity of, 307-8; suits involving different schools of law, 341-42; on wrongful appropriation and destruction, 303-4
majority, age of, 137
makrūh, 99
Mālik: 75; on acts of *negotiorum gestor,* 187; on bride-price, 143; on contract of gift, 199; on fornication involving dhimmī, 340; on homicide as impediment to inheritance, 166; on inheritance by dhimmī, 336; on interdiction of women, 197-98; on liability for damage, 186; on liability for loss of profit, 189-90; on non-Islamic customs, 36; on paternity, 151, 153; reasoning of, 51; on share of grandfather in estate, 171; on suitability in marriage, 138, 140; on support of relatives, 159; on transfer of claim, 202; on wife's financial freedom, 141
Mālikī school of law: 92; on conditions in waqf, 211; on consultation of experts by qāḍī, 247; on contracts between dhimmīs, 340; on criminal cases involving Muslims and non-Muslims, 337; on divorce, 147-49 *passim;* on diyya of dhimmī, 337; doctrine of, 64-67 *passim;* on duration of treaties, 367; on estates under debt, 164; geographic distribution, 69; on illicit contracts, 195; on jurisdiction over dhimmī, 337, 338; on *laesio enormis,* 193; on legal effects of conversion, 343; on length of 'idda, 150; on length of pregnancy, 152; on limitation, 184; on marriage of dhimmī, 335; on maẓālim justice, 268; on perpetuity of waqf, 207; on powers of qāḍī, 260, 263; on prisoners of war, 356; on qāḍī, 273; on recognition of custom, 109; on representation by counsel, 258; on spoils of war, 357-58; on trade with non-believers, 371; on value of wrongfully appropriated property, 189; on witnesses, 254; on written documents, 79
Mamlūk period: and the caliphite, 22-23; position of ḥājib, 271-72
mamlūka. *See* ownership, absolute
al-Maqrīzī: on futya, 249; on ḥājib jurisdiction, 273; on maẓālim hearings by sultans, 269
maraḍ al-mawt. *See* death sickness
al-Marghinānī, 94
maritime code, Ottoman, 289
marriage: 132-51; as affected by conversion 342-43; consummation of, effect on bride-price, 143; consummation of, effect on divorce, 148; impediments to, 134-37; between Muslim and dhimmī, 335; suitability in, 138-40; temporary bars to, 136; termination of, 146-49
marriage contract: conditions in, 140-41; conditions for validity, 133; consideration in, 195; form requirement, 192, 198
maṣlaḥa. *See* istiṣlaḥ
masnūn, 99
matrūka. *See* land, common
maturity, of child and guardianship, 157

al-Māwardī: on caliphate, 17-19; on jihād, 358; on maẓālim justice, 264, 266, 269; on qāḍī, 245, 261-62, 273
mawāt. *See* land, dead
maxims: as found in the Majalla, 103; Talmudic sources, 103
maẓālim: court organization, 267; institution of, 259, 260; jurisdiction, 263-66, 272; procedure, 265, 267-69
Mecca, school of law, 41
Medina, school of law, 41, 45-56 *passim*
Mehmet II, compilation of laws, 280-82
Mehmet Ebussuud Efendi, 282-83
menstruation, significance for divorce, 149. *See also* 'idda
merchant communities. *See* extra-territorial jurisdiction, capitulations
milk relationship, impediment to marriage, 134-36
minor: age of puberty, 196; criminal responsibility of, 225; support of, 157-58. *See also* minority
minority: cause for interdiction, 196. *See also,* minor
misrepresentation, impeding consent, 193
mixed commissions, in Ottoman empire, 326
Mixed Courts, in Egypt: 330-32; abolition of, in Egypt, 332
mixed courts, in Ottoman empire, 329
Modernists, 75, 83-84
modernization of Ottoman law. *See* tanẓīmāt, Western influence on Ottoman law
Mongols, and the supremacy of the sharī'a 24-25
most-favored-nation clause, 313, 317, 322, 323, 325
mufti, 75-76, 248-51
Muḥammad ibn 'Abd al-Wahhāb, 70
Muḥammad ibn Sa'ūd, 70
Muḥammad, Prophet: 30, 31, 33; and arbitration, 367; and diplomatic methods, 370-71; on divorce, 99; and the hadīth, 36-50; and precedents for Islamic international law, 352; relation to imāmate in Shī'ī doctrine, 115-20; sharing in war booty, 356-57; and treaty precedents, 364-66 *passim*
muḥtasib, 59-60, 259
mujtahid, 100, 104
murder: of musta'min by Muslim, 337; of unbeliever by unbeliever, 340. *See also* homicide
mūrith, 164
mushāwar, 251, 252
Musta'lian. *See* Fāṭimid
musta'min: 338, 341; defined, 337; legal effects of departure from Islamic territory, 345-46; murder by Muslim, 337; status of in Islamic state, 361-62
Mustafa Rashid Pasha, 285
mut'a, in Shī'ī law, 128
mutarjim, 255-56
Mutawālī, 119
mutawallī, of waqf, designation of, 204; of waqf, duties of, 204
al-Mutī', Caliph, on consultation of experts by qāḍī, 247
muzzakī, 255

nafaqa. *See* support of wife
nā'ib, 237
Nāṣir al-Dīn Ṭūsī, on the caliphate, quoted, 25
naṣṣ, contrasted with qiyās, 96
national courts in Egypt, 331-32
nationality: difference of as invalidating bequest, 176; as impediment to inheritance, 165-66
al-Nawawī, 98
nāẓir. *See* mutawallī of waqf
neglect, 191
negligence, in Majalla, 304
negotiorum gestor, 187
Netherlands, capitulations with Ottoman empire, 320, 322
Niẓām ul-Mulk, on the caliphate and sultanate, 21-22
Niẓārī Ismā'īlī, doctrine on relative status of imāmate and the Prophet, 117
non-Muslims, inheritance among, 166
Nuṣayrī, 119

oath of allegiance. *See* bay'a
objective responsibility in the Majalla. *See* risk
obligation. *See* contract
obligations, contractual, disproportion between, *see laesio enormis*
occupatio, 183
offense. *See* crime
offer, 191-92; in marriage contract, 133
Ottoman empire: abrogation of capitulations, 329; capitulations with, 315-26; decree legislation, 109; policy on Islamic law, 81; reforms in, 327-30
ownership: 181-85; absolute, defined, 181; absolute, of land, 287; absolute, limitations of, 182; absolute, in Majalla,

301; acquisition of, 183-84; joint, 185; transfer of, 183

pain, compensation for, 190
partnership, 201
paternity: acknowledgment of, 152-53; attribution of, 152; establishment of, 151; repudiation of, 152
penal codes, Ottoman, 286, 289
penal law: as applied to dhimmī, 336-37; in the Ottoman empire, 279, 285-86; principle of territoriality of, 341; procedure, extraordinary jurisdiction, 274-78
penalties: categories of, 224; after death, 226
personality of law: in Byzantine empire, 310; before Islam, 309-12; Islamic concept of, 310-15; in Islamic penal law, 223; Ottoman concept, weakening of, 327-30. *See also* territoriality of law
petty larceny, punishment for, 230
physical injury, punishment for, 228-29
Pir Ṣadru'd-dīn, on the imāmate, 118
Pisa. *See* Italian city states, extra-territorial privileges
pledge: defined, 200; termination of, 201
Portugal, capitulations with Ottoman empire, 325
possession: 183; as estoppel, 184
prayer: infringement of rules on, punished, 232
pre-emption: involving dhimmīs, 340; in Majalla, 302
pregnancy: enforcement of physical punishment during, 234-35; length of, 152. *See also* 'idda
pre-Islam: customary law in, 28-33 *passim;* influences of, 91-92
prescription. *See* limitation
pretium doloris, 190
prisoners of war, 355-56
private international law. *See* conflict of law
private law, in Ottoman empire, 279
prodigality, as cause for interdiction, 197
prohibited actions, defined, 186. *See also,* transgressions
property: attributes of, 179-80; capable of being made waqf, 205; classification of, 180-81; declaration of, as waqf, 205-6; defined, 182; destruction of, 188, 190-91; fungible and infungible, defined, 180; joint, in Majalla, 301-2; in Majalla, 298; measurable and non-measurable, defined, 180; movable and immovable, defined, 180-81; movable as waqf, 205; of a musta'min in Islamic territory, 345-46; offenses against, 230; personal, period of limitation, 184; public, *see* public land; real, *see* real property; restoration of wrongfully appropriated, 189; as spoils of war, 356-58; tangible and intangible, defined, 180; tangible as waqf, 205; transfer of, 183. *See also* land, ownership
Prophet, see Muḥammad, Prophet
protégés, 327-28
Prussia, capitulations with Ottoman empire, 323
puberty, age of, 156
public interest, limiting ownership, 182
public land: defined, 288; in Majalla, 301
public law, in Ottoman empire, 280
public order: concept of in Islam, 338; and jurisdiction of qāḍī over dhimmī, 340
punishment: cumulation of, 234; discretionary, see ta'zīr; for Muslims and dhimmī, compared, 336-38; physical during pregnancy, 234-35

Qāḍī 'Abdu'l-'Azīz, quoted, 124-27
qaḍā' al-'askar, jurisdiction of, 269-71
qāḍī al-quḍāt. *See* qāḍī, chief
qāḍī: 30, 38, 39, 57-60, 76; jurisdiction over waqf property, 209; chief qāḍī, 58-59; composition of court, 244-48; *consilium* in Andalusia, 251-53; as creator of law, 241; declaring person legally dead, 165; functions, 259-63; imposing ta'zīr (discretionary punishment), 231-32; as judge between dhimmīs of differing religions, 340; jurisdiction, 241-43; jurisdiction in cases between Muslims of differing schools of law, 341-42; jurisdiction over dhimmīs, 337-38, 340-41; jurisdiction in penal cases, 275; legal status, 236-43; petitioned by woman for permission to marry, 137; powers concerning mutawallī of waqf, 204; principle of consultation, 244-48; religious function, 243-44; right to establish bequests for poor relatives, 177-78; role as arbitrator, 338; role in divorce, 147, 149; supervision of property guardian, 157
Qadrī Pasha, 83
Qasam (Qāsim), 256
qaṣaṣ, 39
qiṣāṣ, 275

qiyās: 96-97, 101, 102; applied to the Qur'ān, 88, 95; influence of Greek philosophy, 97; in Shī'ī doctrine, 122-27; theory of Rabbinical origin, 96-97. *See also* analogy
Qur'ān: 30-32 *passim*, 35, 41-42, 67, 72-79 *passim*, 90-95 *passim*, 101-4 *passim;* as authority for qiyās, 97; on false accusation of adultery, 229; on fornication, 299; on homicide, 227-29; on intoxicating beverages, 232; on punishment of offenses against peace and security, 231; on punishment for theft, 230; as a root of the sharī'a, 87-90; as source of Islamic international law, 352-71 *passim*

Rabbinical law, influence on Islamic law, 89
Rabī'a ibn Abī 'Abd al-Raḥmān, 44
ra'y, 38
real property: in absolute ownership, 181; classification of, 181; foreign ownership of, in Ottoman empire, 329; in Majalla, 301-4; period of limitation, 184. *See also* land, ownership
reciprocity, limitation of in capitulatory treaties, 323-24
reform movement, Ottoman. *See* tanẓīmāt
relatives: agnate, defined, 167; agnate, inheritance of, 172-73; agnate, order of precedence, 173; cognate, defined, 167; cognate, inheritance of, 173-74; cognate, order of precedence, 174; inheritance of, 167-74; maternal, as guardians, 154; poor, bequest for, 177-78; theft from, 230
release, terminating contract, 202
religion, difference of: and bequests, 176-77; in child care, 154; as impediment to inheritance, 165-66
religious obligations, infringement punished, 232
responsibility: collective, in penal law, 224; criminal, 224-25
right to revolt, 15
rights, injurious exercise of, 186
risk, theory of, in Majalla, 297
Roman law, influence on Islamic law, 89
Russia: capitulations with Ottoman empire, 324; mixed commissions in Ottoman empire, 326

Sabians, status under Islam, 350, 362
Sa'īd ibn Musayyib, 44
Salafiyya, 75
sale: categories of, 198; defined, 198; defined in Majalla, 301; of futures, 194; in Majalla, 297-98, 299-301
al-Sarakhsī, on religious character of qāḍī, 243
sariqa. *See* theft
Saudi Arabia, law on waqf, 221-22
schools of law: ancient, 40-42; development of, 63-71; relations among, 70-71. *See also* Baṣra, Hanafī, Ḥanbalī, Kūfa, Mālikī, Mecca, Medina, Shāfi'ī, Zāhirī
scriptuaries. *See* dhimmī
Seceders. *See* Khārijī
sects, as distinct from schools of law, 71
secular courts, in Ottoman empire, 293
secured debts, payment of after death, 163
self defense, 225
settlement: of debt terminating contract, 202; defined, 201
Seven Lawyers of Medina, 44
Seveners. *See* Ismā'īlī
al-Shāfi'ī: on acts of *negotiorum gestor,* 187; on bride-price, 143; on contracts concluded during drunkenness, 198; on divorce, 149; doctrine of, 53-56, 60, 63-65; on homicide as impediment to inheritance, 165; on inheritance by dhimmī, 336; on istiṣḥāb, 102; on istiṣlāḥ, 102; on liability for damage, 186; on liability for loss of profit, 189; on non-Islamic customs, 36; on paternity, 151; on punishment of repentent thief, 230-31; on services as property, 180; on share of grandfather in estate, 171; on support of relatives, 159; on transfer of claim, 202
Shāfi'ī school of law: concept of dār al-ṣulḥ, 359-60; on consultation of *consilium* by the qāḍī, 246; on contract of gift, 199; on doctrine of jihād, 354; on duration of treaties, 367; on estates under debt, 164; geographic distribution of, 69; on jurisdiction over dhimmī, 337; on *laesio enormis,* 193; on musta'min, 362; on prisoners of war, 355-56; on qāḍī, 245; on recognition of custom, 109; on spoils of war, 357-58; on suitability in marriage, 138-40 *passim;* on support of wife during 'idda, 151; on value of wrongfully appropriated property, 189; on witnesses, 254; on written documents, 79
shahāda. *See* witnesses
sharī'a: 57, 104; devices for evading, 77-80, 107-8; five values of human acts,

98-100; formalism of, 106-7; impact of contact with West, 83-84; influence of Rabbinical and Roman law, 89; and international law (Islamic), 350-51; and Islamic educational system, 86; and jurisdiction over Muslims and non-Muslims, 360; nature and sources, 85-112; in Ottoman empire, 279-83 *passim*, 292; scope of application, 77-78, 80; as system of equity, 105
Shaybāni: 92, 101; doctrine of, 53; on musta'min's return to enemy country, 345-46; on revocability of waqf, 207; on share of grandfather in estate, 171; on validity of will of dhimmī, 339; on wrongful appropriation, 189
Shaykh al-Islām, 76
Shaykh Sa'dī of Shirāz, 102
Shaykh Ṣaduq, 121
Shī'a: 34; on bequests to heirs, 176; on caliphate, 6; definition of, 114; doctrine on allegiance to the imāmate, 120-21; on roots of sharī'a, 97-98; religious organization, 123; theoretical basis of law, 97-98
Shī'ism: aims, 113; doctrines on caliphate, 121-22; doctrines on imāmate, 114-21; legal theories, 113-31
shuf'a, 104, 108. *See also* pre-emption
shūra, *consilium* in Spain, 251-53
shurṭa: 242; jurisdiction, 274-76
Sidī al-Khalīl, on conversion and penal law, 344
silence, when regarded as acceptance, 192
siyar. *See* international law (Islamic)
slavery: as cause for interdiction, 196; of conquered peoples, 356
sources of law, in Ottoman empire, 283
sovereignty, territorial, influence of concept on capitulations, 327
spoils of war, division of, 356-57
state lands: defined, 288; inheritance concerning, 287; period of limitation, 184
statute of limitations, in Majalla, 305-6. *See also* limitation
succession, after death: compulsory, defined, 160-61; compulsory, discussed, 164-65; optional, 160; optional, defined, 160; optional, limited to third of estate, 175; and simultaneous death, 165. *See also* inheritance
suckling: 153-54. *See also* milk relationship
suitability, see marriage
Sulaymān II (the Magnificent, al-Qānūnī), 282-83, 285, 109
sultan, punitive power, 276
sultanate, and caliphate, 20-27; maẓālim jurisdiction, 265, 268
sunna: as a root of the sharī'a, 90-95; as source of Islamic international law, 352; types discussed, 34, 35, 42, 45
support: of minors, 157-58; of relatives, 158-60; of wife, 144-45; of wife during 'idda, 151
al-Suyūtī, definition of property, 182
Sweden, capitulations with Ottoman empire, 323
Syria, legislation abolishing waqf dhurrī, 220-21

tafwīd, in divorce, 147
taklīf, 121
al-ṭalāq al-bā'in baynūnatan sughra, 149
al-ṭalāq al-raj'ī, 149
talio. See lex talionis
tanẓīmāt: 283-95; effect on civil and criminal law in Ottoman empire, 329-30; effect on commercial and capitulatory treaties, 328-29; modification of Western privileges, 329-30
taqlīd, 74, 75
Tā'usī, 119
tawrīth. *See* inheritance
ta'zīr: 231-32; defined, 227; punishments applied, 231-32
territoriality of law: 328, 332; in Islamic penal law 223. *See also* personality of law
testator, 164. *See also* bequest
testimony. *See* witnesses
theft: defined, 230; punishment of, 230; by unbeliever from unbeliever, 340
torts. *See* prohibited actions, transgressions
tradition. *See* ḥadīth
Traditionists, 45-56, 60, 63-68
transfer of obligation, 202
transgressions, 188-91
treaty: form of, 366; historical precedent for, in early Islam, 364-66; as method of terminating jihād, 358. *See also* Hudaybiya treaty
treaty-making power in Islam, 364
triple divorce. *See* divorce, triple
trust: compared to waqf, 212-13; derived from waqf, 213-18; theories of origin discussed, 215-17
Twelvers. *See* Ithna 'Asharī

Two Sicilies, Kingdom of, capitulations with Ottoman empire, 323

'udūl, see betrothal, withdrawal from
'Umar, Caliph, 44
Umayyads: and development of jurisprudence, 36-42; diplomacy of, 370; treaty relations with Byzantine empire, 366
umma, 3-6, 23, 24
United States, capitulations with Ottoman empire, 325-26
unlawful enrichment, 188
'uqūbāt, meaning discussed, 223. *See also* penal law
'urf. *See* custom, customary law
usufruct, 182. *See also* hire, loan, waqf

Venice. *See* Italian city states, extraterritorial privileges

Wahhābī, 70, 81
wakīl, 257-59
walāya, 120
waqf: 100, 108, 111-12; basis for English trust, 213-18; beneficiaries, 204; beneficiaries, determination of, 211; charitable, *see* waqf khayrī; charitable purpose of, 206; compared to trust, 212-13; concept of, 204; conditions of, 210-11; declaration of property as, 205-6; defined, 181, 203; establishment of, 203; establishment of, by dhimmī, 336; establishment of, by musta'min, 346; establishment by testament, 206; family, *see* waqf dhurrī; form requirement, 192, 198; inalienability, 206, 208-9; inalienability, evasion of, 209-10; irrevocability, 206, 207-8; as a juristic person, 208; object of, 206; origins of, 204-5; ownership of, 208; period of limitation, 184; perpetuity of, 206-8; perpetuity and *cy pres* doctrine, 207-8; recent legislation relating to, 218-22; rigidity of, 217; unconditional, 206; validity of, 204-5. *See also* waqf dhurrī, waqf khayrī
waqf dhurrī: abolition of, in Egypt, 219; abolition of, in Syria, 220-21; defined, 181, 204; limitation on, in Lebanon, 219-20
waqf khayrī, defined, 181, 204
waqf property: exchange, lease, sale of, 208-9; permanent right to build or plant on, 209-10
wāqif: 203-22 *passim;* requisite capacity of, 205
war. *See* jihād
waṣiyya, see bequests
weregeld, under Islamic law, imposed on dhimmīs, 335. *See also* diyya
Western influence: on Egyptian law, 330-31; on Islamic law, 82-84; on Ottoman law, 283-93 *passim,* 307-8; 327-30, 346-48
wet nurse, 153
widow, remarriage of, 150-51
wife: freedom to manage property, 141; maximum number of wives, 137; obedience of, 145-46; share of estate of husband, 166-67; support of, 144-45; support of during 'idda, 151
will: in Shī'ī law, 129-30; validity of (dhimmī), 339. *See also* bequest
witnesses: in court, 253-55; to marriage contract, 133; use of, 35
woman: interdiction of, 197-98; right to choose husband, 137, 138
wrongful appropriation: 189-90; definition of, 189; differentiated from theft, 189; in Majalla, 303

Yaman, Zaydī sect in, 132

Zāhirī school of law: 67-68, 74; on illicit contracts, 195; on length of pregnancy, 152; on non-support of wife, 145
zakāt, infringements of rules on, punished, 232
Zayd ibn Thābit, on share of grandfather in estate, 171
Zaydī: doctrine on imāmate, 114; doctrine on relative status of imāmate to the Prophet, 115-17 *passim;* in Yaman, 132
Zoroastrians, legal position of, 335, 342. *See also* dhimmī
Zuhrī, 44
al-Zurqānī, 110

www.ingramcontent.com/pod-product-compliance
Lightning Source LLC
Chambersburg PA
CBHW022007300426
44117CB00005B/69
* 9 7 8 1 6 1 6 1 9 1 1 7 7 *